WORKS ISSUED BY
THE HAKLUYT SOCIETY

AN ELIZABETHAN IN 1582

The Diary of Richard Madox,
Fellow of All Souls

SECOND SERIES
NO. 147

ISSUED FOR 1976

CORRIGENDUM *to the Half Title*

This volume is not issued for 1976
but is the second issue for 1974

HAKLUYT SOCIETY

COUNCIL AND OFFICERS, 1974–75

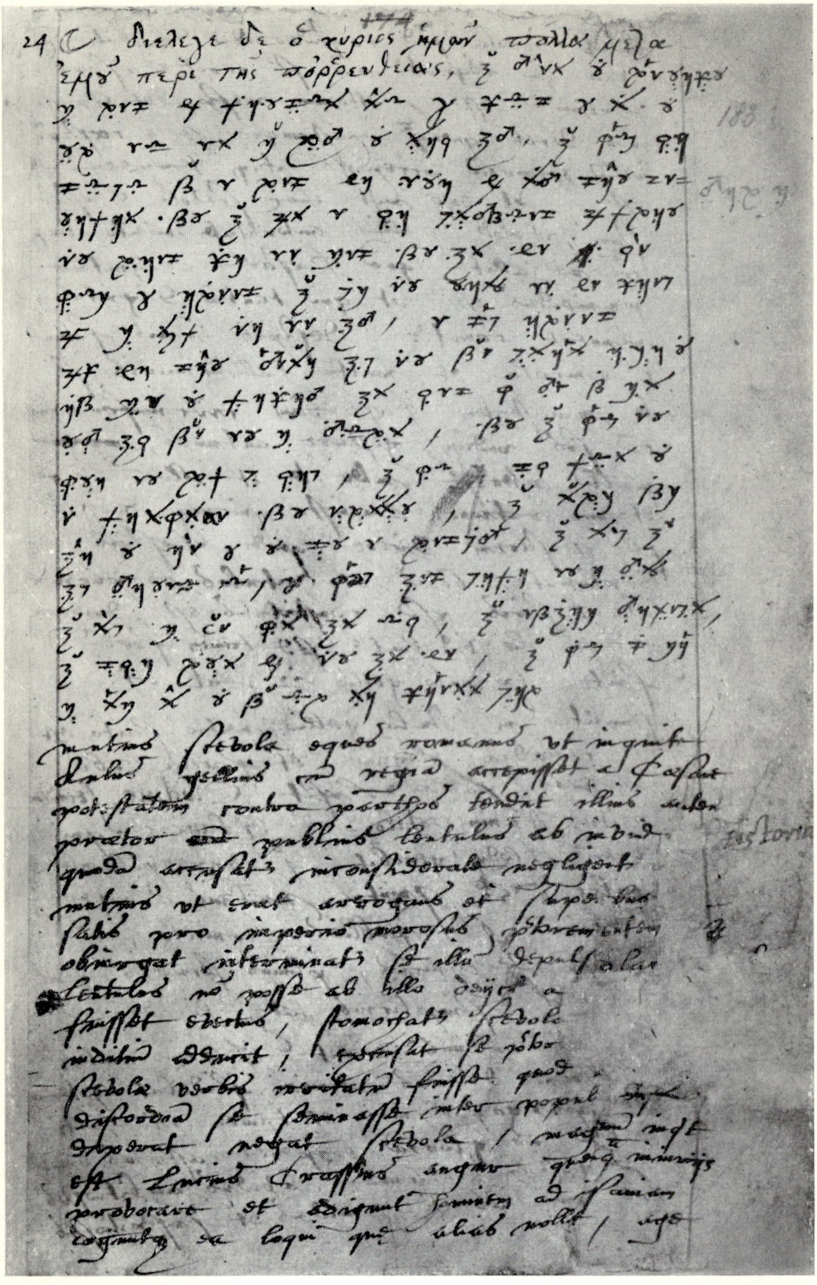

Fig. 1. A page of Madox's Diary, 24 Sept. 1583, showing the cipher with Greek insertions and some of the Latin text (transcribed on pp. 194–5)

AN ELIZABETHAN IN 1582

The Diary of Richard Madox, Fellow of All Souls

by

ELIZABETH STORY DONNO

THE HAKLUYT SOCIETY
LONDON
1976

ISBN 0 904180 04 2

Printed in Great Britain
by Robert MacLehose and Company Limited
Printers to the University of Glasgow

Quid terras alio calentis sole mutamus?

HORACE

In the hande of our Lorde be all the corners of the earth.

PSALM 95

Published by the Hakluyt Society
c/o The British Library
London WC1B 3DG

To Procope S. Costas

In Memoriam

CONTENTS

LIST OF ILLUSTRATIONS[1]

[1] The drawings from Madox's Diary are reproduced by permission of the British Library Board.

ABBREVIATIONS

APC	*Acts of the Privy Council*
Athen.Oxon	Anthony Wood, *Athenae Oxoniensis*, ed. P. Bliss, 4 vols., 1813–20
B.L.	British Library, Reference Division (Bloomsbury), formerly British Museum Library
CSP	*Calendar of State Papers: Colonial; Domestic; Foreign; Ireland; Spanish; Venetian*
Cal. Salisbury MSS	Historical Manuscripts Commission, *Calendar of the Manuscripts of the Marquess of Salisbury at Hatfield House*, 22 parts (or volumes), 1883–1971
M.T.	Merchant Taylors' Company, Records at Merchant Taylors' Hall, London
OED	*Oxford English Dictionary*
PN (1589)	Richard Hakluyt, *Principall Navigations, 1589*, facsimile, with an introduction by D. B. Quinn and R. A. Skelton, 2 vols. Hakluyt Soc., 1965 (the journal of Luke Ward is on pp. 647–72)
SP 12	Public Record Office, State Papers, Elizabeth, Domestic Series
Taylor, *Fenton*	*The Troublesome Voyage of Captain Edward Fenton*, ed. E. G. R. Taylor, Hakluyt Soc., 1959 (the journal of Edward Fenton is on pp. 83–149)

PREFACE

Chronicling, in the main, the initial (albeit abortive) attempt to establish a spice trade in the Moluccas, the Diary of Richard Madox covers a single calendar year. Since five months of that year were to pass before the flotilla of four ships rounded the Lizard, the Diary also records its author's winding up of his affairs at Oxford, his stay in London following upon the problems and false starts incident to departure, and the slow passage from Blackwall to Southampton aboard the *Edward Bonaventure* with the many visits to and from persons interested in the enterprise. The last seven months record the tensions and rivalries that developed in the command, the long sojourn at Sierra Leone, and an account of the subsequent passage to São Vicente, Brazil. It was here, on 24 January 1583, that the English ships, now reduced to two, were forced into an engagement with three Spanish ships, which was resumed the next morning when, in the words of Madox's fellow chaplain, they had that day one very hot breakfast fighting. Although Madox's account stops short of this date – he died within a month – the ignominious outcome of the voyage to 'China and Cathay' can be traced in other documents.

The Diary of Richard Madox has been well known to historians of the sixteenth century, particularly from the fact that some portions of it were calendared in 1862 in the *State Papers, Colonial Series. East Indies, China and Japan, 1513–1616.* More recently, excerpts ('a quarter' of the whole) relating to the voyage were included by E. G. R. Taylor in *The Troublesome Voyage of Captain Edward Fenton* (Hakluyt Society, Second Series, No. CXIII, 1959). Its documentary value is well justified by that part of the Diary which deals with the voyage, for Madox takes many of its aspects into account. Organisational problems relating to the appointing of officers and the impressing of crew, meteorological puzzles relating to winds, tides, and currents, attitudes inhibiting trade with the natives, questions concerning the efficacy of the usual medical remedies – all of these elicited a lively response from him. His recognition of these several aspects, coupled with his acute observation of those in command, does much to help us understand the failure of this first attempt to reach the Spice Islands and establish trade. Moreover, his avid curiosity about natural phenomena, exotic vocabularies, and customs – hence his drawings, including that of a woman 'fynely pynked' – explains how a Fellow of All Souls College could eagerly consort with those for whom 'pitch, tallow . . . dirt and bilge water smelled more sweetly than myrrh and marjoram.'

But the Diary is also of interest because it touches on other aspects of sixteenth-century life. By virtue of his academic training and status at Oxford, Madox reflects the Elizabethan social and intellectual outlook in the period falling just short of its real achievement. He reads Cardano and William Bourne, yet he also looks back to Aristotle and Albertus Magnus. He can quote Chaucer and Spenser (the *Shepheardes Calender*), yet more often he cites Horace, Virgil, and the Roman dramatists. He goes to see a 'scurvy play' in London and stays not to hear the matter only a few short years before Tamburlaine drummed out a 'decasillabon' and 'brave Talbot' triumphed on the stage. His Diary represents multiple facets of the expanding and developing Elizabethan consciousness; if nothing else, it underscores the rapidity of that development after 1582.

That this 'vivid and circumstantial document' (the phrase is E. G. R. Taylor's) should not have been made available before may seem surprising, but a firsthand acquaintance with the manuscript soon makes this omission understandable. Up until mid-September, Madox categorically denied that he was keeping a personal record of the voyage. Though he had been pointedly watching, listening, and recording from its inception, he had been careful to note down his observations surreptitiously. Increasingly aware by September that his General and his 'Vice-admiral' were eager to pry into his personal papers and read what he knew to be frequently mordant comments, he undertook elaborate precautions to disguise his statements by several means: first, by resorting with increasing frequency to the use of cipher, Latin, and, on occasion, Greek. The cipher passages happily present few problems except where mutilations of the manuscript occur; but by any standard, and particularly by the standard of an M.A. Oxon., 1575, the Latin as well as the Greek is often barbarous and, as a consequence, difficult to construe. Second, to mask his comments still more, he devised a complex system of pseudonyms to refer to his fellow voyagers. Many of these designations become clear only after persistent detective work. Third, on at least two occasions he embedded his comments so obscurely in historical and literary allusions that their import, at least for me, remains still disguised. In fact, for the latter two-thirds of the Diary, these three devices to obscure the record may be said to have served his intention far beyond his need. Furthermore, the manuscript has suffered some marks of sea change, the result of staining and mutilation, from the time its author penned his last entry for 31 December to when it was carried home eventually to become part of the great Cotton collection.

To smooth out Madox's Latin in translation and to excise the obscure passages have been constant temptations. In the interests of completeness, the entire manuscript has been transcribed and translated – warts and all – though regrettably the Latin transcription is omitted here. For the same reasons I have included the shorter but still interesting Diary of Madox's fellow chaplain John Walker in spite of the difficulties arising from its having been badly damaged by fire.

For assistance in rendering the Latin and Greek passages into English and, more importantly, for aid in the arduous initial labor of reconstructing them, I am greatly indebted to Procope S. Costas. Thanks to his painstaking efforts, it may truly be said that a portion of Madox has been rescued from oblivion. I hope that the dedication of this volume to him will suggest the measure of my gratitude. The transcription, editing, general interpretation, and annotations, however, are my responsibility.

To Professors George B. Parks and David B. Quinn, I owe the suggestion that I undertake to edit the Diary, and I am grateful to them – at this stage – most especially for their careful reading of the Introduction. To my friends and colleagues S. F. Johnson and William Nelson, I am indebted for many stimulating discussions and wise counsel. To my husband I owe a great deal: with 'the sun himselfe,' as a contemporary said of Sir Francis Drake, he has been 'a fellow-travailer.'

I want also to express my gratitude for permission to utilise archival records and materials at the Bodleian, at All Souls College, at the Merchant Taylors' Hall, at the Public Record Office, and at the British Library. To the last of these I am indebted for their granting me permission to print Madox's manuscript and to reproduce his drawings. I wish also to express thanks to the University Court of the University of Glasgow for permission to include the portrait of John Banister, the surgeon on the voyage, and to the Marquess of Salisbury for permission to include Robert Norman's Chart of the Thames Estuary.

For fellowship assistance permitting me to work on this manuscript over a long period, I wish to express my very sincere thanks to the Simon Guggenheim Foundation, the Henry E. Huntington Library, the Newberry Library, the John Carter Brown Library, and the Council for Research in the Humanities at Columbia University.

INTRODUCTION

I. LIFE AND BACKGROUND

That we should know so much about Richard Madox for the single year 1582 has its wry aspect. For that year we know a great deal about him, not only about his involvement with the first trading expedition to the Spice Islands on which he died, but also about the minutiae of his daily life – where he dined, with whom he supped, and even, on occasion, what he dreamed. But of the preceding thirty-four years we know precious little. Apart from a few records having to do with his academic career, virtually all the remaining information derives from the personal notes he jotted down on the title and on, what proved to be, the final leaf of his Diary – jotted down no doubt while he was lying 'bwelting on the sea' and doing no good.[1] There are also a few hints to be winnowed from comments he made in the course of keeping this daily account.

Although we know from his later academic record at All Souls College, Oxford, that he came from Shropshire – a fact supported by his dialectal preferences and by his acquaintance with and interest in fellow Salopians – we do not know where it was that he was born on 11 November 1546. Comments in the Diary suggest that it was in Uffington, a small village on the banks of the Severn about three miles northeast of Shrewsbury. Held by Saxons in the time of Edward the Confessor, this 'town of the children of Uffa' had been bequeathed to Haughmond Abbey in the twelfth century by the crusader Robert de la Mare whereupon it became an extraparochial liberty.[2]

It remained an Augustinian demesne until the time of the dissolution when Henry VIII granted the Abbey to Sir Edward Littleton.

[1] 'Bwelting' (i.e. 'rocking'; more commonly 'bolting' or 'bulting') represents vocalic *w* and reflects Madox's Salopian dialect with its Welsh influence. Sir Philip Sidney, who like Madox attended Shrewsbury School, also adopts this preferential spelling on occasion ('rwyn' for 'ruin').

[2] R. W. Eyton, *Antiquities of Shropshire*, IX (London, 1854–86), 4–11. In the *Valor Ecclesiasticus* for 1534–5, the abbot of Haughmond Abbey is given £37 9*s* 6*d* of assized rents in Uffington. For the later history of the Abbey, see *Trans., Shrop.Arch.Soc.*, Third Series, VI (1906), xviii–xix.

In 1548, it was purchased by Sir Rowland Hill, citizen, alderman, and lord mayor of London, who then conveyed it to the heirs of his sister Elizabeth and to her husband John Barker of Wolverton, Shropshire, on condition that they agree to occupy the Haughmond estate. Thus, after the marriage of their oldest son James to Dorothy Clive, Haughmond Abbey and its appurtenances passed securely into the hands of the Barker family. Granted a patent in 1562 by William Harvey, Clarenceux King of Arms, James Barker succeeded in making his family of some importance in the area. Two of his sons, Rowland and Richard, attended Shrewsbury School with Madox. The former was to become sheriff of Shropshire, the latter judge of North Wales, recorder of Shrewsbury, and M.P. as well.

The presumptive evidence that, if not actually born in Uffington,[1] Madox at least lived there, derives from three entries in the Diary: on 8 July after being three months at sea 'keeping Thom Beggars cowrse,' he notes simply that he 'drempt muche of Uffington.' A little more than a month later when recording details of the flora and fauna at Sierra Leone, he comments that the parrots come from the north to the hilly south to feed, returning at night 'lyke croes in the Munkmore' – a wooded area located across the Severn from Uffington. And earlier, when still at Oxford, he recorded that he had heard 'Mrs Barker was dead' and added the pious observation, 'The *Lor*d be merciful unto us.'

The earliest record so far discovered in which Richard Madox's name appears dates from 1562 in what is the earliest register of Shrewsbury School,[2] where he is listed as *alienus* and a member of the first class, indicating that he was both a non-resident and in the highest form. Chartered only ten years before as *Libera Schola Grammaticalis Regis Edwardi Sexti*, Shrewsbury School was just beginning to establish its formidable reputation under the guidance of Thomas Ashton, its excellent and worthy master, as Camden was to call him. Besides introducing the first register of students, Ashton is also credited with putting the school on a sound financial basis and with drawing up its statutes and ordinances, which, adopted in 1578, were to continue in effect until 1798.[3]

[1] The parish registers for Uffington date from 1578. While the surname Madox, common in Shropshire, appears in the 1580s and 1590s and subsequently, there is no apparent link with any of the persons mentioned in the Diary.

[2] *Shrewsbury School Regestum Scholarium, 1562–1635*, ed. E. Calvert (Shrewsbury, 1892), p. 1.

[3] Formerly a Fellow of St John's College, Cambridge, Ashton became master at Shrewsbury in 1561 or possibly even earlier. See Thomas Auden, *Memorials of Shropshire*

In 1562, the year of Madox's recorded attendance, the school had 266 scholars, half *alieni* and half *oppidani*, and the master was assisted by two ushers, Thomas Wylton and Richard Atkys. The statutes indicate that during the winter season the day began at 7:00 a.m., in other seasons at 6:00 a.m., school opening and closing with 'prayers sung and said' by the boys 'reverentially upon their knees.' Physical activities included shooting with the long bow, running, wrestling, and leaping; the curriculum included Xenophon, Isocrates, and the New Testament in Greek; the historians and Virgil, Horace, and Terence in Latin. The top form had not only to read but to play an act of a comedy once a week. When some twenty years later he was seeking a means to disguise his acerbic comments on his fellow voyagers, Madox chose to assign them roles in a comedy, prompted perhaps to do so by his early schooling.

Aged sixteen and in the highest form in 1562, we may conclude that at this date Madox had been in attendance at Shrewsbury for some years: the average time spent at the school in the sixteenth century was a little over five years and the ages of the boys ranged from seven to sixteen. As an *alienus*, his charge would have been two shillings (in contrast to the twelve pence required of a resident), and he would have 'tabled' with a householder in the town. Two of his school fellows who continued on friendly terms with Madox were Reginald Scriven, who preceded him to Oxford and to election as a Fellow of All Souls and was ultimately to serve in five parliaments, and Robert Wright, who became a Fellow of Trinity College, Cambridge, and, on the recommendation of his former schoolmaster Thomas Ashton, tutor to the young earl of Essex. In turn, Essex was to recommend *his* former tutor to the office of Clerk of the Stable to Queen Elizabeth and, in 1592, was to support his election, along with that of Scriven, to parliament.[1] Both Scriven and Wright, though the latter was 'meanly born in Shrewsbury,' were knighted.[2]

The names of several other persons who date back to this earlier association also crop up in the Diary.[3] There is no mention, however,

---

(London, 1906) and J. Basil Oldham, *A History of Shrewsbury School, 1552–1592* (Oxford, 1952), from which my information on the school is drawn.

[1] H. T. Weyman, 'Shrewsbury Members of Parliament,' *Trans., Shrop.Arch.Soc.*, Fourth Series, XII (1930), 194–7 and 'Early Chronicles of Shrewsbury,' *Trans., Shrop. Arch. and Nat.Hist.Soc.*, III (1880), 325–6.

[2] The date commonly given for Scriven's knighthood is 1603, e.g. W. C. Metcalfe, *A Book of Knights* . . . (London, 1855). W. A. Shaw, *The Knights of England*, II (London, 1906), 124, says that although he was frequently so styled, he was never knighted.

[3] These include Harry Yomans (20 Jan.), Thomas Elkes (26 Mar.; 1 Apr.), and Thomas

of two of his school fellows who were to gain academic distinction – Meredith Hanmer, historian and religious controversialist, and Andrew Downes, Regius Professor of Greek at Cambridge – whom Simonds d'Ewes termed 'the ablest Grecian of Christendom, being no native of Greece.'

But what of Madox's family, who, presumably, had been living in nearby Uffington? Since there is no mention of his mother in the Diary, we may assume that by 1582 she had been dead for some time. There is a single reference to his father to whom he ascribes an anecdote, but as he records no attempt to see him or write to him before his long departure, it seems likely that by this date his father too was dead.

After going to London in February, 1582, preparatory to sailing, Madox sees his sister Ann on several occasions: they dine together; twice they go to Greenwich together, and once to court. Among his expenditures for the month of February, he reckons seven shillings 'for hats' for himself and his sister. On 17 March as he pulled on his boots to ride to Oxford for a last visit, her arrival at his lodgings deters him: suspecting he had already departed, she 'wept for unkyndnes.' Three days later she falls sick of 'hir old dises,' and Madox administers a purge of hellebore – a remedy variously used for the falling sickness, the ague, and melancholia – which on this occasion produced good results, 'so I thank God she mended.'

During the six weeks (from mid-February to the first of April) that he spends in London waiting out the delays incident to departure, Madox meets with his cousin 'Marget,' his cousin Thomas, and his cousin Nicholas Madox, a haberdasher of London.[1] On Ash Wednesday he assists in the christening of Nicholas's son, named Thomas after Madox's older brother, and makes a gift on behalf of himself and his brother of two spoons costing 17*s* 6*d* with 3*s* more for the nurse and midwife.

Besides his older brother Thomas, Madox, it seems, had a second brother, never specified by name, who was also a member of the University in 1582 though this relationship is evidenced only by three brief references in the Diary. During the New Year holidays Madox visits his elder brother Thomas and family in Wolverhampton. He then heads back for Oxford on 4 January, with his brother riding with

Lawley (1 Apr.). Allusions to two others, George Torporley (18, 19, 22 Feb.; 9 Mar.) and John Powell (16 Feb.) may refer to relatives of the Thomas Torporley and the John Powell who were in attendance at Shrewsbury in 1562.

[1] Merchant Taylors' Acct. Bks. No. 6, 389*v*.

him so far as Perry Hall in Handsworth, Staffordshire, where they take leave of each other 'with prayers and tears.' The next day Madox arrives at Oxford. Two days later (7 Jan.) he records that he dined at Trinity College, 'wher with my brother . . . and others we concluded [on] a clubbing on the moroe.' This particular diversion, as Madox describes it, could involve a very large gathering of scholars, obviously by accretion, since he mentions 400 'owt of al howses' marching with drums and bagpipes and 'other melody' first to one and then to another of the colleges, carrying 'clubs' of holly or other greenery.[1] At each stop they were received by a member of the University who delivered an impromptu oration in verse or in prose to which a member of the 'clubbing' group, crowned with garlands, responded. On this occasion (8 Jan.), Madox records that at the gate of Trinity College 'Sir Wurford' (that is, William Warforde, B.A. and a Fellow of Trinity) received him with an oration while his brother 'had an other of Sir Poticary' (Thomas Potticary, B.A. and a Fellow of St Johns).[2]

The last allusion to his brother at Oxford is the notation that on 12 February he supped with 'M. Thornborowe of Magdalens' (later to be successively Bishop of Limerick, Bristol, and Worcester) at a local hostelry where he found his brother together with three others, two of whom were attached to Magdalen. From the extant college records the only candidate for this unnamed brother, if in fact he was a full brother and if in fact he took a degree, would be William Madox of Magdalen (B.A., 1587) and St Edmund Hall (M.A., 1590). That Madox makes no mention of saying goodbye to his brother at Oxford seems initially surprising, but, in fact, when he does depart for London on 17 February, he records specifically that he 'took leave only' of four people – all of them Fellows of All Souls. It seems clear from the brief allusions in the Diary that among his relatives – his cousins, his sister Ann, and his two brothers – Madox maintained the closest family tie with his older brother Thomas.

Once again there is a wry aspect to the biographical data concerning Thomas Madox: though we know relatively little about him, surprisingly we do know how much he earned annually for a period of thirty-five years, thanks to the excellent records of the Merchant Taylors' Company. The first notice is of his being admitted B.A. at Oxford in 1565, where he probably had begun his studies in 1560 or

[1] For the suggestion that such social gatherings could on occasion develop into unruly frays with the townspeople and the 'clubs' be used as weapons, see n. 2, p. 71.

[2] A candidate admitted to the B.A. was styled in Latin *dominus*, in English *sir*.

1561 at Brasenose College. Seven years later he received his M.A., having been granted a dispensation to perform the final exercises after taking the degree because he was a 'schoolmaster in London.'[1] Two years earlier, that is, in 1570, the Chief Ushership of the Merchant Taylors' School located in the parish of St Lawrence Pountney had become vacant, and Richard Mulcaster, its excellent master, had appointed Thomas to the position. In addition to lodgings, Thomas, like Mulcaster, received £10 a year, though without the master's perquisite of £6 for 'wood and coles.'[2]

In 1572, the year Thomas was granted his M.A., the Merchant Taylors decided to find a replacement for the current master of their free grammar school in Wolverhampton. (Founded in 1528 by Sir Stephen Jenyns, 'some tyme a Beneficiall Brother' of the Company, it had been entrusted to them on his death.) Having considered divers learned men and having resisted the blandishments of Laurence Humphrey, President of Magdalen, and his candidate, the Master and Wardens settled on Thomas, relying, as they stated in a letter to Humphrey, on the experience they had had of his 'hitherto well doinges' rather than 'a good hope' of another 'hereafter well to do.'[3]

Thomas accordingly took up his position on Lady Day, 1573, at a yearly salary of £13 *6s 8d* with an additional quarter's salary to take care of the 'transportinge of his Bookes and stuff thear.'[4] Soon (6 April) Thomas wrote, requesting that some good order be taken for the 'better reparacion bothe of Schole and Dwellinge howse which are nowe in Decaye,' and the Company authorised restoration within a limit of five or six pounds. The expenses amounted precisely to £5 19*s* 11*d*.

Writing to the townspeople of Wolverhampton to announce the new appointment, the Master and Wardens had pointed out that whereas Sir Stephen Jenyns specified a combined salary of £12 for the master and his usher, experience 'in theis late Dayes' had taught them that such stipends were insufficient, and so in order to insure that the master abstain 'from all other exercises hinderinge him' in his profession and devote himself wholly to his calling, they had from time to time increased the salary until it amounted to £17 *6s 8d*, of which the usher was to receive £4. Nonetheless, Thomas found his salary

[1] The dispensation is quoted in *Reg. of the Univ. of Oxford*, ed. Andrew Clark (Oxford, 1885), II.i.79.

[2] M.T. Acct. Bks. 5, 37.

[3] Quoted in G. P. Mander, *The History of the Wolverhampton Grammar School* (Wolverhampton, 1913), pp. 35–6. All quotations of documents, unless otherwise noted, are taken from Mander, pp. 34–61.

[4] M.T. Acct. Bks. 5, 211.

insufficient, and eight months after taking up his position, thirty of the leading townspeople were prompted to write to the Merchant Taylors highly commending their schoolmaster ('A man not only of good and honest life but also Learned, and not only of good life and Learninge but also A man bothe willinge Diligente and as paynefull in his good trade of teachinge as ever any hathe ben in that room and Office') and requesting an augmentation of his salary. Taking cognizance that a schoolmaster cannot live by 'prayses' only, the Company increased his stipend, first to twenty-five marks (£16 13*s* 4*d*) and then to thirty (£20) in the years 1574 and 1575. As the commendatory letter indicates, he early ingratiated himself with the leading citizens. Consequently, in 1582 when his brother Richard celebrated the beginning of the New Year with him in Wolverhampton, he too was entertained by a number of these leading townspeople.

During succeeding years, Thomas ran his school to everyone's satisfaction. In April 1590, a great fire broke out in the southwest part of the town which, not being contained for five days, destroyed numerous buildings including a portion of the schoolhouse. 'Divers back buildings of ease' which belonged to the master's dwelling were burned to the ground and Thomas, as he wrote the Company, suffered 'great losse in his own private estate.'[1] The loss probably included the books and personal things Richard Madox had sent from Oxford before his departure as well as the remaining possessions he had left locked in his study at All Souls, intended by a 'deed of gift' for his brother. Money for reparations was sent to Wolverhampton, this time by means of Thomas's cousin Nicholas Madox.[2]

The townspeople continued to champion their schoolmaster, even enlisting the aid of Gabriel Goodman, Dean of Westminster, in 1599 to seek an increase in salary for him and his usher 'in these hard tymes.' Not until Christmas 1602, however, did the Merchant Taylors see fit to raise the combined stipend to £30. They bestowed, in addition, a gratuity of £10 on Thomas for 'the long experyence' they had had of 'his great paynes and honest conversation.'

After a tenure of thirty-two years, Thomas died on 16 July 1605,[3]

[1] M.T. Court Rec. 3, 211.

[2] M.T. Acct. Bks. 6, 389. Coincidentally, the Chief Usher of the London school in 1590–1 was also named Thomas Madox, son of William, of Wiveton, Norfolk, who had attended the school from 1572 to 1582 and then gone up to Caius College, Cambridge, in 1583 (*Merchant Taylors' School Register*, ed. E. P. Hart (London, 1936)). In May 1591, having given 'just cawse' not only for notable dislike but for violent expulsion, he was dismissed (M.T. Court Rec. 3, 226).

[3] *Wolverhampton Parish Register*, Pt. 1. (Staffordshire Parish Registers Soc., ed. G. P.

and the townspeople wrote to the Company announcing the death of 'our good Neighbor and Schoole-maister M. Madox, by whose dilligence and learning, especially in his younger daies, our Whole Neighborhood hath received much comfort, And noe doubt your whole worshipfull Company noe lesse commendacions, from whose grave discrecions such choice was so well made.'

The evidence of Thomas Madox's long and successful career as a schoolmaster, taken together with the nature of the information which Richard Madox records in his Diary, including careful accounting of financial matters and the kind of attitude it reveals, suggests that they came of modest stock. Though the Oxford registers show that of all students admitted between 1567 and 1622, 6635, or virtually half the total, were the sons of plebeians,[1] one may still question how three sons of persons of modest means managed to attend Oxford. Did one or all of them receive help from such prosperous local folk in the neighbourhood of Shrewsbury as the Barkers, the Scrivens, or the Powells? In settling up his affairs at Oxford, Madox notes on 16 February:

> I payd John Powell [of Salop. He had matriculated at University College 1 Dec. 1581 and was to become M.A. and Fellow of All Souls in 1587] for ther bowser M. Jenyns 5 nobles and 30^{s} to M. Thompson [also a Fellow of All Souls] and gave John 8^{d} so that I am wholy even with hym, and the burser and his tutor have $3^{li}3^{s}4^{d}$ before hand.

Whatever may have been the means by which he managed to finance his studies, Richard Madox followed in Thomas's footsteps and went up to Oxford on 24 January 1567, as he records in the Diary. But vital evidence of his attachment to a College or Hall is missing. It appears not unlikely that he was a Bible clerk at All Souls College as the name of the senior of the four Bible clerks in a list headed '1571' in the College Admissions Book is given as 'Joannes Maddox Salopiensis,' while after the entry the words 'postea socius' ('subsequently a Fellow') have been added. They are partly obscured by an inkstain, but it is not possible to say whether this was by accident

Mander, 1932), p. 141. With Thomas's death, some twenty-one years after that of his younger brother, all certain information about Madox's family ceases, though Thomas left children, including a son named William. *The Visitation of Shropshire, 1623* (Pub. of the Harleian Soc. (London, 1889), 29, Pt. 2, 493) records the marriage of Lettice, daughter and coheir of Thomas Maddockes of Wolverhampton to Henry Davenport, eldest son of Jane Bromley and William Davenport of Hawne.

[1] J. W. Saunders, 'The Stigma of Print,' *Review of English Studies*, 1 (Apr. 1951), 141, n. 2.

or design.[1] No other record of a John Madox of Shropshire has been found and the order of Richard Madox's seniority through the records of the years after 1571 is appropriate to identifying 'John' with Richard, while support is also provided by the posthumous publication of the sermon Madox preached at Dorchester where, as pointed out below, he is called 'John Madoxe, Maister of Arte, and fellow of All soules in Oxforde.'[2]

If the official procedure was followed – for which direct evidence is lacking – Madox as an undergraduate in 1567 would have presented himself to Thomas Cooper, the Vice Chancellor of the University, probably on the Friday following his arrival, and may there have signed the subscription book, signifying his acceptance of the Prayer Book and 'her Majesties supremacye,' though subscription at that date was not enforced.[3] He would then have entered on his course of study, which he dates as beginning on 25 January, the day after he had arrived in Oxford. According to the Statutes of 1565, a candidate was expected to spend four years, or sixteen terms, in study for the baccalaureate – two terms for grammar, four for rhetoric, five for dialectic, three for arithmetic, and two for music. What variations on these requirements would have been made if Madox was indeed a Bible clerk at All Souls is unclear. He records that he spent four years and ten months as an undergraduate. Normally, it would be possible to trace his career through the Buttery Books of his College and through lists of tutors and their pupils, but the records are imperfect in this case. At All Souls there is a gap in the Bursars' books from 1551 to November 1569, but a 'Madox,' without prefix, is recorded in the books in a clerk's place from November 1569 to December 1571 and as a Fellow from January 1572/3 to January 1584/5, which again suggests that 'John' refers to Richard.

From an obscure entry in the Diary, it appears that he may have

[1] Warden Hovenden's Admissions Book, All Souls College Archives.

[2] The precedence of 'Madox' in the Bursars' Books is Nov. 1571, 42 (clearly as a clerk); Jan. 1571/2, 35 (as a Fellow); Nov. 1572, 32; Nov. 1573, 30; Dec. 1573, 23; Nov. 1575, 24; Dec. 1575, 17, and then 10 (on inception as M.A.?) Nov. 1576 and Nov. 1577, 16; Nov. 1578, 11; Nov. 1579, 9; Nov. 1580, 7; Nov. 1581; Nov. 1582; Nov. 1583, 5. He then drops out of the Fellowship in Jan. 1583/4, when news of his death would have been confirmed. I am indebted to Mr J. S. G. Simmons, Codrington Librarian at All Souls, and to Professor D. B. Quinn for giving me the benefit of their researches on Richard Madox. See p. 15 below for Madox's sermon.

[3] In the account of Oxford which follows, I am indebted to the following works: *Reg. of the Univ. of Oxford*, ed. A. Clark, II, Pts. i, ii, iii, iv; Montagu Burrows, *Worthies of All Souls* (London, 1874); and Charles E. Mallet, *A History of the University of Oxford* (London, 1924–7), 3 vols.; and to various archival records of the University and of All Souls College, which W. A. Pantin very kindly arranged for me to see and the Warden, John Sparrow, very kindly granted me permission to cite.

hoped for a Fellowship at All Souls as early as November 1570 but was disappointed. Very soon after his admission to the B.A. he was made a Fellow on Wednesday, 16 January 1572,[1] he reports in his Diary, though his admission, he also reports, was regarded as probationary. The record states that with five others, he was admitted 'in perpetuos socios' on that day, and he notes in the Diary that he was admitted 'sodalis' on Sunday, 18 January 1573.

The College was composed of forty fellows divided into those holding fellowships in the Arts (*Artistae*) and those in Law (*Legistae*). A Warden, who was selected by the Archbishop of Canterbury from among two candidates presented by the Fellows, governed the College with the aid of two bursars, who administered College property, and two deans, who supervised studies. These also were chosen by the Archbishop, drawing equally from both faculties. Fellows received their commons (2*s* 8*d* for weekly commons for an M.A., 2*s* 2*d* for others), annual liveries, and certain emoluments, the latter perhaps including a certain distribution of surplus, which, according to Charles E. Mallet, became a common practice in the early seventeenth century.

Nominations for vacant fellowships came from the Fellows themselves from among candidates who were between the ages of seventeen and twenty-six.[2] Candidates had also to be of at least three years' standing in the University, disposed toward entering the church, and of good birth and character; preference was given to founder's kin. Final selections were made by the Warden.

In 1571 Robert Hovenden had been elected Warden '*summo cum consensu*,' the first instance of a married man being chosen for this office. He was to preside for forty-two years, during which time, among other achievements, he completed the Warden's lodgings and added a garden, pulling down 'The Rose,' a house with a famous well, to make room for them and telling the Fellows that thereafter they could wash in rosewater.

Archbishops were *ex officio* visitors and seemed to have served as sole interpreters of the Statutes. In 1541, following a complaint of certain scandals among the Fellows, Archbishop Cranmer made a visitation and, as a result, enjoined penalties for absence, insubordination, and intemperance ('*compotationibus, ingurgitationibus, crapulis, ebrietatis ac*

[1] All Souls College, Warden Hovenden's Admissions Book. Both Clark and J. Foster (*Alumni Oxoniensis*, Oxford 1891–2) are in error in stating that Madox became a Fellow in 1571.

[2] Madox had just turned twenty-five in Nov. See his bitter comment in 1582, p. 278 below, implying that he had been unsuccessful two years earlier.

aliis enormibus et excessivis commissationibus'). Besides requiring that dogs be rigorously excluded and that the Warden and Fellows wear gowns reaching to their heels, he took cognizance of the Fellows' practice of taking money upon resigning their fellowships. Despite these and other earlier injunctions which had forbidden dicing and gaming, the keeping of hawks, hounds, and ferrets, and the carrying of daggers and swords, the Fellows of All Souls seemed to one observer in 1587 like rich monks in a rich abbey rather than students in a poor college. In 1586 Archbishop Whitgift also felt compelled to write to the Warden about the 'very offensive and infamous maner of buyeng and sellinge of places for excessive sommes of money' which tended to the great discredit and dishonour of the house. Madox did not resign his fellowship in electing to go on the voyage, but he did resign his office as proctor and received from his replacement, Henry Beaumont, Fellow of All Souls, as he noted in cipher, something in excess of the sum of 'twenty marx,' a little more than £13 6*s* 8*d*.[1]

During the next three years (1572–5) Madox concentrated on studying natural and moral philosophy as well as metaphysics; having participated satisfactorily in various disputations and given 'cursory' lectures (that is, reading from a text and making brief comments), he was then presented and licensed to the degree, subject to incepting within a year. At this stage he was incorporated M.A.

In the course of the following year as an *inceptor in artibus*, Madox had to perform two sets of exercises. First he had to dispute in the Vesperiae on three questions in philosophy with the senior proctor responding to the first question, a proproctor to the second, and the junior proctor to the third. Accordingly, on Saturday, 7 July 1576, he disputed in the nave of St Mary's Church on the following *quaestiones philosophicae*:

1. *An mare sit salsum?*
2. *An morbi animi sint graviores quam corporis?*
3. *An terra quiescat in medio mundi?*

The following Monday he fulfilled the second requirement of disputing in the Comitia, in this case with a respondent who had been nominated by the proctors, by addressing himself again in St Mary's Church to three questions:

1. *An putrefactio fiat ab externo calore?*
2. *An mares sint diuturnioris vitae quam foeminae?*
3. *An contentiones sint a bono principe inter cives serendae?*[2]

[1] See entries for 15 Feb.; 9, 13 Mar.,

[2] Printed in Clark, *Reg.* II.i.170. Compare the similar *quaestiones philosophicae* posed

After this forensic display he was presented to the Vice Chancellor, who would give him his insignia – a book, a hood, and a cap – and a kiss on the left cheek. Madox records simply, 'In Commitiis steti 9 Julij 1576.'

Six days later he was in Dorset. His movements during the next three and a half years, recorded at the end of his Diary, specifying the dates and lengths of stay outside of Oxford, are mysteriously unexplained: on 15 July 1576 he notes that he was at Dorchester, where he spent two years and nine months; then, presumably, he was back at Oxford – from 15 April 1579 until the following July; he was next in Paris for three months and returned in October to Dorchester, where he remained until the beginning of 1580. What was he doing during this time? Perhaps he was serving in the entourage of a nobleman or serving as a tutor to his children; perhaps he was serving some kind of ecclesiastical apprenticeship. Whatever it was, clearly he had the consent of his College since he retained his fellowship. In contrast to the 'cause of absens' granted for his voyage upon the solicitation of the Chancellor, the earl of Leicester, which is preserved, there is no record of his having been granted any other leave – or multiple leaves.[1]

Madox was again to visit Dorchester during the Easter holidays in 1580; for Good Friday of that year, he notes down at the end of his Diary, a 'sermon on love.' In October 1581, he again returned to Dorset, this time to Weymouth and Melcombe Regis, where he preached a 'short, sweete, and comfortable sermon' before the mayor, bailiffs, and aldermen. After Madox's death and the return of the abortive expedition, this sermon was published on the initiative of Thomas Martin, who is mentioned in 1586 as 'yoman and Towne Clarke' of the joint borough.[2] The relationship between the two men, if not close, was cordial, since Madox dined with him in London before going to sea and had 'commendations from Dorchester.' Scattered allusions in the Diary show his acquaintance with the area, but exactly what he was doing in Dorchester during the longer sojourns or how he obtained leave remains unexplained.

In November 1580, ten months after his return to Oxford, he was

---

to Madox in mid-sea: Why do the trees in England lose their leaves when those in the Strait of Magellan do not? Why does a monkey smell most sweet when she has eaten a spider? (See entry for 10 Oct.).

[1] Yet the granting of a three-years' leave to William Langhorne, the year before Madox left Oxford, is preserved (All Souls College, Warden Hovenden's Minute Bk.). For Madox's 'cause of absens' see 14 Feb., n. 6.

[2] *Descriptive Catalogue of the Charters, Minute Books, and Other Documents in the Borough of Weymouth and Melcombe Regis*, ed. H. J. Moule, II (Weymouth, 1883), 77.

made praelector or university lecturer, for which he received at least five shillings. He was also studying in the higher faculty of theology. At this time he took priestly orders (24 Nov.) and was licensed under the common seal '*ad praedicandum per universam Angliam.*' This grace was independent of a degree in theology and was restricted, in contrast with the license granted him by Congregation in February 1582, which allowed him to preach '*per universum orbis circuitum.*'[1]

In March 1581, Madox set himself the curious task of copying out in a fine clear hand a tract 'Concerning Succession to the Crowne after Q. Elizabeth' which supported the claims of Lady Catherine Grey. Although this particular answer to the problem of succession had stirred up a storm – *tempestas Halesiana* – in the 1560s, it is difficult to understand its significance in the spring of 1581.

The granddaughter of Henry VIII's younger sister Mary and the duke of Suffolk, Lady Catherine, after the death of her sister Lady Jane, was the next in line of succession in accordance with Henry's will. In 1561 she had secretly married the earl of Hertford, and when it became apparent that she was about to produce an heir, the two were sent to the Tower. The Queen set up a commission under the Archbishop of Canterbury to look into the validity of their marriage, which found it invalid and declared their sons, two by that date, bastards. Nonetheless, the Suffolk line, according to certain views, had provided a candidate for the throne who was, as Conyers Read notes, male, pure English, and of sound Protestant background.[2]

The mood of parliament in 1563 was strong for establishing the succession, and a clerk of the Hanaper, John Hales, known as 'clubfoot,' had prepared a discourse supporting the Suffolk claim. Circulated in manuscript (the work was not published until 1713), his arguments coupled with the prevailing attitude were judged inflammatory. Hales was imprisoned, and his patron Sir Nathaniel Bacon was exiled from court. Lady Catherine, though she was released from the Tower in 1563, was never to see her husband again and was kept in custody

[1] On 8 Feb. 1582, he submitted the following request: 'Inasmuch as Richard Madox, M.A., being engaged to a moderate degree in the study of theology, has shown that he has heretofore devoted his ability to the spread of the gospel to the extent that grace has permitted, he begs the Honourable Congregation, etc., that with your generous consent he be allowed to preach the word of God throughout the entire world. The reason is that, being engaged in the performance of a public duty and about to proceed to the most remote regions of the earth, he wishes to be honoured and strengthened in this undertaking by the wishes, prayers, and support of all of you whom he loves most of all in Christ.' The Latin supplication is cited in Clark, *Reg.* II.i.130. He noted in his Diary (15 Feb.) that this license was granted.

[2] *Mr Secretary Cecil and Queen Elizabeth* (London, 1955), pp. 276–80.

until her death in 1568. It was Hales's discourse, though not identified as such, which Madox finished copying on Tuesday, 23 March 1581.[1]

On Wednesday 5 April, along with Robert Crane of Balliol, Madox was elected to the office of Proctor by direct vote of Convocation,[2] the governing body of the University made up of regents, that is, of masters of arts having less than two years' standing. The two officers, known originally as the Southern and Northern Proctor, were by this date called Senior and Junior. (Crane had been elected at the beginning of Easter term in the preceding year and was thus the Senior Proctor.) Among their duties was the overseeing of the various disputations of candidates. Each bachelor who wished to determine (that is, to go through disputations) had to defend Aristotle, and it was the Junior Proctor's duty to make a speech evaluating the performance of the candidate. In the same way these two officers served at the disputations for masters, receiving fees in each case, with graduates often complaining that they charged too much. Furthermore, as Andrew Clark notes, since they received the bulk of their fees from incepting masters, the number who incepted, either by the regular procedure or by special dispensation, would obviously have a direct bearing on the profits accruing to the two officers. In 1578/9 the fee for a master disputing before he had incepted was a 'dragma' or a pair of gloves, and one notes that when Madox was given a pair shortly before he left Oxford, he immediately 'bestoed' it elsewhere, perhaps because of his own too plentiful supply.

In addition to academic duties, the Proctors were also concerned with the discipline and morals of the students, meting out summary punishment on occasion. Anthony Wood, for example, recalls that when 'the said Crayne with his brother Proctor, walking in the night time in St. Thomas Parish, took a certain person in the act of adultery,' the punishment enjoined was to 'repair the wooden bridge (ready to fall) that leads from St. Thomas Parish unto the castle.'[3]

[1] Madox's manuscript is in Bodleian Library, Tanner MS 79, ff. 24–8. In speculating about his possible motive in copying Hales's tract, one is tempted to recall that when Sir John Harington wrote his *Tract on the Succession to the Crown* in 1602 – in defence of James's claim – he was writing it for his dearest friend Tobie Matthew, Archbishop of York, who preserved the manuscript in the Chapter Library. Madox makes an admiring comment about Dr Matthew, who was at this date Dean of Christ Church, on 2 Feb. and dines with him four days later; one wonders whether the future archbishop may have been collecting documents relating to the problem of the succession.

[2] There is no evidence to show whether Madox's election was owing to the interference of the Chancellor or another official as was the case when he *resigned* the office (see entry for 15 Feb.).

[3] *Fasti*, ed. John Gutch (London, 1786), p. 108.

Six months after he took orders, and on the 'mocion' of Thomas Martin, Madox delivered the 'learned and godly sermon' at Weymouth and Melcombe Regis mentioned above. Based on Matt. 8: 23–25, it was intended, as the title page indicates, for 'all Marryners, Captaynes, and Passengers, which travell the Seas.' Its nautical imagery and homely diction, as J. W. Blench notes, show that Madox had heeded 'the old advice of the preaching manuals to have respect to the audience.'[1] And as Martin explains in his prefatory epistle, he dedicated the published sermon to the mayor, bailiffs, and aldermen not only because they had thankfully received it on its delivery but also 'because you being Marchants, and therfore often travailing the dangerous salt fome, may, (by taking it with you and recording the same) learne how to passe in the acceptable feare of God, your idle times at sea, to the benefit of your own soules, and most of all to the glorye of God.' Martin also makes clear that he was moved to publish it not only out of a certain evangelical fervour but also as a tribute to the 'godly, learned, and vertuous young man [called here and on the title page] *John Madoxe*, M. of Arte and fellow of all Soules in *Oxforde*' who had 'reaped the fruites of his faith,' so that 'his good studyes, in vertuous exercises not buryed in the pit of oblivion, may make him in fame, on earth to live for aye.' The motive was worthy, the degree of achievement questionable.

In assessing the career of Richard Madox during the years he was connected with Oxford, one concludes on the basis of the sparse records that he was relatively successful: he moved up the academic ladder steadily if not conspicuously as B.A., M.A., praelector, Fellow, and, ultimately, University Proctor. His actual academic achievement is more difficult to access. He was curious and knowledgeable about many things, but his interest in theology, his avowed profession, seems to have been scant and his skill in Greek and Latin, at least as attested by his Diary (discussed below), something less than proficient. This, not untypical, lack of proficiency reflects the academic standards obtaining at mid-century and following. As Nicholas Grimald commented in 1556, there were 'such as have english meatly well, and but a smattering, or small taste in the latine: which noumber is great, among the scholars of this realme.'

Madox seems also to have been relatively successful in other ways. His absence from Oxford during the three and a half years he spent in

[1] *Preaching in England in the Late Fifteenth and Sixteenth Centuries* (London, 1954), pp. 172–3.

Dorchester and in Paris suggests that he obtained some sort of special patronage since he did not have to relinquish his fellowship at All Souls. This was also to be the case in 1582 when as Chancellor of the University and prime mover of the forthcoming voyage, the earl of Leicester selected him to be the chaplain on the flagship, the 'admiral' of the small fleet headed for China and Cathay.

Entries relating to Oxford in the Diary show him concerned, if somewhat warily, with political and religious matters. They also show him as gregarious and no respecter of persons, whether he was dining with the mayor of Oxford and wassailing with the chamberlain or being merry with a groom of Corpus Christi and 'Jerom the bruer.' He consorted easily with scholars and fellows as well as with the younger students, participating with alacrity in their festive activities. This pattern of easy social mingling he was to follow on the voyage to the Moluccas but in the seamier and harsher atmosphere of life at sea with something less than success.

II. THE VOYAGE

Origins and participants

Wishing to make himself useful to the state, as he was later to say with some bitterness, Madox made the eventful decision sometime in the late fall of 1581 to associate himself with the first trading expedition to the Far East. This project had the backing of a number of influential people – Privy Councillors (the earl of Leicester, Sir Francis Walsingham, and Lord Burghley); important members of the Muscovy Company (Alderman Barne – the son of 'old Sir George,' William Towerson, and John Castelyn); and (so-called) 'captains of the sea' including Martin Frobisher, Christopher Carleill, and the current hero Sir Francis Drake, recently returned in triumph from his circumnavigation. Despite this stalwart backing, to the persons involved the trading expedition of 1582 was to seem something of a let-down since it was an outgrowth of two daring enterprises (called the First and Second) that had just come to naught; it was, in actuality, a development of a more sober and far-reaching scheme.

Whatever Drake's real motives had been when he set out in December 1577, he returned three years later with the hard evidence that plundering Spanish treasure in the New World was feasible and with the idea that the English might counter the monopoly of the Portuguese in China and Cathay – thanks to his putative agreement with the Sultan of Ternate – by establishing their own trade with the Spice Islands. Both the hard evidence and the vision were to stir tantalising possibilities in the minds of many Englishmen – seasoned councillors, prosperous merchants, intrepid sea captains, and greedy mariners (with the adjectives shuffled more or less at will).

The visionary aspect soon received formulation in a petition in the hand of Sir Francis Walsingham which sought to establish a new corporation for trading beyond the 'Equynoctyall lyne.' Drake was to be the permanent governor, and in consideration of his great travel and hazard, he was to be given a tenth part of all the profits accruing; further, in obvious imitation of the useful *Casa de Contratación* at Seville, a house was to be erected with 'sooche orders' as had been granted to that institution by the King of Spain.'[1]

Shortly afterward, as reported in December 1580 and January 1581 by Bernardino de Mendoza, the resident Spanish ambassador, a new plan was set afoot. This was to send Drake out with ten ships by way of the Cape of Good Hope to plunder in the Indies and then to continue on to the Moluccas, where Henry Knollys, going by way of the South Sea, was to meet up with him; if the weather did not serve for reaching the Moluccas, they were then to winter in Brazil. Mendoza noted that Leicester was being 'very energetic' about this project. In April he wrote that there had been no resolution about it though there had been a consultation involving Walsingham, Leicester, Drake, Hawkins, Frobisher, (John) Winter, and (Richard) Bingham, the last three, he commented, all expert mariners. The irresolution Mendoza noted was occasioned by the desire of the English at this point to initiate direct action that would undermine to some extent the recent success in Portugal of King Philip II.

Following on the death of the childless King Henry the Cardinal

[1] SP 12/140/44. Repr. in Z. Nuttall, *New Light on Drake* (Hakluyt Soc., 1914), p. 430. In pointing out that this plan for an East India Company anticipated by twenty years the formal inauguration of trade with the Far East in 1600, Conyers Read believes Walsingham should be given the credit for it (*Mr Secretary Walsingham*, III (Oxford, 1925), 396–8). On the other hand, Henry Wagner (*Sir Francis Drake's Voyage Around the World* (San Francisco, 1926), pp. 214, 4–5) observes that the proposal was a revival of a scheme set forth in 1573 and 1574 by Sir Richard Grenville and others. But the impetus at this date clearly derives from Drake's voyage and the reported six tons of cloves he had obtained from Babù, the Sultan of Ternate, who controlled the bulk of the clove trade and who had ejected the Portuguese from Ternate (Wagner, *Drake's Voyage*, pp. 177–8).

In the second edition of *PN* (1598–1600) Hakluyt is still urging the usefulness of such an institution as the *Casa de Contratación*; and he includes an account by a Spanish pilot of 'Certaine briefe extracts' of the orders of the *Casa de Contratación* 'touching their gouvernment in sea-matters.'

in January 1580, the Portuguese throne had been beset by numerous rival claimants – the Duke of Parma; the Duke of Savoy; the Duchess of Braganza; Dom António the Pretender; and King Philip of Spain, the last, as Camden observed, if not in right, yet in might, the strongest. It was clearly to the advantage of the English – and the French – that Portugal remain independent so that the East India trade, the commerce in the Madeiras, in the Cape Verdes, Guinea, and Brazil, as well as in the strategic Azores, escape the grasping hands of King Philip. Although Dom António received some popular support (on being proclaimed king, his horse 'at the first steppe . . . stumbled and almost fell, in signe of presaging ill'),[1] he was no match for the Spanish monarch who set about with ruthless efficiency to conquer the country by land and sea. After a fruitless struggle, Dom António fled to France, and King Philip became master in name of an incredibly rich and extensive empire.

The First and Second Enterprises. In December 1580, according to Mendoza, Queen Elizabeth had sent word to the Azores to hold fast to Dom António, and with the exception of São Miguel it was believed the Islands had indeed declared for him. Consequently, the former plan to send Drake to the Indies was shaped into a new project called the 'First Enterprise': Drake, with a fleet of eight ships, pinnaces, and barks was now to establish a base of operation in Terceira and await the Spanish treasure fleet from the West Indies until the end of the year; if he missed capturing it, he was then to proceed to the Caribbean and plunder the Spanish colonies. Naturally, he was to sail under the flag of Dom António with authorisation to assist him against any of his enemies.[2]

That this project with its obviously political motives was also expected to produce profits is indicated by one stage of the financing: Dom António, relying on a loan from the Queen, was to disburse one-fourth of the charges, the adventurers the rest; the crew was to receive one-third of whatever was obtained from the enemies of 'the king' – António[3] – and he and his partners were to receive two-thirds, divided

[1] Girolamo Conestaggio, *The Historie of the Uniting of the Kingdom of Portugall to the Crowne of Castill* (1600), P3.

[2] Documents relating to the First (and Second) Enterprise are to be found in SP 12/148/43–7 and Dudley Digges, *The Compleat Ambassador* (London, 1655). The dispatches of Mendoza to Philip II (*CSP, Spanish*, 1580–6) include information on these enterprises and others, including the voyage to the Moluccas.

[3] The English almost invariably refer to the Pretender as 'king.' One of the obstacles to French support was that Catherine de Medici wished Elizabeth to aid Dom António 'by that name, but not that of K. *Anthony*' (Digges, *Compleat Ambassador*, p. 394). This objection was the result of Catherine's posing of her own claim to the throne of Portugal.

according to each man's adventure.[1] Significant names of interested captains besides those Mendoza had mentioned in connection with the original plan included Edward Fenton, Gilbert Yorke, and Luke Ward, though, according to Burghley, upon some scruples they were later to 'forbear.'[2]

As usual, the Queen was concerned about the increased charges after additional loans were requested – at one point she was to be offered a unicorn's horn, seven feet in length, valued at 180,000 French crowns as security. She was also concerned about obtaining a firm commitment from the French in support of the venture. After repeated 'stays,' on 18 August Burghley reported the Queen 'very cold' to the idea though all such things as ships, victuals, men, etc., were ready.[3] Six days later she was considering sending out only four of the ships under the charge of William Hawkins.[4] Finally, on 29 August, owing to the lateness of the season and the default of the French, three of the adventurers (Drake, Hawkins, and Walsingham through his secretary Francis Mills) instructed Henry Owtread (or Ughtred) – owner of the *Galleon Owtread*, the largest of the eight ships – and Luke Ward – one of the suggested captains – to sell all provisions and victuals 'at the best prises.' Burghley gave the cost of this First Enterprise at £13,000, the loss at about £3600.[5]

An alternative or Second Enterprise was also proposed. This was to send ships to Calicut on the Malabar coast to establish a trade in spices in her Majesty's right as a party with Dom António. This too fell through, and Dom António, who arrived in England in the summer, departed for France to see what business he could do there. In September Mendoza reported that the Queen had now decided to equip three ships which were to effect a landing in the East Indies if Dom António's supporters were numerous; otherwise they were to proceed to the Moluccas with merchandise. Frobisher as captain was to set out at Christmas.

Such was the origin of the voyage on which Madox was to sail. Many of its participants were those involved in the two earlier projects, and it was to be marked by the same irresolution, uncertainties, and delays that had characterised them. Above all, the same confusion stemming from divided intention was to prevail.

[1] SP 12/148/43.

[2] Digges, *Compleat Ambassador*, p. 379. Fenton's brother Geoffrey wrote at this time that they had been 'put from' the Portuguese voyage by Sir Francis Drake (SP 12/85/19). Upon being released, Edward Fenton was promised his charges (Digges, p. 389); Luke Ward continued to be involved in the dismantling of the enterprise.

[3] Digges, *Compleat Ambassador*, p. 388.

[4] Digges, *Compleat Ambassador*, p. 394.

[5] Digges, *Compleat Ambassador*, p. 422.

If, as Mendoza reported, the earl of Leicester had been energetic about sending ships to the Moluccas, now that the Terceira project was at an end he became prime mover of the new expedition to be headed, according to the initial plans, by Martin Frobisher. He agreed to buy the *Galleon Owtread* (sometimes called the *Bear Gallion*), which had been readied for the First Enterprise and which, as Mendoza noted with satisfaction, had been bombarded in Cadiz.[1] This ship, variously listed as of 400 or 500 tons, was four years old. Madox records with some enthusiasm (19 Apr.) that she represented a new type of galleon built on the lines of the *Revenge*. Its owner Henry Owtread was a busy entrepreneur of Southampton, and at times a promoter of privateering, who had built six ships of which this was the largest and finest,[2] valued by Owtread and Frobisher at £2800. Leicester agreed to purchase so much of the ship as amounted to £2000, with Owtread reserving the rest for his share of the adventure. The Earl also agreed to pay for the sheathing, the supplying of munitions and artillery, victuals, and the furniture, including flags and ensigns, whereof one flag was 'to be of the kynge of Portyngalls armes.' There are differing statements concerning his terms for paying Owtread, but in earnest of the agreement he was to give sufficient new and good velvet to make a gown for Owtread's wife, Lady Elizabeth Courtenay.[3]

Along with the earl of Leicester and Henry Owtread, the third major adventurer was Sir Francis Drake. Initially he had offered either to provide money (1000 marks), his ship the *Bark Hastings*, or his new bark and two pinnaces prepared and furnished with an adventure of £1000. As it turned out, he contributed the *Bark Francis*, and his share is variously recorded as £666 13*s* 4*d* and £700. Most importantly, he

[1] *CSP, Sp., 1580–6*, pp. 128, 180. Henry Owtread's petition to the Privy Council of grievances against Spain in 1580–1 is in SP 12/153/73. On this occasion the *Galleon* suffered only loss of merchandise when the master sailed away and left her on shore.

The occasion to which Mendoza refers is mentioned by Richard Carter alias Juan Perez, who was captured off the coast of Brazil by Fenton in November, 1582. He reported that the pilot (probably 'Simon Fernando') told him the *Galleon* had been at Cadiz when Diego Flores de Valdés (General of the Fleet carrying the troops to fortify the Strait of Magellan) was forced to call in, that the Spaniards tried to capture her in order to make her a part of their fleet, whereupon the crew drew up the cables by hand, escaping from seven galleys sent in pursuit (repr. in Wagner, *Drake's Voyage*, p. 399).

The *Galleon*, as Madox records, had made two Spanish voyages with little profit.

[2] See SP 12/156/45 and *APC, 1578–80*, p. 396.

[3] B.L. Cotton MS Otho E VIII, 120, f. 87. Part of the agreement was that Leicester was to procure if possible a commission from Dom António so that Owtread could send out two ships to spoil the Spanish and Portuguese enemies of the 'king.' There are many papers relating to this voyage in this manuscript (cited henceforth as Otho E VIII), but most of them have been badly mutilated by fire. They are calendared in *SP Col., East Indies, China and Japan* and the most important have been printed, with some differences in transcription, in E. G. R. Taylor's edition of *The Troublesome Voyage of Captain Edward Fenton.*

provided advice to Leicester on the best route, urging that the ships go by way of the Cape of Good Hope and avoid the Strait of Magellan, now believed about to be fortified by the Spaniards, and he encouraged some of the 'sufficient men' of his late company to take part.[1]

At one point Alderman Richard Martin of the Muscovy Company intended to furnish the *Mary Edwards*,[2] but the *Edward Bonaventure* of London, a ship of the Levant Company owned chiefly, according to K. R. Andrews, by the merchant Thomas Cordell,[3] was to become the second ship instead. In October the earl of Oxford asserted he would buy her, and Frobisher himself and Richard Bolland offered £1500, but her owners held out for £1800.[4] A ship of 250 to 300 tons, the *Edward Bonaventure* was expected to carry some seventy men; she was eight years old and, like the *Galleon Owtread*, carried heavy artillery.

The earl of Shrewsbury and his co-owners offered the *Bark Talbot* with the Earl's appointees agreeing to serve under Frobisher, provided they might share indifferently in the trading and, more significantly, in 'any prize lawefully to be gotten.'[5] Instead of the £1000 adventure this would have represented, he seems to have ended up by investing £200.

Having experienced the frustrations and expense of the First Enterprise, John Hawkins refused to subscribe despite, as he commented, Drake's involvement. Leicester, however, rounded up his friends, and in due course the earls of Warwick, Pembroke, and Lincoln, Lord Hunsdon and Lord Charles Howard, Sir Christopher Hatton, Sir Thomas Heneage, and Sir Edward Horsey, as well as two fellow members of the Privy Council, Walsingham and Burghley, adventured.[6]

The Muscovy Company was largely involved although its precise contribution is not specified in the extant documents; besides preparing the wares for barter,[7] it may have been responsible for the adventuring of the *Edward Bonaventure*. Certainly three of its members – Alderman George Barne, William Towerson, and John Castelyn – were active in getting the fleet under sail. Some of the intended officers also became adventurers: Martin Frobisher (£300) and Christopher Carleill (£300)

[1] Otho E VIII, ff. 85*v*–86.
[2] Otho E VIII, f. 106*v*.
[3] *English Privateering Voyages to the West Indies* (Hakluyt Soc., 1959), p. 338, n. 3.
[4] Otho E VIII, f. 87. [5] Otho E VIII, f. 104. [6] SP 12/150/96.
[7] An inventory of wares, including kersies, buttons, pewter, spoons, salts, etc., for the Fenton voyage is listed at a value of £2000; this inventory, as Taylor notes (*Fenton*, p. 13, n. 3), is dated 12 May 1582, which is after the expedition had departed (from Southampton) but while they were still at the Isle of Wight.

– neither of whom sailed; Edward Fenton and his friends (£300); and Luke Ward (£200).

Even the Queen may have become involved if belatedly: after the *Edward Bonaventure* (and the bark *Peter*) had passed through the customs carrying taxable merchandise valued at £912 4*s* 2*d*, a warrant was drafted wherein she agreed to surrender for the use of the adventurers the customs (already paid) on the wares 'shipped in the moneth of Aprill last past in the names of our right trustie and welbeloved Robert Erle of leicester and other adventurers for the discovery and finding of Cathaia.' For this rebate she was to be counted one adventurer, 'according as the voyage shall have successe.' Since the customs amounted to £82 4*s* 5½*d*, the Queen, as recorded, was 'the least' adventurer among them.[1]

Thus the *Bear Galleon*, soon to be rechristened the *Galleon Leicester*, 'a name more sownding and significative,' the *Edward Bonaventure*, the *Bark Francis*, and another bark, the *Elizabeth* – added at Southampton because of the great store of provisions – made up the venture. No record of the total cost of the expedition appears to be extant, but there are charges for the two principal vessels, with provisions for thirteen months and 'an overplus' of six.[2] Those for the *Galleon Leicester* come to £6035 10*s* 10*d*; those for the *Edward* £3457 5*s*. The *Bark Francis* is valued at £66 13*s* 4*d*, but there are no charges for setting her out. Two pinnaces ('unsett up') and two Spanish shallops which were to be carried are estimated at £76. The value of the merchandise carried also is not specified. A complement of two hundred men had initially been projected, but with the addition of the *Elizabeth* about 240 persons were expected to sail. This number included three travellers – Richard Cotton and Edward Gilman on the *Galleon*, Samuel Symbarb on the *Edward*; a fourth was put ashore on the Isle of Wight (16 May). With defections and additional impressment,[3] perhaps no one ever knew precisely how many people were on the four ships when they lost sight of England.

[1] B.L., Lansdowne MS 110, ff. 145–7.

[2] They are given in SP 12/150/96. Included in the itemisation is a reference to 'a bark' of Sir Francis Drake's though the name is left blank and its value not specified. Subsequently (see Madox's entry for 24 Apr.), the merchants bought a bark or frigate belonging to Luke Ward which Sir Humphrey Gilbert himself wished to buy. To avoid offending him, the merchants then sold Ward's bark to him on 1 May and bought the *Elizabeth* 'for burden sake,' setting her out for the £40 which they received from Gilbert.

In reference to this venture, Christopher Carleill later reported the cost of preparation was 'not less than xiiii or xv thowsand powndes' (cited in D. B. Quinn, *The Voyages and Colonising Enterprises of Sir Humphrey Gilbert*, II (Hakluyt Soc., 1940), 359, n. 2).

[3] See entries for 1, 2 May and notes.

The personnel, it would seem, was selected in large part by Leicester with the advice of Drake. The general of the whole company was to be Martin Frobisher, whose early career had been as a privateer[1] and who had had extensive experience at sea, most recently in the three voyages in search of the Northwest Passage. A number of those who were to make this voyage had sailed with him to Meta Incognita. Though he had quarrelled with his subordinates, he seems to have been popular with the sailors, and at least some of them he shipped for this voyage refused to sail after he was replaced. With the assistance of Fenton and Ward, Frobisher was in charge of arranging for the provisions. He was later to be accused of having pocketed £1100 of the £1600 allotted for this purpose (13 Sept.), of shortchanging the stores of 20 tuns of beer (16 Oct.), and, through his man Anthony Fisher, of adding rye to the meal (15 Sept.). He had been similarly charged by Michael Lok, Governor of the Company of Cathay, with 'evil victualling' the ships sailing to Meta Incognita.[2]

On 27 February, as Madox noted, Frobisher was discharged of the voyage and Edward Fenton put in his place. The reason for the change of command is unclear. Mendoza reported that because the Muscovy Company wished to force a lieutenant of their own choosing upon him, Frobisher refused to undertake the voyage,[3] and he added that he himself had been secretly inciting the quarrel. (Curiously, a charge was to be made at sea that the voyage had been bought and sold by Fenton before they left England, the ostensible proof being that he had had daily conference with the Spanish ambassador.[4]) Later Mendoza reported that Frobisher (in consultation with Leicester) intended to head another expedition, which, sailing by way of the Strait, would, he boasted, beat the Fenton group to the Moluccas.

Edward Fenton, who was called both 'a Gentleman of my Lord of Warwikes' and Leicester's 'true follower,'[5] had done active service in

[1] See R. G. Marsden, 'The Early Career of Sir Martin Frobisher,' *EHR*, XXI (July, 1906), 538–44.

[2] B.L., Lansdowne MS 100, f. 7.

[3] *CSP, Sp., 1580–6*, p. 306. This is supported by what John Drake, captain of the *Bark Francis*, was to depose in 1587 (see p. 25, n. 1 below): 'as the merchants were for giving a similar commission [to sail to China and found a factory] to another man, he [Frobisher] refused to go.'

[4] This charge was reported (Taylor, *Fenton*, p. 142) as emanating from his Lieutenant William Hawkins. After his return home, Hawkins stated: 'For in truthe this maketh the sayinge of some of our companye thought true, which saied that this honourable voyage (the more the pyttie) was bought and solde by the Spanyards frends, or Sp[anyards] themselves before oure comyng out of Englande' (Otho E VIII, f. 225).

[5] He is termed a follower of Warwick's by Dionyse Settle (*PN* (1589), p. 622); in June 1582, Leicester names Fenton's brother *Henry* as Warwick's servant (*CSP Add., 1580–1625*,

Ireland, where his more literary brother Geoffrey served in various official capacities for nearly thirty years. As early as the 1560s or 1570s, his name appears in a list of 'sondrye gentelmen and Captaynes for the sea' who have not yet served but are 'fitt to serve'[1] as well as in a list dated 3 February 1580.[2] He had accompanied Frobisher on the 1577 voyage to Meta Incognita as captain of the *Gabriel* and again in 1578 when he served as his lieutenant and was designated captain of the company of one hundred that had been appointed to remain. Although Fenton and Frobisher had quarrelled on the last voyage and again after their return when Frobisher 'uppon the sodaine drewe his dagger,' they were sufficiently reconciled to work together for more than five months in preparing for this venture. From the outset of the voyage Fenton, so Madox reports, was to conduct himself in a wilful and arrogant manner, almost, it would seem, as if he were emulating the very qualities which contemporaries had remarked on in his former captain. As the progress of the voyage was to reveal, however, this mode of conduct served only to mask his irresolution and fear of mutiny.

Luke Ward 'gentleman,' appointed 'Vice-admiral' and Captain of the *Edward Bonaventure*, was an experienced mariner, having served on all three of Frobisher's voyages; he had been admitted an adventurer gratis in the 1578 voyage in consideration of his earlier services and he was one of those appointed 'to inhabit' with Fenton. Earlier, he had served the state by transporting munitions to Ireland and had been commissioned to take pirates,[3] an authority which he was to put to use again in 1582 when the *Edward* encountered pirate vessels near Dover – one of which included the men 'shipt by Furbusher' but who refused to sail under Fenton.

John Drake, aged about twenty, was to captain his cousin's small bark, the *Francis*. He had served as Sir Francis's page, first in Ireland, then on the circumnavigation where he became the first to descry the treasure ship *Cacafuego* and so receive the promised chain of gold. The Portuguese pilot whom Sir Francis captured at Santiago called him a skilful painter and said that when he and his cousin shut themselves up in the cabin, they were always painting: Spanish prisoners taken aboard the *Golden Hind* in Guatulco were shown a copy of Foxe's *Book of Martyrs* with the illustrations coloured.

---

p. 63). In a letter to Leicester, 3 Oct. 1580, Sir Nicholas Bagnall (Thomas Wright, *Queen Elizabeth and Her Times*, II (London, 1838), 119) calls him Leicester's 'true follower.'

[1] Lansdowne MS 683, f. 51. [2] SP 12/136/20.

[3] *APC, 1578–80*, pp. 248, 257, 303; SP 12/123/34.

When on 20 December 1582 Fenton took the decision not to go through the Strait of Magellan, John Drake defected from the expedition; but his ship ran aground and was wrecked while trying to leave the River Plate. After more than a year of extreme hardship, he was taken by the Spaniards and interrogated on two occasions, the two depositions providing information about his experience on Drake's voyage as well as on this one.[1]

The Captain of the *Elizabeth* was Thomas Skevington. Listed on Gilbert's 1578 voyage as 'gentleman,'[2] he seems otherwise unknown. Madox's description of him as a 'fyzzeling [farting] taleberer and a pykethank' must suffice. After his ship was sold to the Portuguese in Sierra Leone, his crew was distributed among the other vessels, and he receives no mention thereafter except in the notation of his death from scurvy on 28 May 1583.

William Hawkins the Younger, the volatile nephew of John Hawkins, served as second in command on the *Galleon*.[3] He too had sailed with Drake and at some stage of the planning had been nominated to captain the ship, though early instructions recommended that if he were to do so some other trusty person be joined with him.[4] But Henry Owtread regretted his being an 'underlyng' to the choleric, stubborn, and highminded Fenton and as late as mid-March urged that the command be given to Hawkins in conjunction with Christopher Carleill, Sir Francis Walsingham's stepson.

About thirty-four years of age, Carleill had had considerable naval and military experience. Initially he was appointed to be Captain-at-Land and the official registrar of the voyage who was to keep a secret record of all 'debatements,' but at the wishes of members of the Privy Council, Madox was later to substitute for him as registrar. Carleill was also designated as a meet person to be governor of a company of men to be left in the Moluccas to learn the language, conditions, and commodities of the country. However, after the Privy Council issued

[1] The depositions are printed in Lady Elizabeth Eliott-Drake, *The Family and Heirs of Sir Francis Drake*, II (London, 1911), 351–7; 380–401.

[2] Cited in Quinn, *Gilbert*, I, 211. Taylor (*Fenton* p. xxxv) says he too had sailed with Frobisher but provides no documentation.

[3] He probably was about the age of John Drake though his date of birth is unknown. One of the eleven children of William Hawkins of Plymouth (aged 63 in 1582), he was termed by Fenton, in a moment of pique, 'A knave, villeyn, and a Boye' (Otho E VIII, f. 228).

The account of the later career of Hawkins found in Ch. VI of Michael Lewis's *The Hawkins Dynasty* (London, 1969) is dubious; that relating to the Fenton voyage largely incorrect.

[4] Otho E VIII, f. 85*v*.

the Instructions for the voyage (9 April), he refused to sail, purportedly because he was suffering from 'an ague,' but as Fenton indicates in a (badly mutilated) letter to Leicester dated 22 April,[1] it was rather because young Hawkins had been given precedence over him in the Instructions. Unlike Hawkins – or his own successor as Captain-at-Land – Carleill was not to be included among the Assistants with whom the General was to confer on 'all causes, matters, and actions of importance.' Madox reports his refusal to go simply as 'upon some discurtesy taken.'

As a result, Fenton and Alderman Barne then appointed Nicholas Parker, who in 1579 had served as Fenton's lieutenant in Ireland,[2] to all of Carleill's preferments and charges. On 1 June a 'jar' broke out while they were at Plymouth. With William Hawkins ashore visiting Sir Francis Drake, Fenton intemperately ordered the ships to haul off to sea: he was desirous, Madox commented, to sail without him in order that Parker might be made lieutenant. Yielding, at last, to the muttering of the crew, Fenton agreed to cast about the next day in order to fetch him on board along with the rest of the 'Plymouth men,' including one of the *Galleon*'s pilots. Fenton was to remain at odds with Hawkins throughout the voyage, whereas he remained, at least openly, in accord with Parker.

The two chaplains – Richard Madox for the *Galleon* and John Walker for the *Edward* – were chosen by Leicester.[3] The instructions issued to Fenton enjoined him to take 'especial care' in seeing that they had the reverence and respect due their calling and in seeing that their orders for 'reformation of life and manners' were obeyed. Writing to Leicester in June, John Walker commented on how wonderfully reformed 'both in rule of lyfe and relygyon' his people on the *Edward* were become: they had, he said, daily morning and evening prayers, with special prayers at other times of day, Sunday sermons and conference in the Scripture thereafter. His Diary,[4] which adds interesting supplementary and supporting evidence to that of Madox's, carefully records the text of each of his sermons.

Not so Richard Madox's; his Diary records other matters. But interesting light concerning the religious practices on the *Galleon* comes from the second of John Drake's depositions in Peru (1587),

[1] Otho E VIII, f. 144.
[2] R. Holinshed, *Chronicle*, II (1587), P5*v*.
[3] Madox, it will be remembered, obtained his leave of absence from All Souls at Leicester's request, and Henry Owtread alludes to him as his 'honowres chapleyne' (Otho E VIII, f. 122).
[4] Reprinted in Appendix II, pp. 295 ff.

where he recounts that his men went to the *Galleon* to communicate because there was no chaplain aboard the *Francis*. (He himself never remembered having taken communion in England.) After communion on the *Galleon*, he explained, the chaplain, that is, Madox, told them 'to retire to some secret place and there to confess to God in whatever they might have offended against the Ten Commandments: if they had stolen, etc., etc., and that they should repent of it and that God pardoned them.' He adds, perhaps with conscious understatement, that he 'acted accordingly two or three times.'[1]

Madox, as mentioned before, was selected by members of the Privy Council to be the official registrar or public notary – an officer, as Leicester's secretary noted, that the Spaniards carried with them on every voyage as a means to restrain partial dealing since 'every man shall knowe his doings must come to light and judgement at Retourne.'[2] The extant portion of Madox's direct, lively, and colloquial account as registrar is printed in Appendix I and is discussed below.

Leicester seems also to have selected the surgeon on the *Galleon*, John Banister, who came from Nottingham. Admitted a member of the Barber-Surgeons' Company in 1572, he was licensed to practice in 1573 by Oxford University and was thus both physician and surgeon, an unusual combination in a period when the medical arts were spread among three kinds of practitioners – physicians, surgeons, and apothecaries. Ten years earlier, together with his good friend and colleague William Clowes, Banister accompanied the earl of Warwick in his occupation of Le Havre, where he successfully cured him of a poisoned bullet wound. (His record of cures on this expedition, however, was to be anything but notable.) An interesting portrait (see Fig. 2) shows him delivering the 'Visceral Lecture' in 1581 in the Barber-Surgeons' Hall on Monkwell Street. He is lecturing on a text from Realdus Columbus and illustrating his lecture by reference to a partially dissected corpse (one of four malefactors permitted the Barber-Surgeons yearly); his arms are depicted, and his age is given as forty-eight.[3] A tireless reviser of ancient and modern authorities, he

[1] Deposition in Eliott-Drake, *Drake* II, 382. Writing in 1584 in support of discovery (*Discourse of Western Planting*), Hakluyt remarks on its utility for the 'enlargement of the gospel of Christ.' To the demands of papists as to how many infidels had been converted by these means, he cited the ministers who had gone on the voyages of Frobisher, Drake, and Fenton but admitted: 'yet in very deed I was not able to name any one infidel by them converted.' (His text is repr. in *The Original Writings and Correspondence of the Two Richard Hakluyts*, ed. E. G. R. Taylor, II (Hakluyt Soc., 1935), 213–326.)

[2] Otho E VIII, 85*v*.

[3] D'Arcy Power, 'Notes on Early Portraits of John Banister, of William Harvey, and

had recently published *The Historie of Man, sucked from the sappe of the most approved anathomistes* (1578). Something of a religious zealot, he showed himself to be – in Madox's estimation – an overweening and assertive man, clashing frequently with his fellow voyagers, particularly with his younger colleague Lewis Otmore on the *Edward*.

Other officers on the *Galleon* included Thomas Hood, a pilot from Plymouth, who had served in that capacity for Drake and had been named to serve on the *Galleon* with 170 men in the plans for the abortive First Enterprise.[1] Clearly representing one of the 'sufficient men' of Drake's former company, he was – in Madox's terms – forever gaping after Spanish treasure. His fellow pilot was 'Simon Fernando' (Simão Fernandes), a Portuguese convert from Terceira called 'M. Secretary Walsinghams man.' Despite his active involvement in piracy during the years 1573–78, including association with the notorious John Callice, he continued to retain the friendship of influential men.[2] Madox found him a well-spring of evil and the instigator of Fenton's wildest plans; even the mild Walker was moved to ask that the General restrain his offensive speeches and his bragging of sundry piracies.

The piratical notions of the two pilots were countered to some extent by the master of the *Galleon*, Christopher Hall. He had sailed (and quarrelled) with Frobisher on all three voyages and on the third, like Luke Ward, had been admitted as an adventurer gratis. Recently, he had served as master of one of the Muscovy Company's ships sailing from Russia. Thus he was probably already acquainted with Matthew Tailboys, a merchant on the *Galleon*, and Tobias Parris, master's mate on the *Edward*, both of whom had also been connected with this particular voyage of the Muscovy Company.[3]

The pilot on the *Edward*, Thomas Blacollar of Plymouth, had sailed with Francis Drake. Thus, in addition to sailors, there was at least one officer on each of the three main ships who had gone through the Strait and returned by way of the Cape of Good Hope. Of the mariners, Richard Carter[4] observed that not ten of them were thirty years of age. Some had served with Drake, some with Frobisher; others had been impressed simply for this voyage.

Authorized under her Majesty's Great Seal, dated 2 April, to impress

the Barber-Surgeons' Visceral Lecture in 1581,' *Proc. Royal Soc. of Medicine*, VI (1912), 18–26.

[1] SP 12/148/47.

[2] See D. B. Quinn, *England and the Discovery of America* (London, 1974), pp. 246–63.

[3] *PN* (1589), pp. 440–53.

[4] See p. 20, n.1 above.

and take up the requisite mariners, soldiers, and artificers, Edward Fenton was also given 'absolute power and auctoritie' to 'order, rule, governe, correct and punyshe by imprisonment and violent meanes and by death,' the entire company appointed for his service.[1] Although the Instructions issued to him a week later restricted his authority by specifying, in particular, a Council of Assistants to determine weighty matters, the powers granted under the patent proved heady indeed. Besides Ward as vice-admiral, Hawkins as lieutenant, Parker as captain-at-land, and the two chaplains, all five of the merchants selected for the voyage were made members of the council; one, troubled with an ague and 'fawlen into the black jaundyce,' was put ashore at Yarmouth. Intended as a restraining influence on the officers, the merchants found themselves after three months largely excluded by Fenton.

He was also directed not to pass the Strait of Magellan 'except upon great occasion incident' (and then only with the advice and consent of at least four of his Assistants), and he was specifically enjoined not to 'spoile or take anything from any of the Queens Majesties friends or allies, or any christians.' The latter injunction allowed for liberal interpretation since to some members of the expedition, Spaniards did not fall into the category either of friends, allies, or Christians.

In the eyes of the Muscovy Company and the Privy Council, the voyage was primarily for the sake of trade and secondarily for discovery. Richard Carter (whom Fenton captured off the coast of Brazil) later recorded that the ships carried a richly decorated gilded chair and other presents with many stones for 'the king' in the Moluccas. In the eyes of many members of the crew, however, the voyage was primarily for plunder and only secondarily for trade.[2] With the disparate motives of the earlier enterprises representing in some ways residual elements in the Fenton expedition, the notion of despoiling Spanish property was not very far under the surface when the fleet took leave of its owners on 1 May.

While they were still in the Channel, the master of the *Galleon* reported to Madox that he supposed the voyage would turn to pilfering (24 May), and on 9 June athwart the Burlings, off the coast of Portugal, they took possession of a Flemish merchantman, which, at the insistence of the two chaplains, was let go without hurt. The following day (10

[1] Otho E VIII, ff. 130–43.

[2] Mendoza reported early on (19 Feb. 1582) that one of the captains had been heard to say that the real intention of the voyage was to plunder, the purported intent being only a bait to get the commercial men to adventure (*CSP, Sp., 1580–86*, p. 297).

June) when Madox preached against this attempt at piracy, the response he elicited was that 'we cold not do God better service than to spoyl the Spaniard both of lyfe and goodes.' To which he commented, 'but *in*deed under color of religion al ther shot is at the mens mony.' The incident encapsulates what came to be the established pattern on the voyage: conflict among the officers, would-be emulation of what captains – or mariners – had heard or had experience of in other ventures, and the persistent opposition of the two chaplains, who were supported by the merchants so long as these had a voice. This opposition, which struck a latent sense of responsibility in some of the officers (particularly in Vice-admiral Ward, as Madox refers to him), intensified the fears and uncertainties of others (particularly Fenton himself). The result was that instead of concerted action in the face of difficult situations, there was debate, indecisiveness, and – inevitably – backbiting.

The first stage: to Sierra Leone

Since Madox's Diary details the voyage, it is necessary here only to sketch in the general outline in order to explain its unhappy outcome. The *Edward* and the *Galleon* meeting at Netley, then proceeded to Southampton, where the *Bark Francis* joined them from Plymouth on 20 April and where a few days later the *Elizabeth* was purchased. On 1 May the four ships weighed anchor at Calshot. It was already late for their projected course around the Cape of Good Hope, since this required taking advantage of the 'winter' winds in the South Atlantic. (Frobisher, it is to be remembered, had planned to sail at Christmas.) In addition, the weather in the Channel was to prove most unpropitious, and for twenty days they plied between Yarmouth and Cowes off the Isle of Wight. It was not, finally, until 2 June that they lost sight of the Lizard.

The 'jar' begun at Plymouth was to be intensified over the question of watering in Boa Vista, one of the Cape Verde Islands. At a council held on 24 June off Cape Blanco in Barbary, it was agreed to do so and then upon the advice of the pilots, who had been called in, to make for the River Plate 'in Brazil.' While their correct course, it is true, was to stand away from the 'villanows' African coast, thus avoiding both the unpredictable currents around the Upper Guinea coast and the equatorial doldrums, still it was not necessary for them to sail so far west unless they had missed the season for rounding the Cape or were in need of water and provisions. (Both of these reasons were later to be invoked by Fenton.) But the plan to run down the coast of Brazil and on to the Strait, as Mendoza reported, had been bruited in England even before their departure.[1] This early decision of the council to make for the River Plate, as Madox's official register shows, was really a decision imposed by the pilots, who countered all objections to it by citing 'wyndes and tydes and currents and reconyngs' which were outside the competence of the Assistants.

Despite the decision taken on 24 June, they did not water in the Cape Verdes. On approaching one of the islands ('some sayd was Bonavista but others thowght yt was La Sal but none cold tell'), Fenton would not consent to stay, purportedly because of the surge on the shore and the lateness of the season, so they hauled off again. The pilots then followed a south-south-east course, asserting that they had to fetch an east wind off the coast of Guinea. The opposition of the master and others to this course was answered by the pilots' vaunted expertise: 'thes old beaten saylors,' Madox records, 'set me and others newe to schole.'

About a month later, they caught sight of the Upper Guinea coast – the name was applied to an area extending from the Gambia River to Cape Mount. At this point Ward again urged that they stand in with a harbour for relief of the company, many of whom were sick and all in want of fresh water. Again a council was called (20 July), including the masters and pilots, to ascertain just *where* they were. Since they had not seen the sun or stars for ten days, their reckonings proved at variance, the pilots deeming they were either at Cape Verga or Cape Palmas, points nearly six degrees apart. It was agreed – despite Fenton's disinclination – to turn back and seek out Sierra Leone. No record of individual opinions was kept on this occasion, because, in the General's view, it was but a 'familier debating' between himself and his pilots. After ten days of aimless circling, another council was called on 1 August, and they again agreed to head *back* for Sierra Leone, where, after much uncertainty, they finally dropped anchor on 9 August.

While it was a necessary point of call because of the sickness of the men, the need for fresh water and minor repairs to the ships, the sojourn stretched out to 1 September when they again set sail. Two days later they returned, ostensibly for more repairs to the *Galleon*. This second sojourn lasted until 2 October, a delay which permitted

[1] 20 April, *CSP, Sp, 1580–86*, p. 340. Mendoza was surprisingly well informed about the venture. He stated their plan was to water first at Cape Blanco in Barbary. Madox (14–16 June) recorded that by Fernando's direction they were to have gone between Barbary and Lanzarote, one of the Canaries, 'to make purchase of gotes or I knoe not what els for al our mynd was set on purchase,' that is, plunder.

antagonisms to intensify, morale to decline, and alternative courses of action to be projected. A repeated point of dissension was the victualling of the *Bark Francis* (and of the *Elizabeth*, though it had been brought along to carry the extra stores). On the two occasions (26 June and 7 Dec.) when it was agreed to allot the *Francis* three-months' stores, Ward was dilatory in providing them, so that when Captain Drake defected on 21 December, one of the reasons was said to be the antagonism of the two captains.[1] Furthermore, as Madox recorded, when Drake importuned Fenton for provisions for his ship, he was frequently threatened that his command would be taken from him and given to another.

During their stay in Sierra Leone they did some bartering with two groups of Portuguese *lançados* (resident traders), selling the *Elizabeth* for rice and ivory and making a second exchange of salt for rice, but, to the merchants' great discontent, they did no business with the native rulers. As a consequence, Miles Evans, a merchant of Bristol who could speak French and Portuguese and had been adventuring at sea for eighteen years,[2] asked leave to depart with the Portuguese in the *Elizabeth* and return to England. This served to hamper Fenton's plans in that he recognised, as Madox noted (25 Nov.; 26 Dec.), the chance that Evans would report to the Privy Council the General's disinclination to proceed with the voyage as projected.

Whoever persuaded Fenton to consider alternative courses (and Madox asserts it was Fernando and Hood, though they each urged different ones), during the fifty-odd days they spent at Sierra Leone, he toyed with two schemes. The first was to return (like Evans) with the Portuguese to the Cape Verdes, ostensibly to secure wine for their depleted casks but really 'to pick and steal.' The second was to proceed to St Helena and there await the return of the Portuguese carracks. Famed as a luxuriant, though deserted, spot, the island served as a landfall for the ships laden with spices returning from the East. Hawkins, once back in England, was to assert that Fenton had promised great rewards to 'all the well willers' of this particular scheme – to Ward £10,000; to Parker £5000; and to the two chaplains £2000 each.

The second stage: to Brazil

By 30 September Fenton, fearing both an inadequate harbour for their great ships and an insufficient supply of spices, had become

[1] See note to 22 Dec. where the occasions on which Fenton reproved Ward for his negligence are cited.

[2] Otho E VIII, ff. 107*v*; 83.

persuaded that it would be unwise to go to the Moluccas. Nonetheless, it was agreed at a council, from which the three remaining merchants were excluded, to continue on but by way of the Strait of Magellan.

Another council was held on 1 November and the consensus now was to seek the needed provisions on the Brazilian coast. On the 25th they met again. After examining a chart of the Strait provided by Sir Francis Drake, they agreed to work in towards the shore, and on 1 December they anchored in a bay about eight leagues from the Island of Santa Catarina (about 28° S), dubbing it the Bay of Good Comfort 'in respect of soundrie reliefs' found there.

Five days later on sighting a ship and immediately declaring it 'a prize,' they brought it in and found that it was carrying twenty-three persons, seven of whom were friars. As a result of their interrogations, they learned that the Spanish fleet assigned to fortify the Strait had sailed from Rio de Janeiro on 2 November. After much wrangling, the council agreed to leave the prize and passengers unharmed (though slightly 'plucked' to satisfy the rapacious sailors) and proceed to the Strait, taking along with them a willing Portuguese (Juan Pinto) and an unwilling Englishman (Richard Carter) who was to serve as a pilot on the River Plate. Setting sail on 12 December, they headed south, but the difficulties of passing through a fortified Strait now began to worry Fenton. According to Madox, Fernando advised him to turn back north to the Portuguese settlement of São Vicente and plunder it and even set himself up as king. The old notion of awaiting the Portuguese at St Helena was revived, and a new one proposed – to lurk about the West Indies and wait for the Spanish treasure fleet from Panama.

As a result of his uncertainty, on 20 December Fenton called a council. He included the masters, pilots, and merchants, though these were 'put out' before the decision was made to head back to São Vicente. This decision, as Madox asserted, would at least enable them to vend their wares with as little loss of stock and time as might be.[1] Accordingly, despite the murmuring of the sailors, they reversed directions. The next night the *Bark Francis* slipped away. The effect of this desertion was so generally demoralising that Fenton now dealt openly with all of the Assistants and advocated the merits of 'honest trading.'

[1] About a month later, that is, on Tuesday, 22 Jan. 1583, as Madox's astrological symbols indicate, Fenton caused the Assistants, once again including the three merchants, to sign the statement that they had agreed to go to São Vicente (Otho E VIII, f. 189). Ward says of this *ex post facto* assent: 'about which thing grewe foule speeches betweene the Generall, and his Lieutenant after the olde custome' (*PN* (1589), p. 666).

At this stage of their journey, Madox's Diary ends, and though he must have been involved in the action at São Vicente, his name appears only once more in Ward's account, that is, on 26 January when he accompanied Fenton to the *Edward* to visit the men wounded in the clash with the Spaniards and once more in Fenton's where for 27 February there is the terse note: 'my father Maddox died.' By this date they were in the harbour of Espírito Santo, near modern Vitória. Five months earlier, on 19 October, Madox recorded that he had prevailed on Banister to bleed him in his left arm; on 29 December he added the further notation, 'but myn arm hath byn stif ever syth.' Apart from these entries, his death remained unexplained and perhaps unlamented.

The third stage: conflict at São Vicente

It is unfortunate that we do not have his unvarnished account of what occurred at São Vicente. Except for Walker's, the other English reports were intended for the perusal of members of the Privy Council, while the main Spanish account by Pedro Sarmiento de Gamboa, the long-suffering general sent to colonise the Strait, was intended for the eyes of King Philip.[1] The real nature of the encounter has its puzzling aspects.

Arriving at São Vicente on 20 January, the English were met by three canoes with eighteen to twenty Indians and Portuguese in each. After conferring with them, Fenton, seeking to engage in trade, wrote to the governor and captain, 'called Jeronimo Leitao,' in English 'by reason I learned of one of our Nation (called John Whithall) in good creaditt with him.'[2]

This John Whithall, as he announced in a letter to an English merchant friend in 1578, was locally called 'John Leitoan': 'they have used the name so long time,' he wrote, 'that at this present there is no remedie but it must remaine so.' Wishing to initiate a trading venture with London merchants, Whithall had enclosed a list of commodities desired at nearby Santos and explained that he was marrying the daughter of an Italian, one Joffo Dore (Guiseppe Adorno), owner of a sugar plantation and refinery, and was becoming his factor; further,

[1] The English accounts include the journals of Fenton, Ward, and Walker and the reports of Hawkins, Thomas Percy (master of the *Edward*), and Peter Jeffrey (merchant on the *Edward*); the last three are dated after their return to England and appear in Otho E VIII, f. 224–8; 200; 186–7. For Sarmiento's account, see *Narratives of the Voyages of Pedro Sarmiento de Gamboa*, ed. C. R. Markham (Hakluyt Soc., 1895).

[2] This explanation derives from Fenton's letter to Leicester on his return (Otho E VIII, ff. 180–2).

he had been assured of license to trade by the captain, *provedor*, and his father-in-law 'who rule all this country.' Accordingly, in 1580 a group of adventurers for Brazil had sent out the *Minion*, stocked with merchandise (of the sort Fenton was carrying), including copper cauldrons for the refinery with artificers to set them up.[1] Of the Fenton group, at least William Hawkins knew that a ship from London had earlier contracted to purchase sugar in Santos (see 23 Dec.).

That afternoon the English brought their ships into a sandy bay, anchoring within a musketshot of the castle and some houses. In the evening Joffo Dore, 'an ancient Genoese,' and a Portuguese ('Stephano Riposo'), identifying themselves as assistants to the governor, came to inquire their purpose. After a 'smal banket,' they departed, promising that although the governor had not received the letters, there would be an answer about trading the next day. The English fired a farewell volley of three great pieces from each ship.

Returning the next afternoon, the negotiators delivered the governor's answer, setting forth the reasons they could not engage in trade: they had submitted themselves to the King of Spain, and, as a result, they had been charged by Diego Flores de Valdés (General of the Fleet transporting Sarmiento's forces to the Strait) not to trade with any nation, and particularly not with Englishmen because of Sir Francis Drake's raiding in the South Sea. Moreover, they had heard of an English 'fleet' intended for the South Sea which they judged were these two ships. On the occasion of this visit, Fenton ordered his pinnace to be manned. With Captain Parker and men with firearms in the longboat to serve as his guard and with Ward in his skiff, they provided an escort for the negotiators with drums and trumpets playing and again fired a volley of three great pieces out of the two ships.

On the 22nd, the English sent their merchants to the town, located three miles up the river, with presents for the governor and the negotiators, but being met on the way by Stephano Riposo, they were told to return and await an answer: the governor was not yet ready to speak with them. In the meantime, the mariners took down their maintops, topmast, and shrouds. All through the next day the English waited for an answer.

On the eventful 24th (at four o'clock in the morning, according to Ward; at midnight, according to Fenton), they heard a call from the

[1] *PN* (1589), pp. 638–40. Adorno was still living in this area in 1591–2 (D. B. Quinn, *The Last Voyage of Thomas Cavendish* (Chicago, 1975), p. 23).

shore and Ward sent out his skiff to fetch John Whithall and two Indian servants aboard. At six o'clock he was conveyed to the *Galleon*, where he accounted for the delays by saying that the governor was fearful the English ships were really men of war, that is, pirates, adding that fortifications had been made at the town and the women sent away; still he advised them to go up into the town with their ships. Fenton noted that Whithall had seemed to come to them by stealth.

At mid-morning Whithall's father-in-law arrived with Stephano Riposo. Despite the 'manie p*e*rsuas*i*ons' of the English, the two repeated that while they should have provisions, there would be no trade for fear of reprisal when the Spaniards returned; they also promised that a conference with the governor would be arranged two days hence, with each side to have four persons present. Fenton then withdrew his Assistants to the poop to consider whether or not they should 'stay' the men while they had them. However, at two o'clock they were suffered to depart, bearing gifts of three 'cloke clothes' which the tailor had earlier cut out for them.

Two hours later three ships from the Spanish fleet intended for the Strait came into the harbour, having, as Fenton recorded, 'as by form*er* conference w*i*th those of St. Vincents a determynac*i*on rather to fight w*i*th us, then to suffer us to rest in quiet there.' At ten o'clock or thereabouts, when the tide served, the Spanish ships let slip their anchors and cables, driving upon the English so close 'that the one talked to the other.'

Thus begun, the fray continued until four o'clock in the morning when a heavy downpour forced them to desist. By that time the Spanish vice-admiral, as the English termed her, had been so 'gawled' they felt it powder wasted to shoot at her any longer. At daylight they could see that though most of the people had been taken away, there were about forty still hanging on the shrouds. Of these, they brought two on board the *Galleon*: one, the boatswain (an Aragonese, according to Sarmiento; a Greek born in Zante, according to Ward); the other, a 'Marsillian' whom they heaved overboard 'because he was sore hurt not like to live.' The *Edward* then weighed and went down to fire on the other two ships and for four hours fought unassisted. The *Galleon* being at anchor was unable to come to her, and in the afternoon, she began to stand out to sea, leaving the *Edward* still fighting. At this point, Ward and his chaplain, dodging the shot, took the skiff to inquire what Fenton's intentions were. The defection of the *Galleon*, strongly taken amiss by those on the *Edward*, was later laid to the insobriety of the crew who had drunk a hogshead of wine during the heat of the fight. One man on the *Galleon* and five on the *Edward* were slain, and some twenty more were hurt. From the report the English received at Espírito Santo more than a hundred on the Spanish ships had been killed and wounded.

The three Spanish ships were the *Santa Maria de Begõna*, captained by Rodrigo de Rada, which the English sank; the *Concepción*, captained by Francisco de Cuellar; and the *San Juan Bautista*, the *almirante* of the fleet when it sailed from Spain. How the three happened to appear in the harbour of São Vicente at just this time is puzzling.

In November, a fleet of sixteen Spanish ships had set out from Rio de Janeiro for the Strait, but the General of the Fleet, Don Diego Flores, later decided to turn back north, reaching the Bay of Good Comfort (called by the Spaniards the Port of Dom Rodrigo) near the island of Santa Catarina on the 16th or 17th of December. There, their number now reduced to twelve, they met the little vessel carrying the seven friars and thus learned of the three English ships headed either for the Strait or for São Vicente.

According to the information the English garnered – Fenton's was elicited from the boatswain they had picked up – the Spaniards then decided to send eight of the ships on to the Strait and four back to São Vicente to search for them ('to take us or sinke us'). According to Sarmiento's account, the three ships that engaged the English were the best of the fleet though Don Diego, with dissembling intent, declared them unseaworthy. Stocking them with supplies of munitions, married settlers, and three hundred of the best soldiers, he left them (together with a store-ship subsequently lost) at Santa Catarina under the charge of Andrés de Aquino, and from there they were to proceed to Rio de Janeiro. On 13 January the rest of the fleet had again headed for the Strait though (according to Sarmiento) Don Diego was so fearful of the English he would not hoist his general's banner.

In assessing this incident, the problem is to know how far its reporters were colouring their statements for particular consumption. Clearly all of them reflect a degree of bias. Did Don Diego divide up his fleet with the intention of seeking out the English? The statements of Fenton, Walker, Hawkins, and Thomas Percy show they held this view, though their information may have derived mainly from the captured boatswain. Were these three ships the best in the fleet and only reputedly unseaworthy, as Sarmiento asserted, or were they filled with 'the refuse of all the Spanish fleete' as López Vaz (Lopes

Vas) described them in 1587? According to Sarmiento, the *Concepción* and the *almirante*, the *Bautista*, were able to return to Spain.

Two further questions arise: how did the English conduct themselves at São Vicente and how were they received? From Madox's Diary we know that Fenton had talked on board of spoiling the town and declaring himself ruler. Doubtless the appearance of the two ships with their heavy guns, the ceremonial volleys, and the 'manie persuasions' seemed – and were intended to seem – threatening.[1] What was the role of John Whithall alias John Leitoan? What was his relationship to Jeronimo Leitão? Were the delays of the negotiators, as Hawkins was later to assert, simply 'for a further myschief'? Clearly the Portuguese expected the return of the Spaniards, but when? If he knew of the three approaching Spanish ships, why had Whithall advised the English to take their ships up into the town which was being fortified?

The sequel

The result of the conflict, as Sarmiento discovered when he returned to São Vicente in April, was that the Portuguese had asked the Spanish commander Andrés de Aquino to construct a bastion with artillery to defend the entrance of their harbour and that the Spaniards – to his disgust – had been using the transferred contents of the lost store-ship for brisk trading with the Portuguese. The result for the English was the final overthrow of the voyage. The night following the fray the Spaniards went up the river to Santos, while the Fenton group spent most of two days taking in water and repairing their ships.

On the 29th, the *Edward*, separated from the *Galleon*, by decision of its officers stood out to sea. Walker was now appointed to keep a register of all proceedings 'as Master *Maddox* doth aboord the Admirall.'[2] Seven days later he was dead of a bloody flux and was heaved overboard with a piece shot off 'for his knell.' By 12 February the dire shortage of water dictated that they boil the peas with three jacks of fresh water and two of salt; and on the 27th Ward allotted

[1] Included among the interrogations the Governor Jeronimo Leitão held at São Vicente in February was the question whether the witnesses knew that threats had been offered to him if he did not agree to do what the English wanted. They are printed in Taylor, *Fenton*, pp. 322–3.

[2] On his return, Ward accounted for the separation from his Admiral on the basis of the weather conditions, and this was the view that circulated. In his *Observations* (London, 1622), Richard Hawkins – as a cousin of William, he doubtless received a first-hand report of the voyage – comments on the dangers of an expedition turning back, citing as one example the Fenton voyage: 'for presently as soone as they looked homeward, one, with a little blustering wind taketh occasion to loose company' (ed. J. A. Williamson (London, 1933), pp. 87–8).

half a can of wine for every six men at the setting of the watch. Finally, on 11 March the skiff and pinnace were sent to shore on the island of Fernando de Noronha to seek water and provisions from the Indians. While they got some things aboard – ducks, turkeys, parrots – five men were slain and twelve others hurt by the 'treacherie' of the Indians. At this point the *Edward* headed for England and on 29 May anchored at Plymouth. The next morning 'with much a doe' Ward wrote letters announcing their return and ill success, sending off both Peter Jeffrey the merchant and Samuel Symbarb the traveller to Leicester and Walsingham and young Towerson to his father.

Two days later Walsingham's secretary wrote to Anthony Bacon of their very ill success, remarking that the failure of the voyage was said to be 'their inconsiderate provision of victuals.'[1] Two weeks later when he reported the failure of the venture, Mendoza quoted the merchants as saying that for such a voyage they needed ships of 1000 tons burden, considering the way Englishmen eat. Despite such explanations, members of the Privy Council began an inquiry and obtained evidence from the master of the *Edward* and from Peter Jeffrey while waiting to see whether the other two ships would limp home.

After the departure of the *Edward*, Fenton's course was typically indecisive. In need of water and food, he headed south, intending to go to Santa Catarina or to the Bay of Good Comfort, but four days later he turned back again, finally reaching Espírito Santo on the 22nd. Here he spent ten days attempting to open trade with the Portuguese, sending out the usual negotiating gifts including a piece of white kersey for 'their unhollie fathers.' On 5 March after a small bark from São Vicente appeared in the harbour, the *Galleon* departed, fearing duplicity on the part of the Portuguese. With the consent of his company Fenton later altered his course on 19 May, heading now for England rather than for Newfoundland as had been his most recent intent. On 12 June he decided to make for Ireland and (after '103 daies without sight of any Lande') anchored at Kinsale on the 15th. Here the sailors, forbidden to go ashore, reacted in 'mutinous fashion,' and Fernando was dispatched to Cork to press additional men.

On the 24th they set sail for home; alongside Portland, Fenton threw his Lieutenant into the bilboes, recording simply, 'Hawkins and Tailboyes, beinge dronken Made a Mutynie of me.' Hawkins's account – dated, it seems, on 6 July – is considerably more colourful: being commanded to the bilboes, he knelt, appealing to the Queen's

[1] Repr. in Thomas Birch, *Memoirs of the Reign of Queen Elizabeth*, I (London, 1754), 38.

Majesty, praying his General to adhere to his Instructions (not to remove any of his captains from their charges), and calling on the whole ship to witness, whereupon Fenton threatened that with one word more he would dash him in the teeth, calling him villain, slave, and arrant knave. During the next two days they quarrelled violently. Fenton, according to Hawkins, drew his long knife and would first have stabbed him and then have run at him with his staff, but Banister, Fernando, and others stayed his fury. When they arrived at the Downs on 29 June, Hawkins was in irons.

Fenton wrote at once to Leicester and to Burghley to explain the overthrow of the action – the late start and consequent contrariness of the winds, the inadvisability of going through the Strait with the Spaniards there, and the troubles at São Vicente – and to request an inquiry into the disorderly speeches and great disobedience he had of late experienced. On 2 July Walsingham, responding to a request from Burghley, promised that as soon as Fenton arrived he would obtain the calendar or journal of the voyage,[1] that is, the Register kept by Madox.

According to Mendoza, the two ships' captains were arrested, not – as he deemed proper – for attacking Spanish ships in their own port but for failing to continue their voyage. Fenton wrote again to Leicester (the letter is undated), complaining of ill health and asking that the masters, pilots, and other officers attend the meetings and conferences that had been scheduled. Whatever punishment, if any, was meted out to the captains is not recorded. The surviving mariners – not to speak of the sixty or seventy dead – came out the worst; they had ventured for 'thirds,' their share of the profits, and unless the adventurers took compassion upon them, as Fenton requested, the voyage may well have been their utter undoing.

When Drake, his seventeen men, and a boy disappeared into the night on 21 December, they were, as Drake later deposed, headed for the River Plate to secure provisions to continue their voyage.[2] As Hawkins suggested to Madox (30 Dec.), their aim was to go through the Strait and into the South Sea. Richard Carter, who lived in Asunción, had warned that the river was shoal and dangerous, but Drake believed his small vessel could make it. Proceeding about twenty leagues up the River Plate, they found it so shallow that they

[1] B.L., Harleian MS 6993, f. 52.

[2] This description of what happened to Drake and his companions is based on his two depositions and the account in Eliott-Drake; on the account by John Sarracoll of the voyage set out by the earl of Cumberland in 1586; and on the discourse of López Vaz (both in *PN* (1589), pp. 793–803; 673–4).

tried to enter another. There their ship was wrecked on the rocks. The crew escaped with some arms and clothing and, as they were wet, built a fire which signalled their presence and brought forth a group of 'about a hundred' Indians. When an Indian took one of their hatchets, Richard Fairweather (who had shipped as master's mate on the *Galleon* but had been transferred on 27 September to the *Francis*) struck him with his sword, and the English then thought it expedient to defend themselves. Of their men, two were killed and the boy taken prisoner. The rest rushed for their boat, which capsized. Pursuing, the Indians grabbed them by the hair and stunned them with their weapons. They were all taken prisoner, stripped of their clothes and their boat burned. Those who had been wounded were ceremonially killed.

For thirteen months, moving from place to place, the survivors served the Indians as slaves. During that time five died of sickness. At one point the gunner John Daniel escaped, only to get lost and wander back eleven days later. Then Fairweather escaped. Finally Drake and two of his companions managed to break away. After two weeks of hardships, they were lucky enough to come upon Fairweather who had joined up with some Indian fishermen and their two captive Spaniards, one of whom had been taken twelve years before.

A month and a half later, Fairweather, Drake, and a third Englishman 'Thomas' – no fewer than six of those initially listed on the *Francis* had the given name Thomas – stole a canoe and, using a sail made of skin, crossed a river 'twenty leagues' wide. On the other side, following the tracks of horses, they came to a farmhouse where three Indians serving the Spaniards took them in. After sending on news and obtaining clothes for them, the Indians led them in to Buenos Aires. Here Drake, fearing to tell the truth, declared he was a soldier and was hospitably treated by one Don Ximenes. Three weeks later Richard Carter arrived in the town on a ship from Brazil, recognised young Drake, and informed the Spaniards that he was Sir Francis's 'nephew.' The Captain Alonso de Vera then took the three Englishmen into custody on behalf of the governor stationed at Asunción, and on 24 March 1584 they were interrogated at Santa Fé with Richard Carter serving as interpreter, though he was unable to sign his name.

This deposition was apparently forwarded to Lima since the Viceroy ordered that Fairweather and Drake be sent to him. The Chief Inquisitor, Don Gutierrez de Ulloa, wishing to undertake the interrogation himself, forbade the Viceroy to examine the prisoners, and the matter was referred to King Philip for decision. The prisoners consequently remained at Asunción for more than a year, sequestered in a hermitage where they were allowed to speak only to the hermit, a Segovian by the name of Juan de Espínosa, and to an Englishman who, having been in the country for forty years, had forgotten his native tongue. During this period Drake learned 'good vernacular Spanish' and was able to repeat the Pater Noster, Ave Maria, Credo, and Salve Regina (though he could not recite the Ten Commandments, the Five Commandments of the Holy Church and the Seven Sacraments except in 'a halting and hesitating way'). Fairweather was at times released to work on a ship which the General Juan de Torres, Governor of the Province of Paraguay, was having built. Both Fairweather and 'Thomas' took native wives, probably as a token of their good faith; 'Thomas' was to die some time before 1587.

In the summer of 1586, the Viceroy of Peru, who had learned King Philip's wishes, summoned the prisoners, but only Drake was sent initially. In January 1587 two Portuguese ships were taken by the expedition the earl of Cumberland had sent to the South Sea. Inquiring about Drake, the English learned that he had been in good health the previous year and that Fairweather had married a native wife. One of the pilots of these two Portuguese ships was the Englishman Abraham Cocke who had been left behind when the *Minion* was sent to Whithall in 1580; the other was López Vaz, who declared he had carried the captured Drake, en route to Tucumán, part way in his ship.

En route to the Viceroy, Drake was joined by Fairweather at Potosí, and in January 1587 they both reached Lima where they were thrown into the dungeons. In five sittings on 8, 9, and 10 January, Drake was interrogated by the Inquisitor Licentiate and then imprisoned for another eleven months. Since he confessed to being a Lutheran and was penitent, he was admitted to reconciliation, and on 30 November 1589, he walked in the *auto-da-fé*, wearing the *sanbenito*, a yellow cotton garment marked with a red cross decreed for all victims of the Inquisition; he was then confined to remain under Spanish rule for the rest of his life with the confiscation of his property. Fairweather (called Bonanza), who had been tortured on the rack, was also admitted to reconciliation and also walked in the *auto-da-fé*, but he was condemned to serve four years in the galleys and to perpetual imprisonment.

Even when one discounts the waste in human terms, the positive effects of this attempt to establish the spice trade were scant. But the idea, dating back to its formulation by Sir Francis Walsingham in

1580, continued to tease the adventurous. In 1584 Hawkins, Leicester, Sir Francis Drake, and others were still projecting a voyage to the Moluccas, and though £6000 were expended, nothing came of it, for Drake's energies were now being directed to the West Indies. Again in 1589 a number of London merchants petitioned to send out a fleet, including the *Edward Bonaventure*, but again nothing came of it. In 1591 three ships, again including the *Edward*, were sent out on a reconnaisance voyage. This too proved a disaster. The *Edward* on its return voyage was wrecked near Santo Domingo, and its artillery used to improve the fortifications there. Nevertheless, as Sir William Foster points out, it was the first English ship to sail freely in the Indian Ocean, penetrating as far as the Malay Peninsula. In 1596 Sir Robert Dudley, following in his father's steps, dispatched a venture under Captain Benjamin Wood which also proved disastrous. Finally, on 31 December 1600, the Queen granted a charter to the East Indian Company, nearly twenty years after Fenton's abortive voyage. This time, a factory was established at Bantam, Java, which was to become the centre for trade with the Moluccas.[1]

As for trade with Brazil, the results of Fenton's expedition proved inhibiting, even though he declared that he might have brought home £40,000 or £50,000 in honourable trade. Before Ward and Fenton returned, the *Edward Cotton* of Southampton was sent out to the River Plate, but it 'perished through extreme negligence' off the coast of Guinea. At the end of 1582 William Hawkins the Elder sailed in command of seven ships to the coast of Brazil, but the lading of pearls, sugar, and hides he returned with had been obtained in the West Indies. Having learned of Fenton's experience, he had not ventured to Brazil. In 1586 Thomas Cavendish led a voyage along the coast and through the Strait, where he found the remnant of Sarmiento's resolute attempts to colonise and thus protect the area for the Spaniards. His intent, however, was not to trade but to plunder. (Yet, in following Drake's route, he was the first Englishman to reach St Helena.) In 1593 Richard Hawkins (the son of Sir John) led an expedition through the Strait, which he later described as intended for Japan, the Philippines, the Moluccas, China, and the East Indies. But while plundering on the coast of Peru, his ship was captured by some Spaniards and he himself was sent to Lima. There perhaps[2] he may

[1] See Sir William Foster's edition of *Voyages of Sir James Lancaster to Brazil and the East Indies* (Hakluyt Soc., 1940) and *England's Quest of Eastern Trade* (London, 1933).

[2] As Lady Eliott-Drake suggests (E. F. Eliott-Drake , *The Family and Heirs of Sir Francis Drake*, I (1911), 87).

have had occasion to talk with at least one victim of the earlier troublesome voyage, the penitent John Drake.

The subsequent careers of the main figures involved in the Fenton voyage, however, served to redeem the lapses of 1582–83. In the year of the Armada Fenton was to captain the Queen's ship, the *Mary Rose*. As a result of his marriage to Thomazine Gonson, he became Sir John Hawkins's brother-in-law and in 1589 Deputy Treasurer of the Navy at Hawkins's own request. His epitaph in the Church of St Nicholas, Deptford, dated 1603, sums up his career:

> To the never-fading memory of Edward Fenton, heretofore esquire of the body to Queen Elizabeth, a gallant commander during the troubles of Ireland, first against Shane O'Neal, and then against the Earl of Desmond, who, after having explored the hidden passages of the northern seas, and in other hazardous expeditions visited remote and scarce known places, merited the command of a royal ship in that glorious sea-fight against the Spaniards in the year 1588.[1]

Luke Ward also commanded a Queen's ship, the *Tramontana*, against the Armada, and in 1590 and 1591 he was still patrolling the Narrow Seas.

Even Simon Fernando – that well-spring of evil according to Madox – fought against the Armada, serving under Frobisher in the Queen's largest galleon, the *Triumph*. Earlier, in 1584, 1585, and 1587, he had piloted the English colonists to America, but as D. B. Quinn observed, he may have been responsible for the failure and disappearance of the third colony. An entry through the Carolina Outer Banks had been named in his honour by the colonists in 1585.[2]

Nicholas Parker was to pursue his military career, serving not only in the Low Countries, where he was knighted by Lord Willoughby in 1588, but also in France and in the Islands' voyage under Essex – making thirty years' service in the wars by his own count.[3] In 1598

[1] Quoted in John Barrow, *Memoirs of the Naval Worthies* (London, 1845), p. 160.

[2] See Quinn, *England and the Discovery of America*, and E. G. R. Taylor, 'The English Debt to Portuguese Nautical Science in the 16th Century,' *I Congresso da História da Expansão Portuguesa no Mondo* (Lisbon, 1938), pp. 10–11.

His co-pilot Thomas Hood – thanks to his earlier experience with Sir Francis Drake though not that obtained on the Fenton voyage – was asked to serve as 'Pilot for the Streights' in the voyage sent out by the earl of Cumberland in 1586, which also proved abortive. Hood's logbook as pilot of the *Red Dragon* is preserved in the Henry E. Huntington Library, MS HN 1648*.

[3] *Cal. Salisbury MSS*, Pt. xv, 50.

he was appointed deputy lieutenant of Cornwall and governor of Pendennis Castle, appointments he seems to have retained until his death in 1619. He was to marry four times; by his second marriage to Jane Courtenay, he became, as it were, the stepson-in-law of Henry Owtread (who after 1585 was actively involved in repeopling the province of Munster and was knighted in 1593 by a Lord Deputy of Ireland).[1]

The surgeon John Banister continued to serve the earl of Leicester, attending him to the Low Countries in 1585, and continued to publish medical works: his collected writings published posthumously in 1633 ran to six volumes. In 1586 the Privy Council commended him to the Royal College of Physicians, and in 1594 the Queen herself wrote asking that he be permitted to practice physic. (His younger colleague on the *Edward*, Lewis Otmore, was to become Warden of the Barber-Surgeons in 1596 and again in 1601.[2]) Ending his long career in 1610, he was buried at St Olave's Church in Silver Street, where his lengthy epitaph in verse includes the lines:

> Poore maymed Souldiers, sore sick-hearted Men
> That under Miseries hard Crouch did bow
> Were freely cured, methinkes they cry, Lord, when
> Where shall we find our good Physician now?[3]

III. THE DIARY

As he made arrangements to set out on his journey, despite the entreaties of his brother Thomas and his Oxford friend Owen Davis, Richard Madox was clearly enthusiastic. This is evident in his concern with the preparations and in his election to make the trip in the *Edward* from Blackwall to Southampton for rendezvous with the *Galleon* and the *Bark Francis*, a trip which required seventeen days and brought on his first bout of seasickness. Although this enthusiasm was to be tempered by the tensions developing among the personnel, it was to reappear in his pictorial renderings and detailed reporting of their landfall at Sierra Leone.

[1] Shaw, *The Knights of England*, II, 90.
[2] S. Young, *Annals of the Barber-Surgeons* (London, 1890), p. 7.
[3] Ll. 37–40; the epitaph is quoted in D'Arcy Power, 'Notes on Early Portraits . . . ,' pp. 24–5.

Madox was a shrewd judge of character, and on his second meeting with Fenton when they dined together with Hawkins (and others), he was quick to detect the submerged rivalry between them (20 Mar.). Before they left the English Channel, he had made fairly sharp appraisals of the ranking figures, and part of the interest of the Diary lies in his succinct analyses of their characters. Though he seems to have got on well enough, in spite of private feelings, by the time they were skirting the coast of Guinea, he had become an object of suspicion to Fenton.

The occasion was a letter in Latin sent in reply to one from John Walker on the *Edward* (28 July), which Fenton intercepted and read. Though Fenton could not understand it, as Walker noted, since his knowledge of Latin was imperfect,[1] he nonetheless began to imagine there were 'secrett practyses' afoot between the two chaplains. The one significant statement in the letter was a remark attributed to Peter Jeffrey the merchant: some were muttering, he said, that Madox wished to play the part of Master Fletcher.

As many, besides those who had sailed with Drake, would have known, this was a reference to the friction which had developed between Francis Drake and his chaplain following on Drake's execution of Thomas Doughty (for undetermined reasons) at San Julián.[2] Much later, when the *Golden Hind* was heading home from the Moluccas, it struck a ledge where it remained fast for a number of hours. During this fearful interval Fletcher preached a sermon and administered communion to the company, at which time 'every theefe reconciled him selfe to his fello theefe' and so prepared for death. What Fletcher said in his sermon is unknown, but, as Henry Wagner says,[3] there can be little doubt that he conceived of their plight as punishment for the execution of Doughty – and, very likely, for their piracies as well.[4] Thanks to a change of wind, the ship slipped free of the ledge, but shortly afterwards, Drake excommunicated his chaplain in the presence of the entire ship and charged him upon pain of death never to come

[1] Edward Fenton's single contribution to letters was entitled *Certaine Secrete wonders of Nature . . . Gathered out of divers learned authors as well Greek as Latine, sacred as prophane.* Published in 1569 and dedicated to Lord Lumley, this is a translation from the French *Histoires Prodigieuses* of Pierre Boaistau dit Launay and thus in no way provides evidence to contradict Walker's observation on Fenton's imperfect knowledge of Latin.

[2] Many motives have been suggested, including several scandalous ones (see 12 Sept. and n. 1, p. 184). The copy of Fletcher's journal makes it evident he was not in sympathy with the execution.

[3] *Drake's Voyage round the World* (1926), p. 187.

[4] Though he was content to receive some of the spoil taken from a Spanish chapel in Valparáiso.

before the mast again. He also ordered him henceforth to wear bound to his arm the infamous 'poesy' reading: *Francis Fletcher the Falsest Knave That Liveth.*[1]

A few days after Fenton's intercepting of the letter, Walker reported to Madox that his phrase *partes domini fletcheri agere* had been interpreted to mean that he was used like a fletcher (that is, an arrowmaker), but when the right sense was explained, 'than they were sory, etc.' Whether the pronoun used here has reference only to Fenton and Parker or to others is unclear. Madox, in any case, went about his duties outwardly unperturbed. On 16 August, however, when he recorded Fenton's gift of two shirts, he added the comment: *sed timeo Danaos et dona ferentes.* With the appearance (18 Aug.) of the three Portuguese traders, which, in Madox's opinion, elicited a ridiculous over-response on the part of Fenton and Parker, he took to recording his sharpest comments in Latin.

Yet, curiously, Fenton confided his plans to Madox as to Walker, perhaps in open recognition that, unlike Drake, he could not control his subordinates if the two chaplains were to oppose him publicly. As should be clear from the delineation of his actions during the voyage, Fenton's drive to be 'autor of som great enterpris' – largely in emulation of Sir Francis Drake, as Madox recorded (24 Sept.; 23 Dec.) – was countered by his persistent distrust of his company and his inability to take decisive action. Consequently, he conducted himself in a high-handed manner – excluding the merchants from the council, forcing his master to kneel before him at service and ask his pardon, and threatening to hang the steward of the *Galleon.* This deportment Fenton justified by the powers granted him under the Great Seal, but, as Ward aptly observed, though he had her Majesty's Commission, yet he had not her royalty.

By mid-September Madox was clearly aware that not only Fenton but the Vice-admiral too was eager to pry into his papers. Though he had categorically denied to Ward that he was keeping a Diary, on 17 September he began afresh, as it were. Predating this portion of the Diary 14 September, he started out with a very clearly written explanation in English of his intention henceforth to keep a 'breef remembrance' of things of moment and to write in Greek and Latin 'for the exercise' of his style. He then summarised the voyage to date. This prefatory section thus served to account for the contents of the Diary

[1] This account is from the 'Anonymous Narrative' which reports on the second part of Drake's voyage (repr. in Wagner, *Drake's Voyage*, p. 282).

if anyone gained access to it.[1] As Madox's extensive comments in Latin show, the technique worked. (In contrast, when Francis Drake became suspicious of Thomas Doughty, he forbade him to read or write anything but plain English.)

That Madox anticipated his Diary would be inspected on the sly is further shown by his including – in English – a couple of approving remarks about Fenton and Parker, which were then undercut by passages in cipher. At one point he even went so far as to use the name of the departed merchant 'Evans' (also *persona non grata* to Fenton) as an alias for Walker (identified in cipher). On this occasion his fellow chaplain reported to Madox that there was 'treason wroght' against him (3 Oct.). Before this date, however, he had already resorted to additional precautions to disguise his comments by introducing a complex system of pseudonymic references and by embedding his comments in literary and historical matter.

Once they left the Guinea coast and were at sea, Madox seems to have made a determined effort to act circumspectly, for he recorded (28 Oct.) that those who – undeservedly – had had some reservations about his good faith now treated him with love, honour, and respect. Yet he vowed that, however matters turned out, he would cater to the vices or passions of no one more than was meet, and he continued to disguise his acerbic comments.

It is impossible to know whether Madox's suspicions that his Diary was being inspected were borne out or whether they were reflections of the general uneasiness stemming from Fenton's erratic conduct. Once they were at sea, there would have been scant opportunity for anyone to peruse the Diary or puzzle out its import. But what happened after Madox died? Since only brief cipher passages appear before the departure from Guinea, it is possible that these might have passed unnoticed upon a prior cursory inspection. But it seems inconceivable that Fenton would have allowed the lengthy passages in cipher to reach England if he continued to have reservations about Madox's 'good faith' and had examined the Diary after his death, unless, of course, he accepted the statement that they were exercises of Madox's Greek style. It seems more likely that Fenton's concern would have been directed to the account in English, that is, to the Register, which he knew was intended for the eyes of members of the Privy Council.

[1] That Madox correctly assessed this possibility is shown by Fenton's order on 1 Oct. to Ward, Parker, and Hawkins (*PN* (1589), pp. 654–55) to search the chest of the departing Miles Evans and his apparent appropriation of a letter found in it (2 Oct.).

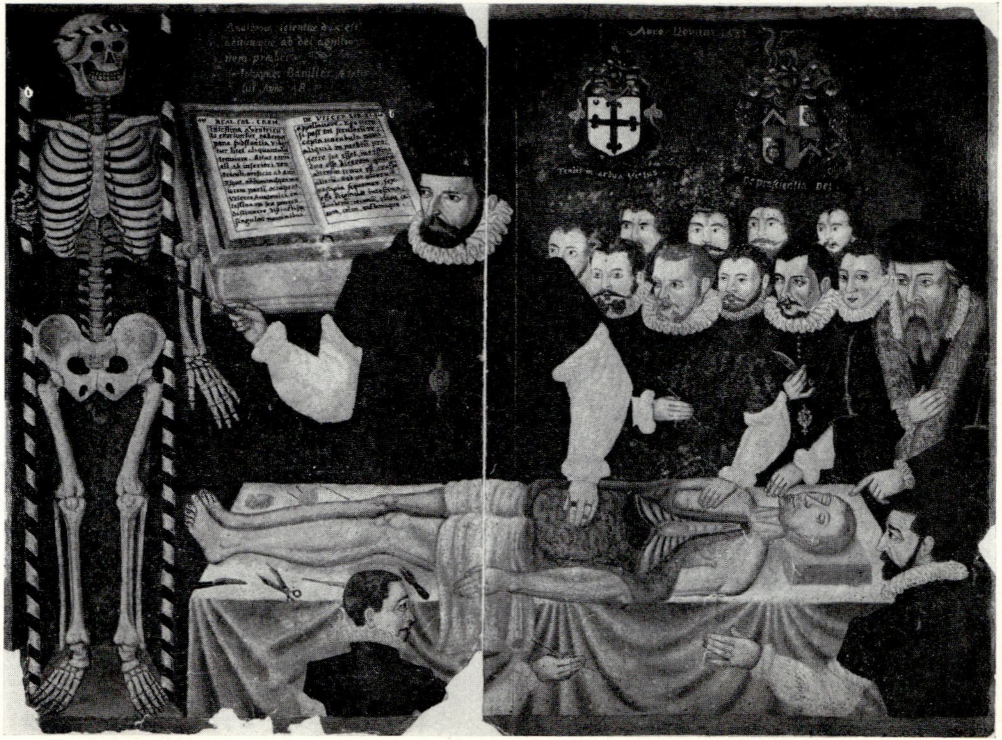

Fig. 2. John Banister, Surgeon on the *Galleon Leicester*, delivering the Visceral Lecture in the Barber-Surgeons' Hall, 1581

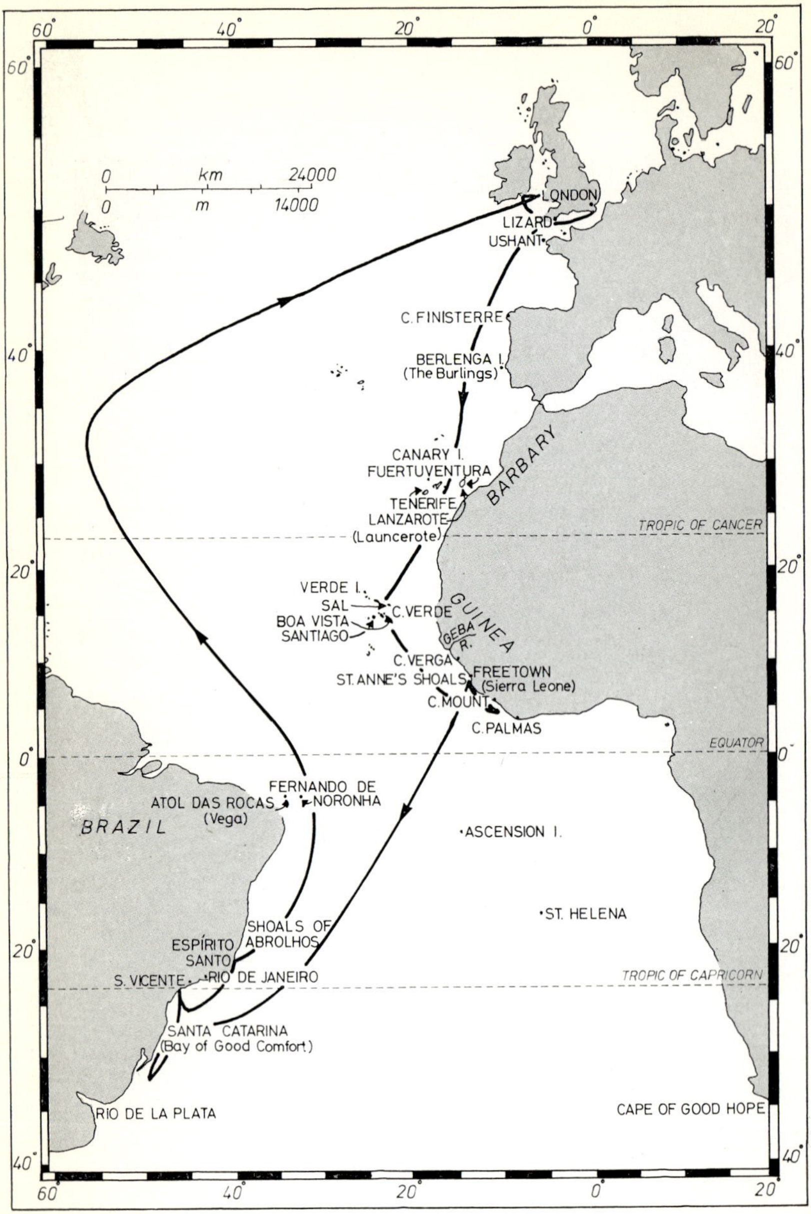

Fig. 3. Voyage of the *Galleon Leicester*, 1582–3. Place-names are in modern form. In cases where the names used by Madox differ considerably from the modern ones, his form is shown in brackets.

In assessing the role – as well as the character – of Richard Madox, certain elements need to be kept in mind. He was quite obviously not only the most educated but also the most intelligent person of the entire company with the surgeon John Banister his nearest rival. (Yet Madox detested him – in part because of his religious bigotry, in part because of his personality.) A conspicuously outgoing person, Madox could talk as easily with the sailors as with his fellow chaplain. He was curious and inquiring about many things – winds, tides, variation of the compass, and exotic vocabularies as well as titillating gossip and trivial (if not jejune) anecdotes. In the tight little shipboard world, his intelligence made him aware of the deficiencies of those in command, and his candour made it difficult to conceal his reactions. Yet a natural wariness, coupled with a realistic sense of the character of the people he had to deal with, inhibited his establishing a forthright relationship. Consequently, in contrast to the less complex John Walker, who also opposed the General's plans, Madox became *persona non grata* to Fenton and Parker.

While the ships were struggling to get beyond the Doldrums and make their way to Brazil, he seems to have become increasingly uncomfortable and, faced at table by such antagonists as Fenton, Parker, and Banister, even somewhat badgered. As a result, his Diary now included accounts of his reading, his speculations on scientific matters and more anecdotes, the latter perhaps indicating that he was now spending more and more time with the crew. Up to the last entry closing the calendar, it served as a sounding board. Strangely, after that date – two months before his death – Madox seems scarcely to have counted in any of the records, even in that of his friend and fellow chaplain.

E. G. R. Taylor has called him a great diarist.[1] This is perhaps excessive. While his day-to-day comments are of great interest, they are not notable for their literary quality. His more detailed and more carefully fashioned account appearing in the Register (Appendix I) reveals, it seems to me, his most effective writing: it is both colourful and colloquial. As a diarist, Madox falls short in his implicit assumption that the recital of an event is sufficient to trigger a response similar to that which evoked his notation. This is as true of the early as of the later part where he disguises his comments but clearly intends to re-evoke their mood. If it is suggested that the Diary is a personal, and the Register a public, record, one may ask whether Madox did not

[1] Taylor, *Fenton*, p. viii.

come to view the second part of his Diary as also intended for perusal by others.

The pseudonyms

To cover up the fact that he is using pseudonyms to refer to the most important (and obnoxious) of his companions, Madox sprinkles a few allusions to the writings of Aulus Gellius, Macrobius, and Livy to suggest he is writing about persons and events they had treated. But, clearly, he selected the names according to his sense of their fitness for the actual situations and incidents he recounts, and he continued to add to their number, varying them almost sportively, so that the texture of allusion becomes increasingly more complex. This complexity becomes most acute in certain Latin passages where he resorts to terms relating to function without appending the relevant pseudonym. This is especially noticeable in his use of the two terms *navarcha* and *gubernator*. Not only do they have more than one signification, but Madox uses them in their different senses at different times, a situation which also obtains with the English term 'master.'

But in order to ensure that certain of these allusions would be identifiable, he appended an Index in Latin and Greek, listing a number of the pseudonyms with what he considered the most important dates on which the personages intended figure in the Diary. The dates are set forth with astrological symbols to indicate the months, a device which – at least at first glance – helps to mask their import (see Fig. 6). By checking out these dates, one finds that all but one of the pseudonyms listed in the Index[1] can be identified with certainty.

Madox saw fit, though, to include only ten of the most conspicuous among his companions in his roster of evildoers. But he provided a solution to the remaining identifications by working out a cross-referencing system and by adding marginalia. Thus when Diary entries for the dates cited in the Index are consulted, cross references to other entries or to the marginalia alongside the specified passages serve to identify additional pseudonyms invented for a particular person. Further, he provided a second cluster of pseudonyms in the Diary entry for 24 September. Here he not only lists the *dramatis personae* of 'an elegant and witty comedy' (reportedly mentioned in Aulus Gellius), but he also gives a succinct characterisation of the more important actors. Thus the various pseudonyms fall into two main groups, those listed in the Index, which are supplemented by marginal

[1] See p. 277 below.

and/or cross references, and those discussed in his account of the purported comedy. Additional information which helps in identifying this multiplicity of names is supplied by other comments and incidents Madox records, and these in turn can often be corroborated by statements in the Diary of his fellow chaplain John Walker, in the account of Luke Ward, or in that of Edward Fenton.[1]

In the discussion that follows, I have given the argument for identifying a pseudonym with its referent, together with the specific entries in the Diary (or in the other accounts) that justify this identification, even at the risk of being tedious: the evidence is thus made available for those who may wish to evaluate it.

Edward Fenton. Edward Fenton, the 'captaine General' of the enterprise – their 'bad headpeese' as Madox was to call him (in cipher) as early as 13 June – is most often and variously denominated. It is as *Clodius*,[2] 'clever, deceitful, peevish, ambitious, and of mean spirit' that he plays the leading role in the 'elegant and witty comedy'; and it should be noted that in ranking the *dramatis personae*, Madox assigns the roles to accord with the official ranking of the persons they represent.[3] But it is as *Hegemon* (ἡγεμών, general) that he is listed in the Index, and this method of referring to Fenton by simply stating his rank is frequently used within the Diary. Two citations in the Index for Hegemon (29 Sept.; 26 Dec.) refer to passages where the account deals with Clodius, thus providing the evidence that Hegemon and Clodius are one and the same person. Other Index listings for Hegemon refer to passages which discuss 'the general.'

Elsewhere Madox designates Fenton by a variety of names and epithets in Latin, Greek, and cipher which comment derisively on his actions in specific situations. Besides the frequent (and expected)

[1] Taylor's partial list of identifications appears in her *Fenton*, p. 320. Because Taylor apparently failed to make use of Madox's Index, which is essential to establishing the referents and because she also failed to check out the cross references in the Diary itself, she did not always recognise that Madox used different pseudonyms to refer to one and the same person. Consequently, there are a number of errors, the most obvious one being the identification of Hegemon (ἡγεμών, general) not with 'General' Fenton but with Thomas Hood the Pilot. Furthermore, since she frequently substituted her conjectured identifications (and misidentifications) for the pseudonyms appearing in the text, the sense of her translation is often vitiated.

[2] A notorious and ambitious Roman demagogue, Clodius was murdered by the accomplices of the partisan leader Titus Annus Milo. This historical fact is doubtless intended to point up the intense dislike which Vice-admiral Ward, frequently called Milo (see below), felt for his General.

[3] That is, General Fenton first in importance; Vice-admiral Ward second; Lieutenant Hawkins third; Captain Parker fourth; Madox himself fifth; his fellow chaplain Walker sixth;nnd the troublesome Miles Evans seventh.

generalis, these include *governowr* (in cipher) 31 May; *imperator* 18 Aug.; *praepositus* 19 Aug.; *popularis tribunus* 19 Aug.; *Theseus* 21 Aug.; *tetrarch* (in Greek) 22 Aug.; *regulus* 18 Aug. *et passim*, and, in a passage including Nicholas Parker, *nostri due reguli* 21 Aug.; *basileus* (in Greek and transliterated) 9 Sept., 12 Sept.; *archaios* (in Greek) 15 Sept.; *antesignanus* 20 Sept.; *monarcha* (in Greek) 21 Sept.; *sophonesteros* (in Greek) 24 Sept.; *kurios* (in Greek) 24 Sept.; *Mutius Scaevola*[1] 24 Sept.; and *mownseer* (in cipher) 24 Sept. In one cipher passage (25 Nov.) where the reference is verifiable from internal evidence, Madox merely terms him *master*, perhaps inadvertently, perhaps intentionally. Fenton's office as 'captaine General' usually makes these random allusions clear.

Luke Ward. The second role in the comedy is taken by *Titus Annus Milo*,[2] 'great in words and sufficiently crafty, bold as well as hard-working, irascible, inexorable, grasping.' This 'second role' accords with the official rank of Luke Ward, 'Vice-admiral' of the *Edward Bonaventure* and thus second in command to Fenton. The identification is corroborated by numerous incidents Madox relates about Milo which are related about Ward in the accounts of Walker, Fenton, and of Ward himself.[3] Allusion to his rank is also indicated in Madox's construction *Hypegemon*, i.e., Vice-general or second to Hegemon, and it is this pseudonym which appears in the Index. The 25 Nov. date listed there refers to a Diary entry dealing with the Vice-admiral, who is then further specified by a marginal cipher reading 'Ward a vilayn.' Again, many specific incidents involving Hypegemon may be corroborated as relating to the Vice-admiral in the other accounts.[4] Elsewhere he is *dux*, 19 Nov., identified by a cipher note 'Ward,' and *hyponauticus* and *hypotholasticus*, i.e., Vice-admiral, 12 Nov.; 25 Nov.

William Hawkins. The third role is that of the 'stupid and indiscreet' yet 'open and honourable' *Glaucus* who 'acts in place of Clodius' but

[1] Madox's use of the name Mutius Scaevola for Fenton on this occasion and his allocating the fifth role in the comedy to 'Quintus Mutius Scaevola, Augur' (Madox himself) is initially confusing and was perhaps so intended.

[2] See p. 51, n. 2 above.

[3] E.g., on 6 Dec. Madox relates that Milo and Pyrgopolynices (easily identified as Captain Parker, see below) were sent out to board the Spanish prize at the Bay of Good Comfort. On this date Fenton records (Taylor, *Fenton*, p. 118) that he sent out 'Cap*t*en Warde and Cap*t*en Parker.'

[4] E.g., on 1 Nov. Madox reports that Hypegemon is summoned with his master (Percy) and his pilot (Blacollar) to the *Galleon* for a conference, a statement verifiable in Ward's own account (*PN* (1589), p. 657).

who 'could not endure' him. This is the position of William Hawkins; as Lieutenant, he was second in command on the *Galleon*. Conclusive identification is provided by the marginal reference to 'Glaucus' alongside a passage relating to 'Hawkins' for 8 Dec., a date which appears among those listed for 'Glaucus' in the Index. Further substantiation appears in specific instances noted by Madox, in particular those revealing the undercurrent of hostility between Fenton and Hawkins and in allusions to Hawkins's experiences on Francis Drake's circumnavigation.[1]

Nicholas Parker. Pyrgopolynices miles,[2] fourth in the *dramatis personae* and 'a swellhead on account of his charge of soldiers,' is clearly to be identified with the Captain-at-Land, Nicholas Parker of the *Galleon*, an identification revealed by the Pyrgopolynices reference in the Index to a 13 Oct. Diary entry where Madox records making an astronomical sphere for *noster miles*. While aware of the hidden rivalry between Parker and Fenton, Madox nonetheless reflects on their intimacy by associating the two as in the *due reguli* allusion mentioned above and in a reference on 20 Aug. to 'Pyrgopolynices and his Theseus.' Again and again Madox derides the cowardice and timidity of Parker, and on 18 Aug. he terms him, ironically, *noster patronus, dux et defensor*.[3] Generally, however, he is simply called Pyrgopolynices, the braggart soldier. Three allusions to the *Big Gun* (*archisclopeta*), Madox's coinage, are not directly verifiable from their contexts although the military figure clearly suggests Parker.

Miles Evans. Menippus Cynicus,[4] seventh in importance in the comedy,[5] is to be identified with Miles Evans, the disgruntled merchant who leaves the expedition in Sierra Leone to return to England with some Portuguese traders. This is proved by the two dates for Menippus listed in the Index (1 Oct.; 25 Nov.), where the passages, one in English and one in cipher, refer to Evans. There is also a cross reference

[1] The hatred of the Lieutenant on the *Galleon* for his General should, by this point, require no further evidence. Madox's choice of a sea-god to designate Hawkins is perhaps intended to give recognition to the exploits of a great sea-faring family.

[2] The 'Tower-Town-Taker' or *miles gloriosus* of Plautus's comedy.

[3] That the reference is to Captain Parker is substantiated by Fenton's journal (*Taylor*, pp. 102–3); Fenton records his own presence at the bargaining session with the Portuguese on 18 Aug., while Madox is specifically lamenting the *absence* on that occasion of their protector, captain, and defender.

[4] A Cynic philosopher noted for his harsh sarcasms.

[5] The fifth and sixth roles are discussed below.

(in cipher) for 1 Oct. to a marginal note (also in cipher) beside a passage in the Diary (25 Nov.) which deals with 'Evans.'[1]

That Madox considered this merchant's role important is to be explained by his observation (26 Dec.) that Evans's departure for England had blunted Fenton's piratical intentions, because the report of these intentions would have preceded the expedition's return. As Madox noted, to return home enriched with plunder was neither safe nor honest, but to plunder and return home in poverty was an offence punishable by death.

Simon Fernando (Simão Fernandes). Two servants are included in the comedy: the first is *Verres*[2] (i.e., swine), 'a notable and open thief' who is to be identified with Simon Fernando, one of the two pilots on the *Galleon*, and who is invoked again and again as 'the persuader and originator' of all their piratical designs. Citations in the Index make the identification clear: in the Diary entries for 1 Nov., 21 Nov.; and 17 Dec., Fernando is identified by name in cipher, and in the entry for 22 Nov., he is identified by name in Greek letters.

Thomas Hood. The second servant is *Galba*[3] (i.e., worm), 'a boasting buffoon' who is to be identified with the second pilot on the *Galleon*, Thomas Hood. This is conclusively shown by the two references to Galba in the Index: the 22 Nov. citation refers to a Latin passage naming him *Hudus*, with a pun on his name in Greek in the margin. The 25 Nov. citation also refers to a Latin passage naming him *Whodus*.

Christopher Hall. Aeneas's steersman *Palinurus*, described in the *dramatis personae* as 'negligent but in every other respect spirited,' is the pseudonym for the *Galleon*'s master Christopher Hall, who is described in similar terms on 20 and 21 Sept. On these two occasions Madox calls him *gubernator* (i.e., steersman), and on 24 Sept. *Publius Lentulus, praetor* to Mutius Scaevola (Fenton). On 21 Sept. Hall so angered his General by his unfit speeches that five of the Assistants were called in to hear the charge and give their opinions. As a result, Walker (see his entry),

[1] As mentioned above, on one occasion (3 Oct.) Madox uses the name of Evans as an alias for Walker, identifying the latter in cipher.

[2] As governor of Sicily, the Roman Cornelius Verres was noted for his extortions and rapacity and was subsequently forced to live in exile.

[3] The name of a buffoon in the age of Tiberius according to Renaissance editions of Juvenal (*Sat.* 5.4). Some of his jests are mentioned in Quintilian (vi. 2, 27, 62, 64, 66).

Ward,[1] and Fenton himself,[2] record and comment on the incident. Palinurus (like a ship's master) keeps a log as part of his duty. He is, furthermore, reported as berating Martin Frobisher for having pocketed sums intended for provisioning the expedition (13 Sept.), a charge in line with other disclosures about Frobisher attributed to the *Galleon*'s master. Having sailed on all three of the Arctic voyages, Hall was clearly alert to Frobisher's practices. Another allusion to the *gubernator* of the *Galleon* appears in a 26 Nov. entry, where Madox comments that he prepared a sailing chart for him; and a 17 Dec. entry records in cipher a comment made by the 'master' of the *Galleon*.

Other allusions to Hall seem intended in the dates cited in the Index for *navarcha*. Of the five entries, three (20, 21, and 24 Sept.) refer to Hall at the time he is called before the Assistants, but the remaining two entries, while applicable to him, cannot be verified outside of their context, that is, either by a cross reference in Madox's Diary or from the other accounts.[3]

? *Richard Cotton*. A final participant in the comedy who also is listed in the Index is *Colax*,[4] 'a kind of parasite who envied everyone for everything, the author of discord and strife, caring only for his own belly and inelegant skin.' Despite the list of dates in the Index and other notices in the Diary, it is not possible to establish his identity with complete certainty.[5] The characteristics of the figure Colax correspond perhaps most closely to the pattern of behaviour – which Madox derides in undisguised form – of Richard Cotton, a traveller who had been recommended to a 'place' on the voyage by the earl of Leicester.[6]

[1] *PN* (1589), p. 653. [2] Taylor, *Fenton*, p. 107.

[3] Thus in translation of Latin passages where the referent is not absolutely certain, the term *navarcha* is given in parentheses.

[4] *Colax* or *The Parasite* was the name of (lost) comedies by Menander, Naevius, and Plautus. See Terence *Eun.*, Prol. 25, 30.

[5] Vice-admiral Ward (as Hypegemon) is the only one of the identifiable figures listed in the Index who is not on board the *Galleon*. Of the *Galleon*'s main officers, merchants, and travellers, the only three not referred to by identifiable pseudonyms are Matthew Tailboys (Tailbush), merchant, and Richard Cotton and Edward Gilman, travellers. This fact suggests that Colax is to be identified with one of these three persons. Scarcely mentioning Gilman, Madox has harsh things to say about both Cotton and Tailboys, though his comments on Cotton are the more extensive.

However, in the account of his comedy, Madox names two (or three) other characters (here the MS is mutilated) who are 'all of the third order' ('Plinius Secundus, Pompil*ius* . . . Simplicius'), and Tailboys or Cotton or Gilman may be signified by one of these. Of those of the 'third order' only Pompilius is ever mentioned again, and this in a passage of utterly obscure import (29 Oct.).

[6] Otho E VIII, f. 182.

John Banister. The last of Madox's companions who figures in the Index is *Lucius Licinius.*[1] He is easily identified as the surgeon John Banister but by a circuitous cross referencing of two of the three dates in the Index: the 19 Nov. citation for Licinius is to an entry relating to 'our Aesculapius' – a patent allusion to the *Galleon*'s surgeon – who while visiting the ailing Walker on the *Edward* quarrelled with Vice-admiral Ward (who is himself identified in a marginal cipher), an event also duly recorded by Ward.[2] The 30 Dec. citation is to an entry relating to 'our Podalyrius,' the son of Aesculapius, who in turn is identified in the margin as Lucius Licinius.

Sir Francis Drake. William Borough. Two remaining personal references in the Index are to *Anas,* identified in the entries as Sir Francis Drake, elsewhere called 'that golden knight of ours' (25 Nov.)[3] and to William Borough (or Boroughs)[4] whose name is transcribed in Greek, apparently a sufficient disguise in Madox's view.

Richard Madox. John Walker. For names listed in the 'comedy' that do not appear in the Index, the identification is circumstantial, though their referents seem clear from the contexts. The fifth role in the comedy is that of *Quintus Mutius Scaevola, Augur* or Diviner;[5] this suggests one of the two chaplains. On 29 Sept. in a disguised account of Fenton's plan to return to the Cape Verdes to plunder, Scaevola is represented as arguing 'scrupulously, devoutly, and at length concerning the power and goodness of the gods.' Both chaplains were of course opposed to piratical ventures. What is to distinguish them?

The sixth (and consequently less influential) role in the comedy is that of *Publius Cornicola.* On 30 Dec. 'Cornicola' is reported as coming from the *Edward* with Hypegemon (Ward) to the *Galleon,* and on that

[1] In the Index Madox lists the pseudonym simply as *Licinius.* Once (margin, 20 Oct.) he writes *Lucius Licinius,* a name I have been unable to identify. Qualities ascribed to the Roman emperor Licinius reflect the very ones Madox abominated in John Banister, i.e., religious bigotry, hostility to learning, and aversion to letters, and Madox may simply have supplied the *Lucius.*

[2] *PN* (1589), p. 658.

[3] On occasion *Anas* appears within the Latin text for John Drake, Captain of the *Francis* (e.g., 9 Sept.) in contexts that readily identify Sir Francis's young cousin.

[4] Borough was the author of a work on the mariner's needle, but Madox attributes to him *The Regiment of the Sea* (by William Bourne), which he was reading on 8 April. On 12 Nov., the single date cited in the Index, Madox duly records the somewhat mysterious but denigrating comments on Borough made by Luke Ward.

[5] Quintus Mutius Scaevola, Augur, was commended by Cicero for his learning and gracious bearing (*e.g., Brutus* 212).

date Ward comments[1] that he and his master (Percy), together with M. Walker, made such a visit. Thus it seems quite clear that Publius Cornicola represents Walker and Quintus Mutius Scaevola Madox.[2] Moreover, Publius Cornicola is reported on 29 Sept. as having predicted to Milo (Ward) that a return to the Cape Verdes would diminish the reputation of all, a statement according with the protests made by Walker to his Vice-admiral on 24, 25 Sept. as recorded in his own Diary (see entries).

Two troublesome aspects to identifying Publius Cornicola with Walker crop up: first, on 25 Nov. Madox cites *Publius* Cornicola as saying he would not commit murder except on the order of one person and then he would not take pity on any soul – a shocking statement for a chaplain and one that duly shocked the chaplain on the *Galleon*. Secondly, there is *one* reference to *Fabius* Cornicola, who, at the meeting of the Assistants called on 24 Sept. to pass upon the fitness of Hall's remarks to his General (alluded to above), asserts that the General is a fool to assume he wields Caesar's majesty everywhere, again rather harsh words for the mild Walker. But only Ward, Hawkins, Parker, Madox, and Walker were called into the presence of the General and the outspoken Hall, so it seems likely that on this one occasion Madox has given only the gens and cognomen and that Walker is intended. Thus we should perhaps assume that the name intended was, in accord with Roman practice, Publius Fabius Cornicola. We should perhaps also recognise in the cognomen a somewhat malicious reflection on Walker's sexual life, to which Madox twice alludes in a jocular way (14 May; 28 June).

To sum up then, the lists in the Index may be checked out against the entries in the Diary and the results correlated by means of Madox's marginalia or by cross references to other entries. The results obtained,

[1] *PN* (1589), p. 664.

[2] Further support for identifying the scrupulous and devout Augur, Quintus Mutius Scaevola with Madox himself is to be seen in a passage for 3 Oct., where at odds with Fenton, he takes comfort in the proverb *Intemerata conscientia frui tutissimum est*, and on 29 Oct. Scaevola is described as endowed with 'a great and intrepid spirit' and an 'unspotted conscience' (*intemerata conscientia*).

One allusion (24 Sept.) to *Lucius Crassus Augur* seems also intended to represent Madox himself. This appears in a passage dealing with Mutius Scaevola and his *praetor* Publius Lentulus (Fenton and his master, Christopher Hall). The name of the Augur Q.M. Scaevola does not appear while that of Publius Cornicola – for Walker – does, thus excluding an identification of Lucius Crassus with him.

The historical Lucius Licinius Crassus was a noted orator who served as a consul with Q.M. Scaevola (distinguished as *pontifex maximus*) in 95 B.C., and the two names are coupled in Cicero's *Brutus* 148. Having already appropriated the name Mutius Scaevola for Fenton in this passage, Madox has to adopt a new pseudonym for himself to keep the *pontifex maximus* distinct from the *augur*.

taken together with the list of the *dramatis personae* of his purported comedy, permit positive identification of Fenton, Ward, Hawkins, Parker, Banister, Evans, Fernando, Hood, Hall (though not in every instance since Madox uses *gubernator*, *navarcha*, and 'master' with differing significations), and of Sir Francis Drake and William Borough as well. The identification of Colax, although the name appears in the Index, remains unverified: the most likely candidate, as already explained, is Richard Cotton. For persons whose pseudonyms do not appear in the Index, that is, for Madox himself and his fellow chaplain, the identifications derive from the contexts in which they appear.

A list of the most frequently used pseudonyms and their identifications follows:

	On the *Galleon Leicester*
Clodius	Edward Fenton, General (see also Hegemon)
Colax	? Richard Cotton, Traveller
Galba	Thomas Hood, Pilot
Glaucus	William Hawkins, Lieutenant
Hegemon	Edward Fenton
Lentulus (Publius, *praetor*)	Christopher Hall, Master (see also Palinurus)
Licinius (Lucius; also Aesculapius and Podalyrius)	John Banister, Surgeon
Menippus Cynicus	Miles Evans, Merchant
Palinurus (on occasion, *gubernator* and *navarcha*)	Christopher Hall
Pyrgopolynices	Nicholas Parker, Captain-at-Land
Scaevola (Mutius Quintus, *Augur*)	Richard Madox, Chaplain
Verres	Simon Fernando, Pilot
	On the *Edward Bonaventure*
Cornicola (Publius Fabius)	John Walker, Chaplain
Hypegemon, also Milo (Titus Annus)	Luke Ward, Vice-admiral

Rather than attempt to answer point blank the question posed earlier – did Madox expect the latter portion of his Diary to be read? – it is better to let the evidence speak for itself. The disguising of his sharp comments was clearly protective and, very likely, necessary once the General with his choleric moods and assumption of royal powers began to regard him with suspicion. The means Madox chose for cloaking his statements doubtless reflects his academic training and interests. The Latin and Greek passages (discussed below); the playful invention of a would-be comedy, which served as an ironic comment on the 'dramatic' action in which he was taking part; and the apt fitting together of figures out of Roman history and literature with those he daily associated with – all of these elements tie in with what we know of his background. (The use of cipher, as I have suggested earlier, reflects an inherent wariness.)

But what of the Index which is keyed to make ten of his fellow voyagers identifiable? What of the marginalia and the cross referencing which serve to make his allusions decipherable? One might conclude that in escaping shipboard tedium, Madox simply wanted to exercise his intellectual energies or give vent to his spleen or – in true academic fashion – set up a system whereby he could easily retrieve the evidence when Fenton would have to answer for his sins at homecoming (25 Nov.). Each of these is possible. But if one takes into account Madox's circumspection as well as his apparently idle statement (28 Oct.) that he would see to it a memory of himself remained 'either by commemorating or rewarding' and puts these two factors together with the knowledge that his Register is extant only up to 21 July, it seems not unlikely that he hoped his guarded statements would serve a useful purpose. He trusted that the Latin, the Greek, and the cipher in which the pseudonyms appeared would prevent his statements from being understood by any of his intellectual inferiors on board the two ships, but he went on to provide a key to the recovery of his material by adding the Index, the marginalia, and the cross references. If he reached home, he had a ready means of furnishing evidence to members of the Privy Council. If he did not, he may have hoped that when Lord Burghley or Sir Francis Walsingham (or his patron the earl of Leicester) inquired for his 'calendar or journal' of the voyage, as they did, his own private record would also be thoroughly scrutinised.

The register

Before beginning his Register, Madox copied out three relevant documents: (1) the Commission granted to Fenton under the Great Seal (2 Apr.);[1] (2) 'Additional Instructions' to those issued on 9

[1] Otho E VIII, ff. 130–31; this has been reprinted by Wagner (*Drake's Voyage*, pp. 45–6) and Taylor (*Fenton*, pp. 59–61).

April which are printed in Hakluyt;[1] (3) a letter from Burghley and Walsingham to Fenton, nominating Carleill as governor of those who were to be 'lefte behynde' in the East and specifying two additional merchants to be included among the Assistants (one of whom did not sail).[2] He also prefaced his account with a note of 'Accidents of Alteration' that had occurred.[3] These included Carleill's refusal to make the voyage, a change which particularly troubled Madox since he had determined 'to have remayned with hym wherever he had stayd';[4] the addition of the fourth bark 'so great was the provision of all things'; and the allocation to Ward, Hawkins, and Madox himself of keys to the one coffer (instead of two) wherein was placed the Privy Council's designation of Fenton's successor 'if it should please God to take him away.' His report of their first weighing of anchors on 29 April follows.

Since he knew that the accounts of deliberations were to be presented to members of the Privy Council on their return, Madox devised a method whereby he could make his report interesting and yet retain its documentary character. As he explained to the Assistants at their first deliberation (24 June), this was to digest in his 'booke' the 'true meaning although yt shold somewhat differ in wordes' from their statements and then append the original minutes 'fyrmed' with their own hands. This 'booke,' as the Privy Council's Instructions to Fenton had specified, was to be kept 'secrete, and in good order' by Madox (or, should he die, by his successor) for exhibition upon their return. In considering the Register, then, one must bear in mind its two parts: Madox's own running account or digest and the minutes signed by those attending the councils. It is in the former part (Appendix I) that he dilates on the motives (sometimes incriminating) which accounted for the opinions the Assistants expressed in councils. He stresses Fenton's particularly and those of the two pilots on the *Galleon* when they were called in to give their expert views on navigational matters.

The last *minute* which is preserved deals with the council called on 20 December to determine whether they should continue to the River

[1] *PN* (1589), pp. 644–47; Otho E VIII, f. 173 (repr. Taylor, *Fenton*, pp. 61–2).
[2] Otho E VIII, f. 129 (repr. Taylor, *Fenton*, pp. 62–4).
[3] Appendix I, pp. 279-280 below.
[4] Madox's decision to have remained with Carleill is reflected in his request for an extension of his leave of absence from All Souls. On 11 March the College officials granted him a second 'cause of absens' of indefinite extent, requiring only that he return to the College a month after he got back to England 'when ever yt be' (All Souls College, Hovenden's Minute Bk.; Diary entry 13 Mar.).

Plate or reverse directions and head for São Vicente, though the signatures to it were not, in fact, obtained until 22 January 1583.[1] This would seem to indicate that after Madox's death on 27 February Fenton either did not assign the duty of keeping the Register to another or he called no further meetings of the Assistants. The last brief entry in Madox's *digest*, however, is dated 21 July ('*Of certaine things which fell owt after this time.*').

Of the 20 July consultation, when the masters and pilots were called in to determine their precise whereabouts on the coast of Guinea and the decision was taken to head back to Sierra Leone, Madox gives a full and frank account in his digest, but there is no signed minute preserved. He notes in his Diary that Fenton directed him *not* to commit the deliberations to the Register. Again, for the 30 September council, when they agreed to go through the Strait; for the 1 November council, when they agreed to rendezvous at the River Plate before proceeding to the Strait; and for the 25 November council, when they decided to make for the Brazilian coast, there are no signed minutes. On 7 December, the council met to consider what to do with the 'prize' (with its seven friars) and to re-consider their decision to make for the Strait. While the Interrogations of the friars, together with their answers, are extant, there is no minute preserved of the decision to go through the Strait, Madox again noting in his Diary that no record of the deliberations was kept.

However, for the next council meeting two weeks later (20 Dec.) six original documents have been preserved, including individually signed statements of the views of the Assistants. It was on this occasion, after all the officers and merchants had been consulted, that Fenton determined to turn back to São Vicente and engage in honest trading. Thus the pattern seems clear – decisions which revealed their intent to go counter to the voyage as projected were not made part of the official record.[2]

At what point did Madox desist from keeping his digest in English? Was it as early as 21 July? On 25 November, the date of a council meeting for which no documents were kept, Madox included in his

[1] Madox's astrological symbol and date at the bottom of the leaf make this clear. It is also confirmed by Ward's account (*PN* (1589), p. 666).

[2] The one exception to this is the early decision (24 June) to water at Boa Vista (which they did not do) and then to make the River Plate their second port of call.

All the extant minutes appear in Otho E VIII except for one document relating to the trial (for mutinous speeches) of Rafe Crane, master on the *Elizabeth*. This has been bound in Cotton MS, Titus B VIII, ff. 280–81, a volume which also includes the second portion of Madox's Diary.

Diary a long cipher passage, with interpolations in Latin, wherein he noted four reasons that he could not keep a 'dayly register.' Since the passage is both mutilated and incomplete, only the first and fourth of these can be made out: they are that Ward told him all notes were to be taken from everyone (an assertion supported by the search of the departing Evans's chest) and that he knew Fenton was eager to read his writings. This is then followed by a short disquisition on the General's malfeasance. Yet, surprisingly, in a Diary entry for 21 December,[1] Madox refers to his opening the Register to 7 December and then comments on the decision taken to go through the Strait. But for this council no record, according to Fenton's injunction, had been kept. The simplest explanation for this apparent inconsistency may be that since the documents relating to the Interrogations of the friars on that same date were preserved, they served to trigger in Madox's memory the only too familiar (though unrecorded) decision.[2]

We can conclude then that Madox adhered to Fenton's injunctions not to keep official minutes of certain of the deliberations. We can also conclude that he may have continued to keep his own running account in English beyond the last extant entry (21 July), but that by 25 November when he listed in his Diary the reasons for not keeping it, he had become aware of the need for caution. Perhaps we should push back the date of this realisation – and the consequent suspension of it – at least to October when Madox learned there was 'treason wroght' against him and in turn relate its having been suspended to his later comment (28 Oct.) that he was now accepted without reservation by those who before had doubted his good faith. In fact, we may perhaps push his decision to suspend it even further back – that is, at least to mid-September when he begins to use his Diary to record many official matters but disguises his comments by resorting to Latin, pseudonymic references, and literary allusions.

If he did continue to keep his official narrative beyond 21 July, it is impossible to know what happened to the portion dealing with events between that date and the time he deemed it expedient to desist. It could have been lost en route home or destroyed by Fenton

[1] See note to this entry for Madox's lapse in writing the date.

[2] There is a suggestion that by the end of December, Madox himself had become reconciled to going through the Strait rather than suffer the disgrace of returning home with their mission unfulfilled (see 24 Dec.). Hawkins (Otho E VIII, f. 225) includes Madox among those who had been willing to go through the Strait but 'in Two dayes weare cleaned turned [around]' – that is, among those who voted on 20 Dec. to head back for São Vicente.

or even by Madox himself.[1] But the more reasonable explanation, it seems to me, is that he desisted after he had devised a counter strategy to Fenton's intimidation. This was to use his Diary, disguising the recitation of the sins of his Captain General and others but carefully indexing and cross-referencing them, to replace the candid account he did not dare to keep in his 'booke.'

The Latin and Greek

Since he was a Fellow of All Souls for nine years, a Master of Arts for six, and, at the time of his leave of absence from Oxford, a Proctor of the University with duties including the examination of candidates, one would expect Madox to be proficient in Latin if not in Greek. This was not altogether the case. As exemplified in the Diary, his style in Latin, as well as the occasional insertions in Greek, abounds – to use his own disdainful comment on another – in barbarisms, solecisms, and hyperbatons. Though this want of proficiency doubtless reflects on the academic level of the college and university at which he had spent almost twelve years (not to mention those spent at Shrewsbury School), in taking his lapses into account, one should bear in mind what his primary intent was in resorting to Latin and Greek. Clearly, despite his avowal, it was not for the exercise of his style.

Consequently, he was content to set down in Latin what he thought in English with scant concern for either correctness or niceties of style. Thus the frequent lack of agreement between subject and verb, the vague or uncertain reference, the shifts of tense and person probably reflect more accurately his informal English style than his academic Latin. That he occasionally slips into English (e.g., *note* for *nota*; *leags* for *leucae*) supports this conclusion. In addition to these and other inadvertencies (e.g., omission of a makron or tilde), like others of his time he is utterly casual in his spelling, particularly in respect to proper names (both *palinurus*, *pallinurus*) and frequently phonetic (e.g., *caesius*, *omphasium*). This casualness extends to punctuation and capitalisation. Lapses in the Greek insertions are even more pronounced: the vocabulary is frequently uncertain, and the accents are often either missing or wrong.

[1] It is equally impossible to know whether or not Madox continued his Diary beyond the 31 Dec. 1582 entry, although for such a confirmed diarist it would seem a likely assumption that he did – at least until he became too ill to do so. Ward's journal shows that Madox was in sufficiently good health on 26 Jan. 1583 to visit the wounded on the *Edward*.

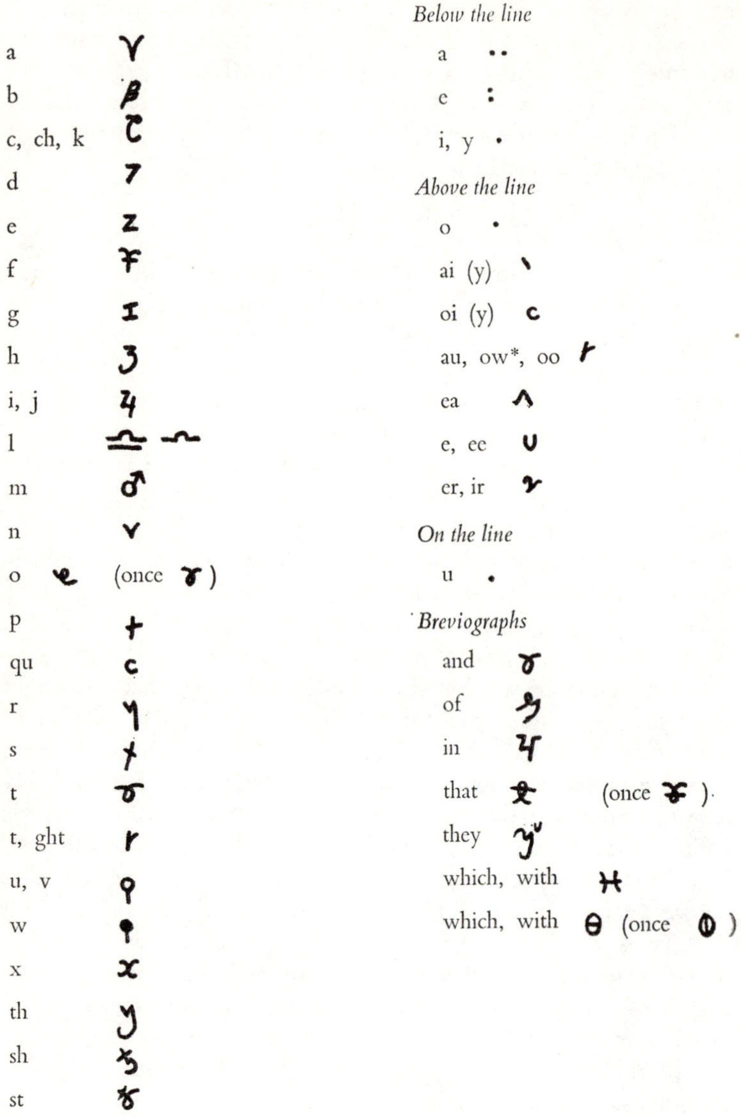

Fig. 4. Key to the cipher

* Since Madox's system is phonetic and since his English spelling pattern is to use *ow* for modern *ou*, in an effort to preserve the texture of the manuscript, I have retained the *ow* spelling in the cipher passages.

The cipher

E. G. R. Taylor performed a signal service in working out a key to Madox's cipher. The identification of the symbols on page 64, it should be recognised, is based primarily on her key (found on p. 318 of her volume), although my examination of all cipher passages in the Diary has resulted in some modifications and minor corrections.

Madox's system, which is phonetic, is based on a combination of Greek, astrological, and private symbols with a variety of vowel sounds determined by the position of the symbol above, below, or on the line – a device which permitted flexibility and ease in writing. He uses breviographs and certain marks commonly used in Latin abbreviations that are frequently carried over into English (e.g., the breviograph for *er*, combined with the letter *M*=M^r^). At times he puts his Latin into cipher. On occasion he slips up in positioning the vowel sounds correctly (e.g., *i* for *o* in aut*o*rity), in adding or omitting a stroke (which results, e.g., in *v*as for *w*as); on occasion too he lapses in the middle of writing a word from cipher into English and once into Greek, making all in all some dozen or more slight errors. But in general his system works consistently and well, though his spelling is of course as variable in his cipher as it is in his English passages. See Fig. 1 for an example of a passage in cipher, transliterated on pages 194–95 of the text.

The manuscript

The first portion of the Diary appears in B.L., Cotton MS, Appendix XLVII (ff. 1–49), formerly Additional MS 5008; the second in Cotton MS, Titus B VIII (ff. 179–221). There is mutilation of the edges and some staining so that while some obliterated words can be reconstructed from the context, others cannot.

Madox uses the secretary hand in general but the Italian for foreign words or for emphases, though not invariably. As mentioned earlier, to the title page he has added various facts about himself and about Oxford and such information relating to the year 1582 as the 'dominical letter' or 'golden number.' This material has necessarily been printed separately. In the very early portion of the Diary Madox used brown ink to indicate the months, Sundays, scriptural citations, and marginalia; green ink to indicate the Saints' Days (but not after 2 February); and black ink for the body of the text. These niceties have been ignored.

Madox's orthography, like his language, is of interest. Often inconsistent in small matters he does have certain preferred spellings, a point of some importance in reconstructing partially obliterated passages. Generally speaking, his spelling is phonetic, again a point of importance both for identifying proper names (*Ellx* for *Elkes*; cf. *halx* for *hawks*) and for understanding cipher passages. Some of his preferential spellings stem from his Shropshire background (e.g., *w* for *ll*, *fawhing*; *w* for *u*, *bwilt*, *bwy*). Equally, his racy and colloquial diction shows many dialectal peculiarities; these are glossed in the text when they offer difficulty.

Editorial principles

In preparing this first complete edition of what is (I submit) a difficult manuscript, I have assumed that, thanks to its particular flavour, it would have interest for a varied scholarly audience. This assumption has dictated the kind of edition I have thought most useful. A photographic facsimile, suitable for a work of a purely documentary nature of specialised appeal, would offer enormous problems to the reader, problems attendant on the legibility of the author's hand and on the condition and complexity of the text. A verbatim transcript, reproducing all evidence of the author's economy and haste in writing (including manifold abbreviations and lapses) would have imposed difficulties, difficulties which would have been eliminated to a large extent by the author or his printer had the work been prepared for publication in the sixteenth century.

For a modern editor to eliminate similar difficulties in no way violates the integrity of the text, and I have chosen a form of presentation which maintains fidelity to the original while providing for minimal changes in accidentals. These changes are spelled out below. Though I have endeavoured to reproduce Madox's orthography scrupulously, I have followed modern typographical conventions for the letters *i/j*, *u/v*, *vv*, and long *s*. Abbreviations and contractions have been expanded except for compass directions, the (infrequent) 'Mistress' and the (frequent) 'master' (here rendered M.).

Capitalisation is introduced at the beginning of sentences as well as for personal and place names. Otherwise the author's irregular practice is followed (e.g., in respect to titles). In some instances, particularly for *l* and *k*, it is difficult to be certain whether or not Madox intended a capital, and in these cases I have given him the benefit of the doubt, determining its presence or absence by the context.

Punctuation in the manuscript consists mainly of spaces between sentences, virgules of varying size, and question marks. Therefore, I have supplied minimal pointing, commas in place of virgules, and final stops when required.

Calendar entries in the manuscript include the date in arabic, an astrological symbol for the day of the week, and, when applicable, the dominical letter and the Saint's Day. As Madox puts the dominical letter sometimes before the astrological symbol and sometimes after, I have regularised the order for calendar entries, identified the day of the week in brackets, and italicised the headings since they constitute divisions in themselves within the Diary. For very long entries dealing with disparate matters, I have introduced paragraphing. Marginalia, which Madox added after completing an entry (shown by his changes of ink), frequently appear a few lines above or below the topics to which they refer, and these have been correctly positioned.

Special symbols

Italic for foreign words and quotations or for emphasis is regularised. Literary quotations in the English passages of the Diary are translated or identified in a footnote; those appearing in translated passages have been retained and a translation added within the text.

Italic substitution is also used to indicate supplied omissions, whether of single letters or of words, resulting from minor mutilation of the manuscript or from the tight binding (particularly of Cotton MS, Appendix XLVII), wherever the sense dictates the reading. If such an omission occurs in what normally would be an italicised passage, the substitutions are in roman.

These two uses of italic are in every case, I think, easily distinguished, for example, *læse majeste* and St Luc*ar*. All reconstructions of the manuscript are rendered in accord with Madox's characteristic orthography.

Square brackets are used for editorial insertions, for supplying a word or letter inadvertently omitted, or for rectifying a lapse (e.g., y^e for y^t); in the latter case, the original reading is given in a footnote.

By means of this double system of indicating omissions – brackets to reflect Madox's own lapses and italic to reflect subsequent impairment of the manuscript – the reader is perhaps enabled to evaluate the condition of the original more precisely.

Ellipsis dots are used to indicate illegible passages resulting from staining or mutilation.

A *blank* is used to indicate a deliberate lacuna in the manuscript, usually of a proper name.

Parentheses mark off passages initially written in Latin, Greek, or cipher, for example (*Latin*:).

Double slant lines indicate the turn of the leaf, and the folio numbering appears in the left and right margins.

The annotation is particularly heavy for the early months, because Madox alludes so frequently to his contemporaries. All dates and college affiliations, unless otherwise specified, are from *Alumni Oxonienses* (1500–1714), edited by Joseph Foster.

All definitions, unless otherwise specified, are from the *OED*. The lack of annotation for an allusion not readily familiar indicates that I have been unable to identify it.

Adhuc erit in loco isto deserto absque homine et absque 1r
jumento et in cunctis civitatibus eius, habitaculum
pastorum et accubantium gregum. In civitatibus montuosis
et in civitatibus campestribus et in civitatibus quae ad
*austrum sunt et in terra Benj*amin *et in circuitu*
Jerusalem et in civitatibus Juda [*adhuc transibunt greges*
ad manum numerantis].

Ait dominus [Jer. 33: 12, 13][1]

*In patera ponder*avit *dominus huius et mensura mensur*avit 2r
tempora et numero numeravit tempora et non commovit
*nec excitavit usque dum impleat prædicta me*liora.[2]

Diarium

Oxon.

1582

[1] The quotation from Jeremiah, of which the last line is obliterated, is written in alternate brown and green ink.

[2] This obscure passage seems to be a quotation imperfectly remembered; it may perhaps be translated as follows: 'Its lord weighed [all things] in a scale and measured the times in proportion and numbered them in arithmetical mean and did not alter or disturb [them] until he had completed the aforesaid task.' I am grateful to Dr Michael Lapidge, Clare Hall, Cambridge, for his assistance with the Latin.

2r

	Christian era	1582
	Founding of the world	5544[1]
	My birth	Nov. 11, 1546
	Reign of Elizabeth	24
YEAR of	Study at Oxford	25 Jan. 1567
	Proficiency in logic	1571 Nov.
	Proficiency in philosophy	1575 Oct.[2]
	Ministry	24 Nov. 1580
	Proctorship	1 April 1581[3]
	Intercalary year	28[4]
	Dominical letter	G[5]
	Golden number	6[6]
	Epact [of the moon]	6[7]
	Circle of the sun	23[8]
	Roman Indiction	10[9]

[1] A date of variant reckoning, but Madox's agrees with that of his friend Cyprian Lucar in *A Treatise Named Lucarsolace* (1590), A3.

[2] Madox indicates his admission to the bachelor's degree and his licensing as a master of arts. The record of the stages by which he proceeded to the degrees given in Clark's *Register* shows minor differences in dates: 'Richard Madox, suppl. B.A. 26 Apr., adm. 1 Dec. 1571, det. 1571/2, suppl. M.A. 10 Oct., lic. 25 Nov. 1575, inc. 1576; suppl. lic. to preach 8 Feb. 1581/2' (II.iii.10).

[3] On 5 Apr., Madox and Robert Crane (of Balliol) were elected Proctors. In the following Nov., Leicester as Chancellor wrote from the Court to the effect that as Madox was about to be employed outside the realm on public affairs, he recommended Henry Beaumont of All Souls to take his place as proctor. Beaumont was duly elected 8 Feb. 1582 (Clark, *Reg.* II.ii.96, 116; i.130). In resigning his office to Beaumont, Madox, as he notes (15 Feb.), received from him 'therfor twenty marx.' See also entries for 6, 9, and 13 Mar.

[4] Relating to leap year.

[5] Used to denote Sundays in a particular year. As the first seven letters of the alphabet are used to denote the first seven days in Jan. and so on in rotation, the letter of the first Sunday is the 'dominical letter.' Thus Madox labels his first entry on 1 Jan. 1582 'Newyersdaie A.'

[6] The number of any year in the Metonic lunar cycle of nineteen years. This number for the year n of the Christian era is $(n+1)\div 19$ and is used to compute Easter. The remainder is the 'golden number,' so-called because its invention, ascribed to Meton c. 432 B.C., was purportedly sent to the Romans in letters of gold (also called 'prime').

[7] The number of days, never exceeding thirty, which gives the difference between the solar and the lunar year. It is computed by multiplying the golden letter or prime by 11 and dividing the product by 30; the remainder is the 'epact' (John Davis, 'The Seamans Secrets' (1594) in *Voyages and Works*, ed. A. H. Markham (Hakluyt Soc.), 1880, pp. 247–48).

[8] The circle of the sun, which contains 28 years, was invented to determine the dominical letter. This number for the year n of the Christian era is $(n+9)\div 28$; the remainder is the number of the 'circle' (Thomas Blundeville, 'The Arte of Navigation' in *His Exercises* (1594), 2S7*v*–8).

[9] Civil reckoning of time which shows the place a given year occupies in an unspecified cycle of 15 years. It is computed by adding 3 to the given year and

Lent	Mar. 4
Easter	April *15*
Whitsunday	June 3
Vicechancellor	Doctor James[1]
Proctors	Crane
	M*a*dox
Mayor	Nobl*e*[2]
Sheriff	Demton[3]

Domini est terra et plenitudo eius 2v
Psal. 24 [:1]

1582 January ♒

1. ☾ [*Mon.*] *Newyersdaie A.* I was at Wollerhanton.[4] This day 3r
abowt 3 a clock in the morning my sister was dylvered of

dividing by 15; the remainder is the 'indiction,' but, says Blundeville (2S8*v*), this indiction is to be counted from Sept., in contrast to the dominical letter which is counted from Jan.

[1] William James, D.D. (1574), Master of University College (1572–84), served as Vice Chancellor 1581–2 and again in 1590 (*Athen. Oxon.*, II, 203; 217).

[2] William Noble, who became mayor in 1581, was a carrier (1562) and wine merchant, living in 1573 with his wife and 'vi pore and yonge' children in a house known as 'The Swynstock' in St Martin's Parish. He was to serve the town in various capacities until his death in 1593 – as chamberlain, 1571–2; bailiff, 1573; alderman and coroner, 1579; mayor; and M.P. in 1584–5.

In a prolonged town and gown controversy, Noble was firmly on the side of her 'Majesties poore subjects' in opposition to the rioting and disorderly students. In exhibiting articles against certain members of the University in 1575, he alluded to the riots, disorders, and misdemeanours on the part of the students, recounting how thirty or forty of them armed with swords and bucklers and clubs had gone about the town at 11 o'clock at night with drum and trumpet 'misusinge both men and women with opprobryous words' (cf. entry for 8 Jan.).

After a series of complaints, matters reached a climax in 1579 when divers students broke the doors and windows of his house and threatened to pull it down and fire it, forcing his wife, children and servants into the street crying 'Murdere, murdere, lyght, lyght, for the passyon of God,' whereupon the townspeople rushed to his defence. With the constable ineffective, they summoned the Vice Chancellor and divers other doctors to come with all speed, but even they could not quiet the fray without proclamation of rebellion. And, as the townspeople affirmed in a petition to Burghley, this vexation was only that they would not witness against Noble in a complaint presented in the Star Chamber by a student of Christ Church. (See W. H. Turner, *Selections from the Records of the City of Oxford* (Oxford, 1880), *passim*, pp. 338–417; Clark, *Reg.*, II.i.315; 325.)

[3] Edward Demton (or Denton) served as sheriff in 1582 (Lansdowne MS 35, f. 140); he had been J.P. in 1580–81 (*APC, 1580–81*, p. 34).

[4] Visiting his older brother Thomas, who was serving as headmaster of the Grammar School. See pp. 6-8 above.

Katherin borne

a girle which at evensong was christened Katherin by me and Mrs Katherin Latham and Mrs Elsabeth Creswel.[1] I dyned at M. Plankneys[2] and playd at cards and gav my wynings to Peg and Sam. Supt at M. Lewsons.[3]

Hopkins

2. ♂ [*Tues.*] *and* ☿ [*Wed.*] I stayd in Hampton and ther dyned
3. with M. Fox and others.[4] M. Hopkins broght me wyne and told me what he wold do for lytle Hanbery.[5]

4. ♃ [*Thurs.*] my brother gave me an ymperial rial and my sister a spur riol.[6] I took my leave and cam with my brother and my man by the wel with 60 buckets to Perry Haul wher we fownd Mrs Stanford[7] at dynner with hir

[1] Mrs Katherin Latham is unidentified but clearly the godmother after whom Madox's niece was named.

Mrs Elsabeth Creswel, perhaps the wife (according to the *Wolverhampton Antiquary*) of Thomas Cresswell of Featherstone, a prebend of the Church of St Mary of Wolverhampton. John Cresswell (whose first wife was Jane, daughter of Richard Clive) was a Merchant of the Staple, a prominent citizen of Wolverhampton, and a supporter of Thomas in the latter's (indirect) bid for an increased stipend. (See *Wolverhampton Antiquary*, ed. G. P. Mander (1933), pp. 13; 170; 274, and Stebbing Shaw, *History and Antiquities of Staffordshire*, II, (London, 1801), 154.)

[2] Merchant of the Staple, Henry Plankney (or Plantney) was one of thirty townspeople (including John Cresswell) who had written to the Merchant Taylors in 1573, commending their newly appointed schoolmaster and urging that his stipend be increased (see pp. 6–7 above). Shortly after taking up his post at Wolverhampton, Thomas had written to the Company by Plankney, commenting on the bearer's good will to their 'wurshipfull Socyetie' as well as on 'his ready furtherance and helpe in seakinge all meanes to Further me towardes the executynge of my Duty.' From 1582 on, Plankney, whose business often required him to be in London, served as liaison man between the M.T.'s and their schoolmaster (Mander, *Wolverhampton Grammar School*, pp. 39–41, 44).

[3] Probably Thomas Leveson (or Luson), Merchant of the Staple and a member of one of Wolverhampton's leading families, whose sister (Anne) Madox was to visit at Perry Hall in company with his brother three days later (see 4 Jan.). Both Thomas Leveson and his brother John, a bachelor, had signed the letter commending Thomas Madox to the Merchant Taylors. (See Shaw, *Hist. and Antiq. of Staffordshire*, II, 168; *Wolverhampton Antiquary*, p. 170; and Mander, *Wolverhampton Grammar School*, p. 41.)

[4] Thomas Fox was one of the signatories of the commending letter.

[5] 'Lytle Hanbery' presumably refers to Walter the young son of Robert Hanbery, who was to matriculate at St Mary's Hall, Oxford, age 14, in Nov. 1582. Robert Hanbery was also one of the signatories of the commending letter; in his will he mentions his son and heir Walter, who was then at Oxford (*Staffordshire Parish Records* (Wolverhampton, 1932), Pt. I, p. x).

[6] A spur riol, which took its name from the star resembling the rowel of a spur on its reverse, was worth 16*s* (R. Nares, *Glossary* (1905)).

[7] The country estate of Perry Hall in Handsworth, Staffordshire, had come into the Stanford family by purchase by Sir William, Justice of the Common Pleas, whence it devolved in 1558 to his heir Robert, one of six sons. Four years later Robert married Anne Leveson (see above), and their son Edward was in turn to inherit the estate. (See Mander, *Wolverhampton Grammar School*, p. 52; *Staffordshire Pedigrees* (Pub. of the Harl. Soc. LXIII), p. 216.)

brother in law and hir kinsman but he and his sone wer rydden to a comyssion yn Brymwyche Heath. With prayers and teares I took my leave of my brother and rode to Henley. The Lord cumfort and guid us both ever. Amen. brother

5. ♀ [*Fri.*] we cam to Oxford the day being fayre.

6. ♄ [*Sat.*] *Epiphanie* I supt at M. Maiors and after wasseld with M. Brush the chamberlayn.[1]

7. ☉ *G* [*Sun.*] I dyned with M. Marvin at Trinyty Colledg wher with my brother and the 2 Paulets and others we concluded [on] a clubbing on the moroe.[2] We supt at Lyncoln Colledg.

8. ☾ [*Mon.*] we went a clubbyng owt of al howses in the town, some, abowt 400, with drome, bagpipe and other melody. At nyght w*e* cam home with . . . torches and at Unyversytie College Latwar*e* of St. Johns[3] welcomed us in verse with a fy*ne* oration in the name of kyng Aulrede, clubbing crown*d* us with 2 fayr garlonds and offered the third but I answering his oration gave hym th*e* third and crowned hym poet lawreat. So marched we up to Carfox[4] where Sir Abbots of Bayly Colledg[5] had an oration in prose

[1] For the mayor, see n. 2, p. 71 above. John Brushe was Chamberlain in 1581–2 (Turner, *Records . . . of Oxford*, p. 417). His duty, with his fellow chamberlain, was to oversee the property of the city, draw the rents, and allocate expenditures (Anthony Wood, *Survey of the Antiq. of Oxford*, ed. A. Clark (1889–99), III, 33).

[2] John Mervin (or Marveon) of Wilts. had matriculated at Trinity in 1581, aged 22.

For Madox's unnamed brother, see pp. 4–5 above.

The '2 Paulets,' sons of Sir Amias Paulet of Somerset, were Anthony and George, who had matriculated, age 18 and 15 respectively, at Christ Church in 1580. Anthony later studied at the Middle Temple and became Governor of the Island of Jersey and Captain of the Guard to Queen Elizabeth.

The term 'clubbyng' is not elsewhere documented, with modern accounts of it deriving from Madox's next entry (e.g., Mark Curtis, *Oxford and Cambridge in Transition* (1959), p. 238 n.; F. S. Boas, who badly transcribes the passage in *University Drama in the Tudor Age* (1914), pp. 160–61; and Mallet, *History of... Oxford*, II, 143). See, p. 5 above and cf. n. 2, p. 71 above, where it appears the conviviality sometimes turned to rowdiness.

[3] Richard Lateware became a scholar of St John's in 1580 and went on to take his D.D. in 1597. Anthony Wood termed him an ingenious Latin poet and writer of epigrams; he served as chaplain to Lord Mountjoy and was slain in Ireland in 1601, aged 41 (*Athen. Oxon.*, I, 709–10).

[4] According to Wood (*Survey*, ed. Clark, I, 61), the street (properly Quatervois) was commonly called 'Carfox' (Carfax).

[5] George Abbot of Balliol, future archbishop of Canterbury, was at this date admitted to the B.A., conferred on 31 May 1582, and hence styled 'Sir'

co*mending* us for taking the savage who did ther an*swer* and yelded his hollyn club being with his . . . al in yvy. So
3v went we to Trynyty *Colledg* // and at the gate Sir Wurford[1] receved me with an oration and my brother had an other of Sir Poticary.[2] Then at the entry M. Marvin had one by Sir   . We supt at the presidents lodging and after had the Supposes[3] handeled in the haul indifferently.

9. ♂ [*Tues.*] yt snoed. I dyned and supt at Lyncoln Colledg with docter Underil[4] and M. Paulets and M. Marvin with us.

*d*octer Underil

snoe

10. ☿ [*Wed.*] Wensday fel a great snoe which driving thro the slates spoyled much of our syling. It was very gret in the north and at the meltyng of yt many wer drowned. My man Thomas browght me a cuple of capons which I gave to the warden.[5]

11. ♃ [*Thurs.*] I had Dyck Smotes trotting mare[6] and rode to

---

(equivalent to the Latin *dominus*). After receiving his D.D. in 1597, he served as Master of University College until his elevation to Canterbury in 1611. He showed, according to Wood, 'more respect to a cloak, than a cassock' (*Athen. Oxon.*, II, 562–5).

1 William Warforde of Bristol had entered Trinity at the age of 13; on receiving his B.A. in 1578, he became a Fellow and was to receive his M.A. in March. Sympathetic to Catholicism, he left his college, friends, and the nation, as Wood notes (*Athen. Oxon.*, II, 45–6), to become a priest in Rome; in 1594 he entered the Society of Jesus.

2 Thomas Potticary of Wilts. entered St John's in 1575, taking his B.A. in 1579, and was to receive his M.A. in 1583.

3 George Gascoigne's translation of Ariosto's *I Suppositi* was originally performed at Gray's Inn in 1566 and printed in 1573.

4 John Underhill was Rector of Lincoln College and served as chaplain to the Queen. Wood notes that he was also Leicester's chaplain and became Rector of Lincoln with his help (*History and Antiq. of the University of Oxford*, ed. John Gutch (1792–96), II.i.187).

5 On his departure from Oxford, Madox assigned his man Thomas to service with Henry Beaumont, his successor as Proctor (see 16 Feb.).

Robert Hovenden, the first married Warden (see 29 Apr.), served from 1571 to 1614, having been elected at the age of 27 (Burrows, *Worthies of All Souls*. pp. 93–4).

6 In Nov. 1581, Richard Smoat (or Smout) had become carrier (*tabellarius publicus Academiae*), which gave him a monopoly of the traffic between his district and the University; as such he was regarded as an officer and common servant.

The charge for hire of a horse to London one way was 3*s* 4*d* with the hirer finding horsemeat by the way. In due course Smoat failed in his business and fled, at which time he was indebted, among others, to the 'Bursars of All Souls' for £74 and to Henry Beaumont for £22 (Clark, *Reg.*, II.i.315–20).

London. Yt rayned and thawed fast and the waters wer very great. *London*

12. ♀ [*Fri.*] *and* ♄ [*Sat.*] som what fowl and cold. I stayed in
13. Queenhyve.

14. ☉ G [*Sun.*] I presented my self to my Lord of Lester who caused M. Green[1] to set me at meat for his own table was ful.

[15. ☾ *Mon.*] I was before M. Alderman Barns[2] master of the Muscovy Howse and sir Frances Drake and others who shewing that I was comended to them by my Lord *dem*aunded what I wold aske. I answered that I sowght not gayn but was glad to serve my *cun*trey or ther honorable howse or my Lord and therfor wold refer my self to them which knew better than my self what was fit for me. Thys answer lyked them so I was alowed xx^{li} for my provision, with great promyses of bowntiful consyderation. I pray God I may deserve yt. I fel acqueynted with Crowther of... in... who goeth with us.[3] Muscovie *House*

16. ♂ [*Tues.*] M. Banyster of Nottingham owr surgion and I dyned at M. Clows in Clement Lane, a surgion also of a good wyt.[4] He gave M. Banyster many gyfts and gave me a booke of 4^{s} agaynst the popes supremacy.

[1] William Green, a follower of the earl of Leicester, in order, according to Thomas Morgan, 'to seeke therby Quietnesse, to live a Christian Life, as many Catholikes more do follow the Counsellors' (W. Murdin, ed., *A Collection of State Papers... left by... Lord Burghley* (1759), II, 449).

[2] As Governor of the Muscovy Company, Alderman Barne, son of the merchant and capitalist Sir George, was importantly concerned with the Fenton voyage. His sister Anne had first married Alexander Carleill and then Sir Francis Walsingham. Thus the refusal of his nephew Christopher Carleill to accompany the venture, although he had invested £300, which distressed Madox (see 21 Apr.) must from a purely practical view have also distressed Barne (SP 12/150/96 and T. S. Willan, *The Muscovy Merchants* (1953), p. 14).

[3] He seems not to have sailed (see 1 May).

[4] For John Banister, who was to prove a constant thorn to Madox, see pp. 27–8 above.

His 'loving frend' William Clowes, who 'had studied and practised this worthy Arte of Chirurgery, sithence the 4. yeare of her Majesties Raigne,' served in 'her Majesties Navy' and in 1575 was appointed surgeon to St Bartholomew's Hospital where he became conspicuous for his scoffing and jesting manner. He was to serve (like Banister) with Leicester in the Low Countries and ultimately as the Queen's physician. The two friends regularly commended each other in their publications, and their prolific writings helped to establish English as a justifiable medium for medical works. (See Clowes' *A Right Fruteful and Aprooved Treatise...* (1602), B3*v*, *The Selected Writings of William Clowes*, ed. F. N. L. Poynter (1948), and J. J. Keevil, *Medicine and the Navy*, I (1957), 130–36.)

[*17.*] ☿ [*Wed.*] ♃ [*Thurs.*] ♀ [*Fri.*] *and* ♄ [*Sat.*] I bowght a
[*18.*] chest and other things *ne*edful for my viage which after
[*19.*] shal be [reckond]. I hard Mrs Barker was dead.[1] The *Lor*d
[20.] be merciful unto us. Herry Yomans cam [to me owt] of
the cuntrey.[2] We dyned at my cosyn [Nicholas][3] and [had]
a . . . at Mrs Wayn*wryghts.* //

4r *21.* ☉ *G* [*Sun.*] yt was very cold and a bytter wynd. Ther
was . . . throowt London. I kno not why. M.
precht at Paules: be not wyse in your own conceyt. I
xxli receaved of M. Aty[4] xxli and gave hym an acquittans for
yt, being my furnyture for the viage. Robert Wryght[5] and
Page I supt at M. Pages and had good honest chere.

22. ☾ [*Mon.*] *and* ♂ [*Tues.*] I bowght aquavite and other things
Coldock [*23.*] in Sowtherk and dyscharged Coldock 40s for my brother
Thomas.

24. ☿ [*Wed.*] I was drinking with Harry Mosen, walked to the
. . . howse with Christofer and Pory,[6] after dyned with
Trencher M. Georg Trencher[7] at the Rose in Chepe at M. Gilberts

1 Apparently a member of the Barker family of Haughmond Abbey, see, p. 2 above.

2 He too had attended Shrewsbury School with Madox (*Shrewsbury School Reg. Schol.* p. 6).

3 For Madox's cousin Nicholas, see pp. 4 and 7 above. His son, born on 22 Feb., was named after Thomas (see 28 Feb.).

4 Arthur Atye, recently appointed private secretary to Leicester, had received his B. and D.C.L. in 1574 from Oxford where he had been Principal of St Alban Hall from 1569 to 1581 and Public Orator from 1572 to 1582 on the nomination of Leicester. He was to resign the latter office on 9 Apr. because of his new duties (Clark, *Reg.*, II.i.250). After Leicester's death, he became secretary to the earl of Essex and consequently involved in the conspiracy. He was to be knighted by James.

5 After attending Shrewsbury School (with Madox), Wright went to Trinity College, Cambridge, whence he was 'carefully chosen' sometime during the mid 1570s to become tutor to Essex (see 7 Mar.).

Knighted by James, he 'so lived and dyed a grave and sober man, meanly born in Shrewsbury, but attayned by his vertue to good estate and quality' (Sir James Whitelocke, *Liber Famelicus*, ed. John Bruce (1858), pp. 20–1).

6 Peter Pory of St Mary's Parish, Oxford, had been admitted to special privileges as a servant of the Warden of All Souls in 1576 (Clark, *Reg.*, II.i.390). From the entry for 1 Apr., it seems he had intended to accompany Madox on the voyage but then desisted. At his death in 1610, he was a baker of white bread at the sign of 'The George,' and the inventory of his 'goods and chattels,' including leases from two colleges, amounted to £598 8*s* 5*d* (Oxford Inventories 'P' for 10 Dec.). His widow Elizabeth, relict of William Tillard, survived him until 1621 (Wood, *Survey*, ed. Clark, III, 122 and n.).

7 Perhaps George Trenchard of Dorset, listed in the musters, Sept. 1580 (SP 12/142/37). See 5 Mar. and p. 12 above for Madox's connections with Dorset.

a goldsmyth.[1] Ther was Christofer Paulet and M. Colbye a lawyer,[2] M. Wast and others. We ran yn to philosophy by a question of fansy wher they herd me attentyvely.

25. [♃][3] [*Thurs.*] I herd how John Conrad had a lybel abowt the hard usage of Campion and Ned Marb*ack* made yt. And how owr Walton was used for saying that Campion was hardly delt with al, Dyxon +, Hargrave + and Porter + accusying hym. M. warden was at Lambeth abowt yt and lykwyse agayn on ♃ [Thurs.] but nothing concluded.[4] M. Myls[5] told me my viage was honorable and of no danger. a libel + *kn*ave

2[*6.*] ♀ [*Fri.*] I rod to Uxbridge, lay at the Crown with Sherburn and Jerom the bruer[6] and on M. Stretford, a man of my Lord Chauncelors.[7] We wer myrry together.

[1] The goldsmith Henry Gilbert was the proprietor of the Rose in Cheapside (Ambrose Heal, *The London Goldsmiths, 1200–1800* (1935), p. 159).

[2] Perhaps Thomas Colbye, who had been admitted to Gray's Inn in 1549 (J. Foster, *Register of Admissions to Gray's Inn* (1889), p. 20).

[3] Madox has misdated and/or misassigned the astrological symbols for 25, 26, and 27 Jan.

[4] Edmund Campion, a shining light at Oxford until his removal from the University and defection to Rome, returned on a mission with Robert Parsons in 1580. He was captured in July 1581, and executed on 1 Dec. along with two other Oxford men, Alexander Briant and Ralph Sherwin. The impact of the execution is made clear by Parsons's reference to the 'countless . . . number of books, dialogues, treatises, poems, satires, which have been composed and published, some in print and some in manuscript, in praise of these martyrs' (*Letters and Memorials*, ed. L. Hicks (Catholic Rec. Soc. 39, 1942), I, 133).

Although this particular libel has not come to light, the Privy Council was busy throughout the spring directing the Vice Chancellor and other officials, including Warden Hovenden, about the 'late libellers' of Oxford. In April the Privy Council informed them of the apprehension and commitment to the Clink of Roger Weekes, who first received the libel from Dodwell (see 5 Feb.). This was Thomas Dodwell, a renegade Catholic who stated in response to interrogations administered in 1584 that he had been persuaded by certain individuals in Oxford to go to Rheims 'to do good to his country' (*APC, 1581–82*, pp. 350, 352, 400 and SP 12/168/35).

'Owr Walton' was Dunstan, of Somerset, who had taken his B.A. in 1580 and was a 'fellow elect' of All Souls though never admitted. The three 'knaves' Madox refers to – Edward Dixon, Humphrey Hargrave, and Richard Porter – were all Fellows of the college.

[5] Francis Mills of Southampton was secretary to Sir Francis Walsingham, although continuing to serve as clerk of the peace for Hampshire. In 1586, having served 'above 13 years in court,' he was appointed to the Privy Seal office. An All Souls man, he had served as Subwarden in 1564–5. (See *The Third Book of Remembrance of Southampton, 1514–1602*, ed. A. L. Merson, III (1965), 33 n.; *CSP, Dom., 1581–90*, pp. 360, 362; and Clark, *Reg.*, II.ii.10.)

[6] For Sherburn, see n. 4, p. 82.

Perhaps Jerome Maye, who as a cook at All Souls, was admitted in Jan. 1568 to sell ale (Clark, *Reg.*, II.ii. 11; II.i. 324).

[7] Thomas Bromley, a fellow Salopian, had become Lord Chancellor in 1579.

2[7.] ♄ [*Sat.*] we rod to Oxford, supt with Sir Reynolds the probationer who apposed and made gawdyes.[1]

Lewise of Yfle a good husband

28. ☉ G [*Sun.*] Rob Breach[2] and Evans wer going ther way. I dyned and Davis at M. Lewis of Yfley[3] wher we supt
[*29.*] also and lay al nyght and after dynner on ☾ [Mon.] with
[*30.*] M. Pilson[4] cam home. ♂ [Tues.] I was dygesting my books and stuffe.

Noble

31. ☿ [*Wed.*] I supt at Ned Nobles going furth general.[5] He gave me a payr of gloves which I bestoed on M. Slater.[6] I had 3 cheses from my brother, one I gave to Jacson,[7] an other to Davis, the third is for Pory. Robert Elx[8] payd the cariage. Spent 10^{li} as folowth: //

1 Having disputed, he then provided the repast; at this date Edward Reynolds was a Probationary Fellow of All Souls. He left soon after to enter the employment of the earl of Essex since he is described in 1583 as his secretary (*Cal. Salisbury MSS*, III, 4). He too was involved in the Essex conspiracy. (See *The Assembly Books of Southampton*, ed. J. W. Horrocks, II (1917), 25–6 n.)

2 Robert Breach of Wilts. attended St Mary Hall, matriculating in Nov. 1581 at the age of 20. See also 6 Feb.

3 Owen (or Ewen) Davis, with whom Madox seems to have been on particularly good terms (see 31 Jan., and 3, 16, 17, 21, and 26 Feb.), was also a Fellow of All Souls. In Oct. the Proctors had nominated him and John Cissel (of Trinity) as Clerks of the Market, an appointment that at times both the Proctors and the Vice Chancellor claimed to have the right to make. Thus in Nov. when Robert Crane, the Senior Proctor, gave them the oath of office, the Vice Chancellor forbade him to give it and the two appointees to take it (Clark, *Reg.*, II.i.254 and n., 251).

Ifley, now a suburb of Oxford, was in the sixteenth century included in a civil parish of that name. The manor house 'Court Place,' so-called because the manorial courts were held there, bears the date '1580 I.L. for John Lewis.' In 1591 his wife Joan, tenant of Court Place, was presented in the Bishop's Court as a recusant (*Victoria County History, Oxfordshire*, v (1957), 190, 204).

4 Edward Pilson (or Puleston) had matriculated in 1580 at Brasenose.

5 Edward Noble, a student at Queen's College, was to receive his degree in 1583. The phrase 'going furth general' seems to mean 'without specific intent.'

6 Probably Thomas Slater of Brasenose who had matriculated in 1579 (although an Edmund Slater had matriculated on 11 Jan. of this year).

7 Henry Jackson of St Mary's Parish was listed c. 1565 as the butler (*promus*) of All Souls, a college servant subordinate to the manciple. During the 1580s he is termed manciple, and his duty was to keep the buttery and buttery books. In 25 Eliz. with Richard Smoat (see 11 Jan.) he was bonded to collect the rents in Oxford; he died in 1619. (See Clark, *Reg.*, II.ii.11; C. T. Martin, *Catalogue of the Archives in the Muniment Rooms of All Souls' College* (1877), p. 162; and John Griffiths, *Index to Wills proved in the Court of the University of Oxford* (1862), p. 33.)

8 Robert Elkes of Shropshire was admitted on 1 Aug. 1578, age 28, as a 'privileged person' – a term applied, in addition to those who served the University community, to actual students unattached at the time of their matriculation to any college or hall (Clark, *Reg.*, II.i.393). Although Elkes is not listed in Foster, he appears in Univ. Oxon. Arch. 'Matriculation Register P,' 1564–1614, p. 177. (The date listed in Clark, *Reg.*, II.i.391, for his admission is 3 Apr. 1579.) He apparently was related to Thomas Elkes mentioned 20 Mar. and 1 Apr.

To Coldock for my brother	40^{s}		4^{v}
for Plato in Greek and Laten	35^{s}		
for an ephemerides[1]	3^{s}	6^{d}	
for Bezaes testament Greek and Latin for my brother	6^{s}		
for a mappa mundi and other od pamphlets		18^{d}	
for a mantil	17^{s}		
for 2 sut of buckram	13^{s}	4^{d}	
for 2 payr of buskins	6^{s}	4^{d}	
for a chest	9^{s}		
for a gallon bottel of tyn	3^{s}		
for a half pint		6^{d}	
for the aquavite	5^{s}		
for 2 dials, one for my brother	2^{s}		
a mappa mundi for my brother and a marker		18^{d}	
for wax kandels		18^{d}	
conserva roses	2^{s}		
conserv green ginger	8^{s}		
dyvers smale[2] pamphlets	5^{s}		
for a flock bed[3]			
for a knyfe	1^{s}		
for cloth left with M. Page	20^{s}		
spent up and down and there	19^{s}	2^{d}	

(*cipher*: reseevd this monith xx^{li}. Disbursed of the sam 10^{li}.) //

Domini est terra et plentitudo eius 5^{r}

Februarie ♓

1. ♃ [*Thurs.*] we supped at Smalmans 12^{d}.[4] At nyght was

[1] A table showing the predicted position of a heavenly body for a given period; the plural form commonly used as singular. See 11 May.

[2] This disyllabic form, common in Middle English, occurs as late as the seventeenth century.

[3] Stuffed with tufts of cotton or wool.

[4] William Smallman of the parish of St Peter's in the East was elected Inferior (or Yeoman) Bedell of Law in 1577. The duties of the six bedells were partly real, partly ceremonial: they kept the matriculation register, collected fees, conveyed official messages, and served as officers of the Vice Chancellor's court; carrying the mace (*baculus*), they walked before the professors of the faculties when they went to give lectures, before students and graduates when

playd cats and dogs and plumping and other wawling sport.[1]

2. ♀ [*Fri.*] *Purification.* Doctor James preched in the forenoon 3 to the Philipians: I pray God that your love may increase. After noon in Alhallows Doctor Math*ew*[2] did as he doth al things excellently of Simeon in the 2 of Luke which signifieth the hearer,[3] concluding that yf he cold never fynd the Saviour but in the temple, we must not absent our selvs from church and yet hope to fynd hym. We supt at Smalmans 12^d.

Mathew

1^s

3. ♄ [*Sat.*] Slater and Davis and Waring[4] and I went to Tytimans and eat fresh sprats and muskels. I herd that my Lord vicownt Bindon was dead on ☉ [Sun.] last in Dorsetshire,[5] that the mownseur was gone and the queen to accompany hym to Dover and that the Lord of Lester, the Lord Charles Haward, the Lord Hunsden and others wold with hym over sea[6] and that my Lord of Oxford had

Cowrt newes

---

they went to perform exercises for degrees, and before the Vice Chancellor when he went to Congregation and Convocation. During the next two years, Smallman was licensed to sell ale and brown bread to supplement his income (Clark, *Reg.*, II.i.256, 325, 337 and n.).

He apparently cut a fine figure: in his will (dated 2 Aug. 1592) he disposed of his 'best gowne,' his 'second gowne either the black or russett,' his 'best fustian dublet,' and his 'second dublet with a spanish lether Jerkin with six silver buttons' together with his boots and spurs (although allowing his wife to use her discretion in bestowing his hose and stockings). (University Archives, Oxford, Reg. Curiae Cancellarii, 1545–1661, f. 175).

[1] 'Cats and dogs,' a game played with a piece of wood called the 'cat' and a club called the 'dog.' 'Plumping' – unidentified; 'wawling,' obstreperous.

[2] Described by Camden as '*theologus praestantissimus*,' Dr Toby Matthew had a distinguished career at Oxford, where, according to Wood, he was much respected for his great learning, eloquence, sweet conversation, friendly disposition, and for the sharpness of his wit. He served as chaplain to the Queen (1572) and became Archbishop of York in 1606 (*Athen. Oxon.*, II, 869–78).

[3] Since it was to him Christ addressed the words '*nunc dimittis*.'

[4] John Waring of Oriel College had matriculated *c.* 1580.

[5] Lord Thomas Howard, second son of Thomas Howard, 3rd Duke of Norfolk, and the younger brother of the poet, had extensive holdings in Dorset, where he served as Vice-admiral. By his first wife he had four children, including his heir Henry, 2nd Viscount Bindon, who in the several years before his father's death was notorious for his debts, his quarrels, and his ill-treatment of his wife Frances, daughter of Peter Meutys, who had served as a lady-in-waiting to the Queen.

The date of Howard's death is given incorrectly in many sources, but see *Complete Peerage*, ed. G. E. Cokayne, rev. by V. Gibbs *et al*, VI (1926), 584. See also entries for 6 Mar. and 13 Apr.

[6] François, duc d'Alençon, having arrived in London on 1 Nov. 1581 to pursue his suit for the hand and the financial support of Elizabeth, was ceremoniously ushered out by the Queen and her court on 1 Feb. Despite the entreaties

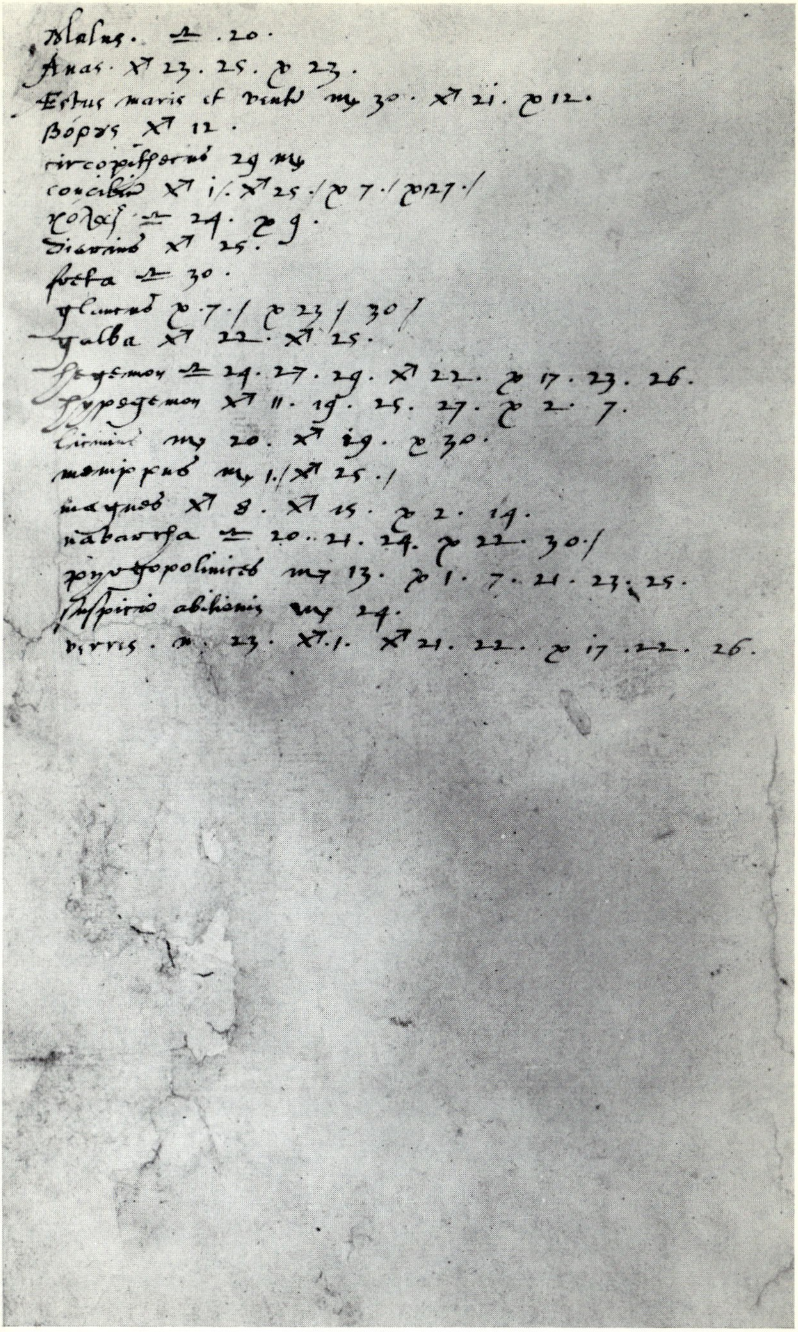

Fig. 6. Index to Madox's Diary, listing the most important pseudonyms and topics

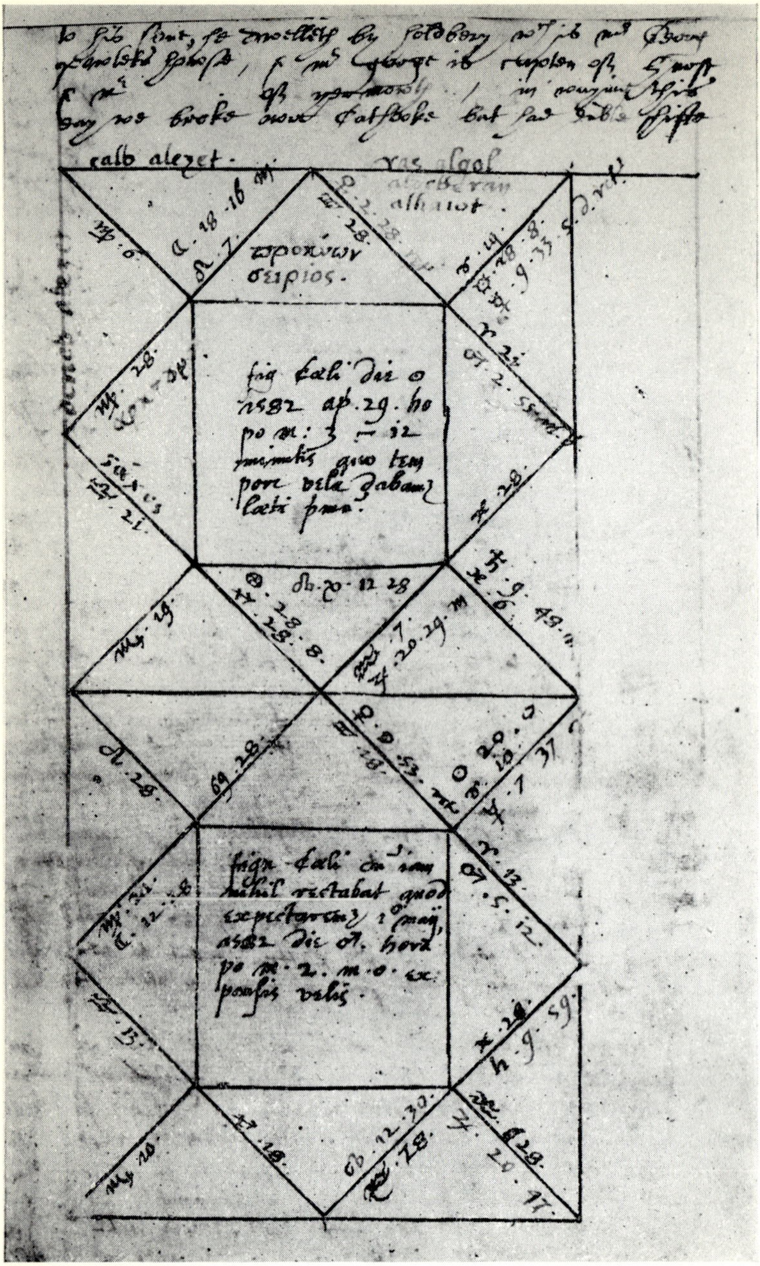

Fig. 7. Two horoscopes of the expedition cast by Madox on 29 April and 1 May

taken his wyfe agayn and that my Lord treasurer shold mary a second daughter to my Lord Wentworth desyring rather a man than money.[1] God send them al to do for the best.

4. ☉ *G* [*Sun.*] Knyght of Corpus Christi[2] preched and did wel. M. Den, Lankford, Pryce and Short[3] dyned with us at nyght. We had musycians and went up with them and 20 clubs to Carfox.

5. ☾ [*Mon.*] I wrot to London to Peter Pory. Ther was an other lybel fownd with Dodwels man abowt Campion.[4] We wer comaunded to keep the gates shut til 8 but to what end I se not.

6. ♂ [*Tues.*] was presented Sir Buckfowld of Brasenose, the least batchler I think in Europe.[5] I dyned with doctor Mathew. He spake frendly of M. Screven.[6] Ther was

---

of the duke, the Queen, wearing black to show her grief (according to the Venetian ambassador) insisted on accompanying him to Canterbury, where 'after one daies tarriance,' they took leave of each other 'not without great griefe and shew of verie great amitie.' On 7 Feb., together with 'the earle of Leicester master of hir horsses, the lord of Hunsdoun governour of Berwicke . . . and the lord Howard the vice admiral,' the Duke took to the sea at Sandwich with three great ships, though others of the English had departed the night before from Dover. (See *CSP, Venetian, 1581–91*, p. 29 and Holinshed, *Chronicles* (1587), 6M4.)

[1] Edward de Vere, Earl of Oxford, who had been Burghley's ward, married his eldest daughter, Anne, in 1571. On returning from his Italian tour, he accused her of infidelity, 'entyced,' as Burghley noted in his diary under the date 29 Mar. 1576, 'by certen lewd Persons' to become 'a Stranger to his Wiff' (Murdin, II, 778). See also 3 Mar.

Burghley's second daughter, Elizabeth, was married on 26 Feb. (see 3 Mar.) to William, son of Lord Wentworth of Nettlested in a celebration which lasted three days. (See Lansdowne MS 33, No. 5 for an account of expenses.) The new bridegroom died in the following Nov. (William Murdin, ed., *Collection of State Papers . . . left by . . . Lord Burghley*, II (1759), 746).

[2] Thomas Knight had become a scholar of Corpus Christi in 1569 and received his M.A. in 1577; he was to receive his B.D. in 1584.

[3] All four of Madox's dining companions were (or had been) Fellows of All Souls: Henry Den (or Denne) became a Fellow before 1564; Charles Langforde in 1565; Edward Price, 1568; and Anthony Shorte, 1570. According to Martin (*Catalogue of the Archives*, p. 379), both Price and Shorte had resigned their fellowships in 1580.

[4] See n. to 25 Jan.

[5] As John Buckfold (or Buckfield) was 'presented' (admitted) to the B.A. on this date, Madox styles him 'Sir.' In view of the comment on his lack of ability, it is interesting to note that in 1593 he became chaplain of All Souls.

[6] Reginald (or Reynold) Scriven, together with three other Scrivens – two of whom were perhaps his brothers since they too were listed as '*alieni*' – had attended Shrewsbury School with Madox. At Oxford he became a Fellow of

doctor Culpeper and his wyf and Thom Furs and his wif and Allen of Gloster Haul.[1] Doctor Mathew told how old doctor Baily took 8^{li}. of M. Tuchiner for bringing in his . . . which Tuchiner being scholmaster had taken for
5^{v} [bringyng] // yn hym before in to the howse.[2] Wil Breach came to town and was sory for the going away of Robyn.[3] He browght me a letter from John Trus . . . to place Phillip Breach at Wollerhanton with my brother and to that end did I wryt to my brother. We supt at Smalmans, spent 6^{d}. I gave hym a payr of spectacles with the case 6^{d}.

Phillip Breache 12^{d}

7. ☿ [*Wed.*] I packt up my stuf ynto the lytle study and took an ynventory of al my books. I payd Sherburn a mark horsehyre[4] which is reconed in the last yere.

8. ♃ [*Thurs.*] my study was new plastered. News came that Anwerp was yelded to the prince of Parma who kept yt with 10,000 men, that the prince of Orenge was taken, that the mownser began to be a fearful suspicion to the king his brother and that the supply of Hugonet*s* wh*ich* cam owt of Franse to fortifie mownsewr in the Lowe Cuntreys wer set on by the Guisian in Champayn and put

News

All Souls and was appointed by Archbishop Grindal to the office of 'bourser' in 1578 (Martin, p. 304. See also p. 3 above).

From the entry for 16 May, it seems he was now in the service of Lord Chancellor Bromley, a fellow Salopian.

[1] Dr Martin Culpepper, who received his D.Med. in 1571 was Warden of New College (1573–99). According to Wood, he was a favourite of Leicester's (*History . . . of Oxford*, ed. John Gutch, II, Pt. i (1790), 231).

Thomas Furs of Christ Church was described in 1569 as living in Allhallows Parish in a house called the Bear Inn (*Fasti*, I, 183).

Thomas Allen, according to Wood, 'the very soul and sun of all the mathematicians of his time,' had resigned his fellowship at Trinity College to retire to Gloucester Hall where he instructed in mathematics, antiquities, and natural philosophy until his death in 1632. Wood also states that he was on such close terms with Leicester 'that few matters of state passed, but he had knowledge of them, and nothing of moment was done in the university, but Allen gave him it in writing' (*Athen. Oxon.*, II, 541–42 and Mark Curtis, *Oxford and Cambridge in Transition* (Oxford, 1959), p. 236).

[2] The allusion is perhaps to Henry Bailey, who was a Fellow of New College from 1534–52 and was to receive his D. Med. in 1563 and Richard Tuchenor, Fellow of New College from 1522–30 and a schoolmaster at Winchester (C. W. Boase, *Reg. of the Univ. of Oxford*, I (1885), 352). The point is the 'infamous' practice of buying and selling of fellowships.

[3] See Jan. 28 and n. 2.

[4] Henry Sherburne is listed as a groom (*equiso*) of Corpus Christi in 1562 (Clark, *Reg.*, II.ii.15 n.).

to slaughter and that therfore the mownsewr was returned to England but the last point was fals how ever the first be.[1]

9. ♀ [*Fri.*] I supt at Smalmans, spent 12^d^. 12^d^

10. ♄ [*Sat.*] I had a war*ant* from M. Screven for an acre of wood to me and Smalm*an*. I (*cipher*: had 9^s^ of M. Lyster for Jenyns wif).[2] ix^s^

11. ☉ G [*Sun.*] *Septuagessima*. M. Robinson[3] preched 2 Philipians. He shewd owt of *racionale divinorum* that the papist thowght not superfluity of word or ceremonyes to hurt, as if one wold say *baptizo te in nomine patris et filii et spiritus sancti et Diaboli* and owt of Scotus the 9 distin*ctio* lib. 4 de . . . sententiarum that yt is agaynst scripture to beleeve transubstantiation[4] and owt of Lactantius that ymages or remembrances of absent frends [be necessary, but] God is always present and therfore we need noe ymage.[5] Slater, Davis and I walked to Wolvercot and had cyd*er* at Besse Jenyns. Lawghern told me that his brother Clark had a benyfyce of an hundred pound for hym and shewd me Tolderburyes letter therin.[6]

[1] This is an example of the rumours following on the military success – the capture of Tournai – of Alexander Farnese, Duke of Parma, while Alençon was wooing the Queen in England. Henry, duc de Guise, and leader of Catholic extremists, supported Spanish rule in the Netherlands.

[2] Thomas Lister had matriculated at Brasenose in 1577, age 18.

'Jenyns wif,' elsewhere called 'Besse,' is perhaps to be connected with John Jenyns, one of the Oxford citizens who rallied to the support of William Noble (see p. 71, n. 2 above) or Frances Jennens who had been admitted to bake white bread in 1566. Both had taken oaths to observe the privileges of the University (Clark, *Reg.*, II.i. 302–4, 337).

[3] Presumably Henry Robinson of Queen's College who was to receive his B.D. in July; he afterwards became Bishop of Carlisle.

[4] Distinctio XI would seem more apt: *utrum transubstantiatio sit possibilis.*

[5] 'For the plan of making likenesses was invented by men for this reason, that it might be possible to retain the memory of those who had either been removed by death or by absence. . . . But in the case of God, whose spirit and influence are diffused everywhere, and can never be absent, it is plain that an image is always superfluous' (*Ante-Nicene Christian Lib.* (1951 repr.), VII, 41–2).

[6] William Lawghern (or Langhorne), a Fellow of All Souls, had been granted a leave of absence in 1578 for three years for study abroad (All Souls College, Warden Hovenden's Minute Bk.). Burrows cites a letter, dated 1581, which refers to him as 'late Fellow of All Souls' and 'servant' to Sir Walter Ralegh (*Worthies*, p. 110).

Christopher Tolderbury (Toldervey, Tollerby) of Christ Church, was to become Canon of Lincoln in 1583. During the years 1575 and 1576 he was cited along with other rowdy students of Christ Church by William Noble (see p. 71, n. 2 above) for breaking into the house of a citizen 'with their weapons readye drawen, as swords, daggers, and bastynadoes,' for dispossessing a poor

12. ☾ [*Mon.*] I dyned with M. Anthony Sherloe at the principals chamber of Herthal[1] and had good cheare and supt with M. Thornborowe of Magdalens at Gilberts wher was my brother, Procter, Bis and Ynkforbye.[2] M. *Thor*nboroes wif is doctor Bolds dawghter of Salsbury.[3] She *p*lays wel upon the lute and virginales. //

6r *13.* ♂ [*Tues.*] having a letter from my cozin Nicholas that our viage was lyke to hold, I prepared my self to be redye.

14. ☿ [*Wed.*] I spoke with M. Marten of Weymowth[4] and had commendations from Dorchester. I wrote bye hym to M. Green.[5] I had aproved me by my lord of Lesters letters to the officers a cause for 3 yere besyde my ordinary days with al profyts rising in the howse the mean season as yf I were present, my lyverey and commines only excepted.[6]

a cawse [for] 3 yeare

---

miller of his horse and whipping him with his own whip, and for upbraiding a certain cordwainer with 'such opprobrious words as are not to be spoken of any eyvill man, and withall savinge your honors reverence, they made water in at the chincks of his dore and windowes uppon him and his men being at wourke in his shopp' (Turner, *Records ... of Oxford*, pp 359, 361).

[1] Anthony Shirley entered Hart Hall in 1579, age 14, receiving his B.A. in 1582 and becoming a Fellow of All Souls in that year as founder's kin (*Athen. Oxon.*, II, 495). He became a protégé of the earl of Essex and then lived a life of wild adventure, ultimately becoming a Roman Catholic exile in Spain. His popular account of his travels in Persia was published in 1613.

Philip Rondell served as Principal of Hart Hall for half a century, whence it became a refuge for adherents of the old religion (Mallet, *History of the University of Oxford*, II, 297).

[2] John Thornbury of Salisbury had received his M.A. in 1575 and was to receive his B.D. in 1582. He served as chaplain to the Queen and ultimately became Bishop of Limerick, Bristol, and Worcester in turn. Wood notes he was commended for his skill in chemistry (*Athen. Oxon.*, III, 4).

James Bisse and William Inkforbie were both Fellows of Magdalen. It is impossible to decide which Procter Madox is alluding to – William, who had matriculated at St Edmund's Hall in 1581 or Samuel, who was incorporated from Cambridge in 1576, or even if it is to his 'brother procter' Crane.

[3] 'Dr Booles' was styled 'a very furiouse man' by Simon Forman in recalling his early study with him (1561–3) in 'the free scoole in the Close at Salisbury.'

On going up to Oxford, Forman gained a great benefactor in the (then) rakish 'Sir Thornbury' of Magdalen, some of whose escapades he details in his *Autobiography and Personal Diary*, ed. J. O. Halliwell (1849), pp. 4, 12.

[4] Thomas Martin, 'yoman and Town Clerk' of Weymouth. See pp. 12, 15 above.

[5] See Jan. 14, n. 1 above.

[6] On 28 of Nov., Leicester had written from the court to his 'very loving frends the warden and officers of Allsouls': 'After my ryght harty commendations wheras M. Richard Madox feloe of your Colledge is presently to be employd on publique affayrs, into farre parts withowt this realme, from whence he is not lykely to returne in 2 or 3 yeres or more, I therfore doe hartely pray and also require you that he may have a cause of three yers absens from the Colledge alowed hym and that his absens for the sayd tyme be noe hynderaunce to his

Wygnole and James[1] wer very ernest for my chamber and my study beyond the cumpase of any desert shewd unto mee. Spent 12ᵈ. 12ᵈ

15. ♃ [*Thurs.*] I resigned my office in the convocation howse to M. Beamunt, being therunto commended by my Lord of Lecester. I (*cipher*: had of M. Beamunt therfor twenty marx).[2] I had also a lycens to preach in al the world.[3] I gave M. Slater my ox and my tynker, M. Beamunt my black pot, had a new key for my study and an other for the dore 10ᵈ, M. D*a*bb my belloes. (*cipher*: {twenty marx)

16. ♀ [*Fri.*] I wrot to my brother by Hortons man and sent books and other things. I payd 6ᵈ for the cariage and spent 4ᵈ. I payd John Powel for ther bowser M. Jenyns 5 10ᵈ Powel

---

comodytye in the Colledge, but that he may enjoy all benefytes therof as yf he were present, and so I byd you hartely farewell.' (All Souls College, Hovenden's Minute Bk. A partially modernised transcription appears in Burrows, pp. 91–2.)

On 14 Feb. the officers responded (in Latin) as follows, with Warden Hovenden, Henry Beaumont as Dean in Arts, Francis Bevans, Dean in Law, and the two Bursars Owen Davis and Richard Shippenge signing: 'Induced by these letters the aforementioned Warden and the officers granted Richard Madox, M.A., and at that time proctor of the university permission to leave the College for the three years immediately following, besides the days allowed him by the established statutes, and they grant him or his legal deputy all the privileges and emoluments which he could obtain in any manner whatsoever from the college if he were present with the exceptions only of the commons and the livery, which they did not grant him at all. In testimony thereof they set their seals on the aforementioned day and year' (All Souls College, Hovenden's Minute Bk.).

1 Richard Wignall had become a Fellow of All Souls in 1577, and he was to be nominated as Dean in Arts by Archbishop Grindal in 1582. In 1588 he served as Vicar of Barking, Great Ilford, Essex, whence he received 13*s* 4*d* from the Bursars of All Souls to give to the poor on Christmas Day (Martin, *Catalogue of the Archives*, pp. 305, 20, 21).

Francis James, who also became a Fellow in 1579, was to serve as Deputy Warden in 1584 and again in 1586 (All Souls College, Hovenden's Minute Bk.). He later became master in Chancery and Chancellor of the diocese of Bath and Wells and of London.

2 Henry Beaumont, who had taken his B.A. at Cambridge and incorporated at Oxford, was elected a Fellow of All Souls as founder's kin in 1571. He was to serve the College in various capacities, as Dean in Arts (signing Madox's cause of absence and its extension), as Bursar, as rector of disputations in theology, and as subwarden (All Souls College, Hovenden's Minute Bk., and Martin, p. 305).

In 1619, King James himself recommended, though to no avail, his selection as warden, commenting that his marriage was 'no impediment to bar him, having no children nor ever likely to have anie' and that he would be a fitter governor by reason of his long experience in the house. (Quoted in Burrows, *Worthies*, pp. 136–7.)

For Leicester's commendation, see p. 70, n. 3 above. For Madox's additional paltering with him, see 6, 9, 13 Mar.

3 For the grace asked on this occasion, see p. 13, n.1 above.

nobles and 30^s to M. Thomson and gave John[1] 8^d so that I am wholy even with hym, and the burser and his tutor
10^s have $3^{li}3^s4^d$ before hand. I gave my man Thomas 10^s and put hym to M. Beamunt. M. Davis and I supt at Robert Cavies.[2] M. Kirpie cam from London with M. Steenton whom he wold have bestoed in owr viage. I locked up al my things and made a deed of gift to my
a deed of gift brother of al.

17. ♄ [*Sat.*] I took leave only with Beamunt, Dow, Davis and Wood[3] and so rode to London. Met Lepye[4] at Wykam. Mrs Waynwryght sent me my supper.

18. ⊙ G [*Sun.*] *Sexagessima.* M. Hearn preched at the Crosse but I was not ther. Wee dyned at Mrs Waynwryght with M. Hynton of Hampshire. M. Torpurley cam to mee.[5] I met M. Web of Henley who bestoed the wyne. M. Torpurley supt with mee. //

[1] Giles Thomson had matriculated at University College in 1575; his election oath as a Fellow of All Souls is dated 16 Jan. 1581.

John Powel, age 18, of Salop had matriculated at University College in Dec. 1581. He was to become a Fellow of All Souls in 1587.

[2] Robert Cavie (or Cavy) of St Mary's Parish had been licensed to sell and bind books in 1573, and in 1587 he was admitted to sell ale (Clark, *Reg.*, II.i. 321, 326). An inventory of his household stuff and shop, taken in 1594, including 'cuttinge presses,' 'sewinge presses' and 'butchers stalls,' amounted to £23 10*s* (Oxford University Archives, Inventories Br–C).

[3] Robert Dowe, Fellow of All Souls, was to receive his B.C.L. in Apr. He died in 1588, leaving a large library of 302 volumes, including works of Guicciardini, Commines, and Machiavelli. (See Curtis, *Oxford and Cambridge in Transition*, pp. 136–67, 239, 285 and notes.)

William Wood, also a Fellow of All Souls, was to receive his B.C.L. in 1583; he served frequently as an officer of the College.

[4] Appointed to accompany Madox on the voyage, Thomas Lepye, becoming ill in London, died on 15 Mar. and was buried at Queen Hive. (His burial cost Madox 20^s 'besyds al drinkings' (see 16 Mar.).

[5] *George* Torporley, a free member of the Glovers' Company in Shrewsbury, was given, together with John Beynyon, the exclusive right in 1564 to make and sell 'silk buttons silk lases gold wire and thrid.' Thomas Ashton, Madox's old schoolmaster at Shrewsbury, served as his surety (W. A. Leighton, 'The Gilds of Shrewsbury,' *Trans., Shropshire Arch. and Nat. Hist. Soc.*, VIII (1885), 317, 320). For a later reference to Torporley, and for his apparent connection with Thomas Elkes, see 22 Feb.; 26 Mar. and n. 2.

Taylor (*Fenton*, p. xxxix) states Madox is referring to *Nathaniel* Torporley, later a noted mathematician and writer, who had matriculated at Christ Church, Oxford, in 1581, age 17. Mark Curtis asserts (*Oxford and Cambridge in Transition*, pp. 238–39, n.) the reference here must be to *Thomas* Torporley, who had attended Shrewsbury School at the same time as Madox, gone up to Christ Church, where he received his M.A. in 1577, and was currently serving as Rector of Didcot, Berks. But as the entry for 9 Mar. makes clear, Madox is referring to *George* Torporley.

19. ☾ [*Mon.*] M. Torpurley and I walked to Ratclif. M. Norman shewd me how the strenth of his lodestone was increased.[1] We cam to Fransis Yomders and had ther good chere. 6v loadston

20. ♂ [*Tues.*] Lepye cam up. Huet wrot to me that (*cipher*: Norwod[2] sayd my dealing abowt the colector was shamful and paltry. I did answer him home and yet[3] with charity.) (*cipher*: Norwod)

21. ☿ [*Wed.*] I wrot to Jacson, to Huet, to my very hard frend M. Norwood, to M. warden for a longer cause,[4] to M. Davis, to M. Owyn Glyn to whom I sent a dosen of very good blew sylk poynts.[5] I hard that the mow*n*sewr was wel receved and my Lord of Lester at Flushing, at Mydleboroe, at Anwerp, that a fat ox ther was 30^{li}, a wether 40^{s}, a capon 10^{s}, wyne 16^{d}, and bear 8^{d} the quart, and that my Lord of Lester was sent for home.[6] I bowght dyvers things which after be pryzed. news of Flawnders

[1] Robert Norman, who called himself 'hydrographer,' was a compass maker, publishing the first original work on the magnetic compass in 1581 (E. G. R. Taylor, *Tudor Geography, 1485–1583* (1930), p. 160). Norman comments in his *New Attractive* (A2*v*): 'How beneficiall the Art and exercise of Navigation is to this Realme, there is no man so simple but sees, by meanes whereof wee being secluded and divided from the rest of the world, are notwithstanding as it were Citizens of the world, walking through everie corner, and round about the same, and enjoying all the commodities of the wor[l]d.' See Fig. 5 for his charting of the 'Sandes of the Thames.'

[2] Richard Hewett and William Norwood were both Fellows of All Souls, their election oaths dated 1578 and 1576 respectively.

[3] Madox inadvertently writes 'yet' in English rather than in cipher.

[4] Madox's request reflects his decision to remain with Captain Carleill in the Moluccas or wherever he would have stayed 'whyl God wold geve me leave.' (See 13 Mar. and p. 279 below.)

[5] Owen Glyn of University College received his M.A. in 1576 and was to receive his B.D. in 1583; he had served as Deputy Proctor on 4 Jan. 1582 (Clark, *Reg.*, II.i.248), replacing Madox who did not return from Wolverhampton until the following day.

[6] On 10 Feb., Alençon entered Flushing where he was received with 'all honour and applause by the Princes of Orange and Pinoi'; in Middleburg, the citizens welcomed him with the 'greatest affection and honour'; in Antwerp, the streets were 'strewn with lilies.' There, following an oration, the Secretary of the States robed him in 'the mantle and the cap of the Duke of Brabant [see 27 Feb.], which was of crimson velvet lined with ermine' and presented him to the people, who swore fealty with indescribable enthusiasm (*CSP, Venetian, 1581–91*, pp. 29–30).

On 12 of Feb., Francis Talbot, reporting to his father on the 'great scarstie bothe of vittels and all things els in Flaunders,' noted that Leicester 'hathe caried over with him L bives and v hundred muttons for his provision duringe his aboude' (Edmund Lodge, *Illustrations of British History*, II (1791), 258).

Mendoza reported that Leicester arrived in England on 26 Feb., 'having been summoned in great haste by the Queen, in consequence of the heavy expenses he and those who accompanied him were incurring' (*CSP, Sp., 1580–86*, p. 299).

a virgin play

22. ♃ [*Thurs.*] we went to the theater to se a scurvie play set owt al by one virgin which ther proved a fyemarten with o*wt* voice so that we stayd not the matter.[1] I had a cassock of Ashley which stood me in 20^s and venetians a mark.[2] Lepee had also a cassock which stood [me] in 11^s6^d but it is all cownted afterward.

a servingman

A gentilman trayning a yong servingman bad hym syt down when he was byd but ever to be a dysh behind hym so the master sytting at the boord in Wales had nothing els but oten kakes wherupon his man being byd sytt down fet a bottel of hey and layd [it] on the table saying that hey was the next dysh under otes. M. Torpurley.

a headknok

Henshaw of Christchurch[3] comyng into a howse with a low dore knoct his head shrewdly to the post. Why, how now, quoth on that cam behind, can not ye see? Yes, quoth he, but yt is good maner to knock before ye enter. *Idem.*

Lady Maners

A yong mayd going to a feast with hir mother wher she was to meet hir lover was instructed at all tymes hir mother twynkt [nodded] on hir to lay hir hand on hir brest, to ryse up, and curchye. Hir mother espying hir gnawing a bone nodded on hir wherupon she puld down hir hands to hir wast and leaving the bone a crosse hir mowth lyk a butchers knife made a very fayr curchye. Pain.

20 aunts

Now truly, quoth an old gentilman to a yong feloe, ye ar far to blame to mislyke your aunt for she may do you pleasure and I wold God I had such an aunt. Fy, quoth he, wold I had your land on condicion you had xx^{ty} such aunts. M. Cornwal. //

7^r

The alewyf and hir husband having long drunk owt the gayn of ther bruying indented twyxt them selvs that

[1] This play has not been identified.

[2] In purchasing 'venetians' (breeches), Madox is taking advantage of his 'cause of absens': in 1576 Convocation had decreed that no one 'shale weare anie Scalions of Velvet, of Silke or of any other colour then black or any Gascons or Venetians at all ether within the universitye or without under paine of forfeyting $xiij^s$ $iiij^d$ for the first time, and for the second time $xxvj^s$ $viij^d$ and so toties quoties' (*Statuta Antiqua Universitatis Oxoniensis*, ed. S. Gibson (1931), p. 403).

[3] Thomas Henshawe was a student of Christ Church in 1569, receiving his M.A. (as Henche) in 1577.

nether shold have a stope [tankard] of the best withowt money; the man being drie was content to lay down a gally halfpeny for watring his throt and began [pledged] to his wyf but swapt [drank] al of. I pledge you sir, quoth she, and going to fil more. Na, quoth the man, pay for yt first, wherupon she was driven to pay back the halfpeny to hir goodman which afterward was cowrsed [exchanged] to and froe so long til that one halfpeny had drawn drie the whole stand [barrel] of drink. My father. drink pay small thrift

23. ♀ [*Fri.*] I passed over in study and other smal busynes of no great importaunce.

25. ☉ *G* [*Sun. Quinguagesima*][1] I went down with my syster and my cosyn Marget to Greenwich. My brother Thomas my brother
[*26.*] and M. Davis cam to Town and on ☉ [Sun.] ☾ [Mon.]
[*27.*] and ♂ [Tues.] they wer abowt and used many perswasions and entreaties to stay my jorney. My Lords that wer in Flawnders came home leaving the mownsewr duke of news Brabant. My Lord of Lester kept a worthy howse in Flawnders. M. Furbusher was discharged of the viage and M. Fenton put in his place.

28. *Ashwensday* my brother Thomas and I and Mrs Robinson chrysened a boy of my cosyn Nyclas and cauled his name Christening Thomas who was born on ♃ [Thurs.] before abowt 10 of the clock at nyght. We gave 2 spoones that cost 17^s6^d and 3^s more to the nurse and mydwyfe. M. Betts of Moregate made my picture and had 12^s for yt.[2]

[1] Madox mistakenly writes 'Segagessima.'

[2] John Bettes worked for the Revels in 1578/9, was mentioned, together with Thomas Bettes, as a painter by Francis Meres in 1598, and described as a 'picture maker' resident in Grub Street in 1599. Ellis Waterhouse (*Painting in Britain, 1530 to 1790* (1953), p. 10) asserts he was a pupil of Hilliard's.

He was perhaps the son of John Bettes, painter, limner, and wood engraver, who was stated to be dead in 1576. Erna Auerbach (*Tudor Artists* (1954), pp. 153–54) in discovering a reference to the younger Bettes in the Certificate of Residence and Subsidy Rolls (E.179/146/390) was the first to distinguish between the two; they are conflated in A. M. Hind's *Engraving in England in the Sixteenth and Seventeenth Centuries*, Pt. I, The Tudor Period (1952).

See Roy Strong, *The English Icon* (1969), Plate 136, for the single signed portrait that has so far been discovered; representing an *Unknown Girl*, it was subsequently overpainted to represent the Queen. Five others attributed to Bettes are also of the Queen.

To M. Page for Cloth	$30^s 8^d$
to Ashley for lase, sylk and making	15^s
for shirts to Lepye	$16^s 8^d$
hose for us both	8^s
hats for my self and my syster	7^s
books	5^s
poynts	3^s
paynter	12^s
a spoone	11^s
Carier	5^s
toys and tokens	5^s
watermen and expenses	6^s

sum $6^{li}4^s$ wherof 20^s was reconed the last month so that ther remaynth now $5^{li}4^s$.

(*cipher*: reseved $13^{li}15^s8^d$ spent 6^{li} 8^d. On ☿ [Wed.] . . . I had gold 14^{li}: in the bag an imperial and a French crown, 30^s gold in my purs and 12^d silver and 5^{li} of my brothers.) //

7^v Ps. 118.15 The voyce of joy and delyveraunce shal be in the tabernacles of the rightows saying, the ryght hand of the Lord hath doen valiently.

March ♈

1. ♃ [*Thurs.*] my brother and syster and I dyned at M. Hardwycks and after we went down by water to Blackwal to the Edward Bonaventure wher we eat and drank and cam home by Ratclif.

2. ♀ [*Fri.*] my brother was at the Merchant Taylors hawl with the cumpany and prepared to ryde. He gave me v^{li}.

3. ♄ [*Sat.*] I rode with hym to St. Albons and at the sowth-east dore of the mynster we parted weeping and comytting ech other to the Lord who restore us one to an other agayn at the tyme of his good pleasure and keep us ever in his fear. I cam to London back.

parted from my brother

My Lord of Oxford fowght with M. Knevet abowt the quarel of Besse Bavisar[1] and was hurt and Gerret his man

Lord of Oxford hurte

[1] Anne Vavasour, related to the Knyvets who had been involved with the royal household since the days of Henry VIII, had come to court in 1580 and been

slayn, which greeved the Lord treasurer so muche the more for that the yerl hath cumpanie with his wyfe syth Christmas and taken hir to favowr but throe this mishap and throe the payns he took at the mariage of an other dawghter to my Lord Went[worth][1] on Shrovemunday my Lord Treasurer was syck. God send hym health for he is the health of the whole land.

4. ⊙ G [*Sun.*] *Quadragesima.* I was at the cowrt but my Lord
[5.] was at London, but on ☾ [Mon.] I spoke with his honowr and with my Lord Haward and with M. Trenchur.

6. ♂ [*Tues.*] (*cipher*: I had a cosoning letter from Beamunt so that I kno him for a wrangler.) I supt in Tuttil with Rob Adyn and Cislye.[2] Rob Adin

7. ☿ [*Wed.*] Robert Wryght broke fast with mee (*cipher*: and told me many great unkindneses of his master).[3] Ther was a ship lost at Blackwal that cam furth of Barbary with sugar and spices by runyng upon hir owne Anchore and we hard of an other cast away at Goreend.

---

appointed Gentlewoman of the Bed Chamber. In the following year when she had a child, the earl of Oxford was alleged to be the father and imprisoned. Although released in June, he had to face the anger of Anne's relatives, particularly that of her uncle Thomas Knyvet, a groom of the Privy Chamber. The duel Madox alludes to occurred, and both participants were hurt, though Oxford the more dangerously. Their respective retainers continued the quarrel with the result that a man was slain on both sides.

In July 1582, Sir Christopher Hatton wrote to Lord Chancellor Bromley expressing the Queen's disapproval over his refusal to grant that Knyvet's cause *se defendo* be determined by a privy session in vacation time: ' "You know," saith she, "who he is, and where he serveth; and therefore, in a cause so little important as this, you might have restrained the malice of his enemies well enough." ' (See E. K. Chambers, *Sir Henry Lee* (1936), pp. 151, 154–7; Birch, *Memoirs*, I, 22, 37; and *Memoirs of the Life and Times of Sir Christopher Hatton*, ed. N. H. Nicolas (1847), pp. 321–4.)

[1] Madox here inadvertently writes 'Wentford' in place of 'Wentworth' though getting the name right in his entry for 3 Feb.

[2] I.e., Tothill, Westminster. Although Madox gives no further particulars about 'Robert Adyn and Cislye,' an allusion in the State Papers suggests his acquaintanceship may date back to the years in Dorset: On 10 Oct. 1580, Viscount Bindon had written to the Privy Council, complaining once again of the untoward actions of his son Henry Howard and asking that his daughter-in-law might be kept in safety 'from the practizes of him and of the queane he keepes who is the only cause of my dawghter in lawes unquietnes' and by whom, he fears, 'she maye bee cast awaye.' Later in the month (24 Oct.) he wrote again, calling attention to two statutes executed by his son, one of which was to Robert Aden of Horsington, the husband of the 'naughty quean' his son had taken into keeping and who was himself the 'instrument' of his wife's lewd behaviour (SP 12/143/13, 31).

[3] That is, the earl of Essex. See entry for 21 Jan. and n.

(*cipher*: bastard)

8. ♃ [*Thurs.*] I (*cipher*: was at Lester hows waiting al day. Ther was Robin my lords bastard by my lady of Esex).[1]

Wagstaffe meteore

9. ♀ [*Fri.*] I dyned at Westmynster at the deans table with M. Wagstaf.[2] We taulked of the great and bluddy meteor which was seen at 9 overnyght from the northwest to the sowtheast, dreading the betokenings therof. I wrot to M. warden that I wold com from Sowthampton to Chard[3] yf I myght, to Beamunt for money, to Peter that he myght take yt up. I supt on Georg Torpurleys cost at M. Fownds with William Strangman, John Wolrych, and M. Osburne.[4] //

8r

an observation of longitude

10. ♄ [*Sat.*] in casting how to fynde owt a perfect longitude in sayling, I considered that al ephemerides which are calculated according to the latitude of any place have certenty of truth noe wher but in the same longitude wher the observation was taken, which is a note ether not heeded or not as I knoe by any yet publyshed. The evident proof hearof is this. Suppoze your ephemerides be calculate for the miridian of Compostella in Galizia which is abowt 44 degrees in latitude, and 14 in longitude. In erecting a figure ryght at noone I fynd the ☾ to be just in the angle of the east, 5 degrees beyond the buls eye. Now yf I wold by the same book erect a figure for the same noontyde at Constantinople, which is of the same elevation, I shal fynd ☾ somwhat within the angle of the east and but 3 degrees and 30 mynuts overpast the buls eye, and this *in medio motu* ☾ because Constantinople being at 59 degrees in longitude, yt fawleth to be 3 a clock at Constantinople, when yt is noone at Compostella, so that yn those 3 howrs ☾ according to hir mydle motion

[1] Leicester had publicly married Lettice Knollys, countess of Essex, on 21 Sept. 1578 (although Camden refers to a private marriage in 1576). Their son Robert, styled Lord Denbigh, died at Wanstead 19 July 1584 and was buried at Beauchamp Chapel, Warwick.

[2] Gabriel Goodman was Dean of Westminster. Thomas Wagstaffe had resigned his fellowship at All Souls in 1580 (Martin, *Catalogue of the Archives*, p. 379).

[3] In south Somerset; Madox apparently never made the trip.

[4] Probably Edward Osborne, a rich merchant, who became the first governor of the Levant Company (1581). He also traded in Spain and Portugal and in 1578 had been invited by John Whithall (see 23 Dec.) to trade in São Vicente, Brazil. (See *PN* (1589), pp. 173, 639.)

passeth a degree and a half, and so at noone in Compostella is 5 degrees past the buls eye. Hens may be gathered this instruction: 1. suppoze yt be fownd by observation that 2 Sept. 1582 the ful moon rising in the east angle be 3 sygnes and 20 degrees behind the hart of the scorpion, at the general meridian, which is the beginning of longitude, and the latitude of 40 or 50 or so furth yt muche matereth not. Now yf the same second day of September I trend an unknoen place, and ther fynd that the ☾ rising in the east angle be 3 sygnes and but 17 degrees behind the hart of the scorpion, and in hir midmotion, I pronownce that I am risen eastward 90 degrees in longitude from the general meridian, which is my first observation, wherunto applying my latitude, I fynd the exact poynt of the yerth wher I am, but yf the moone rising be 3 sygnes and 23 degrees behind the hart of the scorpion than am I fauln to the west of my general meridian and so am at 270 degrees of longitude, and by this proportion judge of al other. And this is an observation as I think never publyshed.[1] //

Walking from Ratley[2] to London ther was a man 8v
bwilding up the bulwark of a dytch with the . . . of ox horns [hoofs] to whom after salutacions, sir, quoth I, wil those quycksets [cuttings] groe think you? Yes sir, quoth he, the seazon is good to set yn and this grownd is very batful [fertile]. Yn good tyme sir, quoth I, and so muche the rather [quicker] for happily you have a lucky hand in planting suche seedes and sure yt wil be a great cumfort to you when you shal se them branch up hygher than your head as no dowt they wil yf they lyke the grownd. I despayre nothing sir, quoth he, and your mastership for your good hansel [inauguration] at the sowyng as you walk this way in the spring, gather of the buds to make you a sallet. A dytcher.

a sallet of hornbuds

[1] For this method of determining longitude, see Taylor, *Fenton*, pp. 311–12 and nn. Richard Eden, in his translation of John Taisnier (see p. 191, n. 2) observing that to find out longitude was 'a thyng doubtlesse greatly to be desyred, and hytherto not certaynely knowen,' stated that Sebastian Cabot on his deathbed had told him 'he had knowledge thereof by divine revelation,' to which he commented, 'I thinke that the good olde man, in that extreme age, somewhat doteth' (*A very necessarie and profitable Booke concerning Navigation* (1579), ¶ 3).

[2] Ratley, co. Warwick, four miles southeast of Kineton, where the hills afforded pasture for cattle.

M. Kyndirsley of Walbrooke having maried M. Tipladyes dawghter of Cheapside and using hir hardly for that she was a yong unbroken girle grewe into the disfavor of hir mother who sayd that hir dawghter had never myrry day syth she matcht with hym, which word when yt cam to his eare, he went and bowght a fydle and bringing yt home at dynner tyme before al the gests told the words, wherat he took the fydle and playd and forsed his wyfe to dance in despyte of hir hart because she shold have at least one myrry day in hir lyfe. Sister Ane.

Mirry days with a pipe

A habberdasher of London comyng down[1] into Wales and ther taulking mirrily with a yoman of the cuntrey, yt fortuned them to enter into the examination of felts. Loe, quoth the Londoner in derision of the yeomans felt, thus can we wer a felt in London and after trym yt up and send yt to you in the cuntrey. The yeoman lawghing in his sleeve and looking on the haberdashers wyfe which was born ther and for a poynt of false doctrine had byn sent away to London, no marvel sir, quoth he, the world is false for even so do wee by our mayds hear whom when we have somwhat overworne we send them to London for newe and you take them and make wyfes on them. Brother Thomas.

New trimed hats

A poore feloe which was a scholler being arayned of felony after his endytement, feloe, quothe the judge, are you come hyther to dispute? I pray you what differens is betwyxt fur and *latro*? Great differens as at this tyme my Lord, quoth he, for the one syts on the benche, the other stands at the barr. //

fur and *latro*

I supt at M. Fownds with M. John Wolrych who gave mee an armyng sword. Ther was M. Strangman and M. Osburne.

9r M. Wolridge

11. ⊙ *G* [*Sun.*] *Lent 2.* M. Gregory of St. Lawrence in the Old Jury[2] preched at Paules. The 11 and 12 verse of the 18 of Jeremys he devided into a charg to the prophet, an exhortacion to the people, ther answer.[3] In the first he

[1] Madox inadvertently writes 'downt.'

[2] A 'fayr and large' parish church in Cheap Ward (Stow, *Survey of London*, ed. C. L. Kingsford, II (1908), 140). The preacher remains unidentified.

[3] See 2 Kings 17:13 and Jer. 25:5; 35:15.

ran over by circumstances *legatio, quando, quibus, a quo, quid et causa*: of the 2 and 3^{d} he spok nothing.

I dyned at sherif Martens in Mylkstreet wher was doctor Julius Cæsar that maried his dawghter[1] who gave me very frendly entertaynment. M. Sherif told mee that my Lord of Lester had geven honorable speches of mee. I pray God long to prosper hym and requyt yt with many blessings. He was in some hope that the other ship of Sir Francis Drake was come home. He comended Sir Frauncis and M. Fenton and the rest of our Capteyns. He and his wyfe be both great favowrers of scholers but better acqueynted with Cambridge men than Oxford men. sherife Marten doctor Cæsar

I supt in Botulph Lane at Mrs Lucars.[2] She hath 3 sones, Ciprian, Mark, John and hir dawghter Mary who plays wel on the lute. She gave me a peece of bark which hir cozin Emanuel[3] that went with sir Francis Drake sent hir. She is a very honest gentilwoman. Mrs Lucar

12. ☾ [*Mon.*] I sup at M. sherif Martons. Doctor Cæsar made much of mee.

13. ♂ [*Tues.*] I had 24^{s} from Beamunt and a promyse to discharge my battils[4] which is $14^{s}9^{d}$. M. warden wrote to mee frendly and approved me a cause of absens til a moneth after my returne to England when ever yt be.[5] I went to Beamunt xxiiii^{s} a cause

[1] Richard Martin, goldsmith at the Sign of the Harp and warden of the Mint, became sheriff in 1581 (and later master of the Min. and lord mayor). His daughter Dorcas, relict of Richard Lusher of the Middle Temple, had married Julius Caesar on 25 Feb. 1582. (See Heal, *London Goldsmiths*, p. 202 and *DNB*.)

Caesar, a stepson of the merchant Michael Lok (see 12 Nov.), had been educated at Oxford; in 1581 he had been appointed 'Justice of the Peace in all causes of piracy, and such like throughout the land' (Edmund Lodge, *Life of Sir Julius Caesar* (1827), p. 20). In 1584 he became Judge of the Admiralty and was to have a distinguished career under James who knighted him in 1603.

[2] Joanna, daughter of Thomas Trumball, had married Emanuel Lucar, a member of the Merchant Taylors, in 1541 (he died in 1574). His eldest son by this second marriage, Cyprian, had attended Oxford and was to become a noted writer on mathematical surveying and gunnery. (See *DNB* and E. G. R. Taylor, *The Mathematical Practitioners of Tudor and Stuart England* (1954).) See also 30 Apr.

[3] Emanuel Watkins (Taylor, *Fenton*, p. 156, n.).

[4] I.e., his account for board and provisions from the kitchen and buttery.

[5] On 11 Mar. the Warden and officers of All Souls had granted the following extension to Madox's leave (in Latin): 'If he shall not return after three years, his right to membership in the society would be safe until either he himself should return (as we hope) or his death should be established with certainty (which God forbid). But if he should return, we grant him a period of thirty days for returning to the college, provided that he not receive any part of the

the cowrt with M. Carleyle and supt at M. secretaries lodging.[1]

14. ☿ [*Wed.*] I dyned with M. Carlil at his brother Hudsons who is governowr of Anwerp.[2] He offered me x^{li} to take a boy with me, (*cipher*: but M. Carlil woold not let me). Ther was M. Brytten once of Oriel Colledge which made wyts wyl.[3] He speaketh the Ytalien wel (*cipher*: but is the vainest fel[o][4] in the world for bosting). I supt at Yongs Key at Clarks howse with M. Banester and M. Web the purser.[5] //

Brytten

9^{v}

M. Ashlei and his opinion

15. ♃ [*Thurs.*] being with M. Ciprian Lucar he browght me to his neybour M. Ashley who maketh plaing cards.[6] This man is of Shropshire. He had prepared beads and other devises to venter with sir Humphrei Gilbert who is now abowt an other viag.[7] He told me that he thowght to se when a letter dated at London the first of May shold be delyvered at China before midsomer folowing *et econtra* for he avowched upon report as he sayd of the Yndians that ther was a saylable passage over America between 43 and 46 degrees throe which he sayd Sir Franses Drak cam home from the Moluccas.

---

stipend as long as he has been absent from the college. This is our decision and our declaration' (All Souls College, Hovenden's Minute Bk.).

This extension related to Madox's intention to have remained with Captain Carleill 'wherever he had stayd.'

1 Sir Francis Walsingham, stepfather to Carleill (see Jan. 15, n. 2.).

2 Christopher Hoddeson had begun as an apprentice to the merchant Sir George Barne and gone on to marry his granddaughter Anne Carleill. As a result of various trade ventures in the northeast of Europe, he had by this date amassed a fortune. He was to be knighted by James. (See Supplement to *DNB*.)

3 'M. Brytten' is not listed in Clark or Foster.

'Wyts wyl' apparently a syncopation of the phrase 'wit, wither wilt,' meaning idle talk.

4 Madox inadvertently misplaces the vowel sign in his cipher, writing *i* for *o*.

5 Walter Webbe, purser on the *Galleon Leicester*. See 1 May.

6 In 1578 John Ashley collided with the monopoly of the 'whole trade, trafficque, and merchaundize' of playing cards which the Queen had recently granted (for 100 marks a year) to two of her gentlemen pensioners, Ralph Bowes and Thomas Bedingfield. Made aware that Ashley's claim had a legal justification and that he set many persons to work who otherwise would be idle, the Privy Council instructed the Master of the Rolls and the Attorney General to look into the matter and, if convenient, to bring the parties 'to some good composicion amonge them selfes,' which apparently obtained (*APC, 1577–78*, pp. 434–5).

7 On 26 Apr. Mendoza reported that Gilbert was fitting out three ships to go to Florida (*CSP, Sp., 1580–86*, p. 349), a report reflecting his intention to establish a 'colonial Utopia' which resulted in his death. (See D. B. Quinn, *Gilbert*, I, 55–62.)

I supt at M. Towrson[1] in Towrstreet with our general, our leeiftenent M. Carleil and M. Ward. Ther was docter Tayler a phisicion,[2] M. Ston a mynyster, M. Wanton,[3] and M. Spenser. M. Towrson hath been 3^{s} at Gynny in queen Maries days and gayned well. He told how the shorks[4] wold eat men swymmyng, of one in Colman street that wold wash his hands in scalding lead.[5] M. Fenton told that before my Lord Bromley and others ther was a pore feloe crept Rownd abowt a hote oven. M. Towrson wonders

Just at mydnyght yt pleazed God to take unto hym Thomas Lepye whom I had apoynted to go in viage with me. He was syck a fortnyght and more, having a great cogh, a lasck [attack of diarrhea], a duble tertian [fever], and a bleeding. He lay 3 howrs speechlesse, we praying by hym til the good howr cam which we all look for, that is a dissolution of this yerthly dwelling that God in the last day may raise us to an everlasting and hevenly tabernacle which the lyving Father graunt for his most loving Sones sake to whom with the Holy Ghost be al prayse for ever. Amen. Lepee dead

16. ♀ [*Fri.*] Lepee was buried in the cloyster at Queenhyve: his burial cost me 20^{s} besyds al drinkings. Ther was Thomas Mall and many of the parysh. I wrot to my brother Thomas and sent hym al my keys in a black box and 16^{li} in gold and 5^{li} of hops to his wyf, 5 grotes, al which was in a hampert [*sic*] sent by Nyghtingal with samon and orenges. 20^{s} wrot to my brother 16^{li}

17. ♄ [*Sat.*] I puld on my bootes to ride to Oxford but did not. My syster suspecting I had bin quyte gone wept for

[1] As a member of the Muscovy Company, William Towerson was importantly concerned with this venture, attending the ships at Southampton. His son Will sailed as a mariner on the *Edward*. See entries for 19, 27, 29, 30 Apr.; 1 May.

Accounts of his three voyages to Guinea, in 1555, 1556–7, and 1557–8, are in *PN* (1589), pp. 98–130.

[2] Richard Taylor was a Londoner with an M.D. from Basel who was to be admitted licentiate of the College of Physicians on 9 Apr. (William Munk, *Roll of the Royal College of Physicians*, I, (1861), 93).

[3] Probably John Wanton who in 1585 was serving as deputy and in 1591 as searcher (*Cal. Salisbury MSS.* XIII, 291; Lansdowne MS 67, f. 100).

[4] The mistranscription in *CSP, Col., East Indies, 1513–1616*, no. 221, has led to the bizarre notion, deriving from this passage, of 'man-eating storks.'

[5] Apparently a common tale since it is told of 'a certaine man at *Millan*,' cited out of Cardanus's *De subtilitate*, in Edward Fenton's translation of *Certaine Secrete Wonders of Nature* (1569), F4*v*–G1.

unkyndnes. I supt at my cosyn Thomas with Mrs Gittins and Mrs Prowse.[1] //

10^r^ doctor Overtune

18. ⊙ G [*Sun.*] *Lent 3.* I went with my syster to Grenwich. Goodman Blewberd caried us, 12^d^. Doctor Overtune bishop of Lytchfild[2] preched in thafter noon befor the queen *quid retribuam domino* etc. He handle*d* the benyfites of our creation by the Father in generaul, our redemption by the Sune in spetial, our preservation by the Holy Ghost in particular. I supt at Mrs Lucars with M. Pingle, M. Fleet, Ciprian, Mark, John, Mary etc.

19. ☾ [*Mon.*] I bowght a bed and other things for Peter.

20. ♂ [*Tues.*] (*cipher*: my sister fel sick of hir old dises but I gav hir a vomit of elebors and so I thank God she mended.[3] My chamberfelo and Wignol wer out to seek me but *ego lautia.*)[4]

(*cipher*: Fenton)

I dyned at M. Carleyls with M. general, M. Parker, M. Carleyl etc. (*cipher*: Hear Fenton fearing lest Wiliam Haukins showld outgo him, he ofered fair speeches to us, promising to caul them 2 brether[n] and me father thensfurth.) We went to Alderman Barns wher we found Haukins and Ward and of our marchants and ther we set down a proportion of 90 saylers and 30 other men for the gallion and 60 saylers with 20 other for the Edward owt of which the An Fransis and the frigot[5] at need must be manned.

21. ☿ [*Wed.*] I wrot to Hary Jacson and comendations to great
[*22.*] manye. I studyed ♃ [Thurs.] and ♀ [Fri.] I prepared to be
[*23.*] goen. I supt on ☿ [Wed.] at my cosyn Nycholas.

*l*ay in the Edward

24. ♄ [*Sat.*] my cosyn Nycholas dyned with me. I [supt on the] Edward and lay in hir al nyght.[6]

[1] Perhaps connected with Lawrence Prowse 'who hailed from London' and became an owner and captain of shipping in the late 1580's in Southampton (*The Assembly Books of Southampton*, J. W. Horrocks, I, 2 and n.).

[2] Educated at Oxford, Overton became Bishop of Coventry and Lichfield in 1579. According to the *DNB*, only one printed sermon of his is extant.

[3] 'A purgation of blacke Hellebor,' an ancient specific for insanity, was also good, according to John Gerard, for those 'troubled with the falling sicknesse' or 'a quartaine ague' or 'blacke choler, and . . . melancholie' (*Herball* (1597), 3F5*v*).

[4] Entertained at the expense of the state, as the next sentence makes clear.

[5] In error for the *Bark Francis*, belonging to Sir Francis Drake, which was to be captained by his young cousin. The *Elizabeth* was later substituted for Luke Ward's 'frigot' (see 24 Apr. and n.).

[6] At Blackwall.

25. ☉ G [*Sun.*] *Lent 4.* I cam to London, receved [*sc.* communion] at Queen Hyve and dyned at M. Huntleys. After cam to the cowrt with my syster. Doctor Humphrey preched the Lord is king, the yerth may be glad therof *that* the multitude of yles etc.[1] He shewd the kingdom of power, of grace, of glory. doctor Humphrei

2[*6*]. ☾ [*Mon.*] I cam to the cowrt. My Lord told me that he wold beg Thomas Elx pardon[2] to go with us as a fyner wherof I was glad. Thomas Ellx

2[*7*]. ♂ [*Tues.*] and Wenesday I was at the cowrt and comyng
[*28.*] a boord M. Screven cam to me. I went with hym to London.

29. ♃ [*Thurs.*] cam agayn to the ship and lay in the captens cabin. //

[1] See Ps. 10:16. Madox mistakenly writes 'the' for 'that' and misnumbers the next two entries.

[2] Thomas Elkes, perhaps the son of the Thomas who served as sergeant for Shrewsbury in 1570–1, had attended Shrewsbury School with Madox. (Cf. his allusion while at Oxford to Robert Elkes, also of Salop, 31 Jan.) The family seems to have had Catholic sympathies since Thomas Browne, a draper in Shrewsbury (and an informant in the Ridolfi Plot), wrote a 'longe and tedious' letter (undated but from internal evidence written before 1576) about two peddlers he suspected as messengers for disaffected papists and implicating Elkes: although imprisoned, the two were released on security of Thomas Elkes (the elder); when on orders of the Privy Council, Elkes was examined about his son 'acongerer' and 'lerynd,' he said he was in France. The bearer of the letter, which concludes with reports on notable papists in the area and invokes Ashton the schoolmaster as witness, was George Torporley, 'a faythfull brother in the lorde' who had been a banished man in the days of Queen Mary. (Whether this is the same Torporley referred to in the Diary or his father is not clear. See 18, 19 Feb.; 9 Mar., Weyman, 'Early Chronicles of Shrewsbury,' *Trans., Shrop. Arch. Soc.*, III (1880), 270; *Shrewsbury School Reg. Scho.*, p. 7; and Lansdowne MS 110, ff. 58–62.) In a second letter to the Queen, ff. 64–5, Browne remarks on the 'comfortable wordes' she has sent him by Torporley.

On 28 Oct. 1580 William Herle (see entry for 24 May), writing to Secretary Wilson on behalf of the imprisoned Rowland Yorke, the later betrayer of Deventer, refers to his accuser 'one Ellks' as a 'partye, that is comm[only] reported, verey ynffamows, a detractor, and of no credyte . . . endyted of felonye, and outlawed upon the same' and avers that though he does not know him, he is delivering some notes to give 'a small Taste (in respect of his lyffe besyde),' and he requests that the notes be returned. (Unfortunately they were. SP 12/143/42.)

On 28 Nov. 1580 one William Randoll was arraigned 'for conjuring to know where treasure was hid in the earth, and goods fellonIouslie taken were become' along with four others, including Thomas Elkes, 'for being present.' Although the four were found guilty and condemned to be hanged, only Randoll was executed; the rest were reprieved (Holinshed, *Chronicles*, III (1587), 6L2).

There is a further allusion in 1586 to the practises of 'Dr. Elkes' in conjuring and withcraft to discover treasure (*CSP, Dom., 1581–90*, p. 308). For the Queen's comment on him, see 1 Apr.

10v generaul dinner at Popes Head

30. ♀ [*Fri.*] M. Fenton our general made a great dynner at the Popes Head[1] for al the captens and Muscovie merchants wher we wer ab*owt* 30 or more. I hard that Peter [Pory] was come and sowght for hym.

Lord of Lester aboord

31. ♄ [*Sat.*] My Lord of Leycester and Sir Fransis Walsingham cam aboord the Edward in the mornyng which was mysty. I was than at London. They comended unto us espetialy love and agreement. My cozin Nycholas dyned with me. We had a cock and bacon. After I cam aboord agayn.

familiar instruction

A fysher man comyng wet from his work was desyred by his wyfe to fet a payl of water. For syth yt rayneth, sayth she, you can be no worse wet than you are alredy and I may save my self drye. The man fretting inwardly to se his wyfe presse hym stil with unresonable service when yt had ben more fyt for hir to have cherished hym with eaze ymagined with hym self that when wyt wold not be lerned by gentil instructions, yt must be rughly tawght by a famylier example, and therfore taking the payl with a smyling cowntenance fet yt ful of water desyring hir to help hym down, which thing as she was abowt to do he powred yt al on hir head. So, quoth he, now mayst thow fet water thy self withowt fear of rayn for thow art as wet as I.

(*cipher*:	reseved	vi^{li}iiii^{s}
	spent	44^{s}
	sent to my brother	16^{li}
	left in my purs	3^{li}
	and 3 peeses of gowld in the color of my dublet.) //	

April ♉

11r

1. ☉ G [*Sun.*] *Lent 5.* we had service and after weyd anchor but the west wynd grew flat and scant so that we wer

[1] The Pope's Head Tavern was in Cornhill Ward. Strongly built of stone, it had several large houses adjoining, one of which carried the arms of England over the door, the size of the complex and the presence of the arms attesting, according to Stow, to its original possession by a 'king of this Realme' (*Survey*, I, 199).

driven ageyn to more in the same place. I went to the cowrt, dyned with M. Schreven [*sic*] and M. Lawley[1] in my Lord chanselors lodging. Doctor James preched Thesallonians, embrace truth and love etc.

Doctor James

I took my leave with my Lord of Lester who told me the queen wold not let Elx go with us lest we shold fare the worse for hym, but in tyme or long he wold get hym furth, wherof I certified Elx. I wrot also to Peter [Pory] that syth his frends were so unwilling and he sent answer that he wold not, therfor I was otherwise provided, and so I cam back to the bark which for lack of mariners which wer very negligent forsloed [lost] a good tyde but the Emanuel[2] weyde anchor and went for Cale [Cadiz]. The Centurion[3] was gone 2 days before. The queen cam by us in a barge.

leave of my Lord of L

the queen

2. ☾ [*Mon.*] the wynd being slack we weyd anchor and went to service and or ever the fyrst lesson the west wind was so large that at a quarter flud we went a head with the mayn topsayl and so lowsyng [getting under way] we towed down past the Retch [Blackwall Reach] and cam to Wolwych wher we anchored abowt none, 3 howrs after we lanched from Blackwal. I walked a shore into the woods and supt at M. Gilburns with the Capten, with M. Barnam and his mother, M. Megs and his wyfe, M. Marsten the chancelor of   and had very good chere.

Initium Itineris

Gilburne

3. ♂ [*Tues.*] the wynd comyng to the east sowtheast we dyned at Alderman Barns who maried alderman Garrets dawghter and had bowght Sir Marten Boze howse for the sone had spent that his father gote.[4] After dynner we rode

alderman Barnes

[1] Thomas Lawley, who had attended Shrewsbury School with Madox, was admitted to the Inner Temple in 1567 and became an M.P. in 1572. He was a protégé of Lord Chancellor Bromley (H. T. Weyman, 'The Members of Parliament for Wenlock,' *Trans.*, *Shrop. Arch. Soc.*, Third Series, II (1902), 317.

[2] The *Emanuel* of London was owned by a company of merchants trading in Spain and Portugal (*APC*, *1580–81*, pp. 235, 299–300).

[3] The *Centurion* of London, owned by Richard Wiseman and John Hawes, and, according to K. R. Andrews, in part by Thomas Cordell, also traded in Spain (*APC*, *1580–81*, p. 274; *English Privateering Voyages*, p. 338, n. 3). See entry for 18 Apr.

[4] Barne, who was to serve four or five times as governor of the Russia Company, had married Anne, daughter of Sir William Garrard (d. 1571), who

Mrs Ward

to a brech cawled Abels Job which they seek to wyn from the sea. This whil Capten Wards mother, M. Farrar and his wyf, Mrs Hil, M. Spenser and his wyf, owr masters wyfe,[1] Mrs Johnson and Mrs Cisly cam aboord, and Capten Carleyl etc.

4. ☿ [*Wed.*] ther was a great fog in the morning but the sone opened with a qualme abowt 9 so that we went to service and ymediatly with a good western gale we hoysed sayle abowt xi of clock and towyng down awhyle we passed by Eryth Retch to Graves End and ther Anchored. Now the number that went was abowt 80 and more having in hir some of those that were apoynted for the gall*i*on, but the number apoynted for the Edward was just 80, vzt. 60 mariners and 20 soldiers, she being abowt 14 score // tune and drawing 17 foot at hir lode mark. At 3 a clock, a quarter eb, we cam to an anchor at Gravesend at x fadome, the wynd being styf at the west. The serchers[2] wer M. Payn and M. Tuck to whom our Capten presented hym self and sent the cocket both for the Edward and the Peter that went to Carye stuff to the gallion. We supt at M. Morryce of the Black Boy[3] with all our trayn of women and sent for a pilat to Dover, vzt. Austen.

11v

Graves-ende

5. ♃ [*Thurs.*] having taken leave of Mrs Ward, Mrs Hil, Mrs Farar and rest we went aboord with owr pylat M. Austyne and when the serchers had byn aboord and bid us

---

had himself served at least twice as governor (Willan, *The Muscovy Merchants*, pp. 14, 29).

Sir Martin Bowes, a wealthy London goldsmith, had served as alderman, sheriff, and lord mayor. His office as subtreasurer of the Mint brought him a £10,000 fine in 1551 (*APC, 1550–52*, p. 188). Thomas, one of his two sons, was involved in a number of shady matters, and at one time his father cut him off with a mourning gown, a ring, and a cup, stating he had already received 'fowre tymes more then ever his parte shuld coom to.' He later restored him to a modest share in his inheritance. (See G. D. Ramsay, *John Isham, Merchant and Merchant Adventurer* (1962), pp. XLI–XLV.)

[1] Thomas Percy was master of the *Edward*.

[2] Officials of the custom house who searched for contraband. The coquet (or docket) was sealed by officers of the custom house, certifying duty had been paid on merchandise. See Intro., p. 22.

[3] William Morris of Milton was an innholder and tavern keeper who in 1571 had been fined 'for selling Beer and Ale in Pots of stone, and Cans not being quarts full measure.' He had served as portreve in 1569 and as jurat, a member of the common council governing the towns of Gravesend and Milton, in 1572–73 (R. P. Cruden, *The History of . . . Gravesend and . . . the Port of London* (1843), pp. 192, 208).

farwel we sayled by the Bolyne at a quarter flud abowt 8 a clock, the wynd stiff at west and northwest westerly spreding al our sayl save the mayn and so kept our cowrse est northest to Blyth Sand, from thence east by the Warp to Blacktayl on the sowth of Burnam Flats in Sussex. Ther we spread owr mayn sayl and shot by a wynd north and by east and east northest leaving Oze Edge and the Mowsetayle a star bowrd and the Showbeacon aport til we cam to the Northeast of the Buxey neare the Gunflet wher we lay all nyght at an anchor. The Sandes in *the* Thames[1]

6. ♀ [*Fri.*] having a smal gale at northwest we hoysed agayn but on the sodayn the wynd cam stif to the east which made us vayl [haul down a sail] and cast owt the starboord anchor with a new cable which being a ging brak a streyn at a quarter lenth so that we wer glad to wey yt and ryd at an other, the wether being somwhat fowle. Ther cam a lynnet and lyght on the shrowds. After diner we hoysed upon a quarter ebbe and making many boords [tacks] at sowthsowthest and north northest by reason of the Gunflet and Mydlland and Su*pe* Sholds[2] we wan 7 myle to wynd ward and hear let fawl an anchor but because the sea was rugh and I very sea syck I cold not mark al as I wold. a cable cracte

7. ♄ [*Sat.*] abowt one or 2 in the morning the wynd stil at east we hoised upon the eb with many boords thro help of the tyde wan owr selvs to the wynward a lytle past the Sands but at 6 aclock when we saw that we cold not bere to Doverward we returned westnorwest to Harwich, the sone bryght shining but the east wynd very stiff and by the way in turning a flaw [gust] snapt in sunder short in the myds owr mayn topsayl yerd. Abowt xi aclock we cam to Harwich and rode before the town. After dynner we walkt with the capten on Suffolck syde to Walton[3] wher the topsaile yard broke Harwich

[1] For the 'Sandes in the Thames,' see Robert Norman's chart (1580) of the Outer Thames Estuary (Fig. 5) and 19 Feb. for Madox's visit to him.

[2] 'Mydlland,' a sand more commonly termed 'Middleground'; Su*pe* Sholds perhaps the same as the 'Black Supes' near Middleground shown in Richard Caundish's Map of the Outer Thames Estuary (c. 1535), repr. in A. H. W. Robinson, *Marine Cartography in Britain* (1962), Plate 5.

[3] Ten miles southeast of Ipswich.

we bowght egs and kild a bitter[1] and gathered broome. We also gathered a basketful of muscles which lay very
12^r thick on the shore when within this 7 yere ther // was not a muscle seen ther but the pore have good releif by them.

8. ⊙ G [*Sun.*] *6 Lent* very fayr but wynd stil at east sowtheast. Many of the saylers went a shore wherat the capten was affended. I red over the Regiment of the Sea made by M. Borrows[2] who is a very proper man for sea matters
Sea rules — and he geveth very familiar rules how to fynd owt the auge or the dragon of the moone by the prime because they both pas abowt in 19 yers and at 1 be in ♈ [Aries], the auge going forward and the ☊ [node] backward.[3]

One having made a *p* upon a can, this is, sayd an other,
a jest at unwares — the pursers can. I knoe by the *p*. Now surely, sayd Georg our Captens cabbin boy,[4] and I wil make a *k* of my masters can that he may kno yt also.

9. ☾ [*Mon.*] after dynner because our pilat was not a boord, the Capten and I and M. Banister went to Harwych wher we fownd hym more heedful of the berol and the ale bowle
M. Grei — then of his business. Ther was M. Grey the cheif of the 4 masters of the queenes shyps, a very skilful coaster and one that had byn muche employd in the taking of French pyrats and had fared the better for them.[5] Hear we bowled and supt at M. Haukins and had 14^s reconyng for

[1] I.e., bittern, a small heron-like bird.

[2] A *Regiment of the Sea*, a simplified translation of Martin Cortes' *La Arte de Navegar* (1551), which had earlier been translated by Richard Eden, first appeared in 1574 and was frequently reprinted. William Bourne, a student of mathematical science who also served as jurat and portreve for the Corporation of Gravesend, was the translator. He had died in March, 1582. (See Cruden, pp. 207, 539, and E. G. R. Taylor's edition of Bourne (Hakluyt Soc., 1963.)

William Borough, to whom Madox attributes the work, was also a writer on navigation. For Luke Ward's unfavourable comments on him, see entry for 12 Nov.

[3] The 'auge' is the highest point of the course of the sun or moon; the 'dragon' is the intersection of the ecliptic and of the circle that carries the moon. The ascending node of the moon's orbit with the ecliptic is called the 'dragon's head'; the descending node, 'the tail.' For 'prime,' see n. 6, p. 70 above. It was held that all the lunations and aspects between the sun and the moon returned to their original places within a 19-year revolution.

[4] George Brodford. The second George among the boys on the *Edward*, surnamed Robinson, was the younger brother of a mariner on the *Galleon* and served as the master carpenter's boy (*PN* (1589), p. 647). He was to die on 16 Aug. despite Dr Banister's ministrations.

[5] Thomas Grey of Harwich was master of Trinity House and in 1580 owner of the *Jonas* (Lansdowne MS 34, no. 66 and *APC, 1578–80*, p. 401).

3 joynts of meat. Ther was with us M. Twynt with a great nose, a good sensible wyse man. But this I perceaved that it is nether good that saylers shold be suffered to go a shore when they lye in harboroe, nether that strong drink shold be suffered in haven towns, for thro lyberty on the one syde and temptation on the other syde many a good wynd and tyde is forsloed, and much disorder both in ship and town commytted and more chardges both to owner and say*ler* than is needful.[1] Wel we browght our pil*at* aboord with a lytle cholor who had not seen us syth we cam to harboroe, and because the wynd *was* east and by north (for any poynt of the north *be* good) we wold gladly have gone but yt was not thowght good to venter by nyght. of saylers shoring

Harwych stands al on fysh and is ruled by a cunstable. Yt stands fayr to the sea on the sowth of Orwel and the haven opens to the sowtheast. I hard the town was rych but I did not perceave yt. Ther is a cunstable. The trade of the haven goeth up to Ypswyche for ther the officers ar and the key and such lyke which shooteth 5 myle up an other ryver that hear at the town joyned with Orwel make the rode.[2] // Harwich

10. ♂ [*Tues.*] we fet home both our anchors in hope to be goen 12v
but the wynd whyvelying [veering] on both syds the east grew so scant that we cold not. After dynner by reason of dyvers complaynts, espetialy the fylching of gowns, the Capten and master cawled us al before them, meanyng to make serch for things missing. Hearin was fownd gilty by proofes the guners boye, and a lost gown fownd besyde in Smyths Cabyn[3] in the gunery. The capten reproving the boy, Furd the master guner took his part and wold have justified hym, behaving hym self after a mutynows maner very prowdly, both in words and actions, telling openly that he myght have byn in a better place, and the capten myght say his pleasure hear, and such lyke, refusing to go down when thryce together he was quarell *with* the gunner

[1] Madox has occasion to make a similar observation when they are anchored at Hamble Hole, 1 May.

[2] At Harwich the Stour joins the Orwell.

[3] John Smith was gunner's mate (see 1 May).

desyred. Hearupon the capten seeing his unsufferable demeaner and advysedly consydering how muche the bad example of one unruly feloe myght hurt in the ship, which by al meanes sowght both to discredit the viage and discorage the cumpany, he cawled hym into his Cabin before the master, his mate, M. Banyster and me. Hear was agayn his behavior as yl as before, saying playnly that he did not lyke the viage, and that he had byn and myght be in better place, and that this was doen to hym on stomake and that he wold be goen and other insolent words, wherupon the Capten with the consent and cownsel of us al discharged hym his offyce, and taking from hym the keys, comaunded hym to passe in the ship to Hampton and ther to attend what the masters of the viage wold say to hym, but when he had gote leav to bring his boy a shore which was beaten for the fault, he cam no more.[1]

letter to the governor*s*

11. ☿ [*Wed.*] we wrot a letter to the governowrs, both of our viage and of Thomas Furds yl behaviowr, requesting that he myght be punyshed. This we sent by Rob Lyddington,[2] havyng these hands: Luke Ward, Thomas Persey, Richard Madox and John Banister. The wynd was ful sowth and therfor we went a shore into Suffolk and dyned at Walton wher we had good chear. At Walton I wrot to my syster An and to Capten Carleyl, desyring hym that our cook of the gallion myght be displased of whom I had herd yl for swering and brablyng.

12. ♃ [*Thurs.*] after noon we went agayn to Harwich to knoe M. Greis mynd but he first encoraging us to be gone, so soon as the wynd cam sowtheast agayn we stayd ther and went to the bowles. //

13r

M. Beacher of London

13. *Good Friday* we went ageyn to Harwich and fet aboord us M. Becher of London, a very curteows gentilman and Parvis also no lesse, and M. Ferris which is maried in Emden, M. Stephens and Chamberlan and M. Jarman which wer bownd to Emden. Ther cam to us also by chance my lady Parkers syster, a dawghter of Sir John

Mystres Goodwyn

[1] On 19 Apr. he was sent to prison.

[2] Lyddington was to serve as purser of the *Galleon*.

Goodwyn[1] and Mrs Doryty Oglethrop and Mrs Beatryce Turner and Mrs Petronell, Goodwyns mayd and one M. Grove ther man. Sir William Parker dwelleth nyehand.[2] Our Capten made them great cheere in his Cabin and did them what honor he cold both with instruments and ordinance. M. Becher told how my Lord Harry vicownt Byndon ryding down with the herawlds to the burial of his father[3] broght an ape and clothing hym in fayr black velvet, moorner lyke, placed hym on a horse next to hym self with a footman leading hym and so they rode owt of London wherat was good lawghing, lawghing I mean not at my Lord but yet at his ape. Lord of Bindon his ape

After dynner bidding the gentilwomen farewel we went with the merchants to Harwich and at M. Greenes, a very fayr howse, we supt at ther chardge having bowled awhyle and so cam abord.

(*cipher*: The capten told me he had but 40^li^ and Fenton 50 towards al charges and therfor wished in causel that[4] we might help our selvs when we cowld.)

M. Grove told of Doctor Pearn who sayd it was a pyke alone because yt had noe feloes and therfore the man browght him back to his feloes. a pyke alone

The Capten told of Mownt Staffords[5] man that because he wold sleep in despite of the wynd which stil *put* hym of his lodging bownd a chest to the ship syde and hym sleep in despite of wynd

[1] Sir John Goodwin had been knighted in 1570 at the Queen's command (Shaw, *Knights of England*, II, 74). His wife and son were included in a list of papists, dated 1581 (Lansdowne MS 33, 145–9).

[2] This person is unidentified and thus whether or not he was connected with Nicholas Parker, Captain-at-Land, undetermined. The house of Arwerton, Suffolk, as Camden noted (*Britain*, tr. P. Holland (1610), 2Q2) 'belongeth to the Parkers hæredetarily.' Madox may have had in mind Sir Philip Parker who served as sheriff in 1580.

[3] The first Viscount Bindon who died 28 Jan. at Marnhall, Dorset (*Complete Peerage*, VI, 584).

The giddy actions of his heir Henry Howard on this occasion derive from the frequent and stormy quarrels between father and son: in 1580 he asserted his father 'had brought him to bee bare, and hadd beggered him in inforcing him to his utter undoing to buye his owen inheritaunce' (SP 12/143/4). For equally extravagant behaviour at the marriage of his daughter Douglas to Sir Arthur Gorges, see Helen E. Sandison, 'Arthur Gorges, Spenser's Alcyon and Ralegh's Friend,' *Pub. Modern Language Association of America*, XLIII (1928), 645–55.

[4] Madox inverts his usual breviograph for 'that.'

[5] Edmund Stafford, like Captain Ward, had sailed with Frobisher on the voyage to the Northwest in 1577 (*PN* (1598–1600), 1904 repr., VII, 285).

self to the chest hand and foot, and a sea comyng yn to hym fel upon the orlop [deck] so deep that every jowlt he lay in the water crying for help and cold not be lowsed. He told also to what use they put muskle shels in Dort.[1]

14. ♄ [*Sat.*] *Easter even* I walked in Suffock by Walton and to Tremley wher ther is 2 churches in one churchyerd[2] and

Ypswych

over the long heath to Ypswych 8 myle west northwest. The town is *great* and fayr with a dozen parysh churches governed by 2 baylyse, sct. this the riche Berker and Goodyn.[3] Ther ar 12 Auldermen in scarlet at the northwest

M. Thomas Sackford

gate. M. Thomas Sackford, master of the requests, hath a notable fyne howse whose bwylding is of the yonyque piller with hawl, parler, chappel, salyes, stayres, chambers, and al of majesty for ther bygnes.[4] An old serving man sheod me al and made me drynk. Yn the haul over the chimney is the story of Sampson and Dalilah gallantly paynted and over the table 2 stories of Joseph and his brethern and at the end the story of Scipio which gave unto Lucius the mayds husband the money that hir parents payd to rawnsom hir.[5] I saw the bryk fowndation by St. Peters

[1] Apparently a long-lived popular notion: 'You among nations have likewise, / Men of severall faculties / In shiting, 'mongst whom we may call, / *Dutch* neatest shiter of them all. / As witnesses his Mussel shells / You find in *Holland*, where he dwells; / Pil'd up as Pewter is in kitchen, / In house of office that he shits in' (Richard Flecknoe, *The Diarium or Journall* (1656), p. 10).

[2] Trimley, a Suffolk village where the navigator Thomas Cavendish was born, has the church dedicated to St Martin in the same churchyard with that of Trimley St Mary.

[3] Camden terms Ipswich 'the eie (as it were) of this shire' with 'fourteene Churches' and 'foure religious houses now overturned' (*Britain*, 2Q2*v*).

The 'riche Berker' was probably John, a merchant, who served as portman and alderman. Edward Goodwyn (or Gooding as he is indifferently called) is referred to as bailiff in 1575 and again in 1581. (See *Bacon's Annals of Ipswich*, ed. W. H. Richardson (1884), pp. 308, 326, 284 and n., 340.)

[4] Thomas Sacford (Seckford) had been sworn in as 'Master of Requests Ordynary' on 9 Dec. 1558 (*APC, 1558–70*, p. 17). His 'great charges and notable enterprise . . . in procuring the Charts of the severall provinces of this realme to be set foorth' are referred to in the dedication (III, A2*v*) of Holinshed's *Chronicles* (1587), an allusion to his patronage of Christopher Saxton, the earliest county mapmaker.

Seckford Hall in the parish of Great Bealings had been held by the family since the time of Edward II (*Bacon's Annals of Ipswich*, p. 252, n. 3). 'Salyes,' apparently for 'sales,' i.e. halls.

[5] For the account of Scipio's returning of the captive maiden to her fiancé Allutius, along with the ransom paid by her family, see Livy 26. 50. A lost play entitled *Alucius* was performed at court in 1579.

which the cardinal layd,[1] and cam to Harwich by water and taulked *of*. . . emerton and other wyches that kyld my Lord . . . and of *how* // Edward Cotton had served the Turk within the Strayts and sold many Christians into the gallies,[2] which thing yf yt be true I cold wysh a precher to exhort the people at the spittal sermons whan Collections be made for captives[3] rather to pay money unto such men of war before and to such that cary ordynance etc. to the Turk as did Sir Thomas Gressam,[4] than to suffer them to sel our Christians fyrst and than we be forsed thro charitye to redeem them. 13

Turkish service

M. Prat is sercher of Ypswych and M. Jud controler. Ther liberty is 7 myle of wher they keep cowrt at a dead loe water; nether can the admyral medle with them. The water is noe ryver but an yngut cauled Ypswich Water.

15. ⊙ *G Easter Daye* the wynd being fresh at the westsowest we set sayl in the mornyng tyde erly according to the Jues passover owt of Ægipt so rare [early] that had not the Peter stayd for them we had left a score of our people a shore ther. *The Lord of heaven passe over us in mercie to bring us from this worldlie Ægipt to the land of the living and passe with us al our viage going before in the daie as a pillar of clowd and all the night long lyke a light of fire, for Jesue Christes sake amen.*

[1] In his remarks on Ipswich, Camden comments in passing on 'thats umptuous and magnificent Colledge which Cardinal *Wolsey* a Butchers sonne of this place, heere began to build, whose vast minde reached alwaies at things too high' (*Britain*, 2Q 2*v*).

[2] A merchant of Southampton, who served as controller. On 27 Nov. 1581, the Privy Council wrote to the mayor of Bristol directing him to find out what sums had been gathered in that city and thereabouts for the redemption by Edward Cotton of Southampton of two Englishmen, captives under the Turks, and to pay him so that he be no loser (*APC*, *1581–82*, p. 266). See 20 Apr.; 1 May (p. 128).

[3] The 'spittal sermons' were delivered during Easter week by especially appointed preachers in the churchyard of the Priory of St Mary Spital, Bishopsgate Ward, where there was a pulpit cross like that in St Paul's (Stow, *Survey*, I, 167–8).

On 1 Apr. of this year the Privy Council had written to the Bishop of London about one Lucas Argenteus, whose wife and children were prisoners of the Turk, recommending that the preachers at the Spital exhort the audiences to contribute towards their ransoming (*APC*, *1581–82*, pp. 375–6).

[4] 'Oracle of the city, merchant prince and trusted financial agent,' he had founded the Royal Exchange in 1566, ending his career with a substantial sum unaccounted for in his transactions in behalf of the Crown (J. B. Black, *The Reign of Elizabeth* (1945 repr.), pp. 218–19). For his involvement with Frobisher's attempts to find the Northwest Passage, see Richard Collinson, *Three Voyages of Martin Frobisher* (Hakluyt Soc., 1867), pp. 344–5. For a later derogatory comment Madox quotes, see 17 Oct.

Awdlyn sleeps on shore

Audlyn the master of the Centurion lyke an yl husband lay *a* shore so that we left hir behynd in the rode. Yet the sea being peaseable she made away a pace after us and cam to an anchor as soone as we, for in rugh sease and rughe wynds comonly the bigger ship goeth before but in smothe seas and *with* owt wynd the lyght barks pryck formost. The [day] fayr and the wynd at westsowest we shot up *est* sowthest on the north Balstey [Baudsey] Sand and abowt 10 a clock meeting the wynd at sowtheast we ran upon the sowest bord [coast] til we cam within 4 myle of the Marget which opened with ther whyt clyfs and the church of St. Johnes. Now because we must trend the cape of the North Furlong [Foreland] which now lay sowth and by east from us, we hawled agayn east and cam to anchor abowt tow leags from yt.

against *se*asickness

I was tawght many medcynes to avoyd the sycknes of the sea as namely a safron paper on the stomak or to drink the juse of wormwod, but I perceaved that the best things [are], to keep very warme, to be sure of hote supping often, to use moderat motion and to bear yt with a good corage til by acqueyntance you become famylier with the heaving and setting of the ship and be able to brook the seas and than the more excerse [exercise] with reason the better, for yf you once fawl to lasynes or unlust [sloth] than is the scarby[1] redy to catch you by the bones and wil shak owt every tooth in your head. //

14r

[*16.*] ☾ [*Mon.*] we set sayl about 7 in the morning and the wynd groying scant and caulme we cam to anchor betwyxt the Goodwyn[2] and the Brakes but sowth them both abowt 4 leags northwest Dover, but anon after 4 the wynd cam fresh at the west so that we set sayle agen. Being in the mayn top I saw at the loe water the whole syte of the Goodwyn dry and discovered a flyght of halx.

Abowt 6 a clock almost 2 leags from Dover ther cam 4 smal barks in our lye, which our cumpany sayd wer men

1 *Qu.* 'scarebabe,' i.e., bugbear. Cf. 'sloath-bred scurvies' (*OED*, 1628).

2 Lambarde describes the ten-mile stretch of Goodwin Sand as 'a most dreadfull gulfe and ship swalower, sometime passable by foote, and sometime laied under water' so it may be said to be 'either sea, or land, or neither of both' (*Perambulation of Kent* (1826), p. 97).

of war,[1] wherfore we prepared [to] fyght and weaving [signalling] in the fyrst she was knoen to be a merchant of Sandwich, but she told us ther wer 2 of them men of war. Wherfor we weaved in the second which was the Lion of Dartmowth, and when she had sent hir men aboord we knew them to be honest, but she told us that the other had geven hir chase, wherfore with our boat we boowrded both the other lytle once, but the one was Byswyck which cam from Gravlyng,[2] whom the man of war having boorded wold not spoyl for acqueyntens sake, and therfore Byswyk promysed to help them to money for ther pillage which was lether that they had taken from a Wallon. This other which was the pyrat being taken by our boat had in hir dyvers of the men which were shipt by Furbusher for our viag, and after, cause Fenton was generawl wold not go, but fyrst stole a bad vessel and after boording a Flemyng changd with hym and so had paltred up 3 barrels of bysket, a barrel or 2 of candels, 30 flytches of bacon, 16 barels of good duble bear. They wer 9 of the cumpany and Watson was the capten. Ther was also *o*ne Willobye, a tawl [bold] feloe of Dover. When we had stoed our men in hir, the Capten and I (being qualme) roed to Dover 2 leags of and comyng thyther abowt 10 a clock at nyght caried with us one of thes felos who begayn but the same day.

wee take a prize

Dover

We went to M. Burdens the controler[3] who maried M. Capten*s* syster. Hear we delyvered our pilat Austyn who is botswayn of the Phillip and Mary,[4] and after that we had wel supt and dyvers of the town cam to us with wyne, because now our ships wer com even with Dover and had shot of a warnyng peece unto us, therfore we tooke leave and abowt 3 a clock cam a boord our ship which ran by the lee with a northeast wynd, who at our comyng spred sayl agayn in hir cowrse. The master shewyng us

[1] Generic for pirate ships.

[2] Gravelines, Flemish Gravelinghe.

[3] William Burden was serving as controller of the Port of Dover as early as 1562 (*APC, 1558–70*, p. 113).

[4] The *Philip and Mary*, listed variously as of 500 or 600 tons, was at this date 26 years old (B.L., Stowe MS 570, f. 159). It was to be rebuilt in 1584 and renamed the *Nonpareil* and again in 1603 when it was renamed *Nonsuch* (J. K. Laughton, *State Papers relating to the Defeat of the Spanish Armada*, II (Navy Rec. Soc., 1894), 335).

peril by negligens

that by neglyge*nce* of some to belay [coil] the haylers [ropes], the mayn yerde *ha*d fawln down and lyke to have kyld 3 or 4, the ve*ry* same thing also happened to us in the boat by defawt and breaking of a haler which was but an old.... Further they told us that the Hopewel[1] of Ypswych *com*yng by from Lysburn informed them of 5 great Cariques [Portuguese galleons] gone for the East Yndies and dyvers other ships for the Trecyras[2] which had gote cownterfet Englysh flags. (*cipher*: The pirats had also as we wer enformed 20 or 40 pownd in mon*y*.) Yn our pri*ce* we had a dog that wold dance and plow and *sin*g prycksō*ng* which made us som sport.[3] //

News

14v

17. ♂ [*Tues.*] after we cam fro Dover which was abowt 3 in the m*orning*, we had the wynd at west northwest somtyme larg, somtyme scant so that holding our cowrse sowth-sowth*west* cam by nyght as far as Bechye[4] halyng our price[5] a sterne. At nyght the wynd being very bold and we frayd of the shore we wer dreven on seaboord far to leeward besowth the Wyght.

The Centurion better than she was thowght

18. ☿ [*Wed.*] we espied the Centurion which had put in on Sonday to the Margat who cam very close by the wynd and left us a stern, keeping hir cowrse toward Spayn, and as we hawled abowt toward Hampton, we descried 2 hulks which some sayd was Capten Heyns,[6] some Coburne the Scot and a price, wherfor we gave them chase to St. Ellyns,[7] wher espying what they wer we cam noe nyer unto them, so they rode heer al nyght, and we hawled betwyxt Portsmowth and the Wyght wher we met with

1 In a 1582 list of vessels in various ports, the *Hopewell* of 170 tons is mentioned under Suffolk though there specified as of Aldeburgh (SP 12/156/45).

2 The Azores, so-called from Terceira, the largest of the nine islands.

3 Harrison describes the 'toiesth curs' called 'dansers,' which are taught 'to danse a measure' and show 'manie trickes by the gesture of their bodies' (Holinshed, *Chronicles*, III (1587), U6). Cf. Mercutio's remark on Tybalt: 'He fights as you sing pricksong – keeps time, distance, and proportion' (*Romeo and Juliet* 2.4. 21–2).

4 Chalk cliff known as Beachy Head.

5 'Price' for 'prize' as 'grace' for 'graze' (see 19 Apr.).

6 Termed a 'notorious English pirott' in June 1582 (*APC*, *1581–82*, pp. 450–1). In 1578 Luke Ward had been commissioned to take pirates (SP 12/123/34 and 31).

7 On the eastern coast of the Isle of Wight.

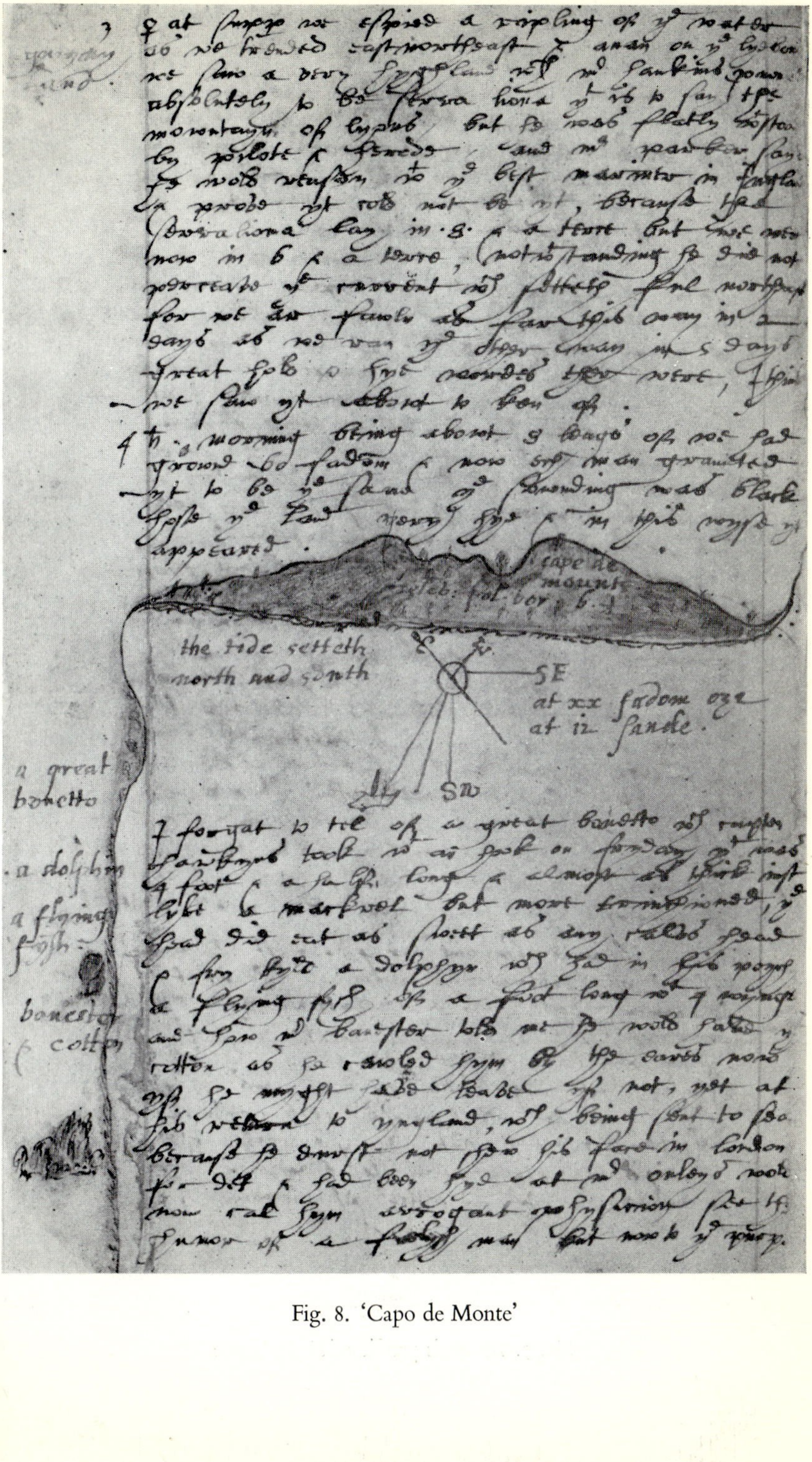

Fig. 8. 'Capo de Monte'

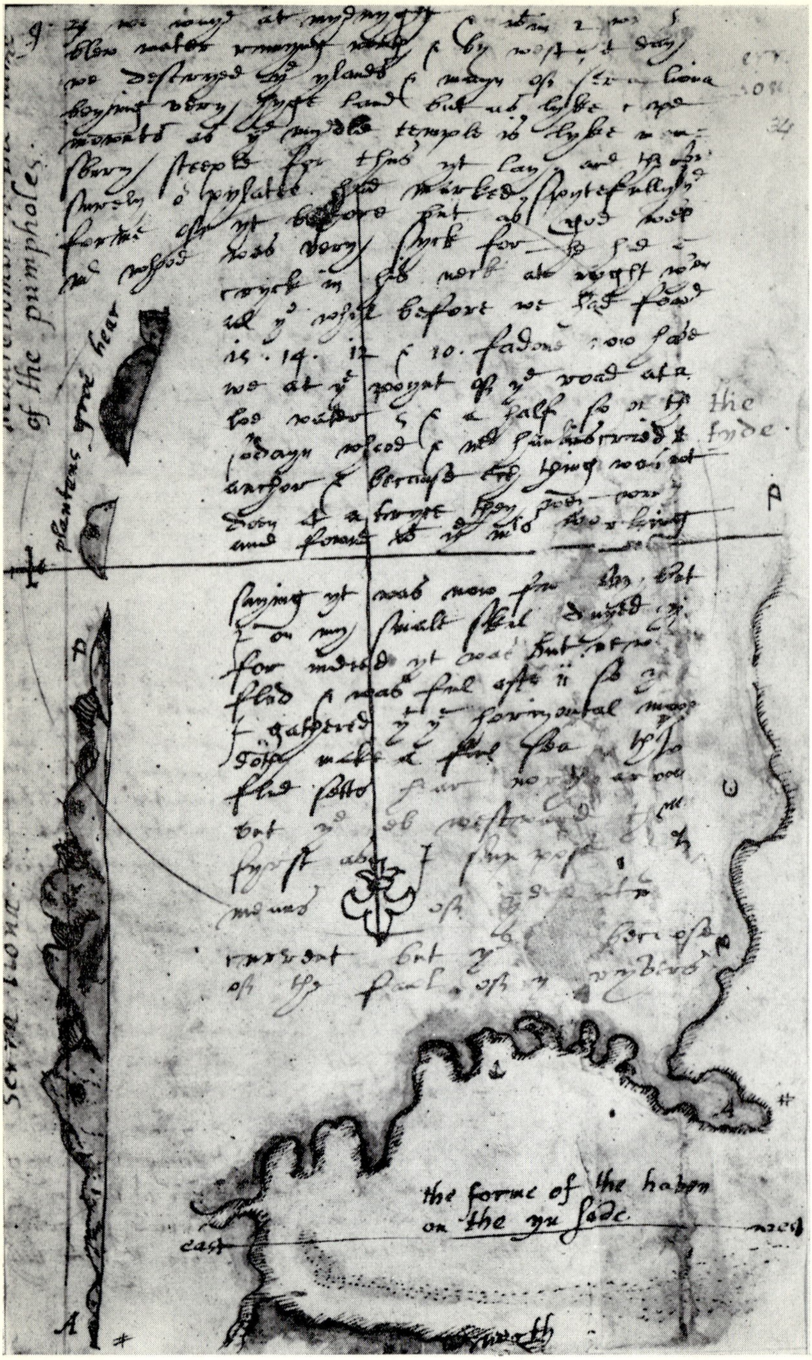

Fig. 9. Madox's profile of Sierra Leone

the Phoenyx of Harwich that is come from Legorn. She belongs to M. Twyd[1] and others. Phoenix

Hear our bark the Peter had boorded a man of war who sayd he had Don Antonios comyssion[2] and had taken a French man laden with salt. This was a lytle before sunset. Hear cam by us in his boot Capten Clark a pyrat whom we did not then know and hayling our ship drank to us and than threw the cup overburd[3] but had we knoen hym he shold also have walked with us. Ther appeared hear a great shole [school] of purposes scowrging above water which som say ar forboders of a tempest and at nyght M. Banyster cauled me up to se a comet but yt was Venus with a great fyery haze lyke a bushlock abowt hir wherupon I told the master M. Percy that we shold have change of wether and anon after that we had mored by east the Cow,[4] the wynd rose tempestuowsly at the sowth but did not long contynue.

a prize

Clark in his bravery

tokens of a tempest

19. ♃ [*Thurs.*] we cam with al our prizes[5] toward Hampton

[1] Thomas Twyd of Harwich commended, with others, by the Privy Council in Dec. 1581; the *Phoenix* was a ship of 100 tons (*APC, 1581–82*, p. 300; SP 12/156/45).

[2] I.e., licence to retaliate on his enemies, known as 'letters of marque' or 'letters of reprisal.' Pirates, both of the lesser and the greater sort, claimed letters of marque not only from Dom António and Alençon but even from King James VI of Scotland, the King of Sweden, etc.

[3] Captain Tom Clark was a pirate of great notoriety whose bravado and daring actions were a source of complaint from 1575 on: depositions in 1578 testify to Clark's method of saluting the men he was about to rob 'with a glass of wyne' in his hand and forcing them to drink with him 'till the tyd was spent,' his men armed with 'swords and calivers' (SP 12/125/66).

A ballad, licensed Mar. 1580, suggesting he had been executed by this date, was entitled *A pastport for pirates wherein they maye marke: and shunn their abuse by the Death of THOMAS CLARKE* (*A Transcript of the Registers*, ed. E. Arber, II, 366 and H. Rollins, *An Analytical Index to the Ballad-Entries (1557-1709) in the Registers of the Company of Stationers* (1924)). However, a petition to the Privy Council dated ?June 1580 refers to goods and merchandise taken by two ships, one belonging to a gentleman of the Queen's Privy Chamber, the other to the 'notorious pirate' Thomas Clark; and as late as 14 Jan. 1586, his wife, M[rs] Julian Ashton of Staffordshire, was still being examined (SP 12/139/54 and *CSP, Dom., 1581–90*, p. 301).

[4] On the Isle of Wight.

[5] These included the pirate ship staffed with the mariners who refused to sail under Fenton, captained by Watson and including Willoughby the Rover (see 16 Apr.), and the 'man of war' with its prize of a 'frenchman,' which had been taken by the *Peter*. On 15 Apr. the Privy Council, crediting Captain Luke Ward with the apprehension of all three, directed the mayor of Southampton and Sir Edward Horsey, Captain of the Isle of Wight, to release the French merchant with the lading and to proceed against the two pirates (*APC, 1581–82*, p. 394).

and gave the castle of Cawshot[1] a bullet which did not grace but she *g*ave us an other that cam close by the stem and both gra*c*ed fynely and ratled gallantly in the wood. Hear met *us* M. Hawl and along we cam to Netley[2] by the gallion whom we hayled with half a dosen sacres and she us with as many, and after that M. Owtread the sherif, M. Alderman Barns, M. Towrson, the mayr of Hampton[3] with others, *nimirum* our general, and M. Parker etc. had vysited us, we went abord our admiral, the gallion Owtread which is a very stately ship with top and top gallant, abowt *400* tune and more. She was bylt at Hemmel [Hamble] which is // fast by, at M. Owtreads charges abowt 4 yer synce and hath made 2 Spaynysh viages with smal profet so that I hope hir best hap be to come, being reserved for this which is a greater action. She is made lyke unto the Revenge but the Edward was bwylt at Rochester 8 yere syth and is lyke the Forsyght.[4] The gallion was molded by M. Baker and framed by John Ady.[5] Hir tymber is very strong and she caryeth 42 cast peeces of culvering, sacre and mynion shot. Hear we dyned and after Furd the guner was sent to prizon and Willoby the rover with others. Lykewyse John of Orkney who had warred in the spreet of Mydleborow and had taken the Bonaventure of Roan was commytted to M. mayr who told hym his comyssion

the gallion and Edward doe meete

gallion *bw*ylte 15r

the Edward bwilte

the pyrate

[1] Calshot Castle served to defend the entry of Southampton Haven. Captain James Parkinson served as keeper. (See 1 May.)

[2] Netley Castle, built by Henry VIII, was kept by Henry Owtread (*Letters of the Fifteenth and Sixteenth Centuries*, ed. R. C. Anderson (1921), pp. 105–6). See also 1 May.

[3] Richard Biston (Bysson, Beeston) of All Saints Ward whose son intended to ship in the *Galleon* (see 1 May and *The Third Book of Remembrance of Southampton*, ed. A. L. Merson, III, 107–8).

[4] The *Revenge*, a ship of 450 tons, belonged to the Queen and was esteemed by Drake as the perfect galleon of his time; he was to select it as his ship in the Armada fight (J. A. Williamson, *Hawkins of Plymouth* (1949), pp. 249–50).

In following the pattern of the *Foresight*, the *Edward* was representative of the new type known as 'galleon-built,' which had, according to William Borough, 'its length by the keel three times its width at the middle, and the depth in hold but 5/12 or 2/5 of the breadth' (quoted in J. S. Corbett, *Drake and the Tudor Navy*, I (1899), n. 1).

[5] Matthew Baker and John Ady were master shipwrights. Baker, the son of Henry, master shipwright under Henry VIII, evolved the first theoretical method to measure the burden of a ship. (See *Autobiography of Phineas Pett*, ed. W. G. Perrin (Navy Rec. Soc., 1918), pp. xxix–xxx, and Monson's *Naval Tracts*, ed. M. Oppenheim (Nav. Rec. Soc., 1902–14), IV, 50–1 and n.)

was forged and taking his wepon sent him also to prizon.[1]

Abowt noon the wynd blew up boysterowsly at sowthwest with rayn and slyt which so contynueth yet, the Lord be praysed who hath browght us to our first desyre which is the cumpany of our Admiral within a good haven. effects of the porpises

M. Walker was hear very gallant in a velvet hat.[2] I was told that he had preched on Sunday in Hampton and he told me that I was register[3] of the viage and that my Lord of Leycester had spoken wel of mee and M. secretary Walsingham great good who indeed doth not knoe me. Nether can I tel wher he shold lern any thing of me otherwyse than by the report of M. Mylls or M. Carleyl, wherof nether the *one* hath had tyme nor the other conversation with me *to* knoe me in deed, but M. Carleils good na*tur*e hath conceved better of me than I can think of my self. I pray God grant me his grace and favowr *that* the effect and yssue of my lyfe may be somwhat answerable to the expectation of thes good nob*l*e men and gentilmen, for as the God of heaven whom I serve and wil do for ever hath kyndled in ther harts a certayn hope of me withowt my desert so I trust his bownty wil bestoe upon mee his spetial blessyngs that I be not altogether left unto my self or to my own wyt and so overthroe all, but I trust that the Lord who hath kept me from my youth up will keep me to the end. *Virga tua et baculus tuus ipsa me domine consolata sunt et consolabuntur in æternam.* || *stimuli virtutis*

20. ♀ [*Fri.*] we went to Hampton and the captens dyned with M. mayr wher I shold also have byn, but M. Banester 15v

[1] Following this action, 'John Orkeney alias Taylor' wrote to Walsingham to protest against his incarceration as a result of his having been picked up by the *Edward Bonaventure.* Asserting that he had a commission from Dom António as well as the consent of the Duke of Brabant and all the states of Flanders, he complains that the *Edward* had taken his own ship *The Flying Ghost* and his prize, a French ship loaded with salt from Lisbon, and having 'rifeled' both of them 'of all the mens apparrell and other necessaries' had delivered them to the mayor of Southampton who now detains both ships 'intendinge to converte them to his owne use' (SP 12/153/26).

[2] For the chaplain on the *Edward*, see p. 26 above. On 23 Apr. Walker was to write to Leicester to request that since he was 'now somewhat in debt,' he intercede with the Queen to allow him to retain his 'poore lyvyngs' until his return 'from the indyians.' These included the benefice of 'fyllack' in the diocese of Exeter which the Queen had bestowed on him 11 Apr. 1579 (Otho E VIII, 145; *Cal. Salisbury MSS*, Pt. II, p. 249).

[3] For his duties as *registrarius*, see pp. 59–63 above. The term 'registrar' had not yet come into use.

Harry Coker

led me (*cipher*; *Latin*: all boastfully as is his custom) to M. Cottons wher was Harey Coker with others who told that the gallion was not so great as she was taken for, but I after fownd affection in his tawlk. I supt and lay at a vitayling howse after I had walked to Redbrydge and so to Hyth and come back to Hampton.

Winchester

Carleil

21. ♄ [*Sat.*] I walked northward to Wynchester 10 myle. I was told that Capten Carleil upon some discurtesy taken wold not goe which was a great greif unto me but the Lords wil be doen in al things. After I cam to Wynchester I visited fyrst the cathedral church which was St. Swythens Abbey.[1] In yt ther be fayr monuments of Brytayn and Saxon kings. I hosted at the George[2] and after dynner went to the castle wher is now bwylt a howse of correction.[3] The old castle was very strong. In the hawl hangs the rownd table with the picture of king Arthure and 24 other knyghts, Galehawt being next hym and than Launcelot. The table is abowt 18 foot in diameter. The town is waled squar and a mayr town[4] and many old monuments of religiows howses therin.

Lord byshop and M Trippe

22. ⊙ G [*Sun.*] *1. after Ester.* M. Phillpot the Lord marques chaplyn preched.[5] I dyned with my Lord bishop who for because he was an Al Sowl Colledge man made me great chear, so did M. Trip that hath maried his kynswoman and

[1] In the eleventh century the shrine of St Swithun was removed from the Benedictine Priory and placed in the cathedral church. Camden notes that the bishops 'ever and anon' consecrated the church to 'new Patrons and Saints, as to Saint *Amphibalus*, Saint *Peter*, Saint *Swithin*, and last of all to the holy *Trinitie*: by which name it is known to this day.' (See *Victoria County History, Hampshire*, v, 51 and *Britain*, Y6.)

[2] Situated on High Street, it was rebuilt in 1769 (*VCH, Hampshire*, v, 8).

[3] The birthplace of Prince Arthur, the son of Henry VII. In 1578 a house of correction was established, and the government undertook to keep 80 men and women at work in skilled occupations or in learning a craft (*VCH, Hampshire*, v, 9, 424).

[4] I.e., a municipality.

[5] William Paulet, third marquess, had succeeded to his title in 1576; he was both brother-in-law and adversary of Henry Owtread by virtue of the latter's having married his sister, the Lady Elizabeth, widow of Sir William Courtenay, and having been named an executor of the estate of the second marquess. At Paulet's instigation, matters moved from the upper house of parliament to the Star Chamber, and in June Owtread was to complain to Burghley of having attended this cause for seven months to his great charge 'besides the losse of my tyme which to me is precious, as one whose industrie yealdeth supplie to his wantes' (Lansdowne MS. 32, 185 [a copy]; see also SP 12/148/18).

at nyght M. Say.[1] We tawlked of our viage and M. Trip willed me to bring home some good seeds. I walked to St. Crosses[2] half a myle of but [I] was not in the Colledge for that I nether sawe M. warden[3] *nor* any other of myne acqueyntance. Sir Fransis Drake was *at* Hampton and dealing liberawly many ways gave M. Ba*nist*er 50^{s} and 50^{s} more twyxt me, M. Wal*ker* and M. Le*wys* Otmore,[4] but in that also M. Banister made *hym* self a part. Upon ♀ [Fri.] at nyght which I forgote M. *Ha*ukyns cam yn with the barque Fraunsys.

Sir Fransi*s* Drake hi*s* liberali*ty*

23. [☾ *Mon.*] the mariners wer mustered at M. Owtreads wher he made a very good and discreet exhortacion to them.[5] At nyght I *su*pt ther and lay with M. Wil Barnes.[6] I had good tawlk with M. Lewys Otmore and fownd hym a good stowt and sensible man both in his owne profession and otherwyse, althogh other that can do lesse by ther arrogant presumption gette among the ignorant an opinion of greater skyl.

M. sherife

Lewyse Otmore

24. ♂ [*Tues.*] we dyned with the generawl. I supt at the Dolphin[7] with the merchants whether cam Sir Humphrey Gilbert and was offended because they had bowght Luke Wards barque.[8] Ther the asse and the moyle [mule] told us

Sir Humphre Gilbert

[1] John Watson, who had been a Fellow of All Souls in 1540 – and was to leave the College £40 in his will – had become Bishop in 1580. He had a M.D. degree.

Simon Trippe, who had taught logic at Oxford, began 'to exercise his faculty' as a physician in Winchester around 1572 (B.L., Add. MS 6251, 36*v*).

William Saye of All Souls had received his B.C.L. in 1570. He was to become chancellor of Winchester in 1587.

[2] A village one mile south of Winchester, which took its name from the famous hospital there, founded by Henry de Blois, c. 1136.

[3] In 1581 Thomas Bilson of New College had become the first Protestant and first married warden of Winchester College, founded in 1382. He was later to become successively Bishop of Worcester and of Winchester. (See T. F. Kirby, *Annals of Winchester College*, 1892, p. 291.)

[4] Otmore (or Atmore), serving as surgeon on the *Edward*, was to come into conflict with Banister, surgeon on the *Galleon*. See 23, 30 Apr.; 7 May; 28 July.

[5] See Madox's official account, App. I, p. 280 below.

[6] The son of Alderman Barne, Madox commends him on 30 Apr.

[7] Southampton's largest inn, the Dolphin is mentioned in 1570 as having 22 rooms in addition to kitchen, cellar, countinghouse, stables, and other offices. John Sedgwick was at this date innkeeper. (See *The Third Book of Remembrance of Southampton*, ed. A. L. Merson, III, 105.).

[8] In 1579 he was using a 'small bark' called the *Sea Bright* to transport supplies to ships being sent into Ireland (*APC, 1578–80*, p. 303). Ultimately it was decided to sell Ward's bark (or frigate) to Gilbert for £40 and to take the *Elizabeth* as 'apter' for the voyage. (See 1 May and Otho E VIII, f. 115.)

There are also allusions in Nov. 1581 and Jan. 1582 to a ship of Luke Ward's

many a tydiows tale. I lay at M. Deas howse with M. Evans the merchant and bowght a Dansk chest of my host 5^{s}. I also entertayned Evan Johns to be my man[1] and gave hym 19^{s}. //

16r

[25. ☿ *Wed.*] *St. Marks* Eve. I dyned at M. Dees, cam aboord and after that we had apoynted men both for the Fransis and the Elsabeth we went to M. sherif Owtread. Ther supt and lay.

26. ♃ [*Thurs.*] made my bedstid and set yt up and dyd order my stuf in the masters Cabyn with whom I was apoynted to be. We dyned aboord the Edward wher according to the cownsels letter a box sealed with hir majestyes privye seal was wrapped in Okam and put into a chest with 3 locks wherof I receaved one key which is in the til of my lesse chest hanged in a black sylk lace, and an other had Capten Ward, a third M. Owtread had to delyver unto M. Haukins which was not than present.

the cofer with 3 locks

27. ♀ [*Fri.*] the paynter paynted our Cabin. I lay at M. Owtreds and was apoynted on Sonday to prech by Alderman Barns and M. Towrson.

M. Harward

28. ♄ [*Sat.*] I was busy al day. Ther cam to me M. Harward of Corpus Christi Colledge, my Lord of Wynchesters chaplyn by whom I sent my Lord a bysket.[2] Ther was with him the prechers of Hampton and other scholers. After cam M. Barloe[3] of Wynchester and saw our cards etc.

a sermon at our setting furthe

29. ⊙ G [*Sun.*] *2 after Easter.* The cumpany being together I preched in the gallion the yerth is the Lords etc., Psal. 24.[4]

---

being used by Gui de Saint Gelais ('M. Lansac') in the enterprise in behalf of Dom António (letter from Cobham, *CSP*, *Dom.*, *1581–82*, pp. 379, 442).

[1] See n. to 1 May.

[2] William Harwood received his M.A. in 1579 and was elected a Fellow of Corpus Christi. For Bishop Watson, see pp. 116–17 above.

[3] Despite his abhorrence of the sea and diversity of calling (he held ecclesiastical preferment at Winchester at this date), Barlow was interested in the art of navigation (*The Navigators Supply* (1597), A4*v*) and experimented with the lodestone from 1597 on. His *Magnetical Advertisements* was published in 1616.

[4] Apparently a favourite with Madox (see pp. 71, 79 above). He gives a précis of his politic development of the text in his official narrative, App. 1, p. 280 below. 'M. sherif Owtred' commented on his performance to Leicester: 'in the Forenoone before theyr depar*ture M.* Maddoxe your honowres chapleyne made

Ther was our general, al our captens save Drake,[1] M. sherif Owtred, M. mayr of Hampton, Sir Reinolds of our howse[2] with others who dyned after under an yawn [awning] on the barbican deck. I wrot by Sir Reynolds *last letters* to M. Davis and to my brother and to Hary Jacson and sent a fyn bysket to Mrs Hovenden ♃ [Thurs.]. ♃

At 2 a clock we wayd anchor and by 3 wer under sayl and by 4 cam to an anchor betwyxt Cawshot and the mowth of Hamble, M. sherif, M. Barns, M. Towrson, M. Caslyn[3] with others being with us which after went home. In waying we broke a cable. *a cable broke*

30. ☾ [*Mon.*] they cam agayne to us and were al day with us in reconyng and musteryng, and others at nyght, M. Alderman Barns and M. Towrson lying in the generauls cabyn, M. Caslyn with the master, and yong M. William Barns with me who is a very honest yong gentilman and *M. Barns* sober. He gave me a fayr fryngd handkercheffe to remember hym and so I shold althoe I had receved nothing.

M. Banester who because he hath not scholership to do *Banester* anything but greedy // of a vayn popular estimation to be *16v* thowght excelent *or* something cast overburd a curious *Banester taketh awai Mrs Lucars beades* payr of bedes *of* myne which Mrs Lucar gave me to exchange at the Yndyes because he wold appear very zealows, for in matters of lerning a man may be tryed and fownd before men when he vawnteth as I have hytherto sufred hym above measure, but in matters of religion only God can se the hart and therfore some men ar therin over ernest many tymes more for desyre of foolysh speche than otherwyse so that I am abashed to se how he overweeneth hym self in comparison of Lewys Otmore who is both for

---

a goddbye w*ith an* eloquente sermon in the shyppe before 300 people as I [think wher] in trewlye he shewed hime selfe to be a chapleyne worthye *of so ho*nowrable a patroane' (Otho E VIII, f. 122).

[1] The disinclination of John Drake to attend services is underscored by Walker's observation (14 Oct.) that he had killed a porpoise 'at sermon tyme (for we sawe hym take it).' See also Intro., pp. 26–7.

[2] See 27 Jan. and n.

[3] The London merchant and member of the Muscovy Company John Castelyn with others of the adventurers writes to Leicester from Owtread's house on 22 Apr. (Otho E VIII, f. 115).

surgery, for personage, for manhod and for wysdom a great deal beyond hym and for modesty withowt comparison.

(*cipher:* reseved $12^{s}\ 6^{d}$
spent[1] $45^{s}\ 6^{d}$
left 27^{s} //

17r

Maye ♊

1. ♂ [*Tues.*] *May day* M. Alderman Barns, M. Towrson, M. Caslyn and the rest tooke a muster of al our men and fownd them to be more than 200 which was our proportion but because the Elsabeth was bowght for burden sake and the frigot sold for 40^{li} to Sir Humphrey Gilbert therfor for hir supply and that we wer by M. Haukins enformed we shold hav vitayl ynogh at the Yndyes, we tooke in abowt 30 more,* but yet this I marked by the slynking away of some knaves after ther pay that yf yt wer possyble, as I knoe not whether yt be or noe, yt wer not amysse to hyre men by the week or moneth to ryg a ship, not letting them wyt whether, and when al is redy than to put men in wages for the viage, cawsing them to come aboord atonce with al ther necessaries withowt sneaking back to the shore for after errands and when they ar once withowt syght of land to poynt officers and orders and se them kept accordinglye.[2] The general muster of our men in the 4 gyngs [crews], being most taul and stowt

a muster of men

*nota

[1] The last three letters in 'spent' are not in cipher.

[2] Madox's complaint is later echoed by Sir Richard Hawkins (cousin of William) when gathering his company for his voyage to the South Sea (1593), he, his good friends, and justices of the town were forced to search all lodgings, taverns, and ale houses: '(For some would ever be taking their leave and never depart:) some drinke themselves so drunke, that except they were carried aboord, they of themselves were not able to goe one steppe: others knowing the necessitie of the time, fayned themselves sicke; others, to be indebted to their Hostes, and forced me to ransome them; one his Chest; another, his Sword; another, his Shirts; another, his Carde and Instruments for Sea: And others, to benefit themselves of the Imprest given them, absented themselves; making a lewd living in deceiving all, whose money they could lay hold of: which is a scandall too rife amongst our Sea-men.' He concludes by wondering how it is that those in great authority 'have not united their Goodnesses and Wisedomes, to redresse this dis-loyall and base absurditie of the Vulgar' (*Observations*, ed. J. A. Williamson (1933), p. 20).

and al in maner lykly men after that we had refused dyvers hansome feloes that made great sute to have gone with us, was this.[1]

In the admyral cawled the gallion Leycester

Edward Fenton esq.	general
Wylliam Haukyns	leiftenent
Nycholas Parker	capten at land
Richard Madox	minister
Myles Evans Thomas Baynam Mathew Taylbush	merchants
Christofer Hawl	master
John Banester	surgion
Symon Ferdinando Thomas Whod	pilots
Richard Cotton Edward Gilman	travelers
Richard Fayrwether	masters mate

[1] Madox's list appears, also in his hand, in a mutilated form in Otho E VIII, ff. 152–5, with occasional variant names and orthography. For example, in both lists he gives 'Robert L*o*ddyngton' though earlier and later in the Diary the name appears as 'Lyddyngton'; Evan Johns, tailor, whom Madox took as his man on 24 Apr. appears in the Diary as 'Evan James' and in Otho E VIII as 'Ivan Jones.'

This second list has been used to supply portions of names obliterated in Madox's manuscript, and it includes two members of the *Galleon*'s crew whom he omitted, a garbeler (to remove refuse from spices) and a carpenter. Madox also omits William Wylkes, a merchant, expert in 'the dying of popingaye greenes' (Otho E VIII, f. 105*v*), who actually made the voyage, shipping in the *Elizabeth* and then transferring to the *Edward*, and 'M. Boze,' who, following legal difficulties (on 16 May), was left on shore at the Isle of Wight (21 May).

The resulting total of 235 men, including the two nameless drum and fife and the cook of the *Galleon* (also nameless), who may have replaced the one Madox had earlier complained of to Captain Carleill for his 'swering and brabling,' plus the garbeler and carpenter and Wylkes still does not represent the actual group that sailed. On 3 May Wyl Wylshire was put ashore because of illness; on 18 May Thomas Baynam, having 'fawlen into the black jaundyce' departed the voyage; Henry Kirkman, Hawkins's man, was left at Plymouth because of his 'abuses'; and on 6 May Fenton sent home the mayor of Southampton's son. Furthermore, though on 3 May they had pressed a tinker and two carpenters, on 8 May they lost a tinker and a carpenter ashore and, says Madox, 'I knoe not whom els.'

Among the nameless members of the crew, one is to be identified as Gideon Sanders, who, in Feb. 1592, age about 34, deposed that of the hundred voyages he had made in his time 'he had made ten or xii viadges with *let*ters of Reprisall,' and he mentions as the first that 'with Captaine Fenton in the Gallion Lecester' (quoted in K. R. Andrews, *English Privateering Voyages*, pp. 155–6).

	Wat Webbe	pursers	
	Robert Lyddynton		
	Edward Robinson	quarter masters	
	John Lynsey		
	Arthure Cotton		
	Wylliam Frye		
	John Gates	master guner	gunners
	John Gore	masters mate	
	Wylliam Kelly		
	John Brandyce		
	Hugh Bowen		
	John Paynter		
	Robert Okyng		
	Nychol Edmunds		
	Henry Kyrkman		carpenters
	Edward Chenye		
	Wylliam Dobson		
	Thomas Blancher	master carpenter	
	Richard Carpenter	mate	
	[John Marshall]		
	Nycholas Wels		
	John Heath		
17v	Mathew Byrd	botswayn	
	Thomas Body	his mate	
	Symon Wood	musicians	
	Thomas Meeke		
	Richard Clark		
	John Kennar		
	[2]	drum and fyf	
	Christofer Jacson	trump*eters*	
	John Rawlyns		
	Ambrose Harrison		
	Esdras Draper	stewar*ds*	
	Thomas Thomson		
	Robert London	cooks	
	[1]		
	Thomas Kydd	coopers	
	John Ashe		
	Lawncelot Robinson	smeethes	
	Robert Whyte		

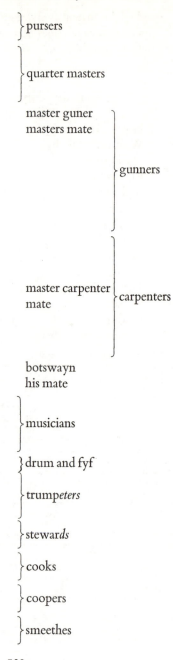

David Evans John Edwards	bakers
John Burden Evan J*ohns*	taylers
John Rawnson Wylliam Rawnson	shomakers
[John Sumerland	Garbeler]
Edward Stokes	platdrawer
Harry Bardsey	Jueller
Nychol Banx	poticary
James Wyn	barber [surgion]
Nychol Butler	distiller

Charles Cæsar
Barth Byston
John Smyth of Hampton
Peter Robinson
John Joanes
John Musgrove
Arthur Rosse
Cyprian Boorman
Roger Parkyns
Richard Bennet
Tege Hues
Gyles Moore
John Hawl
Henry Rising
Denyse Colman
Thomas Belchawn
Opearse Tege
William Field
Zachary Stephens
Robert Hessam
John Wynston
George Gelly
Wylliam Ynglet
Wylliam Foster
Wylliam Gamedge
John Grype
*P*eter Deryckson
Barth Myner

Jasper Norman
Morryce Fydler
John Kent
Water Wood
Roland Peterson
Wylliam Persons
John Legate
Lewys French
John Yngleton
John Bygford
Barth Godchard
Martyn Wylliams
Richard Salt
Henry Mellers
Nychol Collyns
Will Burges
Robert Flynt
Richard Gawyn
Nathaniel Crokey
Wylliam Ceasar
Richard Cove
Morryce Jones
Henry Boorn

John Hurlston	boys
Nych Smyth	
Mathew Fysher	
Moryce Yong	
Valentyn Holt	//

18r In the Edward Bonaventure

Mr Luke Ward	viceadmiral
John Walker	minister
Thomas Persy	master
Samuel Symbarb	traveler
Rondal Shaw	merchants
Peter Jeffreys	
Lewys Otmore	surgion
Thomas Blaccollar	pylot
Tobyas Parris	masters mates
Robert Rosse	

Nycol Chanselor	purser	
John Kyd		quarter masters
Wylliam Duke		
Robert Mawnder		
Wylliam Sherwod		
John Tymberman	master	gunners
John Smyth	mate	
John Johnson		
Robert Seely		
Thomas Dresser		
John Beard		
Nychol Edgerton		
John Maunsfield		
Nychol Allen		carpenters
Wylly Hues		
Robert Barnes		
William Charrol		
Rafe Lorkyn	botswayn	
Wylliam Man	his mate	
Tege Caroe		trumpeters
John Vobs		
Robert Wood		
Davy Lake		dr*um* and fyfe
Robert Pemberton		
John Lyddyn		*st*ewards
Edmund Lytchfild		
Richard Woode		cookes
John Page		
John Rey*nolds*		*coopers*
Thomas Wy*lson*		
Wyllyam Wykers		smethes
John Fawx		
John Whyt	baker	
Edward Davis	shomaker	
Thomas Boze	Jueller	
John Brian	garbeler	
Wylliam Foster	tayler	
Antony Notte	barber	
John Johnson	distiller	
John Pearse		

Robert Pearse
John Hilliard
Wylliam Dee
John Androe
Gryffy Davis
John Wylson
John Read
John Roberts
Thomas Swan
John Fransis
John Austyne
Richard Morryce
John Greene
MarkTowghts
Lawrence Trip
Giles Kyrk
Water Hues
Edmund Driver
Gregory Bool
Water Hooker
Wyllyam Towrson
Launcelot Ashe
Evan Wyn

Georg Brodford	boys
Richard Percy	
Robert Webb	
Georg Robinson	
John Collyns	

In the barque Fraunsis

John Drak	capten
Wylliam Markam	master
John Godfrey	mate
William Reynoles	steward
Thomas Bennet	cooke
John Daniel	guner
Wylliam Hunywel	carpenter
Thomas Myssendyn	surgion
Wylliam Darre	
Thomas Bodnam //	

Christofer Champlyn 18v
Thomas Herdman
George Pyg
Thomas Chater
Thomas Ogard
Robert Brian } boys
Jon Whyt }

In the Elsabeth

Thomas Skevington	capten
Rafe Crane	master
Randall Fox	his mate
[William Wylkes	merchant]
John *Case*	purser
Georg *Cox*	carpenter
Phill *Grene*	guner
Thomas *Martyn*	steward
John Blaccollar	botswayn
Julian Sawnders	[cook]
Sawl Berry	
Richard Shute	
William Wylshire	
Humphrey Bradford	
Peter Owyn	
Edmund Anwyck	
James Robson	

Thus being for the tyme mustered and appoynted til yt shold please our general upon occasion to alter any, abowt 2 a clock we wer under sayle and when we had passed Cawshot and opened the Nyelds, on the syde of the Brambles,[1] M. Alderman, M. Towrson and M. Caslyn took ther leaves with prayer for us and we with weeping eyes comytted them and our selvs to God and so came by the Cows to Yermowth in the nyght, with a fayr east wynd but somwhat lytle wherfor our master fearing lest the wynd *sh*old not bere us thorow dyd ther Anchor, having also in our cumpany the Bridget[2] of M. Owtreads

our owners take leave

Bridget

[1] The 'Needles' were steep chalk stones at the west end of the Isle of Wight; the 'Brambles,' a shoal between Cowes and Calshot Castle.

[2] A vessel of 60 tons (SP 12/156/45).

which was bownd for the Canaries thence to fet. . . . Yt caried away a hulk that he thither sold.

Hampton

Hampton is a gallant cytye seated in the breech of 2 ryvers namelesse, the one fawhing from the norwest throe Red*b*ridge, the other from Wynchester on the northest thro*e* Ytching Ferry.[1] On the sowth is indrawght[2] of the sea and the key. The north only is open to the land, with a rownd castle of old bwylding which was Bevis his Castle.[3] The mayr was M. Byston, a black man whose sone came with us.[4] M. Cotton is controler and M. Smyth customer.[5] Netley Castle is kept by M. Owtread, St. Androes by M. Boyer. Thes stand on the east syde the yndrawght but Cawshot and Hurst[6] be very fayr and strong pyles incompased with the sea safe a smale long croked upcast of beach to come to them. Cawshot is
19r kept by M. Parkinson who hath a fyne sweet boy // to his sone.[7] He dwelleth by Holdbery which is M. Georg Powlets[8] howse, and M. Gorge is capten of Hurst[9] and M.   of Yermowth. In waying this day we broke owr Cathooke but had duble shifte.

19v 2. ☿ [*Wed.*] yn Gods name somwhat tymely we hoysed with a breese of east wynd and a fayr sonshine morning so that

[1] The two rivers are the Test and the Itchin. Madox's 'fawhing' is Salopian (Georgina F. Jackson, *Shropshire Word Book* (1879)).

[2] A term applied to the set of the flood tide in bights and bays along the coast (*Sailing Directions for the Circumnavigation of England*, ed. J. Gairdner (Hakluyt Soc., 1889)).

[3] The 'kynge and knight of great renowne' in popular medieval romance.

[4] Barth Byston is listed as a sailor on the *Galleon* but Fenton on 6 May notes (Taylor, *Fenton*, p. 84) that he sent the 'Maiors sonne of Sowthampton home.' See 19, 29 Apr. for the father's interest in the expedition.

[5] In 1572 the government had leased the collection of customs and import duties in London, an enormously lucrative business, to Thomas Smith, and in 1576 Southampton, Ipswich, and Woodbridge were added to his province. He had become a burgess of Southampton in 1575. (See F. C. Dietz, 'Elizabethan Customs Administration,' *English Hist. Rev.*, XLV (1930), 45–7 and *Letters of the Fifteenth and Sixteenth Centuries*, ed. R. C. Anderson, p. xiii and n.)

[6] Both St Andrews and Hurst Castle had been built by Henry VIII, the latter to guard the western entrance to the Solent.

[7] James Parkinson of Exbury had been keeper of the royal castle at Calshot from 1571 or earlier (*Third Book of Remembrance*, ed. A. L. Merson, III, 115–16) though he was later to be chided for his inadequate care of the site (*Court Leet Records*, edd. F. J. C. and D. M. Hearnshaw (Southampton Rec. Soc. 1905–08), I.i.2, pp. 292, 296).

[8] Younger brother of the third Marquess of Winchester, he was serving as Lieutenant of Jersey in 1579 (*CSP, Dom., Add., 1566–79*, p. 562).

[9] Thomas Gorges was captain of Hurst Castle (*CSP, Dom., 1581–90*, p. 640).

the purposes playd before us by which syghne and by the cawseles workyng and swelling of the sea I dowted fowl wether and indeed when we were thwart the Nields the wynd cam to the sowthwest which caused us to fawl back agayn to Yermowth, wher we supt with Capten Ward aboord the Edward and our general gave to al the ships very necessary instructions for the viage.[1] from Yermowth and back

3. ♃ [*Thurs.*] rayn and rugh wynd. Capten Ward dyned with us. We set Will Wylshire a shore because he was syck and did presse a tynker and 2 carpenters to go with us.

4. ♀ [*Fri.*] fowle and rugh. We tawlked of Yrland and M. Capten Parker concluded that he which cold endure the Yryshe service and pleaz my Lord of Aburgeny myght go for a soldier and a servingman in any place of Yngland.[2] At nyght we sorted our men and I being the 4 person of necessytie must be a larbord man.[3] We cam back agayn to the Cows because the tyde sets rugh at Yermowth. soldier; to the Cows

5. ♄ [*Sat.*] we fel a romeging [arranging] chests and I for example was content to let the musicians have myne cause they wer apoynted 4 to a chest, but I cold se none do so els but my self. chests

6. ☉ G [*Sun.*] *3 after Easter.* Our generaul dyned in the Elsabethe. The master and I walked a shore. He told me how Furbusher delt with hym, very headyly sure, and how that Furbusher was not the mariner he was taken to be as I easyly *be*leave.[4] We supt yn the Elsabeth with the

[1] For the General's instructions, see App. I, pp. 282–84 below.

[2] In 1579 Nicholas Parker served in Ireland as Fenton's lieutenant. For an account of his experience at Kilcolman in that year when set upon by a 'hundred traitors,' see Holinshed's *Chronicles*, II (1587), P5*v*.

Henry Nevill, Lord Bergavenny (d. 1587) was styled 'Sir Henry Nevill, Baron of Abergavenny.'

[3] The custom was, as Sir Richard Hawkins noted, to shift a company into 'Starboord and Larboord men, the halfe to watch and worke whilest the others slept, and take rest' (*Observations*, p. 32.) Madox is commenting on his status as fourth in order on the *Galleon*.

[4] Having served on all three of the Northwest voyages, Christopher Hall had experience of Frobisher's hot temper as well as his navigational errors, both of which are detailed by Michael Lok in his vehement attack on 'The doinges of Captayne Forbisher' (Lansdowne MS 100, ff. 1–15). See also Hall's own narrative, *PN* (1589), pp. 615–22.

Skevington

viceadmyral also, wher Capten Skevington made us good chere but he is a lytle syke of the sextayns evil which thinketh noen in the parysh can chyme the bels lyke hym. Our lieftenent with M. Cotton went to Newport which is 3 myle sowth fro the Cows whether ther runeth a fyne ryver.[1]

7. ☾ [*Mon.*] very fayr and hote but wynd stil sowth west. M. Brown and M. Baker prechers with the baylys of Newport[2] cam to us. M. Banester (*Latin*: hunting for the votes of the most vain masses with dinner expenses and gifts of worn-out clothing) had drawn owt a sheet of paper for to be set on the mayn mast with prayers for morning and evening and sygnes to knoe when they shold be syck which besyde yt was unmeasurably beyond al modesty, the conceyt was also so grosse that yf a mans head had but Aked he wold put them in fear of the frensy, the pestilent

20r

Banester

fever, // the palsey, the pocks, the plage, the scurby, the bubo[3] and such lyke beastly stuffe, which he browght to me to correct as he sayd, but when I had altered some and stryken owt other some he cold not endure to have yt soe and therfore when I see that I plade as in Arte Poetica.[4] He told me thus: *yonder surgion in the other ship althoe he speak mee faire yet I knoe he loveth mee not for he is verie vaine gloriows and hopeth that I will die that hee may take my place, but now sir he hathe noe skil in physique, and therfore I wil send hym this copie and he shal paie one of my men 12^{d} for writing of yt*, wher indeed the other is a good modest feloe and hath more lerning than John Banesters farwel to Notting*ham*. Now sir the sport was that whylst I stood in a studye being wery of his taulk and thowght in my self, surely this is a very vaynglориows asse, he clapt me on the sholder and sayd, yt is true man.

a hawkes pearche M. Parker

M. Parker lykened a servingman that caried a hauk abowt but had no other good qualytie unto a haukes pearch. He is a very honest and curteows gentilman and

[1] I.e., Lieutenant Hawkins and Richard Cotton, traveller. The 'fyne ryver' is the Medina.

[2] M. Iles 'ther new chosen baylyffe' (Walker's Diary).

[3] A swelling in the groin or armpits.

[4] Quintilius, who refused to expend any further words or effort on an author who refused to emend (*A.P.*, 438–40).

lyberawl mynded and one that thinketh modestly of *h*ym self.[1]

8. ♂ [*Tues.*] the wynd cam up to the est but breesed abowt with great uncertaynty. Notwithstanding we cold have wayd betymes but our men were a shore, some drunk and some in dette. Hear lost we agayn our tynker and a carpenter and I knoe not whom els, so that I muse why the masters that with such feloes have so oft byn synged wil suffer any to go ashore.

M. William Haukyns kept lyberawl chere for al saylers in Newport. Yt cost hym 20 nobles very nye, because of good mynde he wold have had our men to have saved ther own money, but al wold not bee. (*cipher*: M. Cotton left 20^s to pay whyl he wold also hav bin cownted prodigayl.) M. Hawkins (*cipher*: M. Cotton)

We hard that the , M. Owtreads ship[2] which he sent to the Yles of Pyckery had geven such a salt to a Frenchman as made hir beshrew hir own self, so that now she lay wonded at Dartmowth. reward of piking

9. ☿ [*Wed.*] we lay stil at Yermowth. M. Whood and M. Blacollar our pylates cam and sayd they wer chased by pyrates. // pilots

10. ♃ [*Thurs.*] M. Capten Parker and I wer aboord the Edward wher Banester with his Robynhood rymes made us good sport. M. Lewys gave me a box of marmylad. We wayd and cam up agayn to the Cows and in waying the larbord cat[3] broke and strok down Cyprian Boorman ynto the water but God be thanked he was recovered withowt any great hurt but had not Gods favowr stood between, that hap myght have slayn 20 men. Lykewyse one May day waying, the starburd cathook brake. 20^v M. Lewis the cat broke

11. ♀ [*Fri.*] the wynd was lowd at the sowth with rayn. We had a generaul communion. Capten Skevington told the generall that Rafe Crane[4] wold not go to the Edward to

[1] This view of Parker is to be altered drastically in the course of the voyage.

[2] In addition to the *Galleon*, Henry Owtread is listed in a paper of 1582 as owning three other ships above 100 tons – the *Henry*, the *Susan*, and the *Elizabeth* (SP 12/156/45).

[3] Device to haul up the anchor.

[4] Master of the *Elizabeth*; for a subsequent 'trial' before the Assistants, see 12, 13 Aug.

receave because of the viceadmyral, wherfore I was sent to perswade hym but when I came thither I fownd that al was nothing els but only the fydle fadle superfynes of Capten Skevington Skevingtons curiosytye. I had Reynoldus Tables of Tobias to correct wher in some places they were false printed.[1]

12. ♄ [*Sat.*] the wynd began to groe toward the westnorthwest but yt heald not.

13. ☉ G [*Sun.*] *4 after Easter.* M. Smyth was aboord us and M. Homes M. Homes[2] of Hampton sent us a hogshead of Claret. M. Capten Ward supt not with us and M. Banester and I had almost fawlen owt reasonyng *de pinquedine*, I saying that the overfatting of any thing cam by cold and he by heate.

14. ☾ [*Mon.*] I went aboord the Edward and fro thence went Newporte with M. Walk*er*, M. Le*w*ys, and M. Tobias to Newport. We dyned and lay at M. Creswels of the Bel who made unto us many a substancial lye. He is M. Symberbs[3] cozyn. After wer we so encumbred with shorehaunters that aboord we cold not get al nyght. M. Walker told mee how *h*is wyfe and he wer parted by consent althoe not dyvorsed. Walker (*cipher*: He told me of many that he had ocupid.)[4]

15. ♂ [*Tues.*] I gote up betymes and gote them ashore for we spent Tobias money. M. Reynolds[5] and M. Caplet Homes browght us an other hogshead of wyne from M. Homes. They told me that M. Cooke of Brazenose and M. Brown procters of Christchurch were procters and that Lycens of New Colledge had lost yt wherby I perceave the canvase of Protestants prevayleth.[6]

[1] Tobias Parris, master's mate on the *Edward*; the 'tables' were probably *Ephemerides trium annorum 58, 59, 60 ex E. Reinholdi tabellis* (1558), see Taylor, *Fenton*, p. 161, n.

[2] Thomas Holmes, listed as a searcher in 1574 (Lansdowne MS 18, f. 139), lived in Holyrood Ward and was to serve as mayor (*The Third Book of Remembrance*, ed. A. L. Merson, III, 18 n. and *The Assembly Books*, ed. J. W. Horrocks, II, 25 n.). See also entry for 15 May.

[3] Samuel Symbarb, traveller on the *Edward*.

[4] As Doll Tearsheet observes, the word 'occupy,' which was an excellent good word before it was ill-sorted, had now become odious. See 28 June for Madox's jocular comment to Ward on his fellow chaplain's sexual proclivities.

[5] John Reynolds was servant to the searcher Thomas Holmes (n. 2 above). See also 20 May.

[6] Both Robert Cooke of Brasenose and John Browne of Christ Church had received their M.A.'s in 1577.

Thomas Lycens (Leyson) had received his M.A. the preceding year; he was to

Sir Edward Horsey[1] having complayned to our generawl that the King of Portingales ship which lay at Meedhole was lykly to be stolen away by the knaves in // hir whom Peryn ther master cold not ru*le* requested us to fet hir nyer, which we dyd so that she gave at hir comyng a gallant volley of shot for an homage. We hard that Capten Lawndrey [and] the French[2] had taken St. Mychaels, one of the Azores in behalf of the King of Portingal. Horsei 21r news

16. ☿ [*Wed.*] we al dyned and supped aboord the Elsabeth wher Capten Skevington bade us as great welcom as that lytle hart cold any wyse conceave, so that Walker sayd, curiows feloes wer good yf yt wer for nothing but to make cheere. Luk Ward and Lewes and Walker and I were on the shore (*cipher*: we puld down 4 gats.) Skevington (*cipher*: knavery)

M. Colman who was M. Wolleys man cam with a broad seal to stay M. Boze tuching some conveance of Land made amysse to Sir William Pellam.[3] The cumpany in the Edward was glad to be ryd of so grosse a man and so great a chest. M. Colman told me that Sir William Pellam wold prefer hym to be my Lord Chauncelors secretary and therfor I wrot by hym to M. Screven,[4] but I hear that the feloe indeed can do very wel but is mervelows neglygent and bold. Boze Colman

---

take his B. Med. in 1583, the year in which he succeeded in being elected Proctor, and went on to practice in Bath, where, according to Wood, he was as 'noted for his happy success in the practice of physic, as before he was for his Latin poetry in the university' (*Athen. Oxon.*, II, 27–8). New College was conspicuous for the number of its students who fled to Douai.

'Canvase' refers to the soliciting of votes before an election – contrary to the statutes.

[1] Captain of the Isle of Wight from 1565 until his death in 1583.

[2] Apparently a reference to Captain de l'Andereau who had embarked in May for the Azores with 600 fighting men (*CSP, For., 1582*, pp. 91–2).

[3] Morgan Colman had served as secretary in 1579–80 to Sir William Pelham, Lord Justice of Ireland (*Cal. Carew MSS, 1575–88*, p. 396); he was now apparently in the service of John Wooley, Latin secretary to the Queen, who was ultimately to become a member of the Privy Council in 1586 (*CSP, Dom., 1581–90*, p. 364).

For M. Boze's exclusion from the voyage, see 21 May.

[4] Sir William Pelham's daughter Elizabeth married Henry Bromley, the eldest son of the Lord Chancellor, and so he may be presumed to have had influence with him.

This passage suggests that Reginald Scriven (see 6, 10 Feb.) was at this time in the Lord Chancellor's service.

Haukins
News

17. ♃ [*Thurs.*] M. Haukins of Plymmowth ryding to London cam to us.[1] He told that the King of Spayn had sent 8 ships to the Moluccas and 5 were cast away on the cost of Barbarye.[2]

saile

The wynd straglyng abowt the east, we set sayl from the Cowse at 2 a clock and 30 mynuts in thafter noone, but yt was so weak that we cold not stem the tyde, yet when the eb cam we fel down to Yermowth and ther anchored – the 4th tyme.

Comet
Bainam
21v

18. ♀ [*Fri.*] we hoysed our boat aboord very tymely. Ther was a smal comete which I sawe 8 days ago in the brest of Erycthonius,[3] but I cold never see yt more than one nyght to judge of his way. M. Baynam the merchant which had been long syck of an ague and was fawlen into the black jaundyce, now despayring of his health returned agayn. // When *the* wynde contrary to our hope began to blow rughly at the sowth we retyred back agayn and cam to the Cows but the vyceadmiral rode yt owt at Yermowth.

Skevington
Bilboes

19. ♄ [*Sat.*] Capten Skevington made a pyttiful complaynt to our generawl of Julian Sawnders his cooke that had geven hym the lye, so that the pore feloe was put into the bilboes, he being the fyrst upon whom any punyshment was shewd for hytherto not so much as a boy felt any correction more than my Lord Awmes, and John Hawlle whom the master combd over for losyng his sownding lead at Hurst Castle when we fyrst went owt. And Captain Skevington was the fyrst that sowght to bring anye quarel to the ripping up, so that dyvers of our saylers were much offended and sayd, set a begger on horsbacke and he wyl ryde unreasonablye.[4]

[1] I.e., William Hawkins the Elder, father of Lieutenant Hawkins.

[2] As Leonardo de Argensola reported from intelligence picked up in 1580, the Spaniards had the 'Design of Usurping the *Molucco* Islands with all their Strength, and to render themselves Invincible Masters of the Spice' (*The Discovery and Conquest of the Molucco and Philipine Islands* (London, 1708), p. 88).

[3] Camden refers to a comet or blazing star that appeared in May with 'a radiant taile streaming above and beyond the right shoulder of Ericthonius' (*Annales* (1635), V6*v*), a constellation in the northern hemisphere more commonly known as 'Auriga,' the 'Waggoner' or 'Carter.' Stow (*Annales* (1600), 4H1*v*) dates its appearance on 15 May.

[4] See M. P. Tilley, *A Dictionary of the Proverbs in England* (1950), B238, where the earliest example is dated 1576.

20. ☉ G [*Sun.*] *after Easter* 5. Ther cam overnyght 2 sayles wherof one caried the Spaynish imbassador Antonio de Castilio,[1] the other was the bark Bur.[2] They both laded corne to Spayn and because they cam prowdly in our loofe and wold nether stryke flag nor top, our master went with comyssion to the Unitye of London[3] wher the Embassador was and fet away Thomas Cleye the carpenter, but Stephen Muns of Lee ther papisticaul master cam with the ymbassadors man to have hym released and shewd us ther passport for hym self and al his company, but we answered that this belonged to the company of Spayniards and no more. We did also sharply rebuke Muns the master for his unloyal pryde and because he went abowt to discorage some of our men from the viage. Antonio de Castilio

Wee dyned in the Frances with Capten Drake wher we had good chere and good frendly welcom withowt curiosyty of words. At 12 the east wynd began to fresh up which caused us to way upon the eb, but before we wer passed a lege yt faynted and we wer fayn to cast Anchor. John Drake

I wrote to M. William Barns of the drye melch lowing Cows and of M. Banesters anotomy of an eg shel and how we spent the day *and* wrot to M. Reynolds to whom M. Banester sent a poticary bil for M. Homes that such physique *sh*old bring a man from *magnificat* to *nunc dimittis*.[4] // My Lord Foster being a lytle dronk went up to the mayn top to fet down a rebel and 20 at the least after hym, wher they gave hym a cobkey[5] upon the cap of the mayn-mast. letters 22r

[1] António de Castilio, who as Portuguese ambassador had taken his leave of the Queen on 24 Feb., then attached himself to Sir Francis Walsingham; preparatory to sailing in Apr., he bade him goodbye with the wish that he might be 'an instrument in a fine enterprise, edifying to this kingdom and all Christendom.' He was to visit Sir Francis Drake at the end of May to settle a suit on behalf of a fellow Portuguese, his happy reception, as he reports to Walsingham, indicating the importance of his being recognized as in his service. See *CSP, Sp., 1580–86*, p. 303; *CSP, Dom., Add., 1580–1625*, p. 57; and *CSP, For., 1582*, p. 49.

[2] The *Bark Burr*, listed in 1582 as of 120 tons, belonged to the London merchants John Newton and John Bird (SP 12/156/45; *PN* (1589), pp. 818–19).

[3] The *Unity of London* perhaps belonged to the London merchant William Hollidayes; it is mentioned in a deposition in 1592. (See Andrews, *English Privateering Voyages*, pp. 165, nn. and 154–55).

[4] I.e., from a hymn of praise to a song of dismissal: Luke 1: 46–55 and 2: 29–32.

[5] I.e., the mariner William Foster, apparently acting as Lord of Misrule.

'Cobkey' (as well as 'cobkin' and 'cobbing') refers to punishment meted out with a stick (Monson's *Naval Tracts*, IV, 200–1 and n.). Citing Madox's use as

fælix auspicium itineris

M. Boze a luckless man

21. ☾ [*Mon.*] before the change the wynd was wel harted at E. northeast so that we set sayl a quarter before 8 in the mornyng upon the half flud, and we tooke a lyer accordyng to the order,[1] for he that telleth the fyrst lye on a ☾ [Mon.] must se mustard made and the ship swept al the week after. When we wer come to Hurst Castle the Elsabeth being behind shot of a peece and stroke sayle which put us in a dowtful mervel, but when we had stayd yt was M. Boze was now come agayn and desyred the pynysse to stay for his chest which was comyng to Yermowth by water, but our general wold suffer noe stay wherfore he was set on shore in the Wyght and when he was ther he cried unto the botsging to take pytty on hym and to take hym back withowt his chest but they refused. Good Lord, the man that had even with very ydlenes spent more than wold set furth 2 of thes viages doth now desyre to have a bad rowme hearin and can not be herd. See what it is to be good for nothing. Wel because we had no chasing [driving] wynd to stem the tyde we lay a hul at an anchor athwart Purbeck al the flud.

22. ♂ [*Tues.*] The next ebbe we cam down to Lulworthe and ther rode yt owt and the next as far as Abbotsebury. The wether was very fayr but in maner noe wynd styrring but small changeable breezes from every quarter.

23. ☿ [*Wed.*] morning we fownd our selves afront Lyme and the next tyde afront Exmowth.

24. ♃ [*Thurs.*] *Ascension* we wayd Anchor in hope to have wethered the Stert but when we cold not (the wynd being ful west) we turned to Dartmowth and rod in the Range at 15 fadome almost a . . . myle fro shore. Hear we sent
22v our boat to furnysh our watering. // (*cipher*: The master told me that had he supposed the viag wowld have turned to pilfering which now he suspected he wowld not hav undertaken it.)

---

well as an example 'cobty' from 1626, the *OED* states one of the two forms must be erroneous; it is clearly the latter.

[1] The 'liar' was to keep the ship without board clean, including the beakhead, performing the task for a week; 'the order' was that the one 'first taken with a lie upon a Monday morning' was proclaimed at the main mast with a general cry 'A liar, a liar, a liar' (Monson's *Naval Tracts*, IV, 60).

At supper we tawlked of tatlers and cownted Hearle that betrayd Madder but a knave[1] as is Nychols the Jesuyt[2] and (*cipher*: Bodnam of the holy hows in Spayn no better for he sendeth letters to the cownsel).[3] We taulked of Richard

Hearle

(*cipher*: Bodnam)

[1] Induced in part by the Spanish ambassador and his secretary, Edmund Mather had plotted in 1572 to liberate the Duke of Norfolk and to assassinate the Queen and Lord Burghley. On 14 Feb. 1572 he was 'hanged, boweled, and quartered' for conspiracy, a conspiracy, as Burghley noted in his 'Memoria Mortuorum,' 'discovered by William Herle.' (See Stow, *Annales* (1592), 4F4*v*–4F5; Murdin, *Collection of State Papers* . . . , II, 194–210; and 26 Mar. and n.)

From Jan. 1571, if not earlier, when in a letter (from the Marshalsea) to the Lord Keeper Bacon, Hearle refers to a 'sormyce' that will be of importance to the Queen, 'without charge to anie,' he seems to have earned his livelihood as a gatherer of intelligence for a number of people, especially Burghley, whom he hails on one occasion as his only patron and refuge. His correspondents included Leicester, who desired him not to come to court too often but whom he accompanied to Antwerp in Feb. of this year, Sir Edward Horsey, and Philip Sidney. His reports allude to Frobisher's being enticed to Spain in 1572, to Captain Ward's forbearing to speak with him after the Mather affair, and, in Mar. 1581, to Sir Francis Drake's proceeding in a second voyage well furnished and well countenanced, and the following month he writes to Leicester that he is most desirous, 'yf your L. so vouchesave,' to make that journey with him. (See SP 12/77/1; 12/86/36; 12/148/13, 55; 12/149/70, 71; T. Wright, *Queen Elizabeth and her Times*, I (1838), 471–5.)

[2] A religious chameleon, John Nicholls, having attended Oxford without taking a degree, became a curate in Somerset. In 1577 he went abroad, first to Douai and then to Rome where he publicly abjured Protestantism, preaching before the pope and the cardinals. Returning to England two years later, he was arrested and imprisoned in the Tower; again he publicly recanted and preached, this time, according to Robert Parsons, before the imprisoned priests and a 'large crowd of courtiers assembled to grace the comedy.' Parson comments that 'this fellow is everywhere talked of in terms of the highest praise. He is held . . . a Theologian, a Philosopher, a scholar of Greek, Hebrew, Chaldæan, most skilled in all languages and sciences,' and in May 1581 the Privy Council urged the bishops to contribute 'some convenient porcion of monie' to supply his wants for apparel, sustenance and continuance of study until an ecclesiastical living became available.

Following the execution of Campion, Briant, and Sherwin, Nicholls was once more moved to confess his error to his Catholic friends, minded this time never to ascend into a pulpit again but to become a schoolmaster. At the end of 1582, however, he was to flee to the continent where, following his imprisonment in Rouen, he again re-affirmed Catholicism. (See *DNB*; *Letters and Memorials*, I, 85; *APC, 1581–82*, p. 40; William Cardinal Allen, *A Briefe Historie of the Glorious Martyrdom of Twelve Reverent Priests*, ed. J. H. Pollen (1908), p. 75.)

[3] Originally a merchant of Bristol, Roger Bodenham became a resident of Seville where he engaged in extensive trading ventures. In 1564 he made a voyage to San Juan de Ulua to recover his fortunes, having obtained the favour of the Spanish merchants by virtue of his 'long abode, and marriage in the Countrey.' In 1577 the Privy Council recommended him as governor of the new society of Spanish merchants trafficking to Spain. In turn, he provided the Privy Council with useful information, writing Burghley in June 1581 of the preparation of men and ships 'to the number of 16/ or 20 sayle and 3000 men' who were to go to the Strait of Magellan by way of the Azores. In Jan. 1582 he wrote to Walsingham of the departure of the fleet to the number of 16 or 17 sail and of their intent to water in Brazil. Significantly, the bearer was 'Christofell Halle.' (See *PN* (1589), p. 522; *APC, 1575–77*, p. 354; Lansdowne MS 32, ff. 141–2; *CSP, For., 1581–82*, p. 449).

On 27 Feb. 1593, aged eighty years and more, he applied to the Court of the

Grafton

Grafton of whom yt was spoken *una voce* that he was a cosonyng merchant and yt was fear*ed* lest he had doen much hurt in our provision for he had bowght green billet, which sweating and working in the close hold did heat al the hold wonderfullye.

25. ♀ [*Fri.*] the wynd being at the west we lay stil in the range northeast from the Start and sowthwest from the rock and sowtheast and by east from the castle: sending our men a shore to mend our boat, at nyght Blancher and his felo carpenters wer missing and whils the rest sowght for them they wer al taken by the watch and layd up. Nether wold M. the mayr delyver them til our general wrot to hym. I wold al harboroes wold hunt aboord thes shore-haunters soe.

the maire of Dartmowth

26. ♄ [*Sat.*] M. Capten Skevington having browght the newes of this matter, who never lyghtly cometh withowt some complaynt, our general sent the master with a letter and M. Haukins also went to whom the mayr delyvered the men, but hear was one Nycholas, mariner, a bankrowt cookhold, which being dronk had made comparisons in the superlative degre and so catcht a box in the posytive, wherfore he was browght a boord and clapt in the bilboes wher had yt not been for Olyfer Knox of Melchom which intreated for hym he might have smarted. At mydnyght M. Hoode cam from Plymmowth and browght me commendations from Sir Fraunces Drake. He browght also some ropes wherof dyvers complayned that we did want but spetiall Ferdinando.[1] He told lykewyse a great wonder that a horse bot his wyfe by the sholder[2] and that the barque Hastings was bownd presently for Brasyle.[3]

a drunken brawle

Ropes

Merchant Taylors as a 'very auncient Brother' and asked for 'some comiseracion of his povertie and neede,' whereupon the Court, recalling he had been 'a Spanishe Merchaunt of great habilitie and state' and considering 'what he was presentlie brought unto,' granted him £5 (M.T. Court Rec., III, 267*v*).

[1] As Madox noted in his 'Booke' (App. I, p. 279 below), 'all other necessaryes as they sayd myght be boroed by the waye, but as for ropes, a man wold not impart them to his own father at the sea.'

[2] Madox again deridingly recalls this remark on 10 July.

[3] The *Bark Hastings*, belonging to Sir Francis Drake, was originally intended for this voyage, Otho E VIII, f. 85).

Many chests were staved [stowed in the hold] and we cam to Torbaye. //

27. ☉ G [*Sun.*] *after Easter 6* Rob Lyddington was sent to Plymmowth for 2 cables but he had a sweet day, for yt rayned pel mel and blew hilter skilter. 23r cables

*Tor*bay as I suppose hath his name of a great work which standeth lyke a towr in the sea at the north of yt[1] and yt is a fayr bay open to the eastnortheast. Torbaie

28. ☾ [*Mon.*] ther cam an Yrysh man of my Lord of Bedfords with a king Harry face[2] both to us and to the Edward and so freely took his drink that he was *slung* down into the skyf. John Case[3] desyred me to be his frend to ryd hym owt of the Elsabeth for Capten Skevington was so curiows that noe man can yndure hym. a beast slinged

29. ♂ [*Tues.*] I took a purgation but yt wroght not with me and therfor I mean to take no more unlesse I have the better physicions.

Frye[4] was set in the bilboes for lying a shore (*cipher:* which was il taken. The master towld me Alderman Barnes thowght our generaul but a folish flattering fretting creeper and so I fear he wil prov.) (*cipher*: generaul)

30. ☿ [*Wed.*] we lay stil in Torbay and dyd nothing.

31. ♃ [*Thurs.*] Capten Ward was aboord us and had a cobkey, and he catcht our lord and caried hym home and hanged hym on the shrowds so had we good sport. Capten Hawkins went to Plymmothe. I wrot by hym to sir Frances (*cipher*: and wold have gon also but our governowr wold not permit, becaus he feareth lest any wis comendashon shold go to Sir Fraunsis.)

At nyght the wynd feared [veered] to the nornorthwest so that we set sayle and by morning had gote past the Stert. //

[1] Torbay is located between Hope's Nose and Berry Head.

[2] Perhaps derived from the 'Harry groat,' coined by Henry VIII and bearing a depiction of the king with a long face and long hair.

[3] Purser of the *Elizabeth*.

[4] William Freye, quartermaster on the *Galleon*.

23^v

June ♋

[*1.*] ♀ [*Fri.*] when some wold willingly have goen to Plymmowth, some, as namely M. Whood, desyred that at least the Frances myght turne in thither and fet M. Hawkins, the generawl wold not in any case suffer yt, which made men thynk that he wold more gladly have goen withowt hym than to have had his cumpany that M. *P*arker myght have been leiftenent. Wherupon great stoma*c*k was taken as the effect did declare, but the wynd fawlyng to the west sowthwest cawsed us in despyte to go to Plymmowth, wher we anchored in the sownd which is a very fayr place.

a jarre begune

Plimmowth

Plymowth stands in the breech of 2 fayr ryvers,[1] for yt hath Cat Water on the east syde, and Saltash Water on the west, and ech of them yeld harboroe for 200 great ships to come furth of the harboro comodiowsly with any wynd. M. Walker and I went thither purposing to have walked only, but M. leiftenent which was now come from Sir Fraunces Drake at Bucland[2] had us to M. Whoodes howse wher we supt with M. Whyticars *that* hath maried M. Hawkins syster,[3] and after we returned to the Edward wher we discoursed with the *vice*admirall of many mens maners and many matters, *ad*vising how love myght best be maynteyned and good o*rd*er kept, but wher overweening pevishnes is once *pl*anted, and myxed with a kynd of creeping dissimulation, yt is hard ther to setle the seeds of any good advice, for now beginneth the hydden poyson to breth owt.

Whil M. Hawkins supposed that consydering Sir Frances Drakes bownty to the whole cumpany and his

[1] The Plym and the Tamar.

[2] In 1581, Drake had purchased Buckland Abbey from Sir Richard Grenvile, albeit indirectly, for £3400 (Eliott-Drake, *The Family and Heirs of Sir Francis Drake*, I, 54).

[3] Henry Whitaker, who had married Judith Hawkins, was Receiver for Plymouth in 1581–2 (Hasted's *History of Kent*, ed. H. H. Drake, Pt. I (1886), p. xxi and *Cal. of the Plymouth Municipal Records*, ed. R. N. Worth (1893), p. 124).

For a report of the scandalous conversation that ensued that evening, see 12 Sept.

endevowr in this viage, yt had been a poynt of curtesy to have doen Sir Francis that honowr as to have come to Plymmowth. M. Fenton on the other syde fownd smal musique on this string, because he supposed that what water cam to M. Hawkins myl was lost from his owne, and besydes also, I knoe not how, he had as leif go by sir Frances howse thirsty as cawl and drink. Whether he lacked money or noe I can not tel, and yet Luk Ward told *nota*
me he boroed 20^{li} of Sir Edward Horsey at the Cows, and 10^{li} of Sir Frances hear, and had withowt any advice of one or other sent a bil of a C^{li} to London, which I ymagin wil be yl welcom, for alderman Barnes befor hand did beseech hym to tak head therof. //

2. ♄ [*Sat.*] In the morning the wynd at northwest, the generall 24^r
wold needs begon, althoe Sir Frances [did] send us word
that this morning he wold se us. The master desyred that the yssue of a
he myght send the pynnyse ashore for the leiftenent and bad grownde
the pilat and others but the general wold not agree, yet did the master send yt. Yn mean season the generaul comanding to wey anchors, the mariners utterly refused, saying that they ventured for the thirds[1] and wold not therfore go withowt the pilats. The general hearat storming, the master bad them way and after he wold ply for ther comyng, so did they. This whyl I was in the Edward. Wel away went the gallion and the Edward after and the Frances was under sayl, but abowt noone Capten Ward and I went to the gallion wher we fownd them in a great murmuring for that some thowght the Frances upon this discurtesy wold stay behynd. Then dyd we enter in to a close consultation (for every impudent boy leaned over our sholders) whether yt wer better hold on our cowrse or turn yn agayn. When the master had desyred to go back, the generaul blamed hym for sending back the boat and sayd that what if you lead me back againe to reise a mutinie ageinst mee. Thes words the master took yl and sayd, yf yt be com to this for my good wil, wold I wer a

[1] It was proposed to divide the profits that accrued after charges had been deducted into three parts: two parts to be allowed to the adventurers and the third part to be allotted to wages and allowances for the captains, factors, masters, and mariners (*CSP*, *Col.*, *East Indies*, *1513–1616*, p. 72).

shore agayn. Some aledged the want of a gret meyny of men, but the gener*al* sayd he wold to Famowth and take us a*s* many *a*s were left. Now al the quarel hearhence did spring that M. Whood and Blaccollar, the 2 pilats, sayd they wold not return til they knew how they shold be used. When every man pel mel and spent his mowth with as smal discretion for hym self as attendance for the hearer, Capten Ward at last sayd that althoe our lat speed hytherto and the fayr wynd presently dyd wysh hast and althoe yt had been reason thes men shold have attende*d* us and not wee them, for on thes 3 poynts the gen*er*al stood, yet becawse they wer al comended by the cowncel, and because we myght have more wynd but now cold have noe more men, he wyshed us to stand back, so did we, and when we had stood *to* the eastward 2 howrs, the Frances was come // but thorow a quarel risen at Plymowth Henry Kyrkman was left behinde for the leftenent had receved abuses by hym.[1] The general took yt il and espetially M. Parker but some thowght us wel quyt of a pykthank [talebearer]. To cowncel[2] agayn wher we cauld and now was every man affrayd of other and those that wold have eaten the backsyde of mowntayns wold not now byte the fore part of a molehil. After muche adoe we were al frends and so knyt up. (*cipher*: In this discowrs I noted the generaul colorik[3] and bas, joined with some craft, M. Haukins open and glori*os*[4] but very childis*h*, M. Parker fine and folis*h* and lordly conseeted, Capten Ward a good rownd wis felo, M. Whood hob glorios.)

24[v]

Henry Kirkman left behinde

(*Cipher*: *vide*)

We had a fayr wynd and abowt xi a clock at nyght wer thwart the Lysard and by morning as far as Ushant,[5] holding our cowrse west sowthwest.

3. Whitsondaye we held on our cowrse sowthsowest and had a fayr north wynd and cold wether so that we

[1] After his return to England, Hawkins noted that because he left Kirkman behind 'for querrelling,' he had not from that time any good countenance (Otho E VIII, f. 224). Kirkman had sailed on Frobisher's voyages and appears among the 'Gentlemen and Souldiers' of the intending colonists (SP 12/123/50 and *Three Voyages of Martin Frobisher*, ed. V. Stefansson, II (1938), 220).

[2] For his official account, see App. I, pp. 284–86 below.

[3] This is the same term Owtread had used in reference to Fenton in his letter of 17 Mar. to Leicester (Otho E VIII, f. 127).

[4] Madox inverts the symbol for *o*.

[5] An island off the tip of Brittany.

4. ran 30 leags, on ☾ [Mon.] 40, on ♂ [Tues.] 30, on
5. ☿ [Wed.] 30 and I think on ♃ [Thurs.] we wer thwart Cape
6. Fenester, but far to the west of yt, for the pole was
7. 46 degres.[1]

Dyvers of our men wer syck and M. Banester had nether skil nor medycine so that I wold advice such as shal note for surgerie hearafter apoynt such a viag to prepare good provision of holsom cumforts and ordynary salves and let them ly in the hands of some honest merchant and let the surgion be prepared to use the salve when need is and some good clean cooke to mynister the other cherishings and so shal x^{li} go further and do more good than a C^{li} in such wyse as owr money is bestoed. All this whyl I was seasike, and no mervel having changed at once both ayr, exercyse and diet. Rumatique I *was* and exceding costyve, and trobled with hartburning which be *a*ppendixes of the sea, wherfore I cold advice hym that is to appoynt such a viag that he have of violet flowrs, borage flowrs, rosemary flowrs, and such lyke which he may gether in Yngland, caphers made to cumfort hym, and barberis sed, and rosemary and tyme to make a lytle broth in a yerthen pipkin. Thes things ar lesse costly but far more holsom than al the suckets and paltry confections. //

8. ♀ [*Fri.*] we held on our way. The wether was al this space 25^r myld and somwhat clowdy and a resonable gale of northwynd.

9. ♄ [*Sat.*] Athwart the Burlings[2] we had espied a sayle which our men sayd was a French man of war but al was to have a A Flemming quarel to his goodes. M. Capten Parker both because he had mynd to the booty and because he wold pleaz the people wold needs have capten Ward to fet hym yn which he dyd but he was a Flemmysh hulk [merchantman] so that thorow my words hear and M. Walkers in the Edward the man had no hurt at all.[3]

10. *Trinyty Sonday* I took occasion at service to speak ageinst ther attempt the day before but they wer al withowt

[1] This headland of Galicia, Spain, is in 42° 51′ N.

[2] Rocks off the coast of Portugal. Now Berlenga I.

[3] Walker reports they again heard news of the Spanish preparations: 'ix ships to go to the Yndies and 11 to the Strayghtes of Brasyl.' See 17 May above.

pytty set upon the spoyl. After noone Capten Ward and M. Walker cam to us and told how greedy they wer and espetially M. Banester who for al his creping ypocrysy was more ravenowsly set upon the pray than any the most beggerly felo in the ship, and those also which at the shore dyd cownterfet most holynes wer now furthest from reason affyrming that we cold not do God better service than to spoyl the Spaniard both of lyfe and goodes, but *in*deed under color of religion al ther shot is at the mens mony.

ypocrysy

11. ☾ [*Mon.*] *St. Barnabyes day* the carpenters boy having stoln a shirt was hoysed to the yerd arme to have been ducked, but I begd his pardon. I shewd them that because we caried felonyows harts, therfore God sent us felons among our selves, as in the XI of Wysdom.

*p*unyshment

12. ♂ [*Tues.*] we kept our cowrse due sowth stil and passed before the wynd with our mayn yerd a crosse al the way, abowt 30 legs comonly or more in 24 howrs, and dyvers say they never cam this way with so fayr a passage.

our waie

13. ☿ [*Wed.*] I wrot letters[1] by M. Austyn of the Bridget to my syster, to (*cipher*: M. Aty of al things and Banesters hypocresy and our bad headpeeses), to M. Wylliam Barn that (*cipher*: Banester *w*as[2] an hypocrit) and sent verses in comendations of John Banesters works. We wer hear at 34 and he went sowthwe*st* to Tenarif. We held due sowth. //

letters

25v
*Ferd*inand

1[4.] ♃ [*Thurs.*] by Ferdinandos *d*irection we kept sowth-sowest on purpose to have goen between Barbary and
15. Launcerot[3] to make purchase of gotes or I knoe not what els for al our mynd was set on purchase[4] but as God wold

[1] Curiously, Madox seems not to have written a 'last farewell' to Leicester though others did. The merchant Miles Evans took occasion to report he now suspected that Fenton, contrary to instructions, would go by way of the Strait (Otho E VIII, f. 146). The surgeon John Banister, after commenting on their 'wyse generall,' 'carefull pilates' and 'zealous and paynfull preachers,' devoted the bulk of his missive to warning the earl of the 'wicked and dissemblinge practyse' of the 'papisticall sorte' (f. 147), while from the *Edward*, Walker remarks on Fenton's leaving Hawkins and two of the pilots at Plymouth, which would have 'bredde a greate myscheyfe' (see 2 June) and on the pleasure the mariners 'who never harde sermon in there lyves' take in his preaching (f. 148).

[2] Madox inadvertently writes 'vas' for 'was.'

[3] Lanzarote, the northernmost and smallest island of the Canaries.

[4] Punning on 'purchase' as illegal gains.

Fig. 10. Madox's sketch of the palmito and the oyster tree

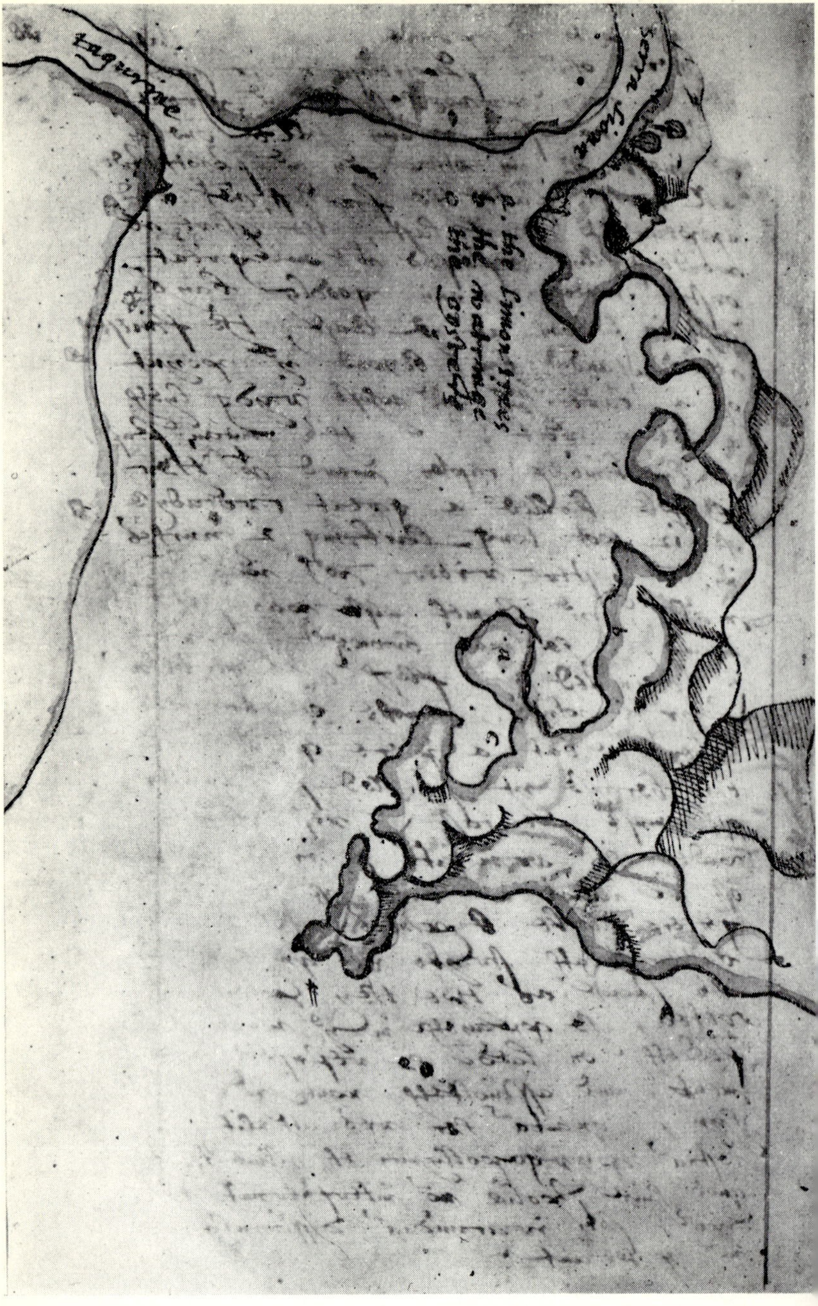

Fig. 11. Madox's chart of Sierra Leone

16. on ♄ [Sat.] morning we wer fawlen to west of yt and so wer forsed to leave yt and Forta Ventura on the larbord and so sayl sowthwest before the wynd.

17. ⊙ G [*Sun.*] *1 after Trinity* we fel yn to west [of] the Graund Canarie leaving Fortventura on the larboord and so passed between yt and Tenarif *wh*ich ar both very hygh lands espetially the *p*yke of Tenarif which we espied above the clowds for being hazie we cold not se the foot of yt.[1] Hytherto we had not one hot daye altho we be within 5 degrees to the ⊙ for the Graund Canarie wher is made the best sugar lyeth in 28 to the northe. Yt is inhabyted by Spaniards. Hear is very good marmaled and great store of fyne suckets. Luke Ward ran yn with the Elsabeth but what he did I knoe not but our general was angry. Dyvers told us what plenty of bonettoes and dolphins we shold have al this *w*ay, but hytherto we smackt no byt of fresh fysh. The lyke they told of gurnet and whyting in the west but our hookes cold catch *n*one, and therfor I perceave men must not go to *s*ea withowt vytals in hope to have flying fyshes to break ther noses agaynst the bunt[2] of the sayle. the Canaries — *No*ta

18. ☾ [*Mon.*] our mayn topmast was taken down and fyshed[3] *f*or that yt had thro lose rocking taken on ech syde a fret. The general cryed owt of M. Owtred, *bu*t the master sayd the fawlt was not so great. topmast

*M*any of our men wer syck which we imputed *to* M. Favours bear of Hampton[4] for that yt *w*as made of brackysh water. Yt took them *e*ver with a sore headach. Old Robert Parkyns *o*f Ratclif dyed. We cast hym overboord and gave *hy*m a peece about 7 a clock at nyght when *w*e wer at 27 degrees. siknese — deathe

[1] See 17 Nov., where Madox, reading and commenting on André Thevet's account of his voyage in 1555 to the 'new found worlde,' remarks on the 'pyke of Tenarif.'

[2] Middle part of the sail; the *OED* cites this MS.

[3] To strengthen the mast by fastening a timber or plank to it with nails or ropes (*Boteler's Dialogues*, ed. W. G. Perrin (Navy Rec. Soc., 1929), p. 86).

[4] The brewer John Favor, who served as sheriff, water bailiff, mayor's assistant, and ultimately (1585) alderman of Southampton, was to run afoul of city officials in 1594 for not brewing 'good and holesome' beer despite an earlier presentment (in 1579). (See *The Third Book of Remembrance*, ed. A. L. Merson, III, 17 n.; Laughton, *State Papers*, I, 159; *Court Leet Records*, edd. Hearnshaw, I.i.2, p. 167.)

26r At service in the // morning a great yron sledge fawling from the mayn top had lyke to have slayn the botson and 2 more and yet God be thanked did no hurt. Yn the after noon a poydrel which is a lytle black byrd cam to the ship, which M. Fayrwether sayd was a token of wynd, and
19. so yt was for ♂ [Tues.] our boat which hytherto we have towed at the stern beyng caried ageynst our poop with a sea brok hir star boord bow but afterwards mended, she was towed agayn with more scope of rope.

danger

token of winde

the boate

20. ☿ [*Wed.*] ther was an eclips of the sone in the mornyng but thro the foggy haze which is hear muche we saw yt not.[1] This morning we passed the tropick of ♋ [Cancer] and soe kept on this cowrse as afore.

eclips

tropik of ♋

21. ♃ [*Thurs.*] in the evening Capten Ward cam aboord and M. Walker. They had taken a tortoyse. Hear was much resoning whether yt wer better break up the Elsabeth or take hir a long but albe the general and others wold hav had hir confiscat, yet Luk Wards word prevayled for hir lyfe. M. Walker lay with me and we ript up much good matter.[2]

Richard Salte diethe

22. ♀ [*Fri.*] *and* ♄ [*Sat.*] we held our cowrse sowthwest
23. toward the Ylands of Cape de Verd. When the ores be a pyke [held vertically] ether the Capten or master is to come yn.

24. [G *Sun.*] *Midsomer* a cowncel was cawled in the gallion with al the asistants at 18 degres latitude wherin was concluded by general consent to seek water at the Yle of Bonavista and from thence to hold cowrse toward Rio di Plata both for the eaze of our men and necessyty of our viage. Luke Ward in al poynts spoke to the purpose with discretion, so did John Drake and M. Walker. The rest *utrunque*.[3] Among al M. Capten Parker yn as much as he

a cowncel

[1] Cf. William Bourne's 'An Almanack and Prognostication' included with his *Regiment for the Sea*, ed. Taylor, p. 354.

[2] See Walker, 22 June: he stayed on the *Galleon* 'because it was nyghte and the wynde blew' and remained until the 24th for he 'lyked not the badd enteringe into a shyppe, the wynde blowinge.'

[3] Madox gives a full account in his official narrative, see App. I, pp. 287–90 below.

was to serv at the land wold needs have leave to appoynt his leiftene*n*t, corporals and sergeants or els he wold do n*o*thing, but the general thowght not meet to have any more leiftenents but his own and so after muche adoe that matter was dashed. A coppy of al things I tooke with ther hands at yt.[1] //

25. ☾ [*Mon.*] I took a purgation being stil syck. We saw many 26v
flying fyshes[2] and took one yn the cheynholes for when flying fish
they be owt of the water they can not se. A number of porpases wer also leaping abowt us which maketh me afrayd of a storme.

26. ♂ [*Tues.*] fawling west yn 16 degrees northward, we fownd an yland which some sayd was Bonavista but others Bonavista
thowght yt was La Sal but none cold tell. Yt rose on the sowthwest of us with 3 hils in the land, the myddest lyk Glastenbury Tor. Capten Parker and Luk Ward after we had anchored in the bay went to descrye the land, but because the rut [surge] went somwhat hard a shore, therfore they wold not bryng the boat a shore and capten Parker lyke a bold soldier thowght every crib [hovel] a castle and every gote an armed soldier. Luke Ward sent owt 2[3] which swyming to land discried a fayr riv*er*, a number of gotes, plenty of byrds but no people, and ther was also abundance of fysh and monstruows great tortuses. Luk Ward took one as byg as a child of the largest fyshe which wold have broken a boat thole [oarlock] in his mowth. Hear be also great shorks which is as yt wer an overgroen dogfysh of 6 foot long or more. In fyne when we returned, the general wold not consent to water hear which thing the viceadmiral took yl, so dyd our mast*er*, but Furdinando

she dyd carie M. Waker on hir bak[4] along the mast

[1] Preserved in Otho E VIII, f. 159.

[2] Walker describes them as the size of 'a hearinge' or larger, with two wings of good length and capable of flying a bow shot, i.e., about twelve score yards (App. II, 25 June).

[3] Thomas Russell and Mark Towghts from the *Edward* (Walker, 26 June). In his official account Madox says that the two were sent out 'with store of men and municion among whom I was also crept to see what wold become of the matter' and he goes on to comment on the fearful reaction at the sight of 'a cupple of goates with long beardes . . . and a lytle kyd' identified as 'towe harnesed men on horsebacke and a dogge' (App. I, p. 291 below).

[4] Walker says 'syttynge upon her backe, layinge my legges a crosse' and comments that the shell was of such hardness 'a carte goinge laden' could ride on her (26 June).

had caried hym to this that the rather for want of water we myght robb and both he and M. Whood which had browght us hyther with promyses of the greatest cumforts in the world do now deny al and say that we have delt madly to rune so far owt of our way. I pray God blesse me from such pilat*es*.[1]

27. ☿ [*Wed.*] yn great displeasure on al sydes we wayd to be
gone but M. Haukins and Furdinando went to descry the
27r sowthwest of the bay wher // they fownd a fayr freshet
and plenty of got*es* but the general sayd we had water
ynogh and therfor would not stay which made the men
the troble of 28. much mislyke[2] and so upon ♃ [Thurs.] Luk Ward cam to
the Elsabethe us to excuse hym se*lf* abowt vitayling the bark for the
general throe ther complaynt had spoken sharpl*y* to hym.
Capten Skevington was hear also with a great complaynt
agaynst his master with gawdy words, for every Jack
sayth, I am a gentilman and I can tel how to governe and I
wil govern that is scarse worthy to syt and keep flyes from
a gawld horse bak. God send me discreet and wyse
governowrs as be gentilmen in deed and not such
crycketcatchers as never cam wher yt grew. In fyne we
made al frends. Luke Ward axed my opinion of M.
Walker. I told he myght be trust with any thing but with a
fayr lasse.

29. ♀ [*Fri.*] *St. Peter.* Hytherto the wynd having byn frank
temperies unto us and northerly met us at sowth and sowtherly at 14
Cæli degrees to the north with muche qualme but yet no rayn
as for our pilots told us many a tale wher we must fet our
wynds and how we shold meet with them as thogh Æolus
or Neptunus had kept market by the way, but all ther
Whoode taulk is nothing but vanyty. As for Whood he doth
nothing but with a bawling mowth rayl agaynst our ship,
ageynst our provision, agaynst our owners, gape for the
Spaynysh treasures swaloyng up the men and spoyling
them of ther money alyve with blasphemows bragging
ageynst God and man. The Lord stay the rage of our syn

[1] Punning on pilot: Pilate; see 3 Aug. For his official account, see App. I, pp. 290–91 below).

[2] See his official account, App. I, pp. 291–92 below.

that yt be not repressed with the rigor of his fury, for wykednes is in our dwelling and among us. So long as the north wynd blew yt was cooler than yn Ingland, but now yt is blomy [close] and hote but yet in no great excesse. //

30. ♄ [*Sat.*] what with qualm and sotherly wynd we gote 27^v
lytle or nothing a head. I took up of Water Web 14 els
of canvase 14^s to make cassocks and breeches for the Cassocks
steward, the cook and my man.

July ♌

1. ☉ G [*Sun.*] *3 after Trinity*. We took 3 shorks of 5 foote a
peece. 2 wer sod, the third was cut in thungs[1] to dry. Yt is shorkes
good sawsed with vynagre, oyl, and peper or garlique. The heads we threw away. The flesh riseth in very fyne and short fybres throowt. They ar made lyke a dogfysh and wonderful gredy. Under ther bellys we fynd lytle blyters of 6 ynches long which hath a flat holo head lyke a . . . so that you wold ymagin his back to b*e* his belly. We had lykwyse 2 martlets that for 3 or 4 days kept us cumpany, being at the least 60 leags from Cape de Verd which was the nyest land.

2. ☾ [*Mon.*] very hote and qualmy. ♂ [Tues.] we took an
3. other shork *and* John Drak sent us a lytle dolphyn of a foot
long, being the fyrst that[2] was kyld, yet M. Hawkins sayd that every day both owtward and homward *b*ound
they drew up 20 or more of 5 or 4 foot long.[3] Yt is dolphine
delicate meat and being fryd did eat just lyke a sole, but the best way is to dresse hym as fresh samon.

4. ☿ [*Wed.*] we had a smal tornado which is nothing els but a
sodayn gust of rayn with a flaw of wynd of which sort I tornado
have seen many in somer tyme at *h*ome. We saved the water in baricoes [casks], which within 3 or 4 days did stink and yet M. Hawkins sayd *th*ey kept some sweet 3

[1] Salopian dialect for 'thong' (Jackson, *Shropshire Word Book*).
[2] Madox writes 'yt' for 'y^t.'
[3] Throughout, Madox emphasizes the untrustworthiness of sailors' reports and their habit of generalising from a single occasion. Cf. 14 Aug.

moneths but *nil temere credendum.* Hear we met with the
sowthwynd — wynd at sowth and we drew yn 5 shorks which the Spaniard cawleth aberone,[1] but dolphin yet cold we not take albe we saw ther azured backs and golden tayles.[2] //

28r

5. ♃ [*Thurs.*] ♀ [*Fri.*] ♄ [*Sat.*] we which had hytherto in maner
6. kept Thom Beggars cowrse sayling right before the wynd,
7. now what between east on the on boord and west on the other, for our ship wold ly no nyer, we gote nothing and yet forsooth our cunyng pilates made us beleeve that the wynd was bownd in an obligation to be at east and east northeast al this tyme of the yer, but M. Hawkins told that they being homward bownd abowt this tyme of yer fownd a sowthwynd at the Cape of Good Hope which browght them to Plymmowth so that ther is no trust.

pilotes

[*8*] ⊙ *G* [*Sun.*] *4* [*after*] *Trinity.* I drempt muche of Uffington[3] and of 3 men drownd in a dytch, but pulled owt with some lyf, and that seing an ylfavored carion fysh above water Jacson dyved to take hir and I also waded in and cat*c*ht hir by the tayle. The God of cumfort geve to my dreame a happy interpretacion. This day ther dyed with us Zachary the swabbe and Edward Kent and a smyth aboord the Edward and in shoting of a pece yt brak a rope wherby the Frances bote was fast to our ship so that she fel away with on man yn hir and an other was fayn to leap overboord to swym for hir and thus have I my whole dreame. I *be*seche the Lord hear to stay the angel of wrath that *he* forrage no farther.

a dreame with the event

9. ☾ [*Mon.*] the wynd cam somwhat westerly so that we lay sowthsowethest but anon chopt into the sowth agayn and is very clowdy. Ned Stoks told how the lions in Affryck kept 100 together in a shole and that they had fyrst spoyled and did now keepe 2 villages and that yf a lyon be hedged abowt with thorns he wil rather be taken than

lions and bores

[1] Sp. *tiburon*; Pg. *tubarão*. Sir Richard Hawkins describes them as like 'Doggefishes' only 'farre greater': 'In the Puch of them hath beene found hatts, cappes, shooes, shirts, leggs and armes of men, ends of Ropes, and many other things' (*Observations*, p. 47). Cf. 8 Oct.

[2] I.e., the dorado, see 17 Nov., p. 229.

[3] Three miles from Shrewsbury; for Madox's possible connections, see pp. 1–2 above.

pryck his foote to come away, and that the wild bores being hunted do gather in a ring which they arm abowt with the greatest and the smaler yn the mydest.

10. ♂ [*Tues.*] we beat up and down and did no good. The general told me that the master was a symple and an obstinate feloe and Thom Whood a wyse, diligent and vertuous man. Come withowt him,[1] quothe *I.* // Al this week we made many boords, some east, some west. We had the wynd at sowth and much rayn but the wether as our Englysh Autume save that the ayr was more thick and foggy and we saw now and than lyke purple bladders swym on the sea which our men cawled carvels,[2] tellyng us that they wold sting sore.

a vertuo*ws* man 28v

red carvels

When I appoynted the boys that wayted to repeat ech meal a sentence owt of Solomons Proverbs M. Whood wold not in any case that his boy shold lern any such thing for he browght hym not hyther for that purpose, and as for hym self he wil not geve a fart for al ther cosmography for he can tel more than al the cosmographers in the world and wil ryde a horse with any man yn England and then [the] mayr of Plymowth shal not set a miller to steal his corn for his wyf eateth as good bred as the best woman in Devonshire and hath every holyday the best of rosting beaf that[3] she *c*an bwy for hir money, save that *a* horse *bo*t hir by the sholder.[4]

Thomas Whoode

M. Banester sayth that he healed 200 in one yer of an ague by hanging abracadabra abowt ther necks and wold stanch blood or heal the toothake althogh the partyes wer 10 myle of and that my Lord of Lester told *h*ym at Rochester that he wold the mownsewr *w*er hanged, and that the queen sayd, I thank *y*ou, good M. Banester, and yf I be able I *w*il requyte you and so she gave hym the advowsons of 2 benefyces which wer s*e*nt to hym by doctor Julio[5] but the doctor s*o*ld them both by the way so

John Banester

[1] Apparently equivalent to 'come off' or 'desist.'

[2] Paper nautilus or Argonaut.

[3] Madox writes 'yt' for 'y^{t}.'

[4] See 26 May.

[5] His surname variously spelled as Borgaruccio, Borgarnaius, and Borgarneins, Dr Julio, a member of the Barber-Surgeons, was a popular physician at court. Burghley, for example, helped him obtain the reversion of a rectory in Middlewich, Cheshire, in 1579, and he was supposedly a favourite of Leicester's, Camden reporting (*Annales* (1635), Y1*v*) that Leicester had supported him against the

that M. Banester *ha*d nothing but yet M. Stanhop[1] offered h*y*m synce C^{li} for his interest in the one, *ye*t he wold not take yt.

29^{r}

a rare balme

Having // byn hytherto very yll and unable to brook any meat, Symon Wood[2] gave me 3 drops of artificial oyl for 3 mornings which he bowght of M. Buntford, a goldfyner at the Mayden Head in Aldersgate street, which dryed up my rewme and did me much good and surely yt is a very excelant balme and cost a noble an ownce.

a tale

The general told of one that was lyke a pye, a fly, and a fart: a pye for he wold have al the talk, a fly for he wold be ever in the dysh, a fart for he wold depart from his norysher with a fowld wo*r*d and never return to his cuntrey to geve yt thanks.

15. ⊙ *G* [*Sun.*] *5 after Trinity* the wynd somwhat larged toward the sowthwest so that we kept very nye sowtheast being now between 7 and 8 degrees to the north and abowt 100 leags fro the cost of Affryck as was thowght but

19. after yt proved lesse for on Thursday we had lytle

barnacles

barn*a*cles which did eat lyk cravisshes [crayfishes] gathered

a dolphin

20. ♀ of *ou*r boat and on Fryday M. Hood took a dolph*in* which was indeed a fyne whyt meat and sw*ee*t but yet not lyke to the samon.

our pilots reconing

Guinye

Being as we suppozed within 5 degrees of the *lyne* or lesse we descryed a hygh *l*and abowt 9 leags of at east northeast wh*ich we* deemed to be Capo de Palmas or Capo de Verga[3] so that Luk Ward with his master and pilat seeing us cast offward cam aboord and wyshed that in as much as we did ly bwelting[4] at the sea and cold doe noe good wee shold stand in with some harboroe for the releif of our cumpanyes. Than was the owncel cawled to

---

opposition of Archbishop Grindal in his marriage to another man's wife. (See Young, *Annals of the Barber-Surgeons*, pp. 314, 363; *Cal. Salisbury MSS*, Pt. II, 236; and Strype, *Annals of the Reformation*, III.i.521).

[1] High sheriff of Notts., Thomas Stanhope was the dedicatee of Banister's first publication, *A Needefull new, and necessarie treatise of Chyrurgerie* (1575).

[2] A musician on the *Galleon*, Wood had sailed with Francis Drake. See 23 Nov. for his comment on Drake.

[3] The one, a promontory on the Malagueta Pepper Coast (4° 22′ N); the other a headland of Upper Guinea (10° 11′ N).

[4] See p. 1 above. Thomas Ellis in his account of Frobisher's third voyage uses the phrase 'laine bulting up and downe' (*PN* (1589), p. 633).

se wher we wer and now every mans reconyng was behind the ships way above 50 leags wherby I did perceav that ether they had not geven yt // alowance to leeward as 29v
the ships lyst required or els ther ran some current which set us to the eastward under the wether bow and so I think yt trew for at nyght we wer in a very rugh race [current] at 65 fadom of soft sandy oze lyke bran and brayd [beaten] pepper, which I judged to be St. Annes Shole.[1]

Wel when the viceadmiral was come aboord with his Madrebona
master and Blackoller, our general, which had cast to the offard west northwest, at the motion of the viceadmiral and others that desyred rather to go on shore for the refreshing of our men than to lye bwelting on the sea and do no *g*ood for some of us wer dead and many syck cauled the matter in cowncel[2] and proposed the question wher we wer, shewing his own *ac*cownt and others. M. Whood sayd the land we saw was Capo de Palmas or els hee wold fyrst be hanged and after cut in 1000 peeces. Such an insolent spech men wold not for modesty sack crose, althogh ther wer reasons to the cuntrary. Than was demanded whether better go forward to the east or go back agayn to the norwest. M. Haukins with good probable reasons shewd that the further we passed eastward the further wer we fro the river of Plate and better therfore to passe to the Surliona for yf we wer ether caulmed or fownd the wynd in any part of the sowth we myght harbor ther with great *s*afety, but yf northerly we myght put of to our great advauntedge. M. Whood sayd that was *lepida responsio*
a villanows coast for when Sir Frances Drake did ther water they set one the potage pot with ryce every meale. *The* general was loth to go thither *pre*tending that he feared the health of his men because al had spoke yl of the cuntrey, but the very truth was, he feared lest fynding ther suffyciency for our provision he shold have than no pretence to passe to the // westward notwithstanding M. 30r
Hawkins objecting that further we went eastward the further we wer from our mark and in more danger to be

[1] Northwest of Sherbro Island and thus south of Sierra Leone.

[2] See Madox's official account, App. I, pp. 292–94 below, where he records Fenton's directive that the debate not be recorded as an 'account in the register' because it was but a 'familier debating' between the General and the pilots.

calmed, he yelded to go back to Se*ra* Leona except the wynd served. Capten Ward as I perceaved undertaking this viage as wel for the hope of his experience as of his profyt and rather more was desyrows to se the shore and on this agreement we departed but presently after the wynd comyng agayn to the sowthwest which was before dew sowth we browght the starboord tack aboord and bore agayn sowthsotheast[1] with dyvers scuds of rayn.

21. ♄ [*Sat.*] abowt noone the wynd agayn began to meet at sowthwest so that we ran agayn westnorwest and spied
22. land agayn and on ⊙ *G* [*Sun.*] *6 after Trinity* being abowt agayn we had land one ech syde to leeward and fownd our selvs so puzzeled that no man cold say wher we wer, not having seen sune or stars for 14 days, but of truth we were not so far to the sowthward by 3 degrees at the least toward the sowth and therfor whether the
the current — current set to the *nornor*est by the reset and [?] yeynwal of Br*azil* or whether the streames of Rio Grande[2] or *oth*er rivers that fawl myghtyly into the sea *ca*use some current or whether yt alway*s do fo*loe the wynd, sure I am we wer n*o* nyer than 8 degrees to the lyne and I *th*ynk fu*rther* of and now agayn we cast to th*e* offward to west norwest.

23. ☾ [*Mon.*] the master went into the boat and grapeled[3] at
current — 300 fadom and sayd that the current did set ful eastwards but indeede the wynd was so byg that I knoe not how he shold wel judge. Hear we met with a number of things
blubbers — cauled blubbers[4] lyke unto red *bry*er bawles a handful stil under the wate*r*. //

30v
dreame — [*24.*] ♂ [*Tues.*] in the morning I drempt of many strange visions that being in Grampole[5] in Oxford I dyd se in the ayr, espetialy an old man as yt were the pope with a sword in his hand and a great rank with hym runyng violently agaynst the steeple.

[1] This statement accords with Fenton's journal though they were soon forced in an opposite direction. See Madox's last extant entry in his 'Booke,' 21 July, p. 294.

[2] Modern Geba; the Guinea currents were notoriously deceptive: see the account of the voyage to Guinea in 1554 by Robert Gainsh, *PN* (1589), p. 92.

[3] I.e., used a small anchor with three flukes to sound.

[4] Jelly fish or sea nettle; for a description, see 3 Oct.

[5] Perhaps the area around Folly Bridge (Clark, *Reg.*, II.i.103).

At the later end of dynner as we wended westsowest with the larboord tack aboord and a bold wynd, the *the* topmast *fa*wleth mayn topmast was bloen down even as the general was drynking and fawling to leewar*d* dyd tear the mayn top much and hanged by the puttocks [shrouds] yt brak 7 foot from the root wher before yt had byn fysht so that on
25. ☿ [Wed.] beyng St. James day we had fayre wether and
26. set up the top agayn beyng amended and [♃ Thurs.] we set up the topmast, beyng so much shorter than before yt had been.

I went aboord the Edward with M. Hawkins wher we had a dolphin. Many of them wer syck and did complayn the want of fresh water so that I bryngïng a letter from M. Walker to the general that 30 were syck, he tooke yt yl and dyd deem yt had byn some practyce of the vice-admiral.[1] Wel God send us wysdom in our governowrs and honest obediens in the inferiors, and al hypocrysy let God trye.

27. [♀ *Fri.*] we had fayr wether but scant wynd.

28. ♄ [*Sat.*] the general went aboord the Edward.[2] I wrot by M. Banester to M. Lewes that they 2 shold one make *mu*che of an other, desyring rather to reape p*r*ayses of others than to attribute unto them selvs anything. I wrot also to M. Walker *up*on the occasion of his letter. I think thus verbatim (*Latin*: Your unpleasant letter distressed me very much. It makes unjust demands; it mentions (*Latin*: The interception of letters) disagreeable things; it makes unfair objections; it complains without reason. Please write, I beg [you], more gently hereafter. *Istaec in me cudatur faba*: I shall smart for that.[3] Fare well, you and your leader. With love to both of you. R. M. Jeffrey said that some were muttering that I wish to play the part of M. Fletcher.[4] Please find out who spread 31ʳ

[1] Both Walker and his Vice-admiral were eager to find a harbour in order to refresh their men. Of the 70-odd men on the *Edward*, Walker reported to Fenton, 30 were 'infected with some sycknesse.'

[2] See Walker's account (28 June) for Fenton's altercation with the Vice-admiral and his reaction to Madox's letter.

[3] Terence, *Eun*. 381.

[4] For Francis Fletcher, chaplain on Drake's circumnavigation, see pp. 46–7 above. For the misinterpretation of the reference, see 1 Aug. As Walker observed, the general could not understand Madox's (ironical) letter 'for he understoode not Latyn perfectlye.'

this rumor and what they expect to gain from it, for I don't quite follow.) Thes letters and others the general did open as I suppoze by the provoquement of M. Banester[1] in whose head ther is some gelosy, for wel assured I am that ther hath not passed me anything wherby the general hym self shold hold me in any suspicion, whoze credyt I have hytherto every way sowght both at land and sea to uphold. What M. Cotton had wrytten I knoe not but tuching the lyke case ther wer sad words betwyxt hym and the general.[2] I pray God setle his love among us els he that seeketh revenge may quycly ether upon pryvy and false accusations or some other conceyt distresse hym self of his best frend and so overthro both hys own safety and the whole action as yn the tale of the oke and the bryar is set down.[3]

29. ⊙ G [*Sun.*] *7 after Trinity.* After clowdy wether in maner al this moneth and coole wyndes, now yt qualmeth and waxeth hote, the wynd at sowthsowest wherupon we cast abowt easterly being between 3 and 4 degrees fro the lyne on the north. M. Evans told me that the hygher the ryver runeth the *d*eeper the tyde ebbeth and floeth and therfor *he* thinketh that by meanes of the great indrawghts the current in ech place setteth toward the shore and in the mydlest of the se is none at al. Hearof lern more of the northeast and northwest and mydleyerth travelers. Before nyght yet agayn we browght agayn the larboord tack aboord and set to the west.

tydes and currents

Capten Skevington supt with us and on the sodayn was a great cry on the Elsabeth and yt was told that one was leapt overboord.[4]

30. ☾ [*Mon.*] the general went thither to examyn the matter and had me with hym to geve them exhortacions. Capten

[1] Banister had conveyed Madox's letter as well as one from Richard Cotton, 'a gentleman,' said Walker, 'with whom I had very small famylyarytye.'

[2] Although allowing Walker to read Cotton's letter, Fenton refused to hand it over because of certain 'wordes conteyned there,' which were, simply, 'that he was sorye there was no better agreement amongste us.' Walker adds, '(in truthe) what his meaninge was herein I understoode not.'

[3] Spenser's *Shepheardes Calender*, 'Feb.' ll. 102 ff.

[4] The cook on the *Elizabeth*, see next entry.

Skevington by the *way* complayned to me grevowsly that M. Wylks wold fart before hym etc. When we cam thither // we fownd that Julian Saunders, a foolysh feloe, 31v had fowght with the masters mate and after leap*t* overboord because they wold not suffer [hym] to come unto us. Yt was determined that he shold be hoysed to the yerd arme and so let fawl. M. Hawl sayd the yerd wold break. Wel hoysed he was and in the swyng the yerd snapt quyt of in the myddle and al cam into the sea not withstanding after he cam yn agayn upon his submission he was pardoned.

farters in the Elsabeth

the yerde breaketh

We went to the Fraunses to dynner wher we had of porpase and dolphyn dyvers ways drest a very fyne and ful dynner, and some we browght home, and of the tayl that is as lyke black lether as is possible which was cut of to throe away we made a meat that none cold have knoen yt from baked calvs feet.

cheer at the Fraunces

M. Taylboise, being a lytle overgone as oft he is, fownd muche falt with this punyshment of the man. The general overhearing cawled hym. What taulk they had I kno not, but M. Cotton was bydden geve place to the commissioners, so was M. Banester. Whether of them t*o*oke the matter worse I knoe not for yt *st*ung them both to the hart, but M. Cotton *som*what and not much better dissembled yt, complayning greatly that the general had his letter and he cold not get yt, so Banester sate beloe and M. Cotton cam not to supper.

newe alter*c*acions

31. ♂ [*Tues.*] ther was hard reasoning betwyxt the general and M. Cotton. What was the effect I kno not, but now is he set at the boords end by the general with great honor. He told me yt was by reason of a letter from my Lord Lumley.[1] Now is M. Banester in worst taking and sayth he shal dye and he can not leave syghing and many foolysh and intemprat words why God shold thus abase hym and for which his synnes. I was with hym and althoe he forge fasting, yet he hath plenty of coole bear and aquavite and I fownd chese parings and bacon stoored in his wyndoe. //

Cotton and Banester bitter enemies

[1] To whom Fenton had dedicated his first and only book.

32r

August ♍ 1582

1. ☿ [*Wed.*] *Lammas day*. M. Banester took on so heavyly that the merchants lest he shold fawl into desperation wer desyrows agayn to prefer hym and al was but the shiftyng of one peg, so that now he is content, saving that he muche repineth at my Lord of Lester that he was not made of the cownsel.

After dynner I knoe not upon what motion in the world, the general fyrst ymparting his mynde to us and than with

Concilium

owr lykyng cawled a owncel wherunto when al were come, he proponed that syth our bear spent faster than our way, whether yt were not good to go seeke water and yf to seek yt than wher? With general consent of al save my self yt was concluded yea and the Surleona appoynted[1] so that at night being from yt as I deem abowt 100 leags we set our cowrse northeast with quarter wynd towards yt in Gods name.

M. Walker told mee that wher in my former Laten intercepted letter I had wrytten *domini fletcheri*, yt was construed that I thowght I was used lyke a fletcher[2] wherat I laffed, but when the ryght sence of al was delyvered, than they were sory etc.

an alcatrashe

Ned Gylman took an alcatrash[3] on the mayntopmast yerd, which is a foolysh byrd but good lean rank meat.

5 Edward Stoks dieth

2. ♃ [*Thurs.*] the Edward sprang hir foremast.[4] Edward Stokes of Henbury or Amsbury, the plat drawer, dyed of a calentowr.[5] God be mercyful to us that lyve. He is the fyfth whom we have throen overboord, and before

6 David Evans

morning died David Evans of Gloester, baker, of an old

[1] Although at this point Madox apparently wished to proceed, he then concurred with the vote of the majority on stopping at Sierra Leone in order to seek water (Minute of the council, in his hand, Otho E VIII, ff. 157–8).

[2] I.e. arrowmaker.

[3] Applied to the frigate bird and later to the albatross: the *OED* cites this passage.

[4] Cracking it, says Ward, three yards from the top, which caused them to be in 'great feare' of it (*PN* (1589), p. 647).

[5] A disease incident to the tropics where the patient in delirium thinks the sea is a green field and desires to jump overboard. Walker was to succumb to the disease on 9 Nov. and not come forth from his bed until 2 Dec.

bruse. This cuntrey is very temperat but yt sercheth old greifs and ether healeth them or els sendeth them to a better physicion. //

3. ♀ [*Fri.*] at supper we espied a ripling of the water as we trended eastnortheast and anan on the lyebord we saw a very hyghland which M. Haukins prononced absolutely to be Serra Liona, that is to say the mowntayn of lyons, but he was flatly withstood by Pilote and Herode,[1] and M. Parker sayd he wold reason with the best mariner in Ingland and prove yt cold not be yt, because the Serraliona lay in 8 and a terce but we wer now in 6 and a terce, notwithstanding he did not perceave the current which setteth ful northeast, for we ar fawln as far this way in 2 days as we ran the other way in 5 days. Great hold [contention] and hye wordes ther were. I think we saw yt abowt to ken of.[2] 32v

Gwynny land

4. ♄ [*Sat.*] morning being abowt 3 leags of we had grownd 60 fadom and now ech man graunted yt to be the same.[3] The sownding was black hose [ooze], the land very hye and in this wyse yt appeared.

[Fig. 8. Capo de Monte]
[sketch 32*v*]

I forgat to tel of a great bonetto which capten Hawkyns took with an hook on Fryday. Yt was 4 foot and a half long and almost as thick, just lyke a mackrel but more trinchioned. The head did eat as sweet as any calvs head, and Fry kyld a dolphyn which had in his poych [pouch] a flying fysh of a foot long with 4 wyngs, and how M. Banester told me he wold have that Cotton, as he cawled hym, by the eares now yf he myght have leave; yf not, yet at his return to Yngland, which being sent to sea because he durst not shew his face in London for det and

a great bonetto

a dolphin

a flying fysh

Banester and Cotton

[1] I.e., Fernando and Hood; cf. 26 June.

[2] A ken (or kenning) is a measure of *c.* 20 miles. Both Fenton (*Taylor*, p. 97) and Ward (*PN* (1589), p. 647) concur that it was about 12–14 leagues distant, that is, about 40 miles.

[3] Ward says they were persuaded by the pilots that it was the entrance to Sierra Leone until within a half league of the shore, they discovered that, in fact, it was a bay (*PN* (1589), p. 648), called by Walker 'Cape de Monte.'

had been hyd at M. Onleys wold now cal hym arrogant physician. See the humor of a foolysh man but now to the purpo*se*. //

33r Abowt noone the master went yn the pynnyse and fownd fyrst 30 fadom oze in sownding and so sholyng to 15 within a culveryn level[1] t*o* shore, and goyng a land he gathered Gwyny beanes and fetches [vetches] and thin[g]s[2] lyke almons and dryed lymes with sea and sun and orenges. John Lynsey browght herbs and fygtrebowes. They fownd a canow and 3 or 4 lytle howses made of reeds lyke unto greate drye seges but saw no people. They gathered oliphants dung and espied a fayr ynlet of water and a goodly fresh spryng fast by the shore, but comyng back they had but cold thanks,[3] for nether dare some men ventur them selvs nor can not abyde that other shal be thowght able to do more than they. Wel now because we cold not se a rock at the norwest end, this was not [Serra Leona], althogh al our pylots 2 howrs before sayd, who knoes not this to be the same? I was desyrows to have anchored hear and march to the hil top for the wether was fayr and trusty ryding in the bay but no help, hall of agayn to the sea and try further, which is to refuse Gods blessing prafered by the fyre syde on a cold day and to tread up and down in the snoe to seeke a warme suny bank.

things gather*d* *a*shore

deepe heades

5. ⊙ G [*Sun.*] *8 after Trinity*. When we had rune westerly al nyght and stil saw the green loe [lee] shore with one fayr tree and est a homock of tr*ees* as is set down, than we fel to recon *wha*t the land is. M. Haukyns and M. Hood to ex*cuse* and clere one fawlt ran into a number, *the* one *tam ficti pravique tenax quam nuntia veri*,[4] the other yf he take an opinion once, aledge what reazon you can, *non magis ille movetur quam si dura silex aut stet marpesia cautes*,[5]

pilotts majors

[1] I.e., sounding shallowly to the length of a culverin (a light cannon), that is from 10 to 13 feet.

[2] Madox writes 'thinks.'

[3] Fenton records they brought him 'Gynny beanes and other triffles' (*Taylor*, p. 97).

[4] *Aen*. IV. 188: as tenacious of falsehood and rascality as prone to report the truth.

[5] *Aen*. VI. 470–1: and is no more altered than if he were set in hard flint or Marpesian rock.

and yet the least wager was ether C^{li} or a goodmans head, and when M. Haukins had rune yn with the ylande at Cape de Verd and sayd he was on yt and that it was Bonavista, now tis fownd tha*t* he came not theron, nether cold for the rut.[1] //

6. ☾ [*Mon.*] because we saw an open, the Frances and *the* 33v
Elsabeth ran yn northward to yt who br*owght* us word that St. Annes sholes
it were the 3 yland[s] in the mowth of Madrebumba, which al 3 we myght see distinctly, wel wodded, being 4 or 5 leags fro them.[2] M. Whood yet wold not *con*sent yt shold be so but rather 3 ylands on the shold ring of Serra Liona. Hytherto we had deep blew water, but being abowt noone athwart the westernmost, we had fyrst green and than whyt and muddy water at 15 fadom and so sholing westward at nyght, being come to 7 fadom wee shran*k* back and anchored at 9 fadom wher we perceaved a horsing eb that set to east north east but the flud not so tyde
vehement. Yt is ful seaz when the moon is an howr past hir meridian.

7. ♂ [*Tues.*] the Elsabeth was gone from us, I kno not how,[3] but we sent the Francis afore who gave us a token of deep water, so that with an eb abowt x a clock we folowed and wer anan in 5 fadom and a half but quycly cam to x and vi agayn keeping northwest. The sowndyng was muddy sand as a myxture of whyt, red and swarfye. Now we confessed that the *pla*ce we wer yn and which at the very fyrst we had seen, as the rippling of the water did wytnes, was Cape de Mownte which . . . by the trending of the land did *in the be*gynning espye and tel us but our pil*a*ts pilotes
wer to cunnyng to be deceaved. I pray God be our pilote, our master, our leader, and al, than shal we not err.

At the nyght ebb we cam to an anchor at 12 fadom because the ebb shold not set us to leeward. This day yt rayned muche. John Heath dieth of a dropsey. 7 John Heath

[1] See 26 June above.

[2] Ward with the *Elizabeth* ventured to within a league and a half of the shore and running along it noted two islands but dared not put in lest the larger ships should follow and be caught on the lee shore.

[3] Having lost their anchor and cable, they were constrained to set sail at night (Ward, *PN* (1589), p. 648; Walker, 7 Aug.).

8. ☿ [*Wed.*] we wayed and ran norwest 4 or 5 leags and at nyght had syght of land to the north and saw the Elsabeth agayn which had lost an anchor and a cable. At nyght we anchored on the norwest edge of the sholes at 15 fadom. The shol*es* lye in rydges in maner east and west lyke falowed grownd. //

sholes

34r

9. ♃ [*Thurs.*] we wayd at mydnyght and within 2 howr*s wer in* blew water runyng north and by west; at day we descryed the ylands and mayn of Sera Liona beying [*sic*] very hyge land but as lyke C*a*pe Mownts as the Myddle Temple is lyke Mamsbury steeple for thus yt lay [see Fig. 9]. And therfore surely our pylates had marked spytefully the forme of yt before but as God wol M. Whood was very syck for he had a cryck in his neck.[1] At nyght when al the whyl before we had fownd 15, 14, 12, and 10 fadome, now have we at the poynt of the road at a loe water 5 and a half, so on the sodayn Whood and M. Haukins cried to anchor and because ech thing was not doen at a tryce, they wer wr*o*th and fownd [fault] with the masters working, saying yt was now . . . but I on my smale skil d*e*nyed y*t* for indeed yt was but . . . flud and was ful after 11 so th*at* I gathered that the horizontal moon doth make a ful sea *and* th*at* th*e* flud setts hear north*ward* but the eb westward. Th*e* fyrst as I suppose *by* means of the *n*atur*al* current but the *other* beca*u*se of the fawl of th*e* ryvers. //

Serra Liona

the tyde

34v

[*10.* ♀ *Fri.*] *we* ran yn with the harboroe and had 9 or 10 *fadom* fast by the shore. Wil Burgesse dyed of *th*e calentour. We tooke hym to land and th*er* on the syde of the hil buried hym with this *e*pitaph which I made.

Burgesse dieth

Thi sowle to heaven whence yt fled
Thi bodi to yearth which fyrst yt bred
Thoe far fro cuntrey lytle WILL
Yet in thi cuntrey BURGESSE stil.

They told that in this river was great daunger of the alligator, which is a water crocadyle, and that under his sholders is perfect muske, al*so* of the seahorse, for one of

seahorse

[1] Madox elsewhere takes occasion to note that whenever the pilots are found to be in error, they feign sickness. See 17, 22, and 26 Dec.

them tooke Capteyn Hawkins trumpeter owt of his *p*ynnyce and did devowr hym.[1]

[*11.*] ♄ [*Sat.*] we went to take the sone a shore, and the declination being 12 degrees 18 mynutes I took the *so*ne on a perfet instrument at 3 degrees 26 *myn*uts fro the zenith so that I pronow[n]sed the place *to* be 9 degrees lacking 8 mynutes. the latitude of Serra Liona

M. Eva*ns*, *M.* Cotton, Richard Fayrwether and I went up into th*e* *woo*d and M. Walker. Ther ar lemmons . . . , *gre*at store of wyld bay, wyld pom*e*gra*nets and* fygs, dyvers strange frutes, dyver*s* strange great trees. We hard the nyghtingales syng sweetly and thrushes. trees

12. ⊙ G [*Sun.*] *9 after Trinity* we had a communion. Af*ter* M. Walker and I wer sent by the general to m*ake* peace between Skevington and Crane, the fyrst a fyzzeling[2] taleberer and a pykethank, the other a hasty foolysh feloe of his tung. With mu*c*h adoe we had them to shake hands, but in th*e* mean Luke Ward had further netled the gene*ral* for Skevington had caried quarels to them both.[3] // Skevington and Crane

13. ☾ [*Mon.*] the cow[n]cel was cawled and the case hard of Skevingtons accusation, so that by wytnes was proved foolysh words of Crane, and he was set in the bilboes but quicly came owt agayn.[4] 35r

[1] Job Hortop, reporting on his voyage to Guinea in 1567–8 with Hawkins, describes how 'in the nighttime we had one of our pinnesses bulged by a sea-horse, so that our men swimming about the river, were all taken into the other pinnesses, except two that tooke hold one of another, and were carried away by the sea-horse. This monster hath the just proportion of a horse, saving that his legs be short, his teeth very great, and a span in length . . .' (*PN* (1598–1600), 1904 repr., IX, 488).

[2] I.e., farting; see 16 Aug.

[3] From the minute of Crane's trial, which Madox set down on 13 Aug., it appears that Captain Skevington considered himself to be Luke Ward's lieutenant by appointment of the commissioners and as such had directed his master to attend on the Vice-admiral whereas Fenton had directed Crane to come to *him* 'twyse a day.'

Skevington also was dissatisfied with Fenton's leadership and had declared, according to Crane, that 'yf M. Frobusher had been general his place shold have been better' (Otho E VIII, f. 280).

[4] Crane had asserted that he would never come to sea again with Fenton 'whyl Fenton was Fenton' and that if he were to be set in the bilboes, John Gates and John Gore (master gunner and his mate on the *Galleon*) would throw them overboard. Several on the *Elizabeth* had heard the threat ('certein wordes tendinge to Mutynie,' according to Fenton, p. 101), but when the accused were called, all denied it. It was concluded that Crane should be set in the bilboes,

We had some rayne. (*cipher*: The generaul sayd befor the master he had as much aut*o*rity heer as had the quen.)[1]

a dragon tree

14. ♂ [*Tues.*] we went furth and fownd a dragon tree of mervelows lenth, crawlyng and wynding with most intricate gires. We fownd great store of lemmons but not ripe, ful many old pomegranats, goodly laundes [pastures] and thorow them pathes beaten 2 foot brood, I knoe not how far, so that I judge the Negroes ether at the tropique of Cancer or ♑ [Capricorn] or both come down ether to fysh, for hear is great store of mullet and others or to gather the frute, and after depart ageyn, and I suppoze the 2 equinoctials be 2 springs as wel hear as in Ingland and most infested with rayne.

a stran*ge* tree

Hear we fownd on the east syde a great tre of a wonderful shadowed top but the bot*tom* of hym was naturally devided by th*ick* butteresses and entercloses [partitions] into so many hawls, parlors, chambers, and cels, that 50 men myght have lodged under yt drye and al in several roomes, not one seing *an other*.[2] Hear we fownd oyster shels and cock*le she*ls and 2 yerthen pottes very thin, which *som* sayd wer of Portingale. We hun*ted oysters* in the fresh rivers, bows of trees *on which* stycked great oysters with thin shels . . . lyke boates of many fashions but . . . holloe, one upon an other, a peck on a lytle spray, sharp and good with vineger, peper and salt. We saw the palmito tre which doth also gro at Cape Mownt. Yt is nothing but a monstruos cane whose pyth is lyke smal rush candles with half pills [husks] on them. As yt groeth up so do the lower leaves faul and the top is a bush of leaves lyke unto segs. Som be 60 or 70 foot high or 100 and a fadome byg and I think lyve not past 20 yer, but this is gesse. //

oyster trees

palmi*to*

35v
turkies

We flusht 3 turky cocks wherof 2 for fatnes cold not fly, the third made a great flyght. We fownd dyvers *f*ewms

---

though he was released, according to Ward (*PN* (1589), p. 649), within half an hour; according to Walker, within ten minutes, the punishment 'mytygated at our req*uest*.'

[1] Madox misplaces the vowel sign, writing *i* for *o*.

Fenton's presumption was increasingly to disturb the others, yet he felt that any disapproval of himself was a 'derogac*i*on of her Ma*j*est*i*es aucthoritie (unworthlie Layde upon [him]' (Taylor, *Fenton*, p. 101).

[2] Cf. Walker's account, 24 Aug.

[droppings] of oliphants in the soyl. On the syde of a bank the stoppel of ther fynting[1] was 28 ynches abowt and the print of ther foot 12 ynches broad and rownd withowt cleft, the rubbing of ther backs agenst trees 9 foot hyge. Many apes and munkeys whom we hard to mop and mock[2] our halowing, but I saw none. Other did. We saw 2 larks with whyt fethers in the tayl, and hard them syng. Some grownd rock, some cley and al good for pasture . . . or medo and corne. I washt with *the m*erchants and layd a buck.[3] We fownd the great whyte dragon tree whose sap floy*eth* lyke mylk in the wild spurg, is just as viscows as glew and after groeth to gume. The fruit is lyke a great yelo apricock. oliphants / Captin Parker said 12 foote / Monkeis / larks / the soile / dragon [tree]

In the nyght comonly yt thundereth and rayneth but the after noone is fayr, hote and drye b*ut* yet clowdy. I speak this as wee *fown*d and as I suppose yt is when the *so*ne is nygh the zenith but to affyrme *that yt* is so alway because we fynd yt *so 4* or 5 days together is scarse to be *a*dmi*t*ted, and yet most places of late ar thus described, and that made Magellanus to caul that sea *mari pacifico* wher Sir Frances Drake had after a hundred and 20 dayes together a sowthwest tempest[4] and that road Porto Infelice wher this [one] did harboroe with most eaze and comodytye. (*cipher*: The generaul was angry becaus I was so far and so long a shore, but the cravenish cowardis of capten Parker.) // temperat / *nota*

15. ☿ [*Wed.*] yt thundred and rayned. The parrets eche day come fro the north to the hilly sowth to feed al day and at nyght returne lyke croes in the Munkmore.[5] We went a shore to take the variation but the rayne dyd hynder us. 36r *parets*

16. ♃ [*Thurs.*] we began to make a net to catch mullets. (*cipher*: The generaul gav me 2 shirts), *sed timeo danaos et* (*cipher: nota diligenter*)

[1] *Qu.* dung; cf. Fr. *fiente.*

[2] I.e., to deride; the more common expressions are to 'mop and mow' or 'mock and mow.'

[3] Put clothes to soak.

[4] During the storm Drake and his company were, according to the deposition of San Juan de Anton, Captain of the *Cacafuego*, 'forty days under bare masts' (quoted in Wagner, *Drake's Voyage*, p. 362). In describing their entrance to the South Sea, the compiler of the *World Encompassed* (1628) observed that it was called by some *Mare pacificum* but proved to be to them a *Mare furiosum* (ed. N. M. Penzer (1926), p. 30).

[5] A wooded area located across the Severn from Uffington; see p. 2 above.

dona ferentes.[1] (*Latin*: It is not necessary to entrust the management of affairs to those who because they are timid dare nothing by themselves, who because they are envious do not suffer others to improve their position; they relate all things to themselves, and, as Terence says, *Labore alieno magnam partam gloriam verbis in se transmovent*: great glory won by someone else's efforts they divert to themselves.)[2]

a fizele

Peter Owen told Capten Skevington that so long as he went fyzeling to the generall with tales to pyke hym a thank, so long they shold never be yn quyet. Hearon was demawnded what was a fyzeler and why privy taleberers wer cauled fyzelers. To this was answered that as he which fyzeleth doth stink worse than a playn farter and doth also lead many into suspition because yt is not knoen whence the fyst [stench] cometh, so etc. //

36v Ned Robinsons brother which cam fro the Edward that M. Banester myght cure hym dyeth[3] so that yf M. Banester had half that knoledge that hym self vawnteth of and that I knoe he wanteth, yet as Chauser sayth wher nature cesseth once to wurck, farewel physique, bear the coarse to church.[4] I was swymmyng in the sea by the watring place.

plenty of fysh

17. ♀ [*Fri.*] we went a fyshing to the sowth bay wher wer great number of mullets but none wold be taken in the net, but one fysh we took lyke a reremowse [sea bat], which swymmeth not flat lyke a place but up and down. Hear I got into the trees to eat oysters. They groe lyk a wythibere [willow] among the mudde and some l*et* faul smal bows plume downe, 50, some 40 foot long and 2 or 3 ynch [in] compasse whe*r* groe the oysters 20 foot above the hyg[h] water, for hear yt hig[h]s [rises] not in al the harboro past 7 or 8 foot at the most, so that I do ymagin veryly the oysters doth gro on this tree naturally. When they ar shakt of with any violence fro the bow, they fal into the

oyster trees

[1] *Aen.* II. 49. [2] *Eun.* 400.

[3] On 2 Aug. Ward had left his master carpenter Nicholas Allen with his boy George Robinson on the *Galleon* 'to take physike' (*PN* (1589), p. 647); Edward Robinson was a mariner on the *Galleon.*

[4] 'Knight's Tale,' ll. 2759–60.

bottom and cleave ether to a stout or one to an other, 10 in a cluster, wherof some gro to be a foot long as I have seen in the gr*eat* piles of shels which we have fownd on the land that the Negroes have made when ether for fysh or fruyt they come hyther, for hear is great store of perch, of pergo [sea bream], of mullet, of breme, of cunner [blue perch] and many strang fruyt, lymmons in great plenty and beans groyng *u*pon trees. Great shels wherof we mad gallant drinking cupps. Much varyety of shelfyshe. //

1[*8*].[1] ♄ [*Sat.*] ymediatly after dynner we espied at the east 37r
poynt a canow which some sayd was 20, and muche adoe, a can*ow*
great terror. Capten Parker styrd abowt to fet men fro the
shore and greatly complayned the rashnes of men, etc.
Well they shewd a flag of truce and we the lyke gladly, for
those that can say *hey corragio*, as God shal help me, this *corragio*
ship is able to beat the kyng of Spayns fleet,[2] now one sylly
canow doth make them creepe into a mowshole. When al
was com yn, yt wer 3 sylly Portingales in a lytle swynes Portingales
troe [boat], the one a sage old man in a capuchio [hood] of black moccado [inferior wool] and shipmens hose of a barbers apern. His name was Fraunces Freer, born at Venyce, dwellyng at the Yl of St. Yago,[3] which had byn spoyld by a Frenchman and his ship broken agenst a rock. The other elderly felo was of his cumpany.[4] The third whose name is Jasper de Wart of Lysburn, being a Portingal leeger with king Farma of the Negroes. His bad cote was noe more patcht than wer his bare leggs splotted [spotted]. He had goodly lips. Being come aboord us with Luke Ward and M. Jeffreis for our merchants wer a shore washing and as the desciples left al and folowed Christ, so when the howbub [hubbub] cam they left al and folowed M. Parker.[5]

[1] Misnumbered '19.'

[2] Madox recalls such boasting statements on 7 Dec., asserting they were voiced by the pilot Thomas Hood and Lieutenant Hawkins, and on 21 Dec., where he attributes comparable remarks to Ward and Fenton.

[3] The main island of the Cape Verde group, the site of Portuguese administrative and ecclesiastical control for the upper Guinea coast.

[4] Called 'Camillo,' see 4 Sept.

[5] Walker terms the canoe of the three Portuguese 'a verye lyttle boate.' Fearing that the Negroes were going to descend on them, Parker manned the

(*Latin*: Piety)

(*Latin*: magnanimity)

37v

(*Latin*: ridiculous)

(*Latin*: Great God! How great our majesty, how regal our countenance. Gentlemen, from you I expect now and demand that honour which you are accustomed to bestow on one who is worthy of it, for I now assume that role. It is fair and fitting, we answer – with bent knees. Let the strangers be called together. They are here. Who are you? Are you going? And where or for what reason? Who lives here? Who lives there? What is the layout of the region? How many cities? How many rivers? What is the food and clothing? What things constitute wealth? Is this a land of fruits, wild animals, beasts of burden or birds? Here is reported to be a very fertile source of gold.

These truly wretched little men, tired by so many questions, [answered] everything splendidly when they should rather have been received with wine (for *in vino veritas*). And when they saw the man [sc. Fenton] on account of his authority wrest his mouth pleasantly with a graceful motion and carefully note down all things from open adversaries, they answer everything at first humbly, timidly and with sufficient caution. But finally when that aged fox [sc. Francis Freer] sitting next to our leader perceived the ass masked in the lion's skin,[1] he placed his bare leg, the better to provide for his repose, on the table itself very familiarly and, so to speak, domestically in the presence of our little king; I could hardly refrain from laughing. But what am I to do? The matter, the people, and the time invite, but the place does not provide the opportunity.

They supply us with much information concerning King Farma, King Torra, King Farre and the Cymboses.[2]

---

pinnace to fetch aboard the *Galleon*'s merchants who were washing ashore while Ward together with some of the *Edward*'s merchants manned the skiff with 'a whyte flagge in the poope . . . in token of peace.' On revealing their identity, the Portuguese were received aboard the *Galleon*, where they reported that 20 sail of Spanish ships had gone to the Strait and 6 French ships had headed for the South Sea (Walker, 18 Aug.).

On 29 Aug. Fenton noted in the margin of his journal: '*Dom diego de flores with a wrie mouthe. generall of the Spanish fleete for the straetes*' (Taylor, *Fenton*, p. 105).

[1] In reference to Aesop's ass who, though base, was enabled by his position to live in ease; by the seventeenth century, the reference was proverbial (Tilley A351).

[2] Called 'Samboses' by those on Hawkins's 1564 voyage to Guinea, the

Asked about the winds, they said that the east and north blow in March, April, and May; in June, July, and August the south and southwest; during the other months the southeast for the most part. (*Latin*: what kind of winds)

Finally, they evaluate and buy our little boat, the Elizabeth, which we had decided to burn,[1] for 80 measures of cleaned rice, 10 quintals of elephant teeth, which weighed 500 pounds, and an Ethiopian. I shall not say how great a commotion arose among us, how much frightened lamentation, how many suspicions, what diverse conversations, every wave a skiff – for whom the painted Ethiopian – *cavete, cavete, tradimur, tradimur.* It was especially ridiculous that our protector [sc. Parker], he whom we procured as our captain and defender, was not there or rather the shell in which he hides himself. The strangers depart to pay off what they promised, and the day for trading was set.)[2] (*Latin*: the Elizabeth sold) (*Latin*: *Cupi*dity) 38r

19. ⊙ G [*Sun.*] *10 after Trinity.* (*Latin:* While our little king – for in the future we may so term that fearsome commander and popular tribune who thinks himself of such worth that the queen of China would court and embrace him – was purging himself, we proceed with Pyrgopolynices to that oyster-producing riverlet. Here indeed we fought it out in the sand very bravely and manfully, not against an enemy (*Latin*: ironically)

Sumbas, as their name implies, were eaters of human flesh. According to Walter Rodney (*History of the Upper Guinea Coast, 1545 to 1800* (1970), Ch. II), they were drafted into the invading army of the Manes in the mid-sixteenth century on its way to Sierra Leone, where the peaceful Sapes were inhabitant.

Tora, a king of the Manes who commanded the islands of the Sierra Leone Channel, was reported still alive in 1605; he was subject (p. 47, though Rodney cites Fenton's journal: Taylor, *Fenton*, p. 108) to Fatima, king of the northern Bulloms, a member group of the Sapes whose kingdom extended from Tagrim Point northwards (Madox's 'Tagurine,' see Fig. 11). Farma, the first Mane king of the Logos (Port Loko) area, was addressed as Emperor of the Sapes, a title retained by his successors. He is reported to have died in 1606 (Rodney, p. 102).

1 Fenton stated that the *Elizabeth* was to be burned because of 'certein Broyles' between the captain and the master [Crane], a 'stubborne knave,' and because it was judged insufficient for further service. On 14 Aug., Ward had brought divers things away; on the 16th he fetched certain things 'of ours,' which Walker records as items which had not yet been divided; again on the 20th and 25th, his company took away additional supplies (Ward in *PN* (1589), pp. 649–50).

The merchant Peter Jeffrey recorded (Otho E VIII, f. 186) that this decision of the general to divest himself of the *Elizabeth* was made without the consent of the merchants.

2 Fenton says it was to be within four days (Taylor, *Fenton*, p. 103).

but playing in turn, not in hand to hand combat with swords or sticks but at a distance with handguns. For it was indeed warlike to hear the clatter of the guns when fire springing out on every side belches forth little balls of smoke. Nor do they destroy anything except gun powder.

Cotton and I proceed to walk. Since we are not to be found anywhere, that Pyrgopolinyces who up to now or in the past never cared about the safety of his soldiers exclaims that these two stupid men, ignorant of danger, inexperienced in public affairs, are devoured either by monsters or cannibals or wandering in this vast desert through devious bypaths have fallen into some evil and cannot return. He complains, he inquires, he calls out like Hercules for Hylas. Meanwhile, we gather love apples[1] and return. At length, with a great crowd following, Pyrgopolynices approaches us in hot anger, magnificently pours out curses and threats to strike terror in us. But I receive him openly with laughter and scorn; I say he acted foolishly in letting two timid and unwary little boys wander off before sewing some message on their clothing so that whoever should find them wandering about might be able to bring them back home. When he realised he was being mocked, he turns everything to a joke. For if I should concede to him even in so small a trifle, clearly ten Nestors would not be able to prevail upon or placate him.) //

38v *20.* ☾ [*Mon.*] (*Latin*: the day was clear, but nothing worth mentioning happened. However, lest it seem devoid of anything, I shall report certain things which come to mind.)

Francise Frere told us that this Farre and Torre ar both under king Farma. Al go naked; nether is the king knoen by any apparel but by a cap. He taketh as many wyves as he list, which soe and reap his rise. The best rice which is the least grayne is 5 moneths from the seed to the sycle and is gathered in May and October; other for comon service is gathered every 7 weeks; the kings riches is slaves and eliphants teath. The fyrst wyfe is queene but the fyrst born boy is prince, and the oldest of kindred is the protector to

the maners of Guynye

[1] The *mala Æthiopica*, called 'golden' or 'love' apples (Gerard, *Herball*, S2*v*).

an orphan. They have *legem talionis* in slawghter or maym; in theft the gylty is sold for the king; for adultery the man only is punyshed. They acknoledge God and mak sayntes mediators such as have been valient men among them whose ymages they keepe and adore.

Yn the woodes be a wonderful cumpany of pysmyres, few frogs, no snayles, no tame beasts; hens just as owrs, some partridges. Tagurina lyeth on the north syde the river. antes

A boy seing his father taking a star with his balla stella[1] cryed, good father, catch one for me, and when he saw the star shoote, ye have hyt hir, father, sayth he, she is fawln, she is fawln. *fabula*

To a theif arayned and making stubborn answers sayth the clark of the syse, I wil prefer you to the gallows. Wer yt awght worth, sayth he, you wold take yt yourself. I wil geve you leav to stretch a rope, sayth the judge. I can do yt yf you say nay sir, answered he. // *acute responsum*

[*21.* ♂ *Tues.*] The general and master and *Par*ker and I rowed up to the poynt of the land at the neck of the sowtheast river and did se the open nornorthest of the great river. We saw many hills, one in the neck of , an other on the sowth syde, all woody save the furthest, which did appear to be the last. The shore is wonderfully defensed with great oyster trees, many goodly bays of 10 fadom at the least. The finest is a sandy bay beyond the poynt of a bare hil on whose rydg lyeth a blew rock. 39r rivers

This mean season M. Hawkins and capten Ward with ther people killed a great crocadyle of 12 foot long lacking 2 ynches in the oyster river which was the male. The femel also was seen aland. He was browght aboord and skynned. The flesh was mervelows fayr and whyte. Muche of yt was eaten. I eat a peece of the hart but because yt smelled so muche of musk, we cast the rest away. Under his armpits and in the joynt of his jaws ar bags of amber greece lyke kyrnels. His 2 lower butter teath [incisors] stryke up quyte throe his snowt as thoe they wer riveted. He *crocadilus* [sic] *alligato*

[1] Cross-staff or Jacob's staff used for taking the sun. Its users were sometimes deridingly called 'star shooters.'

prayeth in the water but feedeth on land. He refuseth noe meat, and assawlteth none that resyst him.[1]

(*Latin*: I will not say how great an annoyance this matter caused Pyrgopollynices and his Theseus because they did not take part in this loot, but they could not conceal their anger.) //

40r [*22.* ☿ *Wed.*] (*Latin*: The merchant returns with rice and ivory. He gave our little king a gift, an Ethiopian eleven years old with a delicate face. He is received kindly. Cotton, seeing himself left out, thrusts himself into the feast. For of all whom I have seen, he is most ready for feasts, but in other matters he is a man of restless and envious disposition, and his language is exceedingly boastful and seeding discord. However, since he could not force himself in at dinner because there was no place, he waited for a while and then went over to the merchants, and there a bitter strife arose between him and them. Did I say arose? Nay, rather it was fomented and encouraged, for it did not first begin now. He complains a great deal. They complain. I take pains to bring about peace but in vain, for whereas before he was in the habit of reporting to me false accusations and complaints against our two little kings, now restored to favour, he acts more boldly and cares for nobody's favour, not even a little, except for the one who can contribute something to his belly.

(*Greek*: Cotton)

The stranger told us many things about the customs of the Æthiopians, and he also made certain inquiries about our queen, with Ferdinando interpreter. But when a painting was brought forth in which a lively likeness of Elizabeth was depicted, that guest recognised the royal countenance instantly. *Greek*: But our tetrarch insolently said: It is not the likeness of the British queen but that of my mistress whom I love. *Latin*: Twice did he impress these things on us and ordered the interpreter to say so. The interpreter did so. The guest smiled. But Walker noted this carefully

(*cipher*: treaso*n*)

The guest reported that there are here among the Brahmans [*qu.* Bulloms] and the Sapies many magicians

(*Latin*: Magician)

[1] See Walker's account of the killing, which, according to Ward, took almost three hours.

as well as jugglers of admirable ability, among them the
king, who is accustomed to put on at will all sorts of
shapes. He is called Fattimai, and through his remarkable 40v
skill in the art he attained to the height of great majesty
whereas before he served another king. He is also (*Latin*: Some astonishing things)
accustomed to kill with a cable and to eat the concubines
with whom he had intercourse all during the night if they
seemed to him something less than agreeable and pleasing.[1]
Certain people tell this and many other stories, partly in
order not to seem ignorant of such customs, partly in order
to scare us and frighten us away from all trade. For he told (*Latin*: The Portuguese deride our timidity)
it as if to deride our timidity once and for all. If you gave
this king a cask of wine or something similar as a small
present, you would have him daily as a guest and he would
satisfy you abundantly, even for a whole month, with rice,
fish, fruit and other food, to say nothing of gold and other
trinkets and [?] baubles. But our leaders are so vigorous 41r
that they tremble even in the face of the flies whizzing by. (*Latin*: Vigorous leaders)
What is more hateful, they know nothing about approaching others and they pride themselves much on the
fact that they can foresee all dangers. But the timid calls
himself circumspect and the mean frugal. Whatever they
[sc. Fenton and Parker] hear they say that this is thoroughly
Irish, for thus the Irish are wont to do in the places where
we obtained and practised our empire. Beautifully and
wisely said. Wonderful, etc.)

23. ♃ [*Thurs.*] M. Cotton and I walked up into the woodes.
We saw marvelows goodly lands and pastures and 2 beastes and birds
loses [oxen] of a brown color with short tayles and rownd
flat horns as byg as 3 yer old bullocks, very grosse and fat.
We saw 2 partridges and he sayd he saw a woodcock;[2]
I knoe not whether he ment me, but surely I saw none
unlesse I shold mean hym. We wer in purpose to have gone
to the top of the hygh hil but he be*in*g weary and fearful,
we returned, and at the water syde in honowr of St.
Bartholomew made a thwacking bonyfyer. They kyld
aboord a fysh which is cawled *herenaceus marinus*, in all herenaceus marinus

[1] See Walker (25 Aug.), who calls the king 'Ferma.'
[2] Also a synonym for 'fool.'

poynts lyke a porcupyne but that he was legles.[1] The skyn is kept.

24. ♀ [*Fri.*] *Bartholomew day* the general and I and capten Parker dyned at the Edward. After dynner the general went aboord but we walked to the lemmon trees.

(*Latin*: Luke Ward told me that in the future our little king would not admit any councillors except those who would smile at him.[2] He added, furthermore, that that
41ᵛ one by his example has proved he rules most arrogantly over the timid and the fearful as well as over the ingenuous and gentle, but when he would see someone full of spirit who could not put up with wrongs and follies, he would revert to his real nature and show a mean and cowardly spirit.

(*Latin*: Chance alteration)

At the table M. Taylbois, loaded with wine, burst out vehemently against Cotton, accusing him, not falsely to be sure, but foolishly and uselessly. Cotton, however, now found his greatest advocate in that Pyrgopolinices whom he is always in the habit of tearing to pieces in secret and privately warring with in addition.

(*Latin*: Decision about the councillors)

After supper the little king called me and ordered me to look into the character of those who would be his councillors. He said that certain ignoble, boorish and witless fellows comported themselves magnificently under the title of councillor. Accordingly, he said he had decreed that henceforth they were not to be used in the council nor admitted to deliberations. For just as the queen summons of all the citizens of first rank only those in whom she has the highest confidence and excludes the others altogether, so he also can and will do.) God send us al wel to doe.

The commodity that hear we fownde

25. ♄ [*Sat.*] the master, John Lynsey, and I with others went to the top of the playn hil whence we myght se the north sand and the red rock and take vew many ways. The master guner was syck. Yt was a hote day. Ther passed not many 24 howrs withowt lyghtening, thunder and rayn, but not gre*at* and the breez ether at the sea or on the hills

[1] See Fig. 12. Walker calls it a 'sea hedgehogge.'

[2] The General and Parker had passed the forenoon 'in talke' with Captain Ward; after supper Fenton repeated to Madox his decision to exclude the merchants from the councils. See also 4 Sept.

was coole and cumfortable, and above 50 men that wer
before geven over to death ar now become lusty and
strong, for the lymmons have scowred ther mowths,
fastened ther teath and purifyed the blud. The fresh water
bathes have suppled ther joyntes, healed the woondes and
abated the swelling,[1] and the foode of the oyster // hath 42r
coct [pricked] them up in hart lustyly so that as long
before I told them the land was nothing so unholsom as holso*me*
yt was heald but no persuasion yn any thing can prevayle lande
til need come to play the orator which rather useth
Carters lodgique than Wilsons rhetorique.[2]

[*26.*] ⊙ [*G Sun.*] *11 after Trinity* the master and I and M.
Hawkins dyned with capten Ward. After we rowed to the
sowthwest bay which is a fayre dry sand when the tyde is
owt. On the land which is the poynt we saw very many
munkeys and I think thos be the spoyl of al the snayls. munkeis
We saw the foyle [dung] of the elephant newly made,
within half an howr of our comyng, so that wer not we
greater beastes than is he, wee myght or this have kild elepha*nt*
more than one of them. His rubbing was 10 foot hygh.
His steps be short and thyck; the pattern of his foot is thus
 18 ynches long and 24 broad. Wee had one tooth
that wayd 50^{li} and hard of 2 that weyd 150^{li}. Hear is at
tyme of yer great resort of the Negroes, as appeareth by the
oyster shels, great store of pergos, brems, dorees,[3] much fyshe
frute, a pleasant and holsome place, but we lack harts to
try yt. We saw also waterfowles in ech respect lyke swans
but that ther bills were whyte, long, and sharp. Thes they
cawled, but I suppose falsely, pellycanes. pelli*cans*

We supt also with capten Ward and so cam home. In
eating the sweet kyrnel of a fruyt lyke unto a whyt plume plumm
that groes by the water syde, dyvers sayd they purged
greatly but with some of us they wroght no allevation. //

27. ☾ [*Mon.*] ther went owt by the cownsel of the Portingale 42v

[1] Cf. Walker, 15 Aug.

[2] In his *Rule of Reason* (1551), V3, Thomas Wilson says, 'Som cal suche rough dealyng, Carters Sophistrie, when the fiste reasoneth a matter by buffites, which the tongue should prove by Argumentes.' (Cited by R. B. McKerrow (ed.), *Works of Thomas Nashe*, IV (1958 repr.), 192).

[3] St Peter's fish, mistakenly called 'golden.'

good fyshing

to the sowthwest rock before day 4 or 5 to fysh and they broght home 50 great dorees and brems. 2 or 3 nyghts we had seen a fyre on the northeast poynt of the land which the Portingal told us was a token that his canow was ther and durst not put into the sea. Now 4 days afore capten Parker with the pynayce wel appoynted went up, but his care to preserve his men cawsed hym not to ventur to far. Now did Fransis Freere request ernestly to have a lytle skyf to go up for his men and with many great intreaties of us al did hardly opteyn yt.[1]

great oringes and plantanes

28. ♂ [*Tues.*] morning his canow cam and the skyfe with great orenges very sweet and delyciows and green, 12 or 16 ynches abowt, also with plantens which is a very delyciows fruyt and groeth lyke a beane 2 or 3 fadom hygh. The cod is 3 square lyke the cod of a segge somwhat bowed. Within this cod is a certayn mello pyth very delyciows and sweet.

(*Latin*: The merchants explain their action with reason)

Our merchants sold them som lynnen cloth and pans for duble the value in gold wherwith the general was offended and indeed not withowt cause, for to sel to merchants is no gayn and thos things also that wold last withowt joperdy, and wher our venture is 3^s duble our ware, to sel for twyce duble gayn is manifest losse, but to have caried some of our perished ware up into the cuntrey, in my opinyon, had been both pollytique and gaynful.[2]

elephant

43r

John Gore and Arthur Cotton saw the elyphant to day wher we sawght hym yesterday // and shot at hym. They say he is a gryzeled brown; his tusks groe in his nether

[1] Freer had come aboard the *Edward* in the afternoon, and at 5 o'clock, Ward took him to the general to gain his consent to use the boat belonging to the *Francis* (Ward, in *PN* (1589), p.650).

Suspicious that the Portuguese might take the *Elizabeth* and depart, though they still owed three bushels of rice (Taylor, *Fenton*, p. 104), Ward sent four men to watch in it that night.

[2] According to Ward, Evans began 'to barter away certaine of the ships commodities with the *Negroes*,' not telling the general until he had finished, 'whereof grew more words then profit, as by the bookes of Marchandise appeareth.' The next night he himself bartered with them, '2. redde cappes for 3. Oliphants teeth,' and on the 30th, the General, Parker, and Drake went aboard the *Edward* to examine the Portuguese and Negroes for things they had bought 'and especially for a stolne cloake, which would not be heard of' (*PN* (1589), p. 651).

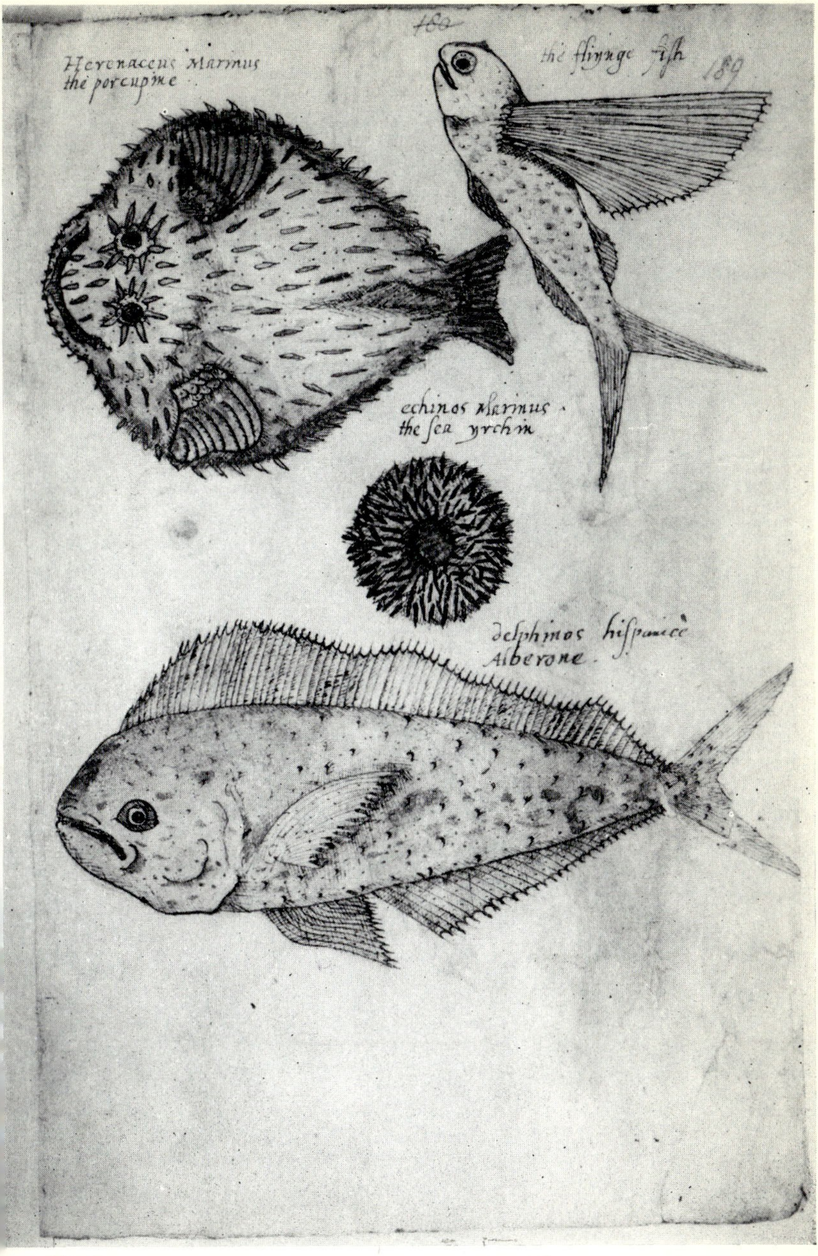

Fig. 12. Madox's drawings of tropical fish

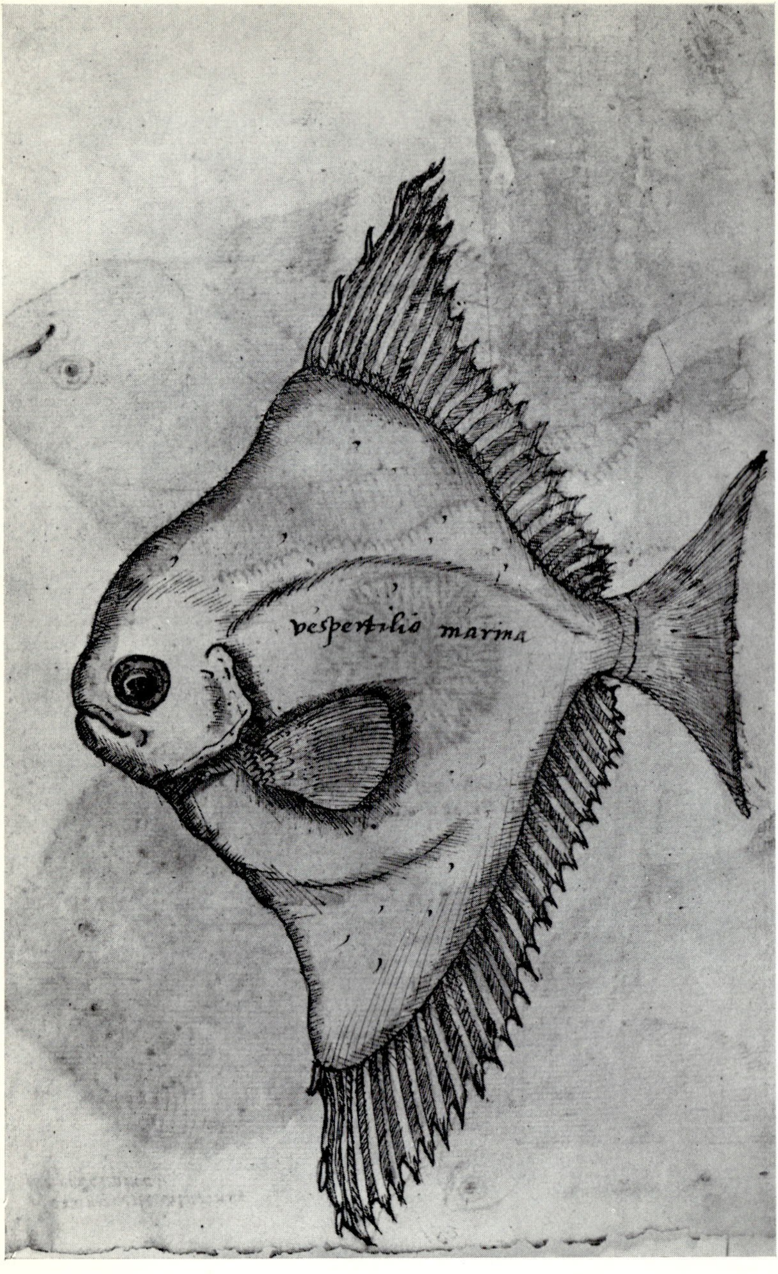

Fig. 13. Madox's drawing of a tropical fish

jawe, his sholders be armed as yt wer with sheilds, wherewith he bears down the woodes.

Jasper de Wart tawght me in the Negroes language to cownt thus. 1. *kink*. 2. *cherink*. 3. *chasàs*. 4. *yaunaleìh*. 5. *chamátra*. 6. *chamátrakink*. 10. *chofàch*. 11. *chofáchekink*. 15. *Bowtrei*. 16. *Bowtrekink*. 20. *cubàch*. *osêmo*, meate. a quo, *arága piá we*. quomodo hoc appellatur: *crow*, deus. *crowfi*, est is quem adorant et mediatorem constituunt. *attamte*, bonum. *allêse*, malum. *urgonỳ*, vir. *ottémera*, mulier.[1] Guiny language

The general caused to be fyxed fast in a stone at the watring place a square plate of copper with this inscription and forme and underneth:

[Fig. 14]

Sketch of the copper plate set up by Fenton

Edwardus Fenton armiger per Elizbetham reginam Angliae, classi praepositus ei quae regiones Chinensem et Cathaiam discooperire destinata est.[2]

August 26, 1582.

[2]9. ☿ [*Wed.*] capten Parker with others went to hunt the eliphant, but indeed althogh they saw hym not, yet they heald al frendly together, and God be thanked notwithstanding al danger came home safe agayn. //

30. ♃ [*Thurs.*] M. Cotton and I and Dic Clark went to the furthest sowthwest poynt. We saw lytle houses of reedes as I think used at tymes of yere for fyshers and a morter of wood, wherin they bray the palmito nutts. 43v fysher howses

At nyght the generawl supt at the Edward. (*Latin*:

[1] This African vocabulary, which seems to be one of the earliest recorded by an Englishman, has been identified (by Dr D. Dalby of the School of Oriental and African Studies, London) as deriving from the Temne language. The modern equivalents, which he has kindly supplied, are as follows: *1* kin; *2* tərəŋ; *3* təsas; *4* yanlɛ; *5* tamath; *6* tamthrukin; *10* tɔfɔt; *11* tɔfɔt + kin; *20* kəgba; *meat* ɔsɛm; *god* kuru; *spirit* kərfi; *malum* aləse!; *man* ɔruni (Baga dialect, orukuni); *woman* ɔwath-bɛra.

[2] The inscription reads: Edward Fenton, Esquire, by the grace of Elizabeth, Queen of England, commander of this fleet which is destined to discover the regions of China and Cathay.

Parker's motto, partially obliterated, seems to read: *nec spes nec metu*: neither with hope nor fear.

Cotton lodged many complaints with me against our merchants and others; nor have I known a man endowed with such odious peevishness.)

oysters with mother of pearle

31. ♀ [*Fri.*] the fyshers browght from the sowtheast rock myghty byg oysters in maner lyk *un*to horse hoofes. The meat was fulsom [cloying] and mylky, but the shel was mother of pearl*e* very thik and good. At nyght yt thundred and rayned and very great lyghtening.[1] //

44r

September ♎

discedimus

[*1.*] ♄ [*Sat.*] we were working upon the flud befor 2 in the morning, and a quarter after 6 in the name of God we wer under our forsayle on the fyrst of the eb having now and than an unsteedy breeze fro the east. *The Lord be thanked for the cumfortable refreshing we have fownd heare, and guide us in mercie the rest of our cowrse to his glorie. Amen.*[2]

44v

When we had fownd the wynd sowthwest at the sea, altho nyghtly before we had a good stif northren breez and eastern fro the land, we anchored 8 or 9 leags on the west the Serra Liona and ther I perceaved that the current setteth naturally to the north for nether was ther wynd nor any sea gale and the flud went with a swyft tyde which made the ship cape [drift] sowth, but the eb strok owt weakly after long tyme, making the ship cap*e* into the east, turning hir buttock agaynst the wynd which was and cawsing the anchor to gro owt of hir star boord bowe.

the current of the sea

2. ⊙ [G *Sun.*] *12 after Trinity* we roade hear stil, having service. This a hote daye and cleere. I sen*t* Luke Ward the names of our people.

3. ☾ [*Mon.*] our general went to the Edward wher he dyned and supt. Yt was verye hote. At dynner we had reasoning

[1] Walker records that as they supped 'under an Awninge upon the sommer decke,' they called for candles, but 'there happened suche aboundance of contynyuall lyghteninge without ceasinge that the same mynystered suffycyent lyghte to suppe by.'

[2] As he had done for their two weighing of anchors in England (Fig. 7), Madox began a horoscope (at 6:15 a.m.) but, since they did not, in fact, sail, left it incomplete.

and whil M. Parker wold comend his own care in keping his men unscattered and safe, the thinge was so ridiculows because ther is at al no maner dang*er* and so odiows because none can be suffere*d* to serch that words began to be multiplie*d*, M. Evans affirming that the Portingal wold have browght the king to hym, M. Parker saying yt was offered to the generall, and indeed yt was offered to both, but was not accepted. Na, we lookt for great thanks to do the Portingal that curtesy to geve hym leav so to do, and for more thanks to do the king that hon*owr* to let hym com into our presens, that he cam not at al. M. Cotton hear agen retching at M. Evans was bydden hold his peace but he medleth to muche. //

contentio

Lusitani se offerant

Because the wynd was contrary and that the tresse [tressel] trees of our mayn mast wer cracked, we loosed to go back agayn into harboro. At mydnyght Harey Mellers dyed of a Calentowr, and he is the 10th that we have thrown over boord.

45r *reditus* 10 Mellers

4. ♂ [*Tues.*] lying at anchor of in the sea the Edward by neglygens let fawl a fayr anchor and cable with a sunken boy, which being not turned on the bytts brok the stopper and ran owt end for end so they were fayn to let fawl an other and to sweepe for yt.

an anchor loste

(*Latin*: At night the little king called me aside. He said that he had seen enough of the insolence and arrogance of the merchants. For this reason he had decided to communicate to them in the future nothing that would not be allowed to be read even in public. And as there was no small scarcity of necessary provisions, especially of drink that had been considerably depleted because of a defect in the casks, he said he wishes to return with Francis Frere and Camillo again to the Cape Verde Islands where he would better supply himself with wine, for he said he had heard that a bitter controversy had arisen between the king [António] and the bishop [governing Santiago]. Thus while favourably inclined to one side, he could seize the opportunity to attack the other.)

(*Latin*: What is proposed)

5. ☿ [*Wed.*] (*Latin*: At daybreak he went away with Pyrgopollinices, and a storm having suddenly arisen, the bark

(*Latin*: Great danger)

was almost overwhelmed by the waves. But we offered them help by letting down from the stern another small bark which he could seize.

Nichol Smith

Today Nichol Smith fell into the sea through a porthole, an unhappy boy and hated both by gods and men. With divine help, however, he kept his head above the waves long enough for Fayreweather and another Smith to swim and take hold of him, already half dead.

Weighing anchor, we set sail again for the southern port; the Edward remained in order to look for the lost anchor but in vain.) //

45[v]

6. ♃ [*Thurs.*] (*Latin*: some went fishing; others made for the shore with Pyrgopollinices, among whom was M. Taylbush, who, because of an offence done to him, threw his arrows into the sea.)

(*Latin*: many curses)

7. ♀ [*Fri.*] (*Latin*: I and others watched the fisherman in the main port, while the rest were looking for the anchor but in vain. We caught two little herrings or rather sea urchins which were armed with a round shell and little black spears [see Fig. 12]. When broken, they tasted very sweet to the palate, even raw. Ward and Walker dined with us.)

(*Latin*: this was done on ♃ [Thurs.])

8. ♄ [*Sat.*] (*Latin*: Cotton and I made for the watering place, and having piled up a heap of wood, we started a fire. We found a sea crab in a grove far from the shore, which fled when he saw us. We built an oven on the shore with very large rocks and with not inept skill. I made the mortar from earth and bitumen.)[1]

(*Latin*: oven)

9. ☉ [G *Sun.*] *13 after Trinity.* (*Latin*; *Greek*: M. Evans thinks that he has been unfairly treated because we always spoke to the Portuguese with Ferdinando as interpreter, and when it was decreed by the little king to send two of ours, John Haul and Peter Owen, with Francis Frere, he insisted, in my presence, on setting out together with them. Of course,

[1] Ward adds that they set up a smith's forge as well (*PN* (1589), p. 652), which suggests that Fenton's dilatory tactics stemmed from his expressed desire (4 Sept.) to return with the Portuguese to the Cape Verde Islands ostensibly for wine but covertly for purchase.

answers the king, I permit you to go now without penalty.

I forgot to say that on Friday we dined with Captain Drake on the Francis and that Walker, the African prince, the king, and little queen and I passed the night there.[1] John Gore and John Kelly,[2] having quarreled at home, enticed two *bowinos*[3] into error so that all four, thrown into fetters, paid the penalty for their stupidity. On the day of the Sabbath weighing anchor in the afternoon, we arrived closer to the watering place.) (*Latin*: they are thrown into fetters) 46r

1[*o.*] ☾ [*Mon.*] (*Latin*: we lunched and dined on the Edward, where Milo did not permit Walker to take away a little dish of mustard to the Francis.[4] *Durum os, et non creta sed carbone notandum*: You brazen face, and to be noted down not with chalk but with charcoal.[5] Fie, is this the way to rule free people? Have we been reduced to such a degree of servitude while we wish to be useful to the state and while we left behind us country, parents, and friends for whose sake we crossed so great a sea? But why? We have sinned, omnipotent Father, before God and man, nor are we worthy to be called your sons. Restore us to your temple and make us your attendants and servants. And although we have angered you grievously, yet do not confute us in your wrath nor reprove us in your rage. Have pity on us, Lord, according to your great compassion and [extend] the abundance of your mercy. Destroy our iniquities and the iniquities of the people and make us safe, O Lord, for we trust in you.) (*Latin*: how to command)

1[*1.*][6] ♂ [*Tues.*] (*Latin*; *Greek*: The king conferred with me about the island of St. Helens between the equator and ♑ [Tropic of Capricorn]; he said it was a land very fertile in (*Latin*: the island of *St* Helens)

[1] Walker records he supped and lay aboard the *Francis*, which is confirmed by Ward (*PN* (1589), p. 652) who remarks that the General also supped there; neither makes mention of the other guests 'invyted by Captayne Drake.'

[2] I.e., John for William Kelly, gunner on the *Galleon*. Gore was gunner's mate.

[3] Meaning undetermined.

[4] Tension, resulting no doubt from their inconclusive progress, is reflected in Ward's increasing concern with provisions which Madox sharply comments on later (7 Dec.) and perhaps explains the unusual dissension between the Vice-admiral and his chaplain. Walker refers to the incident in one word: *sinapium*.

[5] The expletive, from Terence, *Eun.* 806, is added to Horace, *Sat.* 2.3.246.

[6] Madox inadvertently repeats '10.'

all things and wholly without inhabitants; a place, moreover, suitable and convenient for a settlement, where having constructed walls we could establish a colony and there await the return of the Portuguese, who laden with spices come to this place to water in the month of May.[1] It is a remarkable thing how eager we are for fame that is most delusive and how much we thirst to acquire wealth and that too quickly, but we avoid dangers and toil. While we are very much afraid of and shudder at honest dangers, we are threatened with more serious and bitter evils. You, Lord, take heed, and do not spare those who commit
46v evil willingly and do not become angry with those who are compelled to watch and be silent.)

12. ☿ [*Wed.*] (*Latin*: that old merchant came back with our two attendants and three other Portuguese.[2] It was agreed with the oldest of them, whose name is Lewis and who has lived here twenty years, to receive 166 measures of rice in return for 100 measures of salt, a proportion of three to five. This old man reported to us that these Æthiopian people are loyal and compassionate and they ardently love white men if they suffer no injury from them. He added also that this land produces a brazilwood much more effective for dying cloths than that which comes from Brazil itself. But for this reason nothing is produced here lest this region prove harmful to the annual revenues; while he

(*Latin*: feasting)

Brazil

[1] Discovered by the Portuguese on St Helena's Day in 1502, the island was visited by the returning carracks to water and refresh their men. Since the Portuguese had providently introduced a variety of fruits and animals, the little island was frequently described as an earthly paradise, but, as John Pory later commented, it was not so easily found on the outward journey ('A particular description . . . of Africa' in Leo Africanus, *The History and Description of Africa*, ed. R. Brown, I (Hakluyt Soc., 1896), 92–3).

At this point Fenton seems to have been vacillating between returning to the Cape Verde Islands or heading for St Helena. The following day he talked privately to Walker about returning to the Islands, arguing that unless they obtained a store of wine, the voyage would be utterly overthrown, but the chaplain withstood his arguments. It was not until the 19th that Walker recorded (in Latin) Fenton's proposal to head for St Helena.

[2] The 'old merchant' refers to Francis Freer who had taken John Hall (a mariner on the *Galleon*) and Peter Owen (late of the *Elizabeth*) up country to visit one of the local chieftains (see 9 Sept.). The three others were 'Lewis Henriques a dweller here above 20. yeeres,' 'Matthew Fernando,' captain of the carvel, and Peter Vaz, whom Ward terms 'pilot,' Madox (23 Sept.) 'merchant traveler.' Ward mentions that in all seven Portuguese supped with him (*PN* (1589), p. 652).

[King Philip] holds the government in Brazil, here he holds nothing.

He said, further, that the king of the Æthiopians, Massatomba, lives between Cape Verde and the Rio Grande, a noted champion of justice, in whose kingdom, if anything is lost by accident, it is never kept by the founder but is brought to a raised place visible to all.[1] (*Latin*: Justice) Here the queens wear the most magnificent vestments in accordance with the custom of the place. Fatima and Torrea are youths, but Farma is an old man, a little stout and fat yet nimble in war. Here people live a very long time so that many reach the age of 160 years. (*Latin*: old age) According to their sexual urge, they marry a great number of women by whom they beget not a few children. He reported that near the mountains of the moon[2] there is a queen, empress of all these Amazons, a witch and a cannibal who daily feeds on the flesh of boys. She ever remains unmarried, but she has intercourse with a great number of men by whom she begets offspring. The kingdom, however, remains hereditary to the daughters, not to the sons.[3]

47r (*Latin*: a certain facetiousness)

When the stranger had reported these things, our king earnestly inquired whether, as is the case with kings who cohabit with a great number of women, she herself had as many children as the number of men she had intercourse with. I smiled at the man's childishness, but what is not the race of the swift nor the contest of the strong, the Master dispenses at will and, what is more, wisely.[4]

(*Latin*: birds' nests)

They bring from the shore two little nests of birds,

[1] Masatamba, king of the Casangas, a tribe living in the area of the Casamance River with their capitol at Brucama (Rodney, *History* . . . , pp. 89, 7). The story of native justice so impressed Fenton that he too recorded it (Taylor, p. 106).

[2] In the older maps the mountains of the moon figure as a range extending across the continent from Abyssinia to the Gulf of Guinea (Leo Africanus, *History*, ed. Brown, pp. 107–8).

[3] Cf. the account of the traditional origin of the Manes recorded (1625) by André Dornelas, a trader who had spent fifty years on the Guinea coast: he reported that the original chief of the Manes was a woman called Macarico who had offended the emperor in Mandimansa and been forced to leave; taking along her friends and relatives, she formed a conquering army that became so large it was necessary to eat some of the conquered people. On reaching the Atlantic, she proceeded up the coast to Cape Mount where her son was killed in a battle with the Bulloms and she herself died c. 1545; the conquest of the Sapes by the Manes continued for another fifteen years. (Cited in Rodney, *History of the Upper Guinea Coast*, pp. 44–5.)

[4] Echoing *Eccles.* 9: 11.

constructed with remarkable skill of grass woven and joined together in a thousand ways and hanging from slender branches. They are suspended over the river in order that in this way they might be safe from the snare of venomous worms of which there is a marvelous supply here.

We dined on the Edward. Walker disclosed to me that he was told by Whitaker that Thomas Doughty lived intimately with the wife of Francis Drake, and being drunk, he blabbed out this matter to the husband himself. When later he realised his error and feared vengeance, he contrived in every way the ruin of the other, but he himself fell into the pit: he is accused of *læse majeste* because he said that councillors could be corrupted by gifts.[1]

(*Latin*: Doughty is killed)

The days begin to grow hot here. It thundered a great deal and rained occasionally, but the inhabitants say that scarcely three showers will fall here again before the month of March.

Jasper de Wart is accused . . . before us because king Farma would have Francis Frere whipped for his offence, saying this, . . . you would deny that those Anglo-Saxons brought me a bottle of European wine.[2] But we should surely be blamed because we did not answer for him.

I found out for certain that our little king had promised many among us that he would never return to our native land before he rewarded them with wealth. He gave them clothing, but not at his own expense. While he hoped to be able to rule without sailors and a captain, he hated them all worse than a dog or a snake, but after he realised he could

[1] Thomas Doughty had been executed by Drake at San Julián, the site of an execution by Magellan of one of his mutinous officers. Various reasons were subsequently alleged to account for Doughty's offence, including the charge, repeated by Camden, that he had oftentimes accused Leicester of doing away with the earl of Essex.

On 1 June Walker, together with Madox, Hawkins, and John Drake, had dined at 'M. Whooddes' house where Whitaker was also present.

[2] Madox's use of the term *Anglo-Saxons* in its modern sense antedates the earliest reference cited in the *OED*, which credits Camden with having introduced its modern use into Latin in 1586.

King Farma had apparently accused the Portuguese of withholding some of the gifts sent by the English. See the next entry.

become nothing without these people, he now embraces them alone.)[1]

[13.] ♃ [*Thurs.*] (*Latin*: they send wines to king Farma, [which] they contend [must be conveyed] by the Portuguese alone, nor is any one of ours permitted to convey it. Thus I shall enumerate him [? Ward] among the Choroebi who sent a gift provided they should drink it all.[2] But if I shall learn later that they offered our gift to the king in our name, I shall of course cancel the name of our little king entirely from the Book of Fools and record the Portuguese in its place.[3] 47^{v}

(*Latin*: He says he dies from laughing from time to time because he diluted the wine with water)

Pallinurus told me that Furbusher received 1600^{li} for buying victuals and some other necessaries considered useful for the ship, but that he spent only 500 pounds on provisions, reserving the rest for himself. He affirmed that others similarly engaged in such business were able to take care of themselves and to do this destroyed at that instant the whole purpose of the enterprise. . . . Besides we have the greatest provision for the journey, and the king admitted that this ship with the provisions and the merchandise had cost ten thousand pounds.)[4]

Martin Frobusher

[14. ♀ *Fri.*] (*Latin*: I wandered through vast deserts with two companions, but because of the byways I could not reach the top of the mountain. As we supected on account of the

[1] See Madox's cryptic remarks on this subject on 15 and 24 Sept. On the 16th, Walker records that the general gave his men new liveries 'of brodd cloth of popyngay greene.'

In his account, dated after their return, Hawkins reported Fenton's promising to reward all the 'well willers' consenting to take over St Helena, the money to be captured from the Portuguese 'Armathos' watering at the island on their return from the East Indies (Otho E VIII, f 224*v*).

[2] Coroebus was a traditional fool who tried to count the waves of the sea. Familiar to readers of the *Adagia* of Erasmus, the term, with the incorrect *Ch*, is used by both Gabriel Harvey and Thomas Nashe (See McKerrow, *Works of Thomas Nashe*, IV, 181). Madox uses it again on 26 Sept.

On the 13th, Ward notes he gave the Portuguese 'a bottle of wine for one of the savage Queenes' (*PN* (1589), p. 652).

[3] Madox apparently is recalling an anecdote in *The Arte of Rhetorique* (1553 ff.) by Thomas Wilson, whose *Rule of Reason* he also remembered (see n. 2, p. 175, 25 Aug.): a jester belonging to Alphonsus, King of Naples, kept a record of the follies at court in a 'Booke of remembraunce'; queried by the king as to why he was listed among the fools for trusting a stranger who might indeed prove to be untrustworthy, the jester assured him that if he did not prove to be so, he would then take the king's name out of his book and put that of the stranger in its place (ed. G. H. Mair (1909), p. 144).

[4] For estimates and statements of costs, see pp. 21–2 and nn. above.

consumption of fresh bread and abundant drinking of water, all of us to a man purged up and down with the most acute abdominal pains, and this was almost universal.

It should be especially noted that the new moon brings an abundant force of showers in the region, but after it has begun to shine, the rains come to an end, the season remains the same. At night there are few storms, and it rains during the day.

48r Although the soldiers are strong and sufficiently courageous, they are utterly inept at trading and the exploring of unknown lands. Because, indeed, being always among enemies and in a hostile place, they believe they are [here] exposed to the usual dangers; for this reason they can never enter into dealings with others without suspicion. Suspicion, however, breeds hatred and

(*Latin*: Soldier and merchant)

hatred open war, and thus those they ought to attract and attach to themselves by human kindness and clemency, they frighten off by impudence and malice, and in this way all love perishes. Especially because of ignorance of languages, each is a barbarian to the other. And so the Portuguese always looked out very well for their own interests as they condemned and sent away those who had thoroughly learned the language and customs of the aliens. Thus friendship was contracted not through soldiers but through merchants. For it is not likely we should hate any man or wish to do him harm except through fear or cupidity or revenge. And if they are not provoked either by words or deeds and do not fear by some indications that our good faith will be transformed into suspicion, there is no danger of cupidity, while we could easily hope to be able to deserve well of ourselves and our plantations by [serving] their interests from which we stray. And this argument I should not wish to pass over lightly.)

When ther was establyshed in the north *in* Wales and in Devonshire 3 cowncels[1] for *the* ease of the subjects because they shold come to far to the lawe, the old yer*l* of Bedford being made president of D*evon*shire after a terms trial delyvreth u*p* his pattern to the king, saying that thos which

[1] See *Statues at Large*, v (1763), 32 Henry VIII, c. 50.

before refused to law for the travel *and* cost of yt, now having the judgment // so ny ther dores wold not styk to 48v enter an action for the cock scraping in a y*ard*, wherfore he desyred yt myght be cawled in and so yt was, but Wales and the north to ther great troble do so stil remayn.

15. ♄ [*Sat.*] I was stil syk with the collique and lask. We supposed ther was rye in our mea*l* thro some juglying that ANTHONY FISHER, M. Furbushers man,[1] had made, for al*tho* bowters wer payd for and men for ther *w*orke, yet we fownd playnly yt never *h*ad been bowlted. (*Latin*: a gainful but wretched deceit)

(*Latin*: I learned by frequent experiments that the loadstone, which in England declines from the north towards the east by at least 11 degrees, here does not bend more than three degrees from the arctic pole toward the east.)

In the oyster bay the merchants saw an other aligato *and* fownd a fysh almost dead, owt of whose syde he had bytten a great *lu*mp. Yt was a sword fysh lyke *to a* shork and his sword 20 ynches *long*, 3 ynches broad with 13 antleys[2] *on* the on syde and 11 on the other of *a*n ynch and 2 ynches long as hard as *i*ron. The fysh was good and did eat lyke sturgion.

(*Greek*: The leader, having seen much, hoped that those who are concerned about [him] should have the garments.)[3] //

In adventurs of discovery seldom any man bringeth 49r publique good to his own lyfe, more seldom with his own gayn but never yf he be careful ether of lyfe or gayne. (*Latin*; *Greek*: He who does not know this admits he does not know. We are willing to undertake actions of this sort. He did not love them from the heart, but as Perseus says, *callidum* [*sic*] *scis ponere sumen*; *scis comitem horridulum trita donare lacerna*: you know how to serve up a hot sow's

[1] Listed as a 'Trumpetter' on Frobisher's ship the *Ayd* in 1578 (G. B. Parks, 'New Material on the Third Voyage from the Huntington Library,' (*Huntington Library Bull.*, Apr. 1935, 215–33), repr. in *The Three Voyages of Martin Frobisher*, ed. V. Stefansson, II (1938), 223).

[2] *Qu.* for antlers. Walker calls them 'thorny pyckes.' Both Walker and Ward counted 23 and 22 respectively on a side.

[3] See 16 and 24 Sept.

udder; you know how to present a shivering companion with a threadbare coat . . . [Sat. I. 53–4]. For [he thinks] that they are loyal whom he rules chiefly by snares of food and [lure] of garments and . . . he captured and returned them captive.)

16. ⊙ [*G Sun.*] (*Latin*: Ward and Walker dined with us 14 *after Trinity*. Walker told us much about the cruelty toward his [Ward's] boy George who paid the penalty for all those things which they hold evil. Not the wrath but the man's fury swelling up and breathing slaughter and blood easily reveals that his mind was polluted and poisoned by a remarkable stain of foulness.[1] But the sailors suppose, not wrongly, that there was a great cosenage in provisioning the journey and that he had profited much in the obtaining of provisions,[2] for destitute of the necessary food and drink they would almost have perished to a man if they had not helped themselves greatly by the benefits of this shore.) //

49^v

[Dyed on] the gallion[3]

[1	Richard] Salt	[June 21]
[2	Roger or Rob] Parkins	[June 18]
[3]	Yrish [for Edward Kent]	[July 8]
[4]	Zacharie [Stephens]	[July 8]
[5	Edward] Stokes	[August 2]
[6	David] Evans	[August 2]
[7	John] Heath	[August 7]
[8	Will] Burge*ss*	[August 10]
[9	Richard] Cove	[August 19]
[10	Henry] Meller*s*	[September 3]

[1] The allusion to the cruelty of Ward to his cabin boy George Brodford (see 8 Apr. and n.) is unexplained, Walker simply recording that he and Madox 'complayned to the other *de miserrimis nostris casibus* etc.'

[2] On the 14th the sailors on the *Edward* had 'murmured for wantinge there suppers and at there small allowaunce' and consequently, as Walker recorded, refused to set the watch until pacified by Ward.

[3] Madox neglects to record at the appropriate date in his Diary the death of Richard Cove, though he had taken him into account in his numbering. The date here has been supplied from Fenton's journal (Taylor, *Fenton*, p. 103); Fenton records Salt's death as occurring on 22 June and Heath's on 6 Aug. (Taylor, *Fenton*, pp. 90, 99).

1582 September 14[1] 180r
⊙ Sun in ♎ [Libra]

When I perceaved that dyvers made notes of our viage and I had nothing but what remayneth in memory to tel when I come home, I purposed hensforward to keep a breef remembrance of those things that shal happen of any moment, and when lesure serveth me, to wryte rather in Greek or Laten for the exercise of my stile than otherwyse. Therfore of thos things that ar passed to this day is I cam from Blackwal in the Edward Bonaventure the 2 of April and from Hampton in the gallion on Sonday the 29 of April, and on Whytsonday the third of June we wer owt of syght of England and so cam to the Canaries and after to Bonavista and lastly to Serra Liona wher we now of Guny ar. Ther ar many lemons, red peper that groeth on trees, graynes groying in grownd,[2] aples lyke great lylly rootes, many dyvers fyne shelfysh, many other fysh, olyphants, munkeys, dear, buffs [wild oxen] and porcupines, for 5 of our men having leave to walk on Sunday stragled so that they stayd owt al nyght and wer *set* in the bilboes for yt when they *cam* home and that worthely because they [distressed] the general and capten Parker in [thinking] they had byn lost. . . . The Serra Liona standeth in 8 [degrees] . . . 2 terces. Hear be many villan*ows* vermyn lyke wyngles gnats which do muche troble us and make spoyl of bred. Hear be arshires[3] in the fresh water that eat tymber, // almost no snayles but thos that be ar very byg. 180v Hear a very great store of good sugar canes in the woods sugar canes fast by wher our ships road, for the master gunner gote some. Hear ar also marlyns and Cranes etc.

[1] The second portion of the Diary is in Cotton MS, Titus B VIII, ff. 179–221. The beginning of this portion, overlapping as it does in date with the earlier part, seems to have been written as if Madox expected it to be read by Fenton, Parker, and perhaps others. The justification presented here is surely intended for eyes other than the author's, and the handwriting of the early pages is notably clear and careful. Further, such a flattering comment as that on Captain Parker's skill in shooting (9 Oct.) seems intended for *his* consumption, since Madox undercuts it by a cipher passage 'He sayth so.'

[2] Malagueta pepper, called grains of paradise.

[3] *Qu. arske* or *asker*, a water newt considered venemous.

17. ☾ [*Mon.*] yt rayned.

[*18.*] ♂ [*Tues.*] M. Walker supt with us.

[*19.*] ☿ [*Wed.*] the general and we supt with the viceadmiral.

(*Latin*: The mast, source of trouble)

20. ♃ [*Thurs.*] a very hote day. (*Latin*; *Greek*: When the mast is made steadier from above by the double strength of the fish on both sides and the masthead is girded with a new post which was placed beneath what they call the transverses, lo, a new question arises concerning the trunk of the mast itself between the partners which surround it in the lower part. This matter marvelously irritated our leader, especially since he had assigned the care of this thing beforehand to the master. Moreover, he was irritated by the restless murmuring of that Howd who thought he had now obtained what he had long been seeking, the mere opportunity and hope of invading the jurisdiction of another.[1] Thus, our leader, having looked into the matter because the mast had not been sustained firmly enough, calls the master aside, makes many charges against him, threatens his dismissal and exile. He being a little more self-reliant, not however as a result of his special carefulness, I do not know how or by what womanly wile maintains a mild demeanor. He answers that he had not been raised to his dignity by him nor ought he to be dismissed by him.[2] Hence the bitterest controversies have arisen. There was also another quarrel between the steward [Esdras Draper] and [our leader]. In

[1] As one of the two pilots on the *Galleon*, Hood was subordinate to Hall who was a very experienced navigating officer and as master ranked immediately under Hawkins among the ship's officers. See Fenton's account (Taylor, p. 107) of the quarrel which followed as a result of Hall's negligence in repairing the mast. For an earlier conflict between Hood and Hall, see Madox's official account, p. 286 below.

[2] On the 20th Fenton recorded that he and the master had 'some speaches' over the repairing of the mast, wherein Hall declared he would be master whether the general would or no (Taylor, *Fenton*, p. 107). The next day Fenton called him before the Assistants, excluding the merchants, and laying open his fault demanded whether Hall would have dared speak such words to the queen and if not, how dared he speak them to him. While the Assistants conceded Fenton had the right to remove his master, they urged clemency, whereupon the general consented to retain him on condition that Hall should kneel before him at prayer time in the presence of the whole company and ask his pardon, which he duly performed. See the account by Walker (21 Sept.) and Ward (*PN* (1589), p. 653). For Madox's disguised account in Latin, see 24 Sept.

these words he compelled the man to swear most solemnly after this fashion, By God's blood, if you are at fault again, you hang.[1]

It must be noted that the heat of the sun, vaporish and sultry, follows upon very cold nights here, but the days are moderate and differ little from the nights in temperature.) 181r (*Latin*: note temperature)

[Fig. 15]

[Diagram of tides and atmospheric refraction][2]

21. ♀ [*Fri.*] *St. Mathews day.* (*Latin*: Ward and Walker summoned Captain Parker and me to their side. The master is called, the letters of authority are produced. They are scanned thoroughly. Full power is given to one not inferior to the queen. Why say more? Not what the culprit fully deserved but what we decided is fitting. He confesses his guilt. He is forgiven. We counsel mutual love and friendship. May the good God grant that he prove worthy.)

Luke Ward was much moved because that having *lost* an anchor and let fawl an other with a halser and a boy of a barel *which* yesterday seeking he fownd yt also lost and so is groen to great choler.[3] //

The Portingals having browght down ther caravel with great store of Negroes we went to se them wher we fownd 50 of them trameled lyke prisoners, al naked saving a rag lyke a dyshclowt to cover ther members. Ther wer 181v Negroes

[1] See cipher passage for 24 Sept.

[2] His observations derive from Jean Taisnier's *Opusculum . . . de natura magnetis*, a work translated in ?1579 by Richard Eden as *A very necessarie and profitable Booke concerning Navigation*. Madox's diagram results from his conflating those appearing on B1*v* and E1*v*, the one dealing with tides, the other with atmospheric refraction. For Taylor's explanation, see *Fenton*, pp. 310, 311.

A translation of Madox's Latin reads: And thus by the orderly operation of the sun, the moon, and the seasons in the heavens, conjunction and opposition cause the greatest boiling on the points of water that are to be increased.

The English: bi the thickness of the aire the star that is yet in L under the horizon may be seen in V above the horizon by the lyn B o L because the ayr betwixt B and O is thik and moyst.

[3] Having dragged unsuccessfully on the 5th, 6th, and 11th for the anchor and cable lost 'by neglygens' on 4 Sept., Ward comments on the 20th that his master and company 'could neither finde the same nor see our booy, which wee left riding by a small cagger [barrel], for a marke for the other greater ancre, so I accompt all lost' (*PN* (1589), p. 653). On the 23rd, a Negro from the 'North shoore' came to dive for them (Taylor, *Fenton*, p. 107).

women one whose skyn was fynely pynked in this sort[1] [see Fig. 16].

182r (*Latin*: tales not without flavour)

(*Latin*; *Greek*: While some were talking familiarly among themselves and were saying what sailors are capable of, our monarch asserted that their knowledge is easy and obvious to everyone, since the ebb and flow of the sea depends on the course of the moon and is governed by its motion. But it is not possible, said another, for everyone to know what mansion of the moon causes the flood and what causes the ebbing of the waters. That is childish, added that wiser one, for the new moon always causes a full flood at London Bridge.)

M. Ferdinando boasting of the skil he had in ryding which is a thing that few mariners can wel doe, for they ar used to the byt under the tayl not in the teath, told that he was set on a great horse at Sir William Morgayns[2] but I, sayth he, when he began to heave and set and to seel [lurch] abowt, I so bremd hym with a cudgel abowt the beak head afore and the quarters abaft, that before he cam to a byttorn I went as smoth with hym as yf he had ryd in a well, which terms argued that he had better skil in a ship than abowt a horse.

The same man to make knoen how lavysh the king of Portingal is told that ther came one morning half a dosen of the queens trumpeters to hym with banners at ther trumpets and they did but trumpet a lytel trumpet to hym and he gave them a C crouns.

22. ♄ [*Sat.*] I was a shore and wel met. We fow*nd* [others at] the oyster bay wher we gathered h[eaps of] good guaiacum,[3] as good and I think b*etter* than that of the East

lignum vitae

[1] Ward and Walker also went to view them, Ward noting 'their behaviour, and other trifles' (*PN* (1589), p. 653). Walker comments that he would not have been surprised had they cursed their nativity, for 'they laye fettered together ... eatinge there meate lyke dogs.' The captain Matthew Fernando promised Ward a Negro boy; named John Primero and seven years old, he was given to him on the 23rd.

Of the Sapes, John Sparke noted that 'their teeth are all filed, which they doe for a braverie, to set out themselves and doe jagge their flesh, both legges, arms, and bodies, as workemanlike, as a Jerkinmaker with us pinketh a jerkin' (*PN* (1589), p. 526).

[2] Knighted at Bristol in 1574, Sir William was the owner of a ship in 1577 which was purportedly bent on privateering (*APC*, *1577–78*, pp. 5–6).

[3] Called variously *lignum vitae* or *lignum sanctum*, it was valued for its medicinal qualities.

Yndy. Hear ar *also* many vynes that gro naturally *but* the Portingal wil not teach the till*ing of them*, for that Canary wynes are hear mu[che prised], which gayn wold be lost yf they once [planted them to] the benyfte of ther own cuntrey. *We* nyghtly saw fyres on the north shore which the Portingals told us was to draw us to trafique with them, but yet we thowght yt not safe to go trye. M. Whood and I sowed pease a shore. //

Wynes

Ignes

Ther was taken in a cabyn of the Edward a fyne golden green snake of 2 foot long. Whether she cam with wood or water or by hir self yt is not knoen, for ther was a great one taken a moneth past in the ruther of our ship and an other did byte the master of the Elsabeth aboord, but a Negro did suck yt and yt was quyckly whole.

182v

snake

23. ⊙ *G* [*Sun.*] *15 after Trinity*. Fransis Frere dyned with us, being axed of the order of warfar in this cuntrey told us that alway the cheifest must march on fyrst and so the kyng Ferma doth also go before his host brandyshing with his hand an olyphants tayle to keep away the arows, and yf one go abroad with the kyngs spear in his hand he may take up hens, ryce or any thing in the cuntrey, and he sayd moreover that this Ferma was the conjurer and Fattima did cherysh hym self only, which is contrary to that was told us before[1] so that I perceav somtyme they tel us a tale in mockery, somtyme a report of ygnorance, somtyme a tale of deceyt.

the Negroes warre

trustye reports

Ther names be thus that be of the Carvel. Lewes Henry merchant which lyveth in Gwyny and had o*ur* salt for ryce.[2] Peter Vaws with long muchatoes, merchant

nomina

[1] See 22 Aug.

[2] Bargaining with the second group of Portuguese had been initiated on 12 Sept. when Fenton agreed with Henriquez for an exchange of salt for rice and informed Ward of the fact. The following day the Portuguese went up the river with Ward's skiff loaded with 12 barrels of salt. On the 20th Matthew Fernando returned with a carvel loaded with slaves; when on the 24th he desired to depart with his carvel, the English insisted he delay until their bargain had been fulfilled, and so he agreed to go up the river to fetch Ward's skiff. On the 29th Ward removed the sails both from the *Elizabeth* and from the carvel lest the Portuguese depart and so deceive him of his boat and the salt, but on the 30th they returned with the skiff and another 'great boate laden with rice.' The following day the English took in enough to make up the 20 barrels of rice due them. See Ward, *PN* (1589), pp. 652, 654; Walker 12, 13, 20, 23, 29, 30 Sept.

traveler. *Ma*thew Ferdinando capten of the Carvel. *Jo*hn Lewes Carelew purser and notarye. *Fr*ansis Frere browght a note of bargayn of sale to the general in Portingal for the [Elsabeth] wherunto 4 of us did fyrm [sign] and the [general] receved the drawght therof with his [signature and] the pursers which I have to keepe.

Testimonium

(*Latin*: If one should ask about the history and customs of the Æthiopians we can report many things. But if one hesitates to aver anything, we can; so the Portuguese boast in the manner in which Rudolph is wont to do when he lies magnificently about some thing.) //

183r

24. ☾ [*Mon.*] (*Greek*: Our lord discussed many things with me concerning the journey ahead. *cipher*: He means to cownterfet the king of Portugals seal and flag and so to tak al as they cam to serv him. He wowld very gladly be a king or autor of som great enterpris but he is a very disembling ipocrit, not caring for any thing but his oun vayn welth and rekoning. He doth not trust any on frend in the ship nor any him. A good rekoning if our great mownseer had not been desirows rather to rob than to perform his viag, we might b*y* this time hav been at the Molucas, but he wowld not water at Cap de Verd. He wil giv plas to no persw*a*sion but necessity. He seeketh both hear to rayn and to get a kingdom. He sayd he had martial lau and wowld hang Draper at the mast. He sayd the queen was his lov. He abhoreth merchan[t]s. He giveth cotes of not his oun. He wold go throo the Sowth Sea to be lik Sir Fraunsis Drak.)[1]

(*cipher*: mark this)

(*Latin*: Mutius Scaevola, a Roman knight, when he accepted the royal power from Caesar, as Aulus Gellius records, marches against the Parthians. However, his praetor, Publius Lentulus, is accused rashly and carelessly by some jealous person. Mutius, being arrogant and proud and sufficiently peevish by virtue of his command, scolds the praetor intemperately. He threatens to cast him out, torn to pieces. Lentulus cannot be deposed by him who has

(*Latin*: A story)

[1] Cf. 23 Dec., and 31 May where Madox remarks on his ill-concealed envy of Drake.

Madox writes 'bo' for by, 'u' for 'a' in 'perswasion' with 'o' in roman not cipher, and omits the 't' in merchants.

not raised him to his position. Scaevola is angered and he brings him to trial. The praetor justifies himself, saying that he has been irritated by Scaevola's words because . . . he had said he spread discord on various occasions among the people. Scaevola denies it.

It is a serious matter says Lucius Crassus, Diviner, to provoke anyone with insults, and they drive the man to madness and force him to say those things which at another time he would be unwilling to say. Come, says Scaevola, 183v
we must carefully consider in whose presence they are said, for if in the presence of Caesar, the penalty would be death. For all that, answers Crassus, it is not fitting for anyone to deem that he has received an injury [on the part of] Caesar, and thus we must forbear. But, said Scaevola, I am Caesar, seeing that I am a soldier by his authority, and he who addresses me otherwise than as Caesar must be punished as one who is trying to diminish such dignity.

You are a fool, says Fabius Cornicola, and you greatly delude yourself if you affirm that you wield Caesar's majesty everywhere in the market place. There is a great deal of difference between you and that one, for indeed on this principle any purveyor could call himself Caesar because he has decided on his letters of authority to hoard up oxen and calves for Caesar's use.[1]

These things seem to Scaevola rather harsh, but he had to put up with them. From Aulus Gellius 12 Kal. Oct.

Similarly in Aulus Gellius there is mention of an elegant and witty comedy[2] in which the leading role is played by Clodius, the second by Titus Annius Milo, the third by Glaucus who was acting in place of Clodius, the fourth by Pyrgopollynices, a soldier, the fifth by Quintus Mutius Scaevola, Diviner, 6th Publius Cornicola, 7th *Meni*ppus Cynicus; Plinius Secundus, Pompil*ius* . . . Simplicius – all these were of the third order. *Dramatis personae*

Clodius, beloved of none, trusted no one except Pyrgopollynices, and yet he was also jealous of him lest he should take glory away from him. He was clever,

[1] For the basis of this disguised account of Fenton's quarrel with Hall, see 20 Sept. and n. 2.

[2] For the identifications of the *dramatis personae*, see Intro.: *Pseudonyms*, p. 50 ff.

184r

deceitful, peevish, greedy, ambitious and of mean spirit, timid and suspicious. Glaucus was stupid and indiscreet, very boastful but open and honourable in his fashion, yet one who could not endure Clodius. Milo, great in words and sufficiently crafty, bold as well as hardworking, irascible, inexorable, grasping, serves very humbly, but he rules very arrogantly. Pyrgopollynices, a swellhead on account of his charge of soldiers, has a very dull intellect and yet he thinks himself remarkably above the others. He curries favour and is ambitious. Read about the others in Aulus Gellius.

But there was also Colax, a kind of parasite who envied everyone for everything, the author of discord and strife, caring only for his own belly and inelegant skin. He always murmured secretly, he bit everyone openly, but yet he fawned upon all and he constantly boasted of being of the knightly order.

There were also two servants, Verres, a notable and open thief, and Galba, a boasting buffoon.

Pallinurus was another, a little negligent but in every other respect spirited.)

(*cipher*: Cotton)

(*cipher*: Cotton shoywth his tars [penis] to Water Web as he was washing. Witnes Evans, Taylbush and others.)

(*Latin*: sparrows peacocks swallows)

[25.] ♂ [*Tues.*] (*Latin*: they brought to us in their nests two little sparrows, similar to our own but ever so beautiful, which M. Parker was rearing. M. Ward saw a peacock with a long tail, and though he took direct aim, he did not kill it.[1] There appeared swallows which we had not seen before, and so I affirm that the autumn equinox here is earlier than the spring.

Markham dieth

William Markham, master on the Francis, died today of a burning fever. Exhausted through dysentery beyond his strength, he was never afterwards sound or out of danger. Bad beer also aggravated this evil.)

184v
(*Latin*: deliberation)

26. ☿ [*Wed.*] (*Latin*: I wandered toward the east with Walker who recounted how much reproach we should bring on ourselves, what shameful disgrace upon the church of

[1] See Walker, 22 Sept., for his recording of their hunting of a peacock and an encounter with bees.

God, what lamentable sorrow upon our friends if, turning back to the islands again, we tried to load our ships with the spoils of good and innocent men to enrich ourselves.[1]

I respond that it cannot be otherwise than that we should be punished with the greatest hurt on account of our sins, for he who broods the eggs of malice what wonder that he hatch the chicks of punishment. But why? We have warned him secretly and openly; we have admonished him often; we have spoken out in the name of Jehovah; we have threatened him lest he perpetrate wrongdoing. What did he reply? His blood and that of those he compels to sin be on his head. We, I am confident, will be accounted free of all crime in the eyes of God. And insofar as our strength should permit, we will resist with words.

[A legate] of King Farma [for Fatima] came in a boat to us from Camera.[2] His teeth were serrated by a file, his chest and shoulders marked with characters, and he was circumcised, a common thing on account of their religion among all the Æthiopians whom I have seen up to now. And yet they do not worship Mohammed. He brought our general an elephant's tooth and a long-tailed monkey, which pleased him inordinately as a result of that sympathy which I believe exists between them. But after he had twice fouled his guardian with urine and aroused enmity between his master and others on two occasions, he was finally given to Pyrgopollinices, a matter which marvelously vexed Colax.

(*Latin*: a legate from king Fatima)

The king signified he would gladly confer with us. The

[1] On the 24th, Ward, after 'many debatements' with Fenton on the previous day, had called his master Percy and Walker into his cabin and rehearsed the general's plan to return to the Cape Verde Islands to 'gyve chase to everye shyppe' he could find in order to secure a 'longe tyme provys*ion for a* further purpose,' whereupon the three resolved they would continue on to the Moluccas 'whether the generall dyd or no.' (See Walker's, 24, 25, 29 Sept. comments.)

That Fenton had broached his plan to both of the chaplains before discussing it with his Vice-admiral indicates their influence, it would seem, with the rest of the company.

[2] Walker says it was the king's son and his chamberlain, Ward 'a *Negro* of some accompt' (*PN* (1589), p. 654). The Portuguese had sufficiently confused the English about the status of the local chieftains – with intent as Madox noted – so that Walker and Fenton, as well as Madox, record information variously about the kings Farma and Fatima, though here Madox has made a slip.

king was Fatima, as the Portuguese whom we exclusively 185r employ, call him. But I would say that they are abusing us unless we were even more foolish than the Choroebus himself. For we wish to try nothing by ourselves, and if they do not deceive us, they must be considered very stupid.

(*Greek*: a cure) John Burden, afflicted with fever and falling by accident into the sea, was taken out and recovered his health, but because of bad diet he relapsed into fever.)

(*Latin*: Gifts are sent) *27.* ♃ [*Thurs.*] (*Latin*: the general sent by means of the Portuguese an ell and a half of red cloth to king Fatima and a woman's smock to the queen, together with a mirror, all to the value of four marks. He also wrote a letter to the effect that he was so tied up with the ships that he could not visit him but he very much wishes that this should be the beginning of trade between him and the subjects of our queen.[1]

I urged that a gift be sent by means of any one of us, but he intensely despises a counselor lest he himself appear devoid of counsel. And thus he has yielded to no advice at all up to now, nor is there any hope that he will give an ear to any in the future. The woman's smock in London cost 25^{s}, the ell of cloth 10^{s} and 10^{d} worth of gunpowder. He gave some canvas cloths to the others.)

28. ♀ [*Fri.*] (*Latin*: I fished with Ward, and we caught a torpedo torpedo fish and a large number of fish called mullets, of which he had caught 207 in one haul in a small net the day before. We saw more than 40 long-tailed monkies on the rocks as if they were in turn conspiring or determining dubious matters.)

(*Latin*: Chancellor died) *29.* ♄ [*Sat.*] *St. Michael.* (*Latin*: *Nycolas* Chancellor, the purser on the Edward, died, a simple and honest man but timid. In the first place, four days ago he approached this shore where walking by himself off the main route he became so exhausted by fear of danger that death followed fear. His father was an explorer in Muscovy.[2]

[1] For the letter to Fatima, see Fenton's journal, Taylor, *Fenton*, pp. 108–9. Again reflecting information obtained from the Portuguese on the king's '2 or 300 wyves' (Walker, 22 Aug.), he specifies that the smock and looking glass are intended for the queen he loves best.

[2] Richard Chancellor, who had made two voyages to Russia, was drowned in

When hope came upon Julius Caesar of occupying the Parthian kingdom while he was attempting many great things, he sent Clodius and Annius Milo as explorers with the army to investigate the secrets of the region. But when they reached the vast wilderness of Tigrania[1] and received a rich supply of provisions at Rama,[2] they complained they had been forsaken. Clodius would turn back into Lydia[3] toward the sources of water, for Verres had persuaded him this was profitable. But Milo, to whom Publicus Cornicola had predicted that this matter would diminish the reputation of all, protests, rages. From the beginning Clodius and Pyrgopollinices are nourished with the hope of plunder, but Scaevola the Diviner argued scrupulously, devoutly, and at length concerning the power and goodness of the gods and concerning the Vestal Virgin, whom Clodius terms a whore because he had once taken part in the rites of Ceres.[4] Finally, Glaucus comes and says [we] will be able to pass beyond this wilderness in a short time and then abundant supplies will be at hand. When this was affirmed, all concurred.[5] 185v

(*Latin*: a story out of Titus Livy)

1556 at Pitsligo Bay, Scotland, while transporting the Russian ambassador to England. His orphaned son Nicholas was apprenticed to the Muscovy Company and sent to Russia in 1560, where he was charged (in 1568) with engaging in pirate trade. He sailed on all three of Frobisher's voyages and was one of those intending 'to inhabit' with Fenton. In 1580 he was appointed a merchant on the Pet-Jackman voyage in search of the Northeast Passage, and his account is included in *PN* (1589), pp. 476–82.

[1] I.e., 'Tagurine' or 'Tagrim' [Tanguarim] – Bullom territory marked on Madox's chart of Sierra Leone, Fig. 11.

[2] Apparently an allusion to the 20 barrels of rice they had obtained from the Portuguese (see n. 2, p. 193 above).

[3] I.e., Cape Verde Islands.

[4] An allusion to Clodius's profanation of the rites of the Bona Dea held in the house of Caesar, where he gained entrance by disguising himself as a woman. See Plutarch, *Lives*, ix.4–x.4.

The story is referred to in Juvenal II.27, where, in a constellation of allusions that Madox probably remembered, Juvenal asks of those who discourse upon virtue but prepare to practice vice:

> Who would not confound heaven with earth,
> and sea with sky, if Verres should denounce
> thieves or Milo cutthroats [or] Clodius
> condemn adulterers ....

Madox, like Walker, was clearly shocked at Fenton's boasting of his purported familiarity with the Queen. See entries for 22 Aug. and 24 Sept.

[5] On this date Ward and Walker decided 'to deale playnely' with the general about their determination not to return to the Islands of Cape Verde but to go forward, and Madox records, again in disguised fashion, the results of the 'sundry debatements' among the Assistants, with the exception of the merchants

But Colax was so besmeared with the excrement and urine of the long-tailed monkey that no one not beshitten would receive the man.)

He that pisseth cleere may thro the urinal at the phisicions head,[1] which proverbe being lerned of a simple servingman that was sent with his mistress syck water to the phisicion, because he pissed clere hym self brok the urinal in the phisicions face, taking for his excuse this proverbe.

[*30.* ⊙ *G Sun.*] *16 after Trinity* Capten Ward sent for the general to se a fysh with whom I went and other*s*. Yt was 7 foot long, 4 foot 9 ynches in compasse, a head lyke a cowe

186r
a strange fysh

but lytle eys, noe eares, to great // fyns which, ript, wer joynted lyke a mans hand and arm fro the elboe down. Yt was the femel, a very thik skyn. She brethed at the nostrils and grizoned as a beast. The breth was sweet as a melch cow at fresh grasse, the blud hote, the meat was whyt and mervelows savory and enterlarded.

consultacio et propositum de freto tentando

Ther dyned wee and agreed to go thorow the Strayts, the general, Ward, Haukyns, Parker, Walker and I; the rest wer not cauled.[2] After dynner the general walked to the lymmon garden. We supt at the viceadmiral. Henricus cam down with some of the ryse that we barganed for but not all.

(*cipher*: Hear Whood cauled, sayd that Sir Fraunses Draks vitayl in Java cost the valu of 4 thowsand pownd. Bein[g] therof rebuked by Haukins, he sayd it was much and that the peeple esteemed nowght but the best silk and fyn linen. The generaul demaunded wether ther wer

---

who were not involved. Ward later told his master, pilot, and the two merchants the results. See Ward, *PN* (1589), p. 654 and Walker.

[1] Tilley, P269, where the earliest instance is 1591.

[2] From Walker's account, it would appear that Fenton was making another attempt to persuade the Assistants of the inadvisability of proceeding to the Moluccas, mentioning the extremities that were like to occur from want of food and water, the great size of the ships, and their unfitness for discovery. He also summoned the pilots Hood and Blacollar to give their opinions, and when it was agreed to go forward, he then posed the question whether to proceed by the Strait or by the Cape of Good Hope.

To the decision to go by the Strait, Ward adds that being in the South Sea it was agreed 'to deale as occasion should be given' (*PN* (1589), p. 654). Fenton (Taylor, *Fenton*, p. 110), Ward, and Walker, as well as Madox, note that this was a meeting of the Assistants without the merchants.

water inau throo the Straits. He answerd 4 fadom at least: in Molucas they sau no great ships nor think ther is harborow for any nor that we shaul thear get spis inau. Haukins no[t]withstanding afirmeth al. The generaul sayth that fast by the shor at Molucas he is informed that thear is 80 fadom and roky and therfor no riding for us. But he speaketh dowting to go thither. Whood becaus he wold rob in the Sowth See: Haukins al at a venture.) (*cipher*: the generaul bad me tear the not of this[e] hot comparisons and folish with Parker and Haukins)[1]

October ♏

[*1*.] ☾ [*Mon.*] we dispatched our busynes to be goen for the Strayts. M. Evans had articles and quarelsom words put up agaynst *hym* by M. Barsey wherupon he was examy*ned* and so sent back by Francisco as a *man* unworthi of the rowme.[2] I pray God graunt love and charytie and honest dealing amonxt us all that his grace may prevent our wyckednes and his mercy the punyshment of our syns. // Evans sent home (*cipher*: . . . more . . . of the 25 of November and my rem[em-brance] book)

2. ♂ [*Tues.*] the sone 42 degrees hygh, we wer under sayl having our 2 Negroes of whom for the one they took 15 yerds of kersey; for the other they refused yt.[3] In thafter 186v from Serra Leona

[1] 'In this conference grew many hotte, and disdainfull speaches and comparisons betweene Captaine *Hawkins*, and Captaine *Parker*, and also the Generall, as offended with Captaine *Hawkins*, used speaches to him very displeasant, which with much adoe was all in the ende pacified' (Ward, *PN* (1589), p. 654).

In the cipher passages Madox omits the 'g' in being, the 't' in notwithstanding and the 'e' in 'thise' (margin).

[2] At dinner the merchant Miles Evans, who on 28 Aug. had begun to barter independently with the Negroes in the company of the Portuguese and on 9 Sept. had expressed his dissatisfaction to Fenton in not being allowed to establish trading directly with the natives, objected to the tactics of the general in his absence, whereupon the jeweller Harry Bardsey reported his speeches and 'articled' against him. Fenton then called together the Assistants, with the exception of the merchants, to consider the charges. It was agreed Evans should be allowed to return in the *Elizabeth* with the Portuguese. Madox, Walker, and Tailboys initially tried to dissuade him, and later Hawkins, Parker, and Walker tried again, but (says Walker) 'he was obstynate.'

[3] Ward reports that the Portuguese had not delivered so much rice as promised and so Parker and others searched the *Elizabeth* and the carvel and 'found good stoare' which they appropriated in part. In addition, the English purchased for certain 'carsey' and 'pease and bisket' two Negroes for the *Edward* and two for the *Galleon* to replace mariners who had died although the crew from the *Elizabeth* served in part to replace them. The two Negroes on the *Edward* were to escape at the Bay of Good Comfort, commended by Massau and Zingo, the two on the *Galleon*, who were themselves to die before reaching England.

On this date, Ward exchanged his seven-year-old for a bigger boy (*PN* (1589), p. 655).

none we anchored almost a leag fro the west shore and north fro the rock wheron M. Whood was and gathered great oysters for therwith yt was clad.

friar Evans

Report was that M. Evans wold be a fryar which thing yf yt prove true I wil never trust man after, ether for fayth or religion til I have eat at least a peck of salt in his company, but sure the general used hym with curtesy, althoe in serching his chest ther was a letter fownd, for he gave hym wyne, pork, bisket and pease ynogh for a moneth.[1]

3. ☿ [*Wed.*] abowt 2 in the morning we wer under sayl agayn and anchored abowt 4 leags fro the shor at noone. Some

hermodactilus

wer syk with eating hermodactilus[2] which yesterday they fownd on shore. M. Haukins and M. Cotton went aboard the Edward wher they stayd al nyght. At supper the general told of plate stole from the duke of Suffolk.

a figure

M. William Burdeyt by a fygure was detected but after Wylliam Burdying 2 yere was fownd to have yt, resembling the other in al poynts and privy marks.[3]

Before 8 at nyght with a northeast tornado which in the nyght happeth muche we wer under sayl. Whil yt was [blowing] ther wer as thick[4] as tadpoles ab*owt* the ship

blubbers

blubbers which ar lyke to the head of a seedyng thistle or dawndilion with 3 or 4 strings therat wherwith they swym.

kandels

He that sayleth this way let hym get wax candle or very good talloe for al ours meace lyke butter. //

187r

a dreame

Today yt fel in my remembrance that on Sunday nyght as I think I drempt that my 2^{d} goome toth [molar] on the

[1] Fenton recorded that from their first coming into harbour, Evans had practised to go to Santiago to become a friar.

Madox's reference to the 'courtesy' of the general again suggests that he anticipated perusal of his Diary, for his later comments (in cipher) on 25 Nov. reflect distaste for Fenton's directive that the belongings of the departing Evans should be searched by Ward, Parker, and Hawkins (*PN* (1589), p. 655).

[2] Species of colchicum or meadow saffron. Walker records that he fell sick with vehement vomiting and extreme purging.

[3] This tale relates to Henry Grey, Duke of Suffolk, involved in the Wyatt conspiracy, and one William Burdet, a servant to the Duke's secretary Thomas Rampton: during the conspiracy, Suffolk had fled from his estate at Sheen to his seat in Leicestershire and directed his servants in Jan., 1554, to send up his plate. Captured on 2 Feb. 1554, Suffolk was executed within the month; Burdet was pardoned in June. (See D. M. Loades, *Two Tudor Conspiracies* (1965).)

[4] Madox repeats 'as thick.'

left syde was fawln owt. M. Evans (*cipher*: alias Walker) told me that ther was treason wroght agaynst me[1] wherat fyrst I was astonyshed but presently cawling my consciens to wytnes that I had born an honest and frendly hart to al men, espetialy to the general, althoe indeed I perceaved my self in some suspition as one condemning other of presumption, for wher always I exhorted men to charyty in hart, to humblenes in opinion, to a myld conversation and to truth in dealing according to my duty in the fear of God, yt myght perhaps be ymagined that I accused them therby of pryvy mallyce, of overweening conceyts, of lofty behavior, of deceytful reconyng, but fynding my self utterly cleer and having my whole trust in God I was myry and pleasant remembring thes proverbs: *Intemerata conscientia frui tutissimum est. Quo periculum eminentius eo maior animus; quo mors propinquior eo vita sanctior. Cernit deus omnia vindex.*[2] The Lord be praysed for all. suspicion

4. ♃ [*Thurs.*] the general chose Arthur Cotton and the master John Davis to be masters mate in Richard Fayrwethers Roome who cast lots but the lot fel to John Davis which had the place.[3] John Davis

5. ♀ [*Fri.*] being at least 40 leags of the shore we took a quayl aboord and dyvers martlets. M. Hawkins kyld a goodly dolphin. I reared up my bed hygher and had taynted blue cut owt for my man and my boye. // a quaile blewe

[6.] ♄ [*Sat.*] beying falne abowt 40 leags by supposal fro the coast of Gwyny but nothing in maner yet to sowthward and by reason of the qualmes which had setled the sea the water therof was somewhat fowle and therin we saw lyke snakes pyed red and blew ylfavored monsters. We 187v snakish monsters

[1] This information was given to Madox when he and Walker talked alone on shore 1 Oct. and exchanged promises to remain '*fratres in Christo*.'

Clearly from 28 July when Fenton intercepted Madox's letter to Walker, Madox increasingly had become an object of suspicion to his general, whose fear of mutiny, aroused at Plymouth, had been steadily aggravated by the troubles on the *Elizabeth*, the dissatisfaction of the merchants, and the frustration of his officers and crew deriving from their stay of almost two months at Sierra Leone.

[2] It is safest to enjoy an unspotted conscience (cf. 29 Oct.). The greater the danger, the greater the spirit; the closer death, the holier life. God the avenger sees all.

[3] Following Markham's death on 25 Sept., Fenton had sent Richard Fairweather to the *Francis* so a master's mate was needed for the *Galleon* (Taylor, *Fenton*, p. 108).

also saw many great sculs of small frye which as we do ymagyne some great fysh huntyng kept stil at the water brym and over them wer crying as great a flyght of byrdes with small bodyes and long wyngs to pray upon thys frye.[1]

store of byrds

A man that had been a beadmaker in queen Maryes [tyme] cometh to the byshop at the comyng yn of queen Elsabeth for orders, not for desyre of the function but to have wherwith to get his lyving. The byshop having spied his smal abilytie and bad devotion which was drawn by need demaunded whether he cold do nothing but make beades. Yes, sayth he, I was also prentyce to a fawcet maker but of long tyme I have not used yt. Na than, quoth my Lord byshop, go thi way and dowt not to get a good lyving for the beades be layd away, yet spygots and fawcets were never so much used. M. Percy.

a tale of a beadmaker

[7 ☉] G [*Sun.*] *1*[7] *after Trinity* Gregory the smyth dyed and being cut up ther was nothing amysse but cluttered [clotted] blud in his back which some thowght he took lying down hote on the shore on Sonday nyght last in the rayne. I suppose also his brayn was peryshed for he was hote and kekheaded[2] but his brayn was not seen. //

Greg*ory* the smi*th* dieth

188r

8. ☾ [*Mon.*] many of our men wer syk of a burning fever, some cause wherof I gesse to be this: whil we were at harboroe thro plenty of water and other refreshing, blud did fast increase. The people traveled sore in the heat and had water ynogh but now coming to the hote qualmes and scanted sodaynly of beverage they dropt down shrewdly on after an other.

cause of siknesse

Ther was a shork taken with 6 yong in his belly of a cubyt long a peece, which cut owt and cast overburd swam away as thogh they had been old knaves. Simon Wod sayth 4 more fel owt of his mowth in haling fro the galery to the ship and that she wil let them yn and take

the shork whelps

[1] In a statement reflecting the Vice-admiral's provident concern for his men, Walker records on this date how Ward and others manned the skiff to shoot at fowl and then used their fishgigs (harpoons) to obtain great store so that they ate nothing else but fowl and fresh fish; in fact, having such plenty, they heaved overboard that night two great sharks ten feet in length.

[2] Apparently, delirious, ? from *keak*, to cackle.

them owt lyk an adder.[1] Wee took a fayr dolphyn. Our way was withowt speed by reason of qualmes. The wynd that did bloe was at the sowth.

the generawls gift

The general gave me 4 yerds of blew cloth to make me a gown. He gave also to other men some. His curtesy I take in as frendly maner as yt had been velvet. I pray God I may in part deserve yt. I took also 7 yerds and a half therof to make capuchios and breeches for my self, my man, and Mathew.[2] Fernando told many prytty tales of king Sebastian for his execution of Justyce: how he examined 2 justices what they had left by ther parents, what ther anual rents wer and what ther offices and what ther expences and fynding ther welth beyond the reconyng of ther accownts accused them of bribery and so put them to death. He loved to se men ryde fast when he was a boy, and speking to 2 judges to ryde apace, they answered, we use yt not but after theeves. Than, quoth he, ryde one after an other. The same being a Protestant was by the clergy entyced to mak war yn Barbary and so was sleyn.[3]

lyvereis

king Sebastian Justice

lepide

(*Latin*: From available signs and indications I inferred that the current of the sea follows a natural motion from south to north although the general told me otherwise.) //

(*Latin*: Flux of the sea)

9. ♂ [*Tues.*] in the morning watch Rob Lyddyngton told mee a long story of M. Jervish of Chelsee which not induced to mary til he wer 40 yer old, at the dynner talk of one woman the same day took horse and rode to Mrs Ridleys in Shropshire to se Sir Georg Blunts[4] daoghter but lyking

188v

of M. Jervise

[1] Sir Richard Hawkins (*Observations*, pp. 47–8) describes how when any danger threatens, 'the Damme receiveth her Whelpes in at her mouth, and preserveth them, till they be able to shift for themselves.'

The sentence beginning 'Simon Wod...' is written sideways in the margin.

[2] I.e., his boy Matthew Fisher.

[3] The posthumous son of Prince Juan of Portugal, Sebastián became king in 1557 (at the age of three); he was killed in 1578 during an expedition against the Moors. His death evoked the rise of a cult known as 'Sebastianism' which promulgated the notion of his return to restore the greatness of Portugal. Educated by Jesuits, Sebastián was a religious fanatic and mystic.

[4] Sir George Blount of Shropshire (d. 1581), who as a youth had served in the French and Scottish campaigns and been highly favoured by Henry VIII, married Constance, daughter of Sir John Talbot. He excluded his daughter and heir Dorothy from inheriting his great estates by leaving them to a nephew.

His sister, the mother of Henry VIII's natural son, Henry, duke of Richmond, married first Gilbert, Lord Talbois (for a later shipboard comment on their daughter Elizabeth, see 14 Oct.), and secondly Edward, Lord Clinton and Say. (See *Trans., Shrop. Arch. Soc.*, Third Series, II (1902), 312–13.)

better Mrs Ridleys dowghter at the fyrst dynner demaunded hir of hir parents and fynding them tractable rode the same day to Wooster, browght a lycea[n]s made hir a joynter and was maried to her on the moroe, and having than dyned put his foot in the styrrop, leaving his wyfe as he foond her, and cam to London, ther kept M$^{[r]s}$ Churchman the vicars wyfe, spent on hir 1000^{li}. His brother Stedam plaged the priest. He was degraded, prisoned and muche a doe. In conclusion none good of all 4 – priest, Jervise nor these 2 wyves.

much fysh and fowl kild

(*cipher*: he sayth so)

The Edward kyld 15 bonettoes with fysgees and we a dolphin. They also kyld with caleivers 2 dosen of water byrdes which I think was rather by chaunce than good cunnyng for Capten Parker doth shute as well or fayrer than any of them and yet we kyld none. Yt was very sultry hote because ther was no wynd stirryng, for in wynd or rayn yt is ever cold ynogh at the sea, but at nyght we had a good fresh gale.

a hobby

a purpose token of wynd

10. [☿ *Wed.*] a hobby [small falcon] cam and cowrsed the swallows which folowed our ship wherof some we took with hands, som dyed as I suppose for want of water. The hobby fled away. We kyld a purpose wherof ther cam myghty great sholes by us which put us in hope of wynd and rayn as after yt fel owt. The general went aboord the Edward wher al wer wel save the master gunner. M. Walker had byn syck but was amended. God contynue health among us. //

190^{r}

trees still greene

box, eue, savin, pryk-home,[1] misseltew with whit beries

(*cipher*: Parker)

Talking of the Streyts which lye in 52 of the sowth according to the hyght of Ingland, I was demaunded the reason why ther the trees did always remayn green not withstanding the cold snowy hils and in Ingland the trees fal the leaf. I had no other answer but that happyly they myght be of the same nature as was yvye, holy, bay, broome, rosemary, and furs which in Shropshir ar cauled gorst, in Suffolk whyns, which meethinketh ar muche strange and lytle marked for the[y] cary blossoms al the yere long, how cold so ever the wynd or season bee, but this reason was thowght lytle worth (*cipher*: of Parker).

[1] Savin is *juniperus savina*; prykhome, not identified.

Being axed why the munkye smelleth most sweetly when she hath eaten a spider, I cold not gesse at other cause but that the heat of the spider did make hir spiryts fume furth more hotely and to cary with them a muskysh smell of hir humors or flesh. John Paynter dieth. the munky eating a spider 12 John Painter

11. ♃ [*Thurs.*] at day breake, having fownd our selvs abowt 7 degrees the day before, wee had a sooping [sweeping] tornado fro the norwest but yet ever and anon the wynd hanged sowtherly that lytle which was. wynd and wether

The general told that the flesh of a peacock wold not corrupt,[1] no not cast on a dunghil and that he had eaten a peece geven hym by Mrs Barret which was rosted at hir dawghters mariage 2 yere before. He told also a prytty tale of 2 cuntrey men that comyng before M. Beamunt in a controversy when the fyrst had told his tale with many false accusations, the second comyng to his answer sayd to M. Beamunt, Sir, wil yt please your worship to gyve me leave to borow a lye of hym. As who say he was able to lend. // a peacok uncorrupt*ible* the borowing of a lye

12. ♀ [*Fri.*] (*Latin*: about midnight the east and northeast winds began at last to inflate the sails, and this imbued us with great hope that everything would turn out happily with respect to the expediting of our journey. After 12 o'clock we had a favourable breeze: first the SE by S warm then hot. A calm increased our anxiety somewhat. 190v (*Latin*: east wind)

M. Hawkins told me that the reedbearing palmito was not much different from the Indian cocoa tree except that the former bears smaller nuts clustered as it were into one bunch. The latter produces larger ones hanging separately from the branches. The natives extract from both wine, oil, bread, fruit, and a medicinal wine. From the hull of the nut and the outside covering they extract the best oil of a saffron color, first crushing the bark of the tree in a mortar. I myself have found a mortar of this kind at the place where we are in the habit of fishing and where we saw some small huts. There is a great abundance of palmitos in this place and for that reason the Æthiopians flock together (Latin: concerning the palmito and cocoa)

[1] Also asserted in the twelfth century by Alexander Neckam in his *De naturis rerum* (Ch. 39).

here annually, whence the valleys are covered with so many footpaths and trails. The wine, however, they extract from the suspended reed by penetrating with a borer into the branch which supplies the juice to the nuts.[1] The aforesaid [Hawkins] gave me a strip of Javanese paper, very large. This is usually immersed several times in water and washed, and it then becomes very white.[2]

(*Latin*: staunching of blood)

The general told me nothing conduced more toward the staunching of blood in a wound than nettles crushed and applied to it. M. Parker added that the excrement of a pig is very suitable for this. They related, furthermore, that when a horse's hoof was hurt by an improperly driven nail and the horse began to grow lame, M. Nicholas Malbey[3] was in the habit of doing nothing before
191r applying to the hoof nettles crushed and mixed with salt, but if the horse's foot, because of cold and improper blood resulting from previous excessive sweat and subsequent sudden cold, is seen to be contaminated, take the blood in the furrow of the hoof and mixing it either with the white of an egg or hot dung, smear the back of the horse with it, and he will quickly get well.)

for a fownded horse

[*13.* ♄ *Sat.*] In Ships Land which is the back syde of Labradore and as M. Haul supposeth nye therunto Sir Frances Drake graved and bremd his ship the[r] at 48 degrees to the north.[4] The people ar for stature, color, apparel, diet, and

[1] In his narrative of Hawkins's voyage to Guinea (1564), John Sparke reports on palmito wine, 'which is gathered by a hole cutte in the toppe of a tree, and a gorde set for the receaving thereof, which falleth in by droppes, and yeeldeth fresh wine againe within a moneth' (*PN* (1589), p. 527).

[2] Charles de l'Écluse, who visited England after Drake's circumnavigation and inquired from members of the voyage about exotic flora, received a similar gift, which he acknowledges in his illustrated volume *Aliquot Notae in Garciæ Aromatum Historiam* published in this year: 'Through the kindness of these same people I received the white bark of a tree like a very thin parchment on which any kind of writing can be ascribed just as on ordinary papyrus. Drake's companions acquired this in the island of Java in exchange for other merchandise' (B6).

[3] Sir Nicholas Malby, gentleman servant to the Queen, served long and actively in Ireland. In 1576, 'moved by sundry friends,' he published his brief pamphlet *A plaine and easie way to remedy a Horse that is foundered in his feete*. It was to be reprinted in 1583 and 1594.

[4] This is the earliest record that Francis Drake on reaching the Northwest coast of America had gone as far north as 48°. In his two depositions (1584, 1587) to the Spaniards, John Drake stated that they found land at 48° (called New England in the first deposition, Californias in the second) where they remained for a month and a half to take in water and repair the ships.

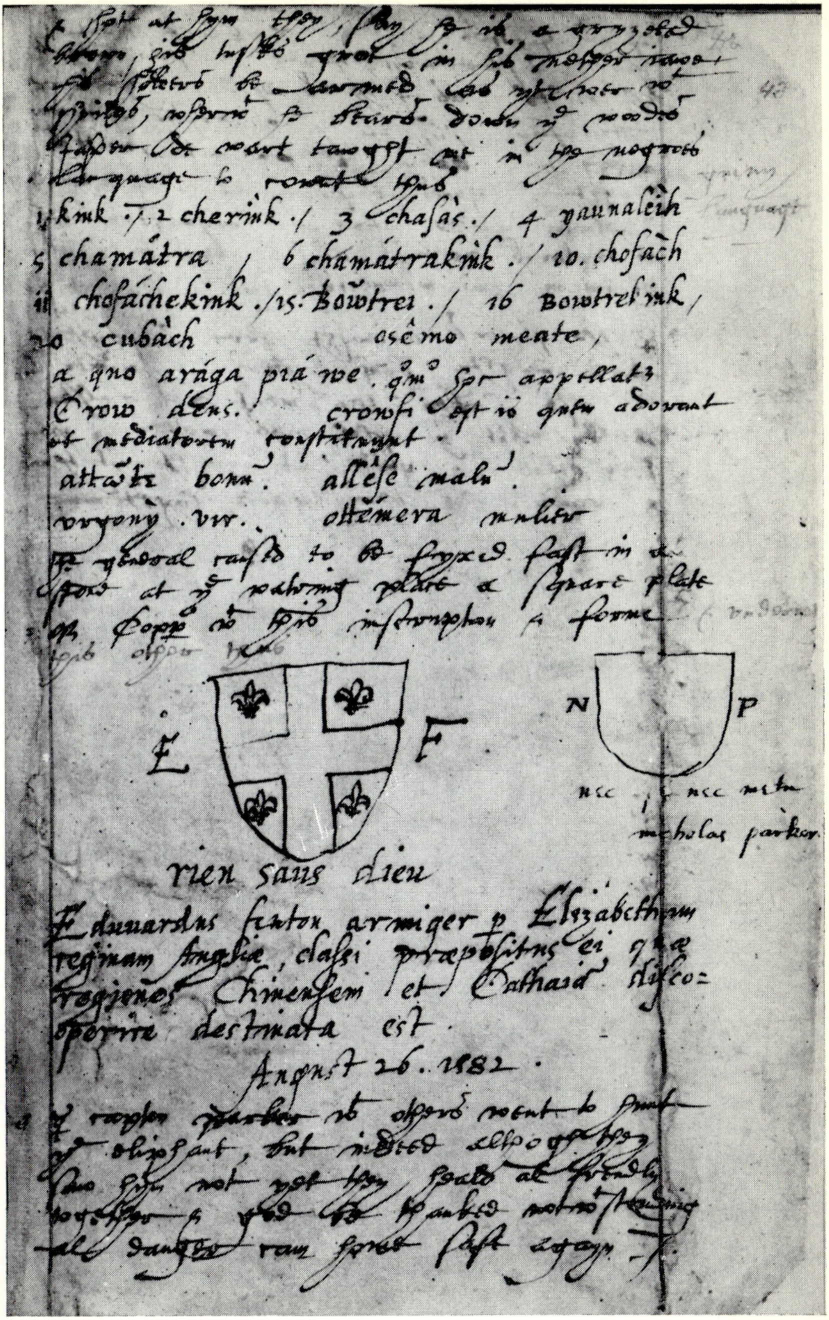
1 kink ./ 2 cherink ./ 3 chasas ./ 4 yaunaleih
5 chamatra / 6 chamatrakink ./ 10. chosach
11 chosachekink ./ 15. Bowtrei ./ 16 Bowtreikink,
20 cubach osemo meate,
E F
N P
nicholas parker
rien sans dieu
Eduardus fenton armiger p Elizabetham reginam Angliae, classi praepositus ei quae regiones Chinensem et Cathaia discooperire destinata est
August 26. 1582.

Fig. 14. Sketch of the copper plate set up by Fenton

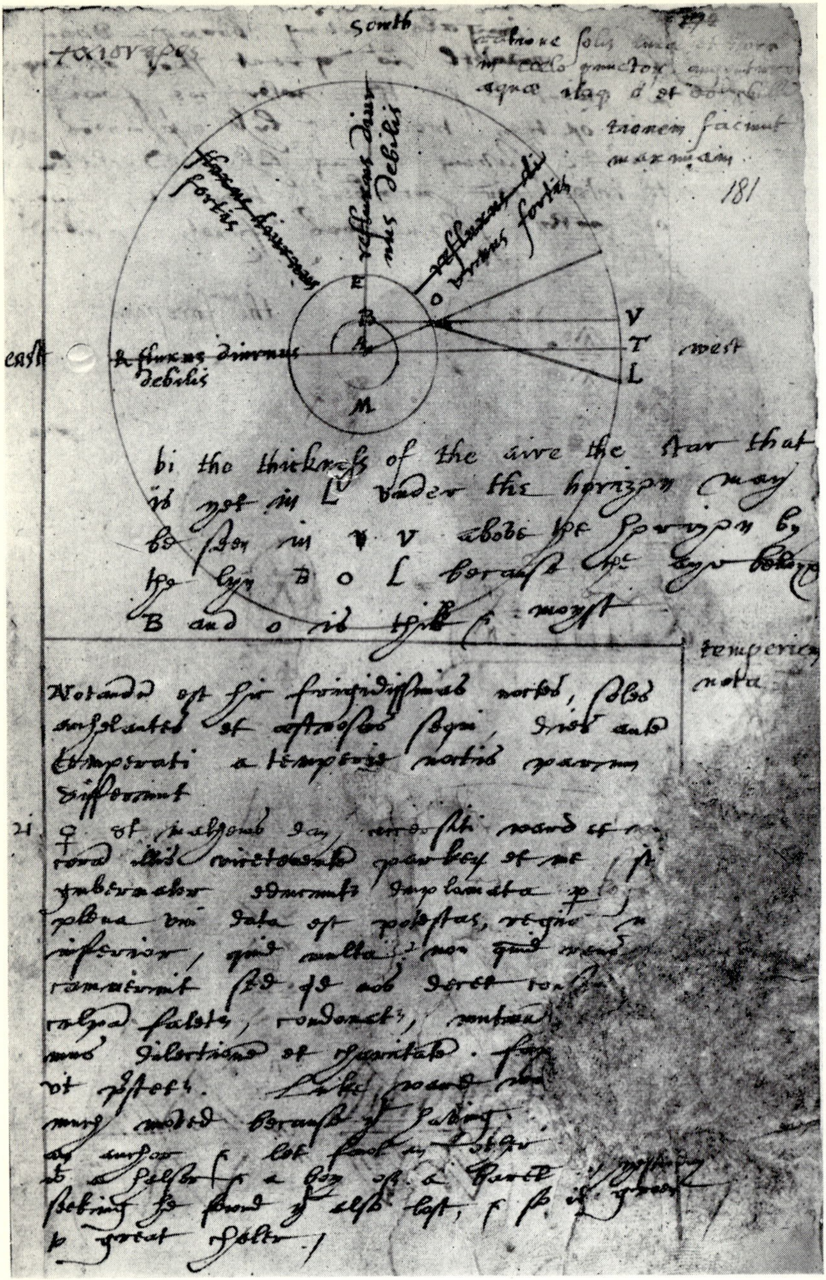

Fig. 15. Diagram of tides and atmospheric refraction

holo speach lyke to thos of Labradore and as is thowght kyngles for they crowned Sir Frances Drake.[1] Ther language is thus. *cheepe*, bread. *Huchee kecharoh*, sit downe. *Nocharo mu*, tuch me not. *Hioghe*, a king. Ther song when they worship God is thus: One dauncing first with his handes *up* and al the rest after lyke the priest and people, *Hodeli oh heigh oh heigh ho hodal*i *o*h. Yt is thowght that they of Labrado*re* worship the son and the moon but [whether they] do of Calphurnia I kno not.

A batu made of planks fastened together wher on thei carie botisioes of wyne at Peru.

[Fig. 17]

A batu *a* raffe

The language of Java[2] 191v

sera	1	*Jownge*	a ship
dua	2	*Brass*	ryse
talu	3	*carbo*	a buffe
opat	4	*vadosh*	a gote
lima	5	*bebeck*	a ducke
ganado	6	*Hiame*	a hen
toido	7	*gerock*	a lemon
delapan	8	*goola*	sugar

[1] In the anonymous account published by Hakluyt, the author describes how the Indian king and divers others set the crown on Drake's head, 'inriched his necke with all their chaines, and offred unto him many other things, honouring him by the name of *Hioh*' (*PN* (1589), *H*).

On the basis of the few words recorded by Drake's chaplain (*The World Encompassed*) and the additional words recorded here, Robert F. Heizer and W. Elmendorf identify them as the dialect of Coast Miwok Indians ('Francis Drake's California Anchorage in the Light of the Indian Language Spoken There,' repr. in *Elizabethan California* (Ramona, Calif.), 1974).

[2] Like the piece of Javanese paper and perhaps the Indian vocabulary, the source for this wordlist was probably William Hawkins. John Drake is a possibility, but since they are again at sea, there seems to have been little chance for this sort of exchange. Thomas Hood, the third person among the officers who had been with Drake, seems an unlikely source because of Madox's intense antipathy to him.

Interestingly, a shorter list than Madox gives appears in *PN* (1589), at the end of N.H.'s account of Cavendish's circumnavigation (1586–88), but in Hakluyt's second edition (1598–1600), it has been transferred from that account to the end of the account of Drake's voyage, XI (Glasgow, 1905), 132–3); this suggests that the list originally derived from some one who had been with Drake.

Eleven of the words Madox records appear in *PN* with three variants: *chricke* for Madox's *chrese*, *sapelo* for *sopolo*, and *larnike* for *larink* (perhaps simple metathesis). Bracketed words derive from the list in *PN*. Madox writes *cocust* for *cocus*.

sala lapan	9	*bownting*	a cowcumber
sopolo	10	*gushanka*	a beane
dopolo	20	*ape*	fyre
patanpolo	40	*prao*	a canow
Chrese	a dagger	*deballe*	a knife
Augenge	a dog	*chae*	fresh water
opiah	a hat	*tolskin*	satyn
busse	yron	*cabo*	golde
tumbake	a pyke	*colabe*	a shyrt
larink	drynk	*liat*	let me se
clapa	cocus	*bebange*	garlick
parnk	a pot	*manche*	no more
sabat P amyt	fare you well	*vade*	a bagg
Babec	a hog	*chanany*	sypres
pala	a nutmeg	*cassedne*	geve me this
salaca	a royal	*apanamanana é ne*	what cawl you this
Sevet	lynen cloth		
	a bilhook	*shaklack*	green cloth
[*gardanga*]	a planten	*ape gene*	rost yt in the fyre
	a turtle	*habis*	al is gone
	a china dysh	*samisere*	a rapier
	a boy	*faccange*	the sand
[*tadon*]	a woman	*rabe*	a wyfe
	a man	*catur*	a taber
	a coate	*betan*	a candle
catcha	a glasse	*cashe*	I thank you
alle	a ringe	*tuttuccaron*	I wil sel you this //

192r (*cipher*: giants)

(*cipher*: Taulking of the giants of Cap Saint Julians[1] M. Parker had a great desir to encownter with them but he swar, as God shal jug[e] me, I wil doo the best I can to sav ther livs, which I beleev, for he wowld sur run away if any daunger wer.)

Yf Guyny geve a good dynner, yt yeldeth a bad supper.

audacter dictum

The yerle of Desmunt being one of the owts yn Yrland was taken prisoner by his utter fo, the yerl of Ormund who demaunded of Desmunt in this sort. What woldst thow do with mee now were I in thi power? What?

[1] Magellan's famous Patagonian giants. Thomas Hood was one of the half dozen who went ashore with Drake and had been shot at by the Indians, with the loss of two of their men (*PN* (1589), *D*).

quoth Desmunt, now by the mantil of St. Patryck, Than I wold kyl thee.[1]

14 ☉ G [*Sun.*] *18 after Trinity* yt was very hote and no wynd. Capten Drak browght us some purpose. M. Taylbush being somwhat with heat effebled fel owt with M. Banester at supper and som unkindnes was rubd up. Launcelot the smyth died of a calentowr which he took on the shore. I lay with M. Tayboys to quiet hym. He told me that the earle of Warwyk maried first the Lady Taylboys by whom he had 1000[li] a yer.[2] He was divorsed from hir. 13 Launcelot [Robinson] dieth

[*15.*] ☾ [*Mon.*] hote stil and no wynd but at nyght a lytle rayne.

[*16.*] ♂ [*Tues.*] (cipher: the generaul told at diner that he dreamt Capten Ward had taken in M. Evans and that he was ready to fight for it and was sor trobled[3] being very angry. He told me that 20 tun of bear was wanting by Furbushers meanes. Haukins told that the generaul furbad him to gev cloth away which was his own and for this caus by Parkers mean did he gev livris which I kno to be tru.)[4] // (*cipher*: note thes)

[*17.*] ☿ [*Wed.*] the day somwhat hote. At nyght began a good sowtheast gale so that being by accownt abowt 6 degrees northward and 70 leags fro the shore we heald on sowthsowest. Sir Thomas Gressam dyd lyve drinking and dye pissing *ut ferunt*.[5] 192v *our* height *and* cowrse Thomas Gresham

[1] The earls of Desmond and Ormond were the heads of two powerful Anglo-Irish families, the southern Geraldines of West Munster and the Butlers of Kilkenny, Tipperary, and Wexford. Gerald Fitzgerald, earl of Desmond, was to be killed in Nov. 1583 and his head sent to London for display on London Bridge, a 'rebell of quality' (Birch, *Memoirs*, I, 32 n.).

[2] Lady Elizabeth Talbois, daughter of Gilbert, Lord Talbois and Elizabeth Blount, had become the second wife of Ambrose Dudley, earl of Warwick, before Sept. 1553.

[3] Madox writes the last three letters of 'trobled' in Greek not cipher.

[4] See 8 Dec.

[5] In a letter to the Privy Council in 1554, Gresham (d. 1579) wrote that he was going to avoid bringing treasure through the customs because 'the Cappitayne and serchers will banckett me; and all their chere is in drynke, wyche I can very ill away withall' (quoted in J.W. Burgon, *Life and Times*, I (1839), 143–4). This statement has sometimes been taken to mean Gresham was opposed to drink, but the reported saying would indicate a different interpretation.

18. ♃ [*Thurs.*] (*Latin*: *St. Luke's day* became mild by reason of the wind which relieved us with its sweet breeze.

(*Latin*: London beer)

As far as London beer is concerned, I have never drunk anything purer. It seemed to all of us to be the very nectar of the gods. Life and health to M. Duffil[1] from whom we got it, and would God all that beer that we look forward to and bought with silver could be found in the hold of our ship. But it is greatly to be feared that Furbusher has played us a trick, which if it's done, it's done unless the all powerful and merciful Father benignly comes to our aid as is his custom, in whose divine will and help all our trust is set, all our hope is placed.)

a speare

I made a spher for M. Parker but did not fynysh yt.

19. ♀ [*Fri.*] (*Latin*: we enjoyed a favourable and pleasant wind, but not the northeast wind which we desired nor the east which the Portuguese had promised us but the eastsoutheast and the SE by S sufficiently robust, which swelling with excessive fury refreshed us and our ships with a welcome chill. We sailed today . . . 30 miles toward the southwest. . . . At this noontide we wandered in the 12th degree of the Ram.

(*Latin*: wind)

(*Latin*: the way and the place)

At 80 leagues from the shore of Senega, John Waklyn accidentally fell from the prow, but because he had learned to swim as a young man and because the ship was proceeding at a very low speed, he was immediately picked up and recovered the ship.

193r

(*Latin*: Waklin fell into the sea)

When I realised that my blood was boiling with excessive heat, partly by reason of the air which had become inordinately hot and partly because of the victuals which consisted of dry and salty foods and abundant drink, I prevailed upon our physician to open the vein in my left arm and let out 10 ounces of blood), but myn arm hath byn stif ther ever syth. December .29.[2]

(*Latin*: letting of blood)

20. ♄ [*Sat.*] (*Latin*: a cloudy day. At night the weather became threatening. A storm from the south snatched my hat from my head and carried it with one motion into the

(*Latin*: my hat is lost)

[1] Anthony Duffield had served as 'bruer' for Frobisher's first voyage. See the payments of Michael Lok (*Frobisher's Three Voyages*, ed. Collinson, p. x).

[2] Madox's added comment in English indicates that he reviewed his Diary on occasion. Walker had been bled on 6 Oct.

sea. We also collected some rain water during this shower which we used for drinking.

Our poet[1] once again comes to himself and now he fills the whole ship with alluring strains and enchanting songs set to meter. He annoys everyone everywhere. He addresses all in order that by a false hope of little glory, he may bring forth his inept compositions, thrust his wares upon someone and as Vergil says, *per compita stridenti miserum stipula disperdere carmen*: murder a merry song with a strident pipe at the crossroads.[2] But now he scrutinises the recesses of books; he teaches, corrects, reproves, interprets, piles insults on the papists, murders the absent, tortures, confutes, lacerates, flays, tears at, and destroys them. For thus he becomes a man if he is graced with some praise and he begins on the spot to swagger most insolently and arrogantly if he considers himself esteemed. If you tighten the reins a little, he humbly dispenses benefits to all, and whatever he cannot win by sound arguments, he purposes to strengthen under the coloring and guise of piety. He cannot endure anyone saying, God be with you or May God bestow his grace on you or A Christian may not pray against sudden death or Through the mystery of incarnation, let us invoke Christ, etc. This is characteristic of a contentious and vain man.) // Lucius Licinius

21. ☉ G [*Sun.*] *19 after Trinity* (*Latin*: during almost the whole day the skies threatened rain, but not even the sails became damp. With the south wind blowing, we sailed forward slowly and almost imperceptibly 10 leagues toward the west.) 193v (*Latin*: the course)

Hear is the ymage of Dover Cowrt, 24 speakers and never a hearer, quoth Ferdinando.

22. ☾ [*Mon.*] (*Latin*: we caught a quail on our ship when we were now at least 100 leagues from every known shore. There are some swallows from Guinea which followed us hither from the port, but a great number of them died (*Latin*: a quail a swallow)

[1] As indicated by the marginal reference to Licinius (see p. 56 above), Madox is alluding to Banister and his 'Robynhood rimes' (10 May) as well as to his excessive Protestant zeal (see n. to 13 June).

[2] *Ecl.* 3.27.

in our hands, long since exhausted by thirst, hunger, and fatigue. Those which remained in the water were somehow revived by the rain, and if they did not recover their strength, they at least did not utterly lose it.)

candels

My Lady Cowrtney, M. Owtreads wyfe,[1] served us candels which being made of flote [scum] and other fylthy stuffe do burn so badly and so beastishly that the cookes in Oxford be not so oft cawled knaves as she is hear remembred with a bad prayer and the candel wyshed in the sluts tayle that made them and yet the poor mayd cold not do therto Sir reverence. Of my uncle and my aunt he is the veryest botcher that ever prict nawl into an old shewe, quoth John Gates.

Verres

23. ♂ [*Tues.*] (*Latin*: when now the waxing moon had reached seven days' growth, which the astronomers call the first quarter, but which is in fact the beginning of the second, we were annoyed by frequent rains from the south and by thunder. At times Verres persuades us to visit the western isles located under ♋ [Tropic of Cancer] where he hopes to find booty, but if we should go farther, he realised he could say nothing. Now and then he dreaded the calm west wind lest – as I suspect – his consummate ignorance of it when noticed would make him appear ridiculous to all. *Greek*: For they do everything not for the sake of truth but for some advantage.) //

194r

(*Latin*: the wind)

(*Latin*: the ships)

24. ☿ [*Wed.*] (*Latin*: we sailed the whole day with a sufficiently strong wind, not however sufficiently adequate for the speed of our journey, but which cooled our ship as much as possible and inhibited us from following the southwest wind rapidly with outspread sails. We are glad to reach our two consort ships which were sailing at a great distance from us and concerning the good faith of which many were in doubt because we had had no words with them for 14 days.[2] We rejoice on coming together under the

[1] Owtread had married Elizabeth, daughter of John Paulet, Marquess of Winchester, and the widow of Sir William Courtenay of Powderham Castle, Devon. Her daughter Jane by this first marriage was later to become the second wife of Captain Parker.

[2] Madox, it seems, should have said ten days since both Walker and Ward record that on the 14th Drake who had killed a porpoise ('at sermon tyme') carried a piece to the *Edward* and to the *Galleon*. An 'extreme' tornado on the

shadow of our wings, and we congratulate one another.

A bird flew over us which we call split tail, nor did it (*Latin*: A bird) appear tired since it did not struggle either to settle down or land. Therefore, I suspect we are not far from some island (*Latin*: An island) whence the quails flew off which we caught the day before yesterday. We were bending 200 leagues, as I believe, from the eastern coast, three degrees and a little more north of the equator.)

25. ♃ [*Thurs.*] (*Latin*: we felt a strong eastsoutheast wind which hurried us on, solacing us greatly and most pleasantly.)

A merchant of Portingal being in Spayne preferred his soverayn in majesty before the Spaynish king which hard [that] a Spanynish merchant told hym he lyed and gave hym a box of the ear. This Spaniard was after espied in *fabula* Lushburn and the Portingal thinking to have advantedge of him *in*formed the king of al, who hearing the matter sent this man agayn to say as much as he before had sayd and at his return, how now, quod the king, what doth the Spaniard answer. He graunteth yt now, quoth he. Lo than, quoth the king, thow seest the man hath that wyt to consyder that his master is the greater in Spayn and I hear in Portingal. Go thow and do lyke and fear no more boxes. M. Butler.[1] //

[*26.*] ♀ [*Fri.*] *and* ♄ [*Sat.*] (*Latin*: we advanced by the same 194^{v}
[*27.*] eastsoutheast wind, nor did anything remarkable happen which seemed worthy of being recorded except that (*Latin*: ravens) during our conversations I learned that ravens were very often seen by Francis Drake in Labrador and Caliphurnia, but we have not seen any as yet.)

28. ☉ G [*Sun.*] *20 after Trinity. Simon and Jude* (*Latin*: I made an astronomical sphere for the military one, who wishing to repay me for my good will gave me two pairs of silk (*Greek*: gifts) slippers and a garment of very thin cloth and fine thread. I receive this gift with grateful heart as is fitting, and I

22nd caused the ships to lose sight of each other, though, as Walker records, the *Edward* and the *Francis* came together on the 23rd because they had shown a signal whereas the *Galleon* had not.

[1] Nicholas Butler, the distiller.

understand it to have been given me by the favour and spontaneous providence of the Almighty so that those who before had had some reservation, undeservedly, about my good faith now treat me with love, honour and respect. Even if one thing be hidden in the heart and another avowed by the mouth, I am on this account neither anxious nor apprehensive, since I have placed my trust not in men in whom there is no strength but in the fountain of mercy and in the tower of fortitude, in him who is able when he wishes and wishes when it seems good to him to succour his servants and to snatch them from all evil. Here, indeed, I take comfort in this important victory. But in respect to those who are my companions in this voyage, I shall strive with the approval of the Holy Ghost to prove as worthy as possible. But if they load me with more benefits than I wish, I shall see to it that a memory of me remains either by commemorating or rewarding. And although that truth for me is certain that he who receives a favour sells his liberty, I vowed, howsoever this matter turns out, to cater to the vices or passions of no one more than is meet.

In the mountain of Jehovah there will be provision for (*Latin*: gaping cracks) our boat, cleft with cracks in its prow which let in the waves of the sea in abundance. Today we examined it and repaired as much of it as possible with lead plates.[1] //

195r (*Latin*: gold) Gold is tested by a stamp, a woman by gold, and a man by a woman. Wind is aroused by a breath of air, a flame is kindled by the wind, and the flame is fed by the timber (*Latin*: lust) under it. Thus drunkenness incites lust, lust titillates the members, and all erupts into flames and fury when love is present.)

(*Latin*: A tale from Macrobius) *29.* ☾ [*Mon.*] (*Latin*: Galbio plucked the erect hairs of Silvanus with a razor and his beard as well, so that he left him looking like the ghost of a Jacobite. When Clodius strove to obtain approval of this thing from Scævola and anxiously queried how this would please him, Scævola scolded him severely and reprehended the deed. He

[1] Ward states that Fenton 'was faine to slinge three men over boord' to repair the leaks (*PN* (1589), p. 656).

directs and admonishes him not to copy the Curii from the pontifical annals and not to live dissolutely nor to reproach the wicked with mocking and scoffs or follow a rather shameful way of life, since the nymph Ægeria had especially requested this thing of Pompilius so that from his chaste example other refractory ones might come to their senses, enticed to virtue. Therefore it is not proper for one who is viler than any wanton satyr and more lustful, dedicating so much to the woodland deities (Sylvani), to connive at such infamy and shame. Galbio is angry. Clodius accepts the matter with the greatest indignation. They zealously inquire about Scævola, and when they discover no charge against his character, they seek to come upon what they can impute to him against the ancient rites or ceremonies and whether they can find he has pronounced something against Ægeria. They murmur secretly and they plot in every possible way so they can apprehend the man trapped in a snare.

Pyrgopollinices proclaims silence and enjoins dissembling, but Scævola, as he was endowed with a great and intrepid spirit and, even more, as he enjoyed an unspotted conscience, answers that he will deal openly with all nor will he fashion a refuge under the wings of the impious since he has learned that sufficient aid against the nefarious devices of the infamous has been placed for him in the power of Jupiter alone.[1] Thus Macrobius On the Dream of Scipio. //

We read in Terence's Eunuch that Thraso because he thought Thais had done him some harm stormed her house in order that he might recover Pamphila by force whom Thais had won over by fraud. But when he had gathered his men and arranged them in military formation Sannio [for Sanga] appeared, armed with a sponge. This, handled in such a ridiculous manner, however, proved disgraceful not so much to Thais as to Thraso. Thus those who contend with taunts and very unseemly deeds against the most powerful enemies, while He readies the 195v (*Greek*: Eunuch)

[1] This passage is utterly obscure; the pseudonyms of Galbio, 'Silvani,' and Pompilius remain unidentified. The Clodius-Scaevola portions of the passage suggest that once again Madox's outspoken comments have brought him into disfavour with Fenton.

Proverbs 1: 21
Jude 18

sword of the word of truth, make blush not so much the enemies of God as divinity itself.)[1]

30. ♂ [*Tues.*] (*Latin*: with breezes neither too violent nor too weak, the eastsoutheast blowing for many days, we were driven always in the direction of southwest, sometimes southsouthwest, but we did not gain even one degree of latitude. We were all struck with great fear lest we be carried unknowingly into the Mexican Gulf, for indeed the tidal stream proceeds in the northwest with such surge that it drives the ship by its force and violence toward the west as it were unwillingly. The explanation of this matter seems to me the more abstruse and difficult as according to the testimony of Albertus in the second book of his Meteora, the source of water is most abundant in the north.[2] Since of necessity the waters there abound in perennial springs, they flow toward the south where they are absorbed again by the heat of the sun; when because of its eccentricity the sun comes closer to the earth, it becomes stronger and thus dries up the vapors and consumes them. But yet the south wind brings rains and clouds in sufficient quantities, which the north wind drives away. Since the currents in this manner seem to be fighting out of the center of these waters . . . they lead to a difficult and inextricable course. . . . Just as Albertus says, the surge of the sea and the inundation come from the north. There are those who think that it is caught by some violent motion from the east to the west of that which carries with it everything and rolls around the primum mobile,[4] but I do not remember having read the author who is able to decide on good faith anything certain or experienced about these things; this pertains also to the

(*Latin*: reason for the tide of the ocean
Qu. Cardano De rerum varietate and Ashcham's Toxophilus[3]

The rainy south wind)

196r

(*Latin*: generation of waters in the north)

[1] The relevant import of this passage not determined.

[2] *Meteora* II, Tract. 3, ca. 6.

[3] Cardanus, Basel, 1557, Bk. I, c. 1, 'Universum, comitae, ventorum ratio.' Madox seems to be vaguely recalling the passage in *Toxophilus* where Ascham compares the good archer who takes account of winds and weather with the good master of a ship who does the same (*English Works*, ed. W. A. Wright (1904), pp. 106–16.)

[4] The standard view was that the flow of the oceans followed the heavens in moving east to west: '. . . the diurnall motion is violent, caused by the first mover, or *primum mobile*, who in every 24. houres doth performe his circular motion from the East to the West, carrying with him all other inferiour bodies whatsoever' (John Davis, *The Seamans Secrets*, H4*v*).

ebb and flow of the sea, which in ports and straits seem to be governed by the motion of the moon alone. On some shores the tide overflows and subsides 3 feet at the most but in some places 30 feet. Whether as it were a boiling cauldron and seething water swelling up in the middle of the ocean extends itself, rebounding in all parts, and whether thus some influence of the light is drawn out so that it is carried now this way, now that, is not in my power to investigate. (*Latin*: ebb and flow)

We sighted today three or four terrestial birds and a duck as well, which flew around the ship on all sides to such a degree that I think we are not far from some island, but we are sailing under one degree of the Ram and, as some think, not far from the Brazilian coast. We also sighted some red bladders and mushrooms in the form of crests of cocks swimming on the top of the waves, which we never observed before except on the Guinea coast.) (*Latin*: a duck) (*Latin*: mushrooms)

31. ☿ [*Wed.*] (*Latin*: we follow the same course as before and I see nothing new, but we are not very distant from the equinoctial line, no more than 17 degrees from the sun and yet we feel a strong southeast wind. Thus even below the equator we must not despair about the winds, which are likewise produced by the sun, nor are they lukewarm as in England. The poles incline toward coldness. From this I gather there is nowhere a fixed or stable explanation of the winds. Furthermore, M. Glaucus reported that he had learned from Drake that although he had crossed this sea more than once, he never twice found the same condition of air or winds but always different one time from another.) // (*Latin*: the wind)

November ♐ 196v

1. ♃ [*Thurs.*] *All Saints.* (*Latin*: We crossed the equinoctial line almost half way between, so they say,[1] the Guinea (*Latin*: The equinoctial line)

[1] Of the conference held that morning (see below), Ward comments on the diversity of their reckonings: 'by some it appeared, we were 115. leagues, by some 150. leagues, by some 140. leagues, and some a great deale further short of

coast and Brazil, but verging rather toward Brazil, and we never enjoyed a more suitable, more temperate or equable climate than that which we happened to enjoy for 16 days but one from the new moon. And even now during the full moon the breeze began to be fuller and more easterly so that the prows look toward the southwest, but it is not yet possible to sail with loose sheets and cables.

(*cipher*: a consultashon)

Hypegemon came to us accompanied by his master and pilot to deliberate our course with us. We thought that we were closer to the Brazilian coast than he did. It was agreed to proceed farther in that direction but if some occasion should separate the ships to proceed to the north shore of the river Plate and remain there for 15 days and then to proceed to the Straits of Magellan and to wait there.)

(*cipher*: Fernando)

(*cipher*: Fernando sayd that what so ever comes fro the Sowth Sea paseth throo the Bay of Mexico and therfor as good steal it hear as thear. He sayd at super that many a tim being at the comaundement [religious service] on hath cried, a sayl, so they hav left al and folowed theft. Ther wer at our cownsel the generaul, Ward, Haukins, Parker, Madox, Fernando, Cotton, Haul, Whood, Blacolar, Fayrwether, Drak, Persay, but Taylbois was not cauled ether to diner or cownsel. Amonxt thes was no order of asking or answering but al confused, which mad me silent. Ward wowld go forward. His reasons wer the benifit of the shor, the hop of sayls, the suposaul to seas Brasil in 8 degrees and sertany therof exept we sau land at
(*cipher*: Persay) 2 degrees. M. Persay sayd ther is no curent any wher but //
197^{r} a tid by the shor. Whood wil stand to the wind and current for look how he findeth it oons, ether the on or the other, and so is it with him for ever.)

(*Latin*: signs of wind)

(*Latin*: Note,[1] when the waves of the sea sparkle or shine like twinkling flames, it is a sign of southerly winds as I learned from the master.)

(*cipher*: When Fernando sayd, generaul I told you[2] that

Brasile, next hand northeast [for southwest] of us: but all agreed to bewith in 20. minutes of the line, some in the line, some to the north, some to the south of the line' (*PN* (1589), p. 657).

[1] In place of *nota*, Madox uses English.

[2] Madox slips in an English 'you' in this cipher passage.

we wer slipt to the westward, the generaul as not hearing at first wold hav passed it, but the felo folowing it stil, tush, sayd the generaul, I fownd it my self, therby noting that he can not abid to be seen lern any thing of any body which is a prowd mind, and for al this, we wer not [westward], for Fernando sayld a month on dry land.) (*cipher*: all my self)

2. ♀ [*Fri.*] (*Latin*: at night we captured two flying creatures similar to doves, with goose-like feet and a sharp beak, which on account of their grey head tops they call baldies. We likewise sighted larger birds, and those which the English call geese are called, I believe, gannets from the sound of their gaggling.) (*Latin*: birds)

He that wil face owt a [lye] manifestly for nothing wil not styk to make a probable lye for something. (*cipher*: Coton sayd Thom Horsman was hangd.) Aurelianus[1] having at the complaynt of one capten executed an other for a suspicion did after demaund how the thing was accepted of the cownsel. Truly, answereth one, ye have used one hand to cut of an other. M. Parker. *acute responsum*

3. ♄ [*Sat.*] (*Latin*: I passed the time without profit.)

4. ☉ G [*Sun.*] *21 after Trinity* (*Latin*: nothing unheard of or remarkable. We went our old way toward the south pole, but we advanced about three degrees.)

5. ☾ [*Mon.*] (*Latin*: I learned from the Big Gun that a Florentine leader built a ship of noteworthy size, of 2400 burden – which he termed a fair-sized galley – with a crew of at least 200 sailors and a mast 30 feet in circumference, and its crown was 24 feet in diameter. The width of the middle was feet, but the length was feet. It was destroyed within these two years, dashed and broken against the Sicilian coast.) // (*Latin*: a Florentine galley)

6. ♂ [*Tues.*] (*Latin*: we proceeded toward the south with a stronger wind. It was, I believe, an east wind. We sighted a bird not unlike a kite, but with wings extended in length more than usual on each side. Its tail, so much of it 197v

[1] Roman emperor (after Flavius Claudius) noted for his military prowess and severity to his soldiers by whom he was assassinated.

(*Latin*: longtail) as we were able to discern, consisted so it seemed of a single oblong feather of two feet. It is safe to believe that we are positioned between the two little islands located (*Latin*: Islands) 4 degrees south of the equator. The larger is called Y de Fernando de Lorhen [Fernando de Noronha]; the smaller and more westerly is called Vega [Atol das Rocas].)

(*Latin*: An account of the loadstone)

7. ☿ [*Wed.*] (*Latin*: by means of the true poles of the loadstone I investigated the setting of the sun, which according to the needle was 27 degrees distant from the west toward the south, when it should differ 19 degrees, for the sun was situated 24 degrees in ♏ [Scorpio], and we were 6 degrees south of the equator near the coast of Brazil. From this I conclude that the true north was 8 degrees distant from
8. the north pole of the loadstone and today ♃ [Thurs.] similarly carefully investigating the rising of the sun by the same instrument, I found it by accurate observation about 20 degrees distant from the east which at the time of setting was more than 19 degrees from the west, and thus it declines only 12 degrees toward the south. This is most certain proof that the north pole of the loadstone declines at this point 7 degrees 30 minutes toward the east. But in England the loadstone declines 11 degrees from the north toward the south, and in Guinea where we set foot it is more easterly from the north by 3 degrees. But now we plough that arc of the sea which is 7 degrees to the south of the equator but yet on Mercator's globe it has a longitude of 347 degrees and in the St. James' meridian, . . .[1]) //

198r

9. ♀ [*Fri.*] ♄ [*Sat.*] (*Latin*: We are still using the eastsoutheast
10. wind, and daily we advance a degree or more now entirely by means of certain stars which should be noted down. They are situated near the south pole and revolve with a very slow and visible revolution.)

[1] The latter portion of this passage on the variation of the compass is garbled, the result of a few words and a marginal cipher having been torn from f. 204v and mistakenly pasted here over the original script. The transferred marginal cipher calls attention to a cipher passage within the text proper on f. 204v, where (25 Nov.) Madox records reasons for not keeping up the register. The relevance of the marginal comment to the text (f. 204v) makes this clear as does the correspondence of strokes in the cipher with those of the portion pasted on f. 197v.

11. ⊙ *G* [*Sun.*] *22 after Trinity*. (*Latin*: The day of my birth which completes the thirty-sixth year of my life. The thirty-seventh begins. The number three is indeed the number of perfection, but the number seven is the number of saintliness and repose. May He who alone opens the seven seals of the book [Rev. 5: 1] and who is both one and of the eternal triad grant that according to the law of the most loving God and my Savior I may henceforth walk perfectly during the remaining time of my life and, sanctified by the Spirit in this life, I may enter into the peace of the Lord after death through Jesus Christ the Redeemer of the whole world. Amen. (*Latin*: My birthday)

We heard that Walker was sick with a fever, so after dinner the general graciously and kindly gathered together some sweetmeats and with me visited and consoled him.) (*cipher*: He told me that Fayrwether sayd the generaul bad him shute at the Edward, and Blacolar did harten them to part, and if he had not wel handeled the mater, they had been gon for the capten was prowdly bent, thinking to shar best when he was from under an overseer.)[1] (*Latin*: Walker is sick) (*cipher*: *nota*)

12. ☾ [*Mon.*] (*Latin*: when I heard that Walker was worse, I hastened to him with the physician as quickly as I could. I found a very weak and sick man. However, my presence consoled him. He said that the day before yesterday he had dreamed that 8 terrible misshapen and black musicians approached him as he was walking on the street and asked him for his money. He kindly promises but they demand all his money, snatch what he has, stab him in the back with a poniard and leave him for dead. In this he sees a certain sign of death when on the royal day, the (*Latin*: Walker's dream)

[1] On the preceding Friday, Walker had fallen dangerously sick of a 'burninge Cala[n]ture,' so that this Sunday morning all the gentlemen of the *Galleon* visited him. Despite his extreme sweating and burning, Walker apparently revealed to Madox information he had obtained on 29 Oct. from Richard Fairweather, now master of the *Francis*. Having come aboard the *Edward* with 'Master Dore' (Ward, *PN* (1589), p. 657) – apparently a reference to William Darre on the *Francis* – to obtain a hogshead of pork, Fairweather had reported Fenton's instructions to his gunner (John Gates) to shoot at them for 'ther keepinge so mutche into the wether etc.'

The *Edward*'s pilot, Thomas Blacollar, like its captain had become restive under Fenton's command.

17th, the engines of war will bellow forth their burst of harmony, a terrible melody and inimical to life.

198v (*Latin*: another dream)

He dreamed further that he saw boys [ascend] up the mast to the body of the sun itself, grasping the rays as they climb. When he is unable to do this and even more marvels at the boys, they showed by clear proof that this could very easily be done by any man born of woman. I devise a plausible and a consoling and, as I hope, relevant interpretation of this dream. And there I spent the night.

Viceadmiral Ward makes many inquiries of me concerning the orderly movement of the stars and reports that William Borows[1] is one who could fill his honeycombs with someone else's honey and so far he is accustomed to feed French dogs while they bring in the hares. Thereupon he sneers at such men and thus he admonishes me with promises and bland courtesy when I return home not to impart more than enough to him who, fully informed concerning all things, like a mule seeks his mother with his heels. For thus he made use of a certain learned and noble Scot.

(*cipher*: Wiliam Borows)

He also conjectured that he had thrown Lock into prison as the master reported. Lock, however, is a man of great wit and admirable honesty, as the master reported to me, but unhappy.[2]

A certain gladiator, after having instructed a disciple

[1] A writer on navigation and, with his older brother Stephen, a chief pilot for the Muscovy Company after the death of the 'incomparable' Richard Chancellor (see 29 Sept.). In 1582 he became Treasurer of the Queen's ships and ultimately Controller of the Navy. His brother Stephen had persuaded the Muscovy Company to support Richard Eden's translation (in 1561) of Martin Cortes' *La Arte de Navegar*, a work which was to provide 'substance' and 'inspiration' for William Bourne's popular *Regiment for the Sea*, which Madox (8 Apr.) ascribed to William Borough, terming him 'a very proper man for sea matters.'

In 1581 Borough's own discourse on the variation of the compass appeared, together with what has been termed one of the first 'truly scientific' books ever published in England, *The Newe Attractive* by Robert Norman whom Madox had visited on 19 Feb. See David W. Waters, *The Art of Navigation in England* (1958), pp. 127–63.

[2] This paragraph appears as a horizontal insert in the margin.

Michael Lok, who served as governor of the Cathay Company following on Frobisher's first voyage to the Northwest, had been arrested and thrown into the Fleet in June 1581 at the suit of 'William Burrowes.' In a petition dated some six months later, Lok refers to the £5000 he himself had lost in the voyages and to his fifteen poor children (*CSP, Dom., 1581–90*, pp. 19–20; *CSP, Col., East Indies, 1513–1616*, pp. 70–1).

in his art, is at length mocked by this same disciple, and thinking he has been unjustly treated, complains. He attacks the disciple with menacing words. The disciple, believing himself skilled both in the practise of the art and in strength of body, in ability to surpass his master by far in nimbleness of footwork and strength of arms, and inflated with pride, challenges the man to combat. He appoints the day. The teacher sluggishly pledges himself. They fight. Weighing the matter on a just scale, the old fox acknowledges himself unequal to his disciple and so breaks forth in these words: Why you rascal, you good-for-nothing, are you so afraid and unsure of yourself that you have readied at least six supporters and defenders, you who have promised to fight legally with me in single combat? Am I, he answered, a boastful young man? Where are they? I utterly deny it. Look around, said the other, and admit it. The foolish and impudent young man looked around. As he did so the other dealt him such a terrible blow on the head that there was no longer any question of a contest. Then the teacher said, Come, I have educated you liberally in my art; I have generously and thoroughly taught you many things, but not all. Since you are swayed by false opinion and think yourself superior, I add still another precept of this art and an uncommon test, and because you do not pay heed but boast about yourself and proclaim your skill everywhere, you are beaten the more grievously. At this point I still have 20 precepts torn from the center and marrow of this art, a number of them very secret, so you will always find yourself so long as I live unequal to me. The young man blushed, confessed his arrogance too late, and taught by an evil turn finally came to his senses and paid due honor to his teacher.[1]

(*Latin*: a wise tale)

199r

In the same manner when you are instructing unequal students, hold the reins in such a manner that when you wish, you will be able to hold back a fierce and refractory

[1] Compare Andrew Marvell's statement: 'My Fencing-master in *Spain*, after he had instructed me all he could, told me, I remember, there was yet one Secret against which there was no Defence, and that was, to give the first Blow' ('To a Friend in Persia,' 1671, *The Poems and Letters*, ed. H. M. Margoliouth, II (1971), 324).

horse. He who does not know this confesses he is ignorant of the manner in which soldiers are to be trained.

(*Latin*: a pretty tale)

A certain beardless boy emitted a rattling noise when his mistress was standing near. Come, said the mistress, how dare you thunder so familiarly before me? Nay, if I had known, he said, that you had in mind what your pipe could prove, I would have relinquished priority and not attempted such a thing before you. This in English has its charm where there is no distinction between *coram* and *ante* but where both are expressed loosely by one word.

(*cipher, Latin*: Ward da[r]es)

199v

The viceadmiral asked me whether I kept a diary of the voyage, and he persuades me that it can be safely secreted with him, for before our return they will all be carefully searched. I denied it absolutely since as I was sickly before, I could not keep one, afterwards I wholly neglected to do it. He says the councillors will expect it of me. I say then that I am willing to put together the log of Palinurus, and thus I get rid of an insatiable and covetous man. For who willingly subjects himself to an irritable and prideful man except he who enjoys exchanging liberty for shameful servitude?)

13. ♂ [*Tues.*] (*Latin*: I make out Walker's will.[1] I return home. At night I visit him again. I spend the night there. I find him somewhat fearful, for he is terrified of sleeplessness on account of his melancholy. Otherwise he is not greatly suffering.)

(*Latin*: the wind)

14. ☿ [*Wed.*] (*Latin*: I return home. In the meantime, the wind began, I believe the day before yesterday, to extend its wings slowly and gradually, first toward the southeast, then toward the northwest, soon toward the east, and now toward the eastnortheast, which we are using today. Thus we proceed toward the southsouthwest with looser ropes lest we should encounter the greatest danger in the shoals of Abreoius [Abrolhos][2] between the continental shore and Ascension Island, 18 degrees from the equator.

[1] Walker, having disposed 'all thinges orderly,' made Madox and Ward his executors.

[2] Of the shoals they were avoiding, Ward says they were 'called by us *Powles*,' (*PN* (1589), p. 658), located 0.23 N and 29.23 W; those of Abrolhos extend thirty leagues off the coast of Brazil.

Now, however, we are sailing at 14 degrees. May God be propitious to us.)

15. ♃ [*Thurs.*] (*Latin*: at luncheon Hegemon seriously charges us that being privy to the brawl and quarrelling on the viceadmiral, we did not inform him. I protest I am ignorant and unknowing of these things. We go there. We make inquiries, we investigate, we find nothing of the sort, but all is feigned and falsely contrived by Glaucus's suspicion and the hasty exaggeration of the Big Gun. (*Latin*: exaggeration)

Pallinurus told me for certain that when they were sailing near the shore toward the northwest, which is commonly called Labrador and were in a latitude of 63 degrees, the midday sun came out after the climb of the loadstone by two degrees, whence one may conclude that there it deviates 22 degrees from the exact north toward the west. If this is true, the reason by which it deviates now this way, now that, from the poles of the world seems inscrutable to me, and I do not know by what secret force it is impelled. See above. (*Latin*: the loadstone)

16. ♀ [*Fri.*] (*Latin*: Investigating the setting of the sun today, I found it to decline 3 degrees from the west toward the south, falling under the horizon in its accustomed course. It is distant 21 degrees passing through the fourth degree of Sagittarius so that here the loadstone declines 12 degrees from the north toward the south. However on the 17th we saw the seventh degree to the south.) //

17. ♄ [*Sat.*] (*Latin*: *the anniversary of the reign of queen Elizabeth* who has now completed 24 years and begins the 25th. God grant that she reign in peace as long as possible, that she be honoured without exception and that godliness be embraced by her subjects. We expressed our joy with engines of war with a festive ceremony of banqueting and a general assembly. 200r (*Latin*: 25th of Elizabeth)

Walker, attacked by sickness, bids goodbye to all separately, and he urges us to repent and embrace virtue. He was convinced he would die that night[1] because he Walker

[1] See 12 Nov. Despite the daily visits of Madox and others exhorting him to be of good cheer and the bloodletting and various waters and conserves administered by Banister, Walker thought himself on this date past recovery as

ardently sought God to be freed from this prisonhouse before he should see us contaminated by quarrelsome wits and the hands of all of us shamefully defiled with blood and plunder, which we daily yawn for and belch forth.

(*Latin*: Andre Thevet) I began cursorily to read the New Antarctic of Thevet[1] who describes not ineptly, at least not falsely, many things which we experienced. On Pliny's testimony he reports Ch. 5 that the Canaries were named from the dogs which Juba of Mauritania led thence, but rather it seems to him they obtained their names from reeds [*i.e.*, *canna*]. In Tenarife Ch. 6 there is a mountain with a great peak, resembling an Ω, extending fifty-four miles in height and twenty in circumference at the base, which is visible to navigators fifty leagues away. He reports it was known to Ptolemy. He says that many times the Spaniards attempted to climb the top of the mountain with pack horses and mules laden with provisions for the journey, but they were never seen afterwards. Thus it is suspected that they were killed by the natives of that mountain who are wild and savage. I say rather that they were overcome either by cold or hunger or noxious vapors. I believe it likely some such thing to have happened.

From his words you gather that the juice of the trees Ch. 8 which we collected in Guinea was cinnabar rather than dragon's blood. Madeira is derived from the word in Spanish for wood or grove. Here they came on the 1st of September, sailing out from New Haven [Havre de Grâce] in France on the 6th of May 1555 and up to that point using the northnortheast wind, which is between the east and the north. //

200^{v} He writes in the fifth chapter that on the 1st of September they sighted the peak of Tenarife at daybreak, but this

---

did all those about him. He was, in fact, unable to rise from his bed until 2 Dec., by which time, as he recorded, his flesh was so consumed that he was 'lyke to an anatomye.'

[1] *The new found worlde, or Antarctike*, the English translation of André Thevet's *Les Singularitez de la France Antarctique* (1557), had appeared in 1568, dedicated to Sir Henry Sidney. At a cost of 6^{s} 8^{d} for the 'Englishe and French,' it was one of seven books (including Mandeville's *Travels*), which Frobisher had taken on his first Northwest voyage (*Three Voyages of Martin Frobisher*, ed. Collinson, pp. ix, x). The errors of Thevet, who made his voyage in 1555 under Villegagnon, were exposed by the Protestant minister Jean de Léry in his account in 1578, where he terms him 'impudent menteur.'

island lies below the Tropic of Cancer.[1] Thence he says they had prospect of a watering place at Cape Verde after they used a favourable northnortheast wind, but owing to a change of air and wind which around Guinea never remain constant they were compelled to call in at Guinea, ch. 17. He does not name the place or the latitude, but I believe it to be on the Rio Grande, 13 degrees on this side of the equator since he states that it is below the ♋ [Tropic of Cancer].[2] By means of sails he landed here on the 4th of September, as in ch. 17. And yet he writes that he supplied himself with water in the islands of Cape Verde. I do not see how, since between the island of Tenarife and this river there are 12 degrees. We were never able up to this time to cover more than two degrees in the space of twenty-four hours.[3] Yet our ship is not an ordinary one but famous and notable for its swift course.

(*Latin*: contradiction)

(*Latin*: Perhaps here 4 in place of 14, as Ch. 18)

He says that he saw an infinite number of fish below the equator. We found what he said concerning the dorados, which we call dolphins, not at all true,[4] because they are visible and accompany the ship for a long time. Even wounded by slingshots they are not put to flight, but all of us bait them with hooks on three-pronged poles and spears made for this purpose: we catch the ones we see. What he says about the marsovini is true, that they forecast storms, but they neither follow ships nor are they without flavor, for I do not remember anything to have tasted better to my palate than their meat.[5]

Ch. 18

Ch. 20

(*Latin*: dorados gilthead in Greek)

[1] Although the Madeiras are a hundred miles north of the Canaries, Tenerife has a northern latitude of 28° 15′.

[2] Seeming so large to the Venetian Cadamosto at first sight as to appear a gulf (*Voyages*, ed. G. R. Crone (Hakluyt Soc., 1937), p. 75), the Rio Grande, in 12.09 north latitude, is now called the Geba.

[3] While rightfully questioning Thevet's claim, Madox's own assertion that they were unable to cover more than two degrees in a day is itself notable. Writing in 1594, Robert Hues stated that vessels going to the Cape of Good Hope sailed a degree a day (that is, 60 nautical miles), and his assertion has been accepted as accurate by modern authorities plotting the tracks of ships. See David Waters, *The Art of Navigation* (1958), p. 37 and n.

[4] In what way Madox found Thevet's statements about the dorado untrue is not clear: 'There are founde great ones like Samons, others that are lesser: from the head to the tayle it hath a creste and all that parte coloured lyke fyne Azure, in such sorte that it is unpossible to excogitate or thinke a more fayrer colour. . . . This fish folowed our shippes the space of seven wekes without once forsaking of them, yea night and day, untill that she founde the sea unsavery or not for hir nature' (E8*v*). For Madox's account of the dolphin, see 3, 4 July.

[5] The marsovini, called sea hogs (from L. *maris sus*, as Thevet explains E7*v*),

Ch. *18* But when he says that the sea water below the line is insipid, it seemed to us not to be so. For some on purpose, to avoid danger [in the future] tasted and found the brine sufficiently heady and piquant. However, we noticed this, that near the tropics sea water . . . is very useful for softening meats but below the equator it is suitable and pleasant. Ch. *11* He notes correctly that palm in Greek is called phoenix because both that tree and that bird, dead and reduced to ashes, come back to life again and by a happy circumstance spring forth. In chapter 18 he describes the pole of the heavens and the equator in a crabbed way, not clearly enough or accurately.

About the Island of Assumption, which he calls Assen- Ch. 21 cion, I heard it to be true that there is a great supply of birds there, 8 degrees to the south. And those which he calls *aponars* we call in Welsh penguins from their white heads.[1]

201r Concerning the southern stars he writes in a frigid . . . manner and not as befits an astronomer, ch. 21. Nothing in the entire book has been treated methodically, but it has been translated even more ineptly inasmuch as he who translated it did not know how to correct the printer's errors.[2] Thus author Thevet, though often naming many

---

are 'like almoste to Hogs on the earth, for he hath the lyke grunt or noyse, and hath the snoute lyke the ende of a Canne, and on the heade a certayne cundite or opening, by the which he yaunneth or purgeth even as the Whale.' He records their swimming 'a mayne against us . . . a certayne sign and forshewing, of that parte from whence the winde ought to come' and acknowledges that the mariners 'doe eate but little thereof' (E8). Cf. Madox's entry for 22 Nov.

[1] Discovered by the Portuguese navigator João da Nova on Ascension Day, 1501, the island was noted for its multitude of birds. Thevet describes the 'Aponars' as 'great and hye, lyke hearnshawes, the belly white and with the backe blacke as cole, the byll lyke to a cormorant' (F1v).

The attribution of the name *penguin* to the Welsh (from *pen gwyn* 'white head') also appears in David Ingram's 'Narrative' (*PN* (1589), p. 560); in a copy of Francis Fletcher's manuscript (included in *The World Encompassed*, ed. Penzer, p. 128); and Sir Thomas Herbert's *Travels* (1638), p. 13. Expressing dubiety, the *OED* records these examples but omits that of Madox although recording citations from the English portion of his manuscript on occasion. For additional instances of this derivation, see the account of Gilbert's voyage to Newfoundland (*PN* (1589), pp. 507; 709); and the *Observations* of Sir Richard Hawkins, pp. 75–6.

In the sixteenth century, a penguin was generally what was later called a great auk, a northern bird, now extinct, and quite unrelated to today's penguin. Neither has ever been reported on Ascension Island.

[2] The STC (23950) assigns the translation to the publisher Thomas Hacket, apparently on the basis of his dedication of the work to Sir Henry Sidney; however, this statement makes it clear that Madox did not automatically accept the translation as Hacket's.

ancient writers, seems to me to have gathered together many absurd things. Moreover, he observes no order in writing.

He seems to call *petun* what we call tobacco, and what Ch. 32
we call plantanes he calls *paquovere*. The Americans bind Ch. 33
their dead and bestow upon them all their possessions, [ch.] 37. They number the years by lunar months, and they Ch. 40
celebrate the new moon. The Island of Zebut is a wealthy one, [ch.] 47. The tide of the sea hurled Magellan for five Ch. 56
days without sails into the southern part of the Straits toward the south. He says that there are 56 rocks in the sea which attract to themselves ships built with iron nails and thus they are forced to use wooden ones there, but this I do not believe, fol. 90.

He describes the astrolabe not sufficiently clearly or appropriately, ch. 68. Rain water [at the equator] produces pustules on the hands, [ch.] 69. With great scrupulousness the natives of Perou preserve a bag whence they believe Ch. 70
all the water of the sea once flowed and issued out. Around Florida the sea is covered with vervain, [ch.] 74. These Floridians, succumbing in war, kill their king, even as the Persians do nowadays, but I scarcely believe it, ch. 74.

Jaques Quartier [Cartier], a Breton French, captured 7 men in Canada; but he brought back two who had been instructed in religion and the French language on his second voyage.[1] Here the enemy are put to flight by means Ch. 79
of a noxious smoke, which, in the face of a strong wind, also seems incredible.

18. ☉ *G* [*Sun.*] *23 after Trinity* (*Latin*: the general visited Walker. We found the man weak and prepared to die; however, we discovered great signs of health.

201v

19. ☾ [*Mon.*] (*Latin*: sailing beyond the equator, we again sighted the sun at the zenith, 21 degrees and a half. Here we saw a great flock of birds, which we call *pleriks* from the sound, following and pillaging schools of little fish. (*Latin*: ☉ at the zenith for the third time)

Our Æsculapius today again visits the sick one. I stay

[1] Of the seven men Cartier captured, 'he reserved twaine, which he brought into *France* and at his second voyage did carie them backe againe, and also they returned againe, and were made Christians, and ended their lives in *Fraunce*' (R3*v*).

(*Greek*: a bitter strife)

(*cipher*: Ward)

at home. A bitter contention arose between him and the captain.[1] While that shipmate of ours by being greedy, by corrupting others, by preaching about himself causes tedium to some and arouses the wrath of others, the other, exhausted, impatient of trouble and vexation, wishes, as it were, to be a cock on his own dunghill; he cannot bear with equanimity that something of which he is not reputed to be author and originator be fitly or dutifully done or spoken. In this way he suffers sorely when wine, sweetmeats and such other things are consumed by others. For he is not a little heedful of the matter. Indeed, if one may speak the truth without injury, he is more greedy than is meet, not to speak of his insolence and innate irascibility which he is wholly unable to dissemble although he conceals the extreme depravity of his greed with sedulous guile.)

(*Latin*: the weather)

20. [♂ *Tues.*] (*Latin*: with a favourable breeze and a truly cold and salubrious NE and by E wind, we speedily made our way toward the southwest, advancing 30 furlongs, more or less, in 24 hours. On the basis of what I can surmise from past recollection, I sighted ☿ [Mercury] early this evening, 20 degrees distant from the sun, a star slightly red, sufficiently bright and apparently of the first magnitude.

(*Latin*: tropic of ♑ [Capricorn])

(*Latin*: Andre Thevet)

(Verres)

This night we also crossed the ♑ [Tropic of Capricorn] not far, as I conjecture, from Cape Frio and the river Jænuario [Rio de Janeiro] on the Brazilian coast, but as yet we have not sighted land. However, Thevet describes verdure, flowers, and aromatic herbs growing here in sufficient abundance, which send forth a most sweet odor and an emanation from some balsam when by and by at a distance of 50 leagues they came near to or saw that part of the land. But no such thing has happened to us up to now, although certain people daily threatened danger from the rocks and high places, who though they said we were hemmed in and entangled in the Mexican Gulf, even now swear that we are a hundred leagues from shore; yet I would dare affirm that daily we have drawn closer and closer.) //

[1] Ward notes tersely: 'there passed speeches betwixt Master *Bannister*, and me' (*PN* (1589), p. 658).

21. ☿ [*Wed.*] (*Latin, Greek*: the north and northeast winds blew more frequently with stout and violent breezes, but to us pleasant and agreeable on account of our old friendship, our common homeland, the ease of our journey, and the coldness of the air. You cannot search out or thoroughly look into all the causes of the winds, but I readily believe that the sea itself provides a richer supply of material to the windy stars than the earth whence the winds spring, but [I do not know] whether this material giving way again to violent turmoil is finally consumed in such a way as to disappear, or being rarified and diminished by excessive heat, it becomes weak and faint, or whether influenced by other planets and stars, it is changed to something else, and that material which just now was rushing with furious force toward the south is now carried at a slow pace toward the setting sun; whether the wind is at times silent and goes to sleep so that aroused by the course of the planets, it afterwards behaves itself strenuously and valiantly; whether some wind goes around the whole earth and traverses it and having completed its course returns to itself again and having rolled around and rotated around its axes and poles, leaving its place, it yields to another wind so that no storm or tempest ever results unless two winds, coming together in a mighty effort, struggle in the heads and tails of the dragons, ascending and descending in the same manner as usually happens in the case of an eclipse. The knowledge of these things is hidden and abstruse, lurking secretly in the very entrails of nature. I have elicited this in my labors. He wholly denies it.[2] It is true that the discussion is connected with the tide of the sea, which seems to me a phenomenon in the water equivalent to the wind in the air, seeing that each alters violently and disturbs the quiet and peaceful condition of its habitat. I do not know how thus with its own effort the wind is forced now here, now there, into all parts of the world, in one place being lusty, in another humble and inane. Does the sea seethe with the heat of the heavenly bodies so that rarified it boils and gives out foam? 202r

(*Latin*: comparison of wind and tide)

(*Latin*: *Qu.* Cardano De varietate rerum and Toxophilus and the philosophy of flux)

(*Latin*: *Qu.* Cardano De navigatione)[1]

[1] See Bk. x. c, 54, 'Navigandi ars' in *De rerum varietate*.
[2] No referent indicated.

Does it follow the course of the primum mobile? Does it rotate around its own axis as something would as a result of planetary influence? By finding itself indiscreetly on the rocks and high promontories and some watersheds and

202v

windings, is it driven and beaten back as among peasants the ball in the game of stakes is knocked about or being kicked rebounds?

So much does the expert pronounce about these matters, but the gain is large and their number is great who have the audacity to express and deliver an opinion like judges easily and firmly about anything whatsoever and wish to die by hanging and to be thrust with the lowest shades of the departed if those thousand discoveries are not equally reliable and certain as the oracle of Apollo or the gospels themselves. And so our own Fernando is wont to do, who

(*cipher*: Fernando)

finding certain observations in Portuguese, which he shamefully acquired with talons more rapacious than those of any vulture while he actively practised his vocation of piracy, and translating these ineptly since they are not, so he avers, yet elucidated in English, they come out disguised in a swill of many languages and everywhere abound in barbarisms, solecisms and hyberbatons; these he sells as his own and boasts of himself as a notable author and inventor when rather he should be called a perverter of books, an extorter of readers, and a tormentor of writers. In these books nothing else is contained but trivialities and vulgarities and what the wit of a sailor would know, dull, obtuse and, what is worse and almost common to all of this class, rash and stubborn and intolerant of all instruction and learning.

(*Latin*: a tale of sickness concerning a husband and wife)

A certain paterfamilias because he was sickly never crept forth but confined himself among his own lares. The neighbors, especially the women who inclined toward these duties also have more leisure, approach the man and comfort him. As he is recuperating in bed, they persuade him he should attempt to expel all pestilent and noxious humours by binding his temples with a thick warm towel and sweating and steaming. His wife gives him the same advice; she knows that hitherto she has solemnly given this counsel, but the old women deny she has a recalcitrant

and peevish husband, and they declare him a worthy man who is seized by disease or old age. What is her husband to do? He complies although with an unwilling and complaining stomach which rather hoped for some savory and healthful food, but shame or nausea does not allow the sick man to ask for it. As a result of fasting, he finally recovers. Bereft of physician and guardian, he looks out for himself. In the course of time his wife becomes sick. Once more the old women and cup-gossips approach her; 203r
they urge her to be of good cheer; they persuade her to take some broth made of herbs, wine and spices in order to restore her stomach, then to eat a chicken or a capon or a partridge either properly boiled or nicely roasted with very fine little pieces of cake soaked and moistened and sweetened with sugar and vinegar. Thus, God willing, she would be able to recover her health anew. Incensed by the malice of the old women on hearing this advice, her husband says, Indeed, my wife is most dear to me, and so I do not permit that she rashly try these new and unheard of drugs in which there is always more danger than hope. But since I have always found her similar to me in all respects, I do not doubt that that which is fitting for me will also be useful and salutary for her. But suffering from pain and with you as my counselors, I drove out and banished the disease by sweating. If sweating and fasting have profited me, they will also certainly profit her. Away, you who are so willing by your impudent extravagance to be the contrivers of bereaving me of such a sweet wife so that when she is dead some one of you joined to me in marriage may hold dominion and spend out her days here. But it will never come to this, so enough of words, go. But you, my gentle and brave wife, my sweet little heart, retire to your bed as quickly as possible. Believe me, I will zealously and carefully see to it that you are not annoyed by nausea resulting from food.) Edward Fenton.

22. ♃ [*Thurs.*] (*Latin*: I devised certain theorems and clear proofs by which our general could perceive the motion of the heavens and the planets, the use of the globe and sphere, the declination of the sun and the stars better and

(*Greek*: Proofs for the sake of Hegemon)

more accurately than the ones which used now with uncertainty cause him to fall into error. I also drew up proofs by which he is able to visualize the course of a ship anywhere (but especially when using winds that are little favourable, he is forced to stray a great distance and wander from his course) and to measure at first sight how far he is from his proposed goal and how much he has wandered off. These proofs, even though they are easy, clear and evident, are understood with difficulty, and they found the access very difficult as if the entire entrance, having been ascertained, were fenced off with a wall, briars, thorns and thistles. Yet they think they can be instructed by a single little word concerning these matters over which learned men have sweated all their lives.

203v (*Latin*: the rainy south wind)

At the fourth hour of daylight the north wind becomes gentle and gives way to the westnorthwest, the westnorthwest to the NW and by N, the NW and by N to the westnorthwest, the westnorthwest to the westsouthwest, the westsouthwest to the NE and by E and the NE and by E to the west. Each heir is milder than its father, and each previous king stronger than its successor. Finally they all disappear. Calm reigns. This is annoying to us, for it is the custom here for the prince to kill no one but to throw into prison in chains all of his subjects which he sees in the midst of his kingdom, and there if the prospect for food allotment is less, to waste them with languishing and fasting.

For this reason throughout the battle with that one the southwest is chief although he was hostile to us on our proposed voyage and in his hatred [dealt] us such great and slow punishment. In the twilight of the evening he inflates his cheeks, he brings rain, he announces war through calm, he conquers, he reigns. A most vigilant king indeed who through the entire period of his reign does not permit his eyes to close. On his death his nephew the southsouthwest succeeds him. Lacking both strength and counsel, he in turn is overcome and he is overcome by

(*Latin*: Sharks follow the rain, the calm, and the south wind)

calm. The sharks dance for joy; they rejoice in southern rains and in calm no less than the sea hogs delight in winds and storms, which like swine are accustomed to run about here and there in the cold but to remain quiet in the heat. On the other hand, sheep are excited and run about when the weather is hot and seek hiding places when it is cold.

(*Greek*: Fernando a false prophet)

This also I think must not be passed over: the day before yesterday when he saw the NE and by N wind bristling, our Fernando burst out with these words, *Indeed, I am not a vain prophet; I had always predicted to you that the north wind would never fail on this coast, and I now add that the farther we advance, the more violently this wind will press upon us.* Some giving credit to his words, lest it appear that a secret escape them, likewise proclaim the same thing not as acquired or heard or perceived from any other quarter but as born of themselves and gathered by skilful investigation from many observations. I who look into the whole matter cannot control my laughter; nor am I ignorant of these things, but they proceed more like fish on dry land.

(*Greek*: Hood is a nobody)[1]

Hood boasts that he is a great one at home and that here he is held in no esteem even though he was brought here not without royal authority; if he had known beforehand the whole business and the conditions that prevail, he, transformed into a dog by Circean potions, barking like Hecuba, would have published these things everywhere 204r
rather than suffer them. He also adds that he is bound by an oath to her royal majesty never to proceed beyond the equinoctial line unless in the company of three counselors. This should have been recognised before because if she had known how scanty his skill is and, on the other hand, how notable his boasting, it would not have been necessary for her to exact an oath from the man unless she would ultimately bring to pass what he cannot accomplish by his own strength and knowledge.)

23. ♀ [*Fri.*] (*Latin*: the sky is cloudy and threatening rain; the sea, not roused by any wind, swells with seething waves. Finally, with an eastsoutheast wind blowing, we head toward the southwest.)

(*cipher*: of sir Fraunsis Drak)

(*cipher*: At super Haukins and Wood toold that sir Fraunsis Drak was in ther det and that he had used them very il, and that he went to his cabin at 8 a clok and wind

[1] The Greek pun is lost in English (ὄυδος ὄυδεις ἔστιν).

or rayn never stird.[1] This ros of that the generaul told Haukins the last of September that sir Fraunsis sayd Ned Gilman was a better mariner than he.[2] The generaul toold me also that sir Fraunsis sayd to a nobl man that we showld never com hom agayn, but I tr[u]st in God we shaul prov him a fals profet in that.)

(Latin: temperature)

24. ♄ [*Sat.*] (*Latin*: the sky is darkened by clouds which distilling the heavenly dew affect the temperature slightly. So it is that if you are thinly dressed, you do not feel the rigor of the cold, and if dressed in heavier clothing, you are not vexed with excessive heat. At noon the northeast wind began to reign again, but there was a great battle between it and calm as to which would prevail or which would command, an extremely doubtful contest and an uncertain outcome of the strife. Since we can do nothing by force, we align ourselves with prayers on the side of the northeast wind.)

(*Latin*: uncertain deliberation)

25. ⊙ *G* [*Sun.*] *24 after Trinity* (*Latin*: a trip to the viceadmiral to console my brother whom we found slightly better. There Hegemon decreed we consider whether we should make for the shore since owing to the decay of the casks, gaping with cracks, almost our entire supply of water was emptied and exhausted. The viceadmiral did not think we should draw near the shore, being afraid now of the mist, now of the calm. Its tyranny which we now suffer happens, he thinks, from the fact that the strength of the northeast wind is weakened and broken by promontories. Thus on account of its force all approaches are blocked and shut off so as to deny entrance to us. Thrust into this recess, the wind is able to come there where by the shelter of the sides extending most widely it is then driven away by such ramparts. A certain

[1] The musician Simon Wood like Hawkins had sailed with Drake; the Portuguese pilot captured at Santiago also referred to Drake's shutting himself up in his cabin together with his young cousin and page, now Captain John Drake.

[2] Edward Gilman, a traveller on this voyage, was to serve in 1585 as Captain of the *Scout* in Drake's West Indies expedition (Corbett, *Drake and the Tudor Navy*, II (1899), 15 n.). In 1588 Drake was to lease his town residence in Plymouth with garden adjoining to him and to Florence Plott, née Gilman (C. W. Bracken, *A History of Plymouth* (1934), p. 95).

probable reason but such is the man's insolence and so great is his estimation of himself that he is willing to annex and gather up reasons deliberately so that either he quarrels with others or comports himself as a wiser and more acute man. This is considered a vice by many but not all. He is 204v
accustomed to decorate and conceal his vices by the trappings of words or by the specious mask of reasoning. However, this seems to me evidence of a most villainous man. (*cipher*: Ward a vilayn)

Very much to the point seems to be what Publius Cornicola reported when he had a conversation with certain people concerning some one named Smedley who was in the habit of stealing secretly into the bed chamber of a lady unknown to me. He said he had once been ordered to kill this adulterer, but, he says, I shall not defile my hands with human blood for the sake of anyone except by order of one person only, which if he should give it, he swears he would not take pity on any soul nor wish to refrain from any crime so atrocious. But if he should be ready to perpetuate evil and to plan a villainous act for the sake of anyone, I will trust him then no more than the vilest combatant defiled by the most loathsome filth.

But back to business. The charts and plans are taken out, even the drafts so that examining all arguments we might more easily ascertain in what place we are. We examined, as it happened, the sketch of the Straits of Magellan which that golden knight of ours who had once passed through had made. Then the question arises by what art or industry he could express so vividly all the islands he had drawn there or decide for certain that they were so (*cipher*: sir Fraunsis Drak cards fals) situated when he had gone through the Straits within the space of only 17 days and for 8 days had been sedulously struggling with much circuitousness and many windings to round one single cape. His companions confess to having seen certain gaps in the land and long recesses of the sea, and thence they surmise that it had been some such thing. But I am convinced that that Drake of ours either found some kind of draft among the Portuguese or Spaniards and thus put forth their little commentaries as (*cipher*: his theft *of* the por*tingale* [charts]) his own or I believe him to be a man who cast off all shame

and dared boldly to determine things unknown and to
present them to her majesty as explored and already
claimed. Either of these things should be reproved.)

(*cipher*: causes of not keeping a register[1]

(*cipher: th*e [causes] I can not keep a dayly register of
things ar [four]: f*i*rst Luk Ward told me that al notes
showld be [taken] from al men, and therfor wiled that he
might keep my boox [which] Robert Lydyinton told me
his master gav him warning therof. Th*e* cauling for and
Evans) serch of Evans baux aproved this tru. . . . words.) (*Latin*:
Give me, put aside for me, for I am writing . . . commentaries of things done by me. This I do with scorn and
threats and not without the greatest reproaches and although he changed them, he raged sufficiently and roused
205r himself in addition. The viceadmiral himself like an
executioner did not blush to rend a suppliant with cruel
imprecations and provoke him also and load him with
abusive insults.)

(*cipher*: Fowrthly the master [sc. Fenton] is s*au*sy to read
al my writings, but on may say he loved me wel and mad
much of me. To this I answer that he used so to do even
to them whom behind ther bax he much disprayseth to
me and therfor had I great reasin to suspect the lik,
espeshaly be[cause] he intersepted my letters, which he had
not doon had he trusted me. But he must answer al this
homcoming. But he that durst put the merchants fro the
cownsel, and keep al juels him self, and threaten martial
lau, and devis to rob the Portingals, and to dwel in Saynt
Helens and not return, careth he for answers? But he hath
not so doon. A good caus for being crost in his reconings
[is that] he cowld not, and therfor did never openly
attem[pt] it fo[r] Walker and I devised how to prevent
such mischif.) (*Latin*: Because, however, my vote is found
(*cipher*: Evans departing) among those who *cipher*: sent Evans hom was caus him
self desired it becaus we might stand in the mor fear to do
il when on was turned bak to complayn, becaus the
generaul swar openly that both of them wold not go to
(*cipher*: spitfully spoken) gether and sayd he was the wurs that day he sau him.
Ward so soon as Evans wa[s] gon out of the cabin sayd he

[1] This marginal cipher, as explained above (n. 1, p. 222), has been torn from the MS and pasted on 197*v*.

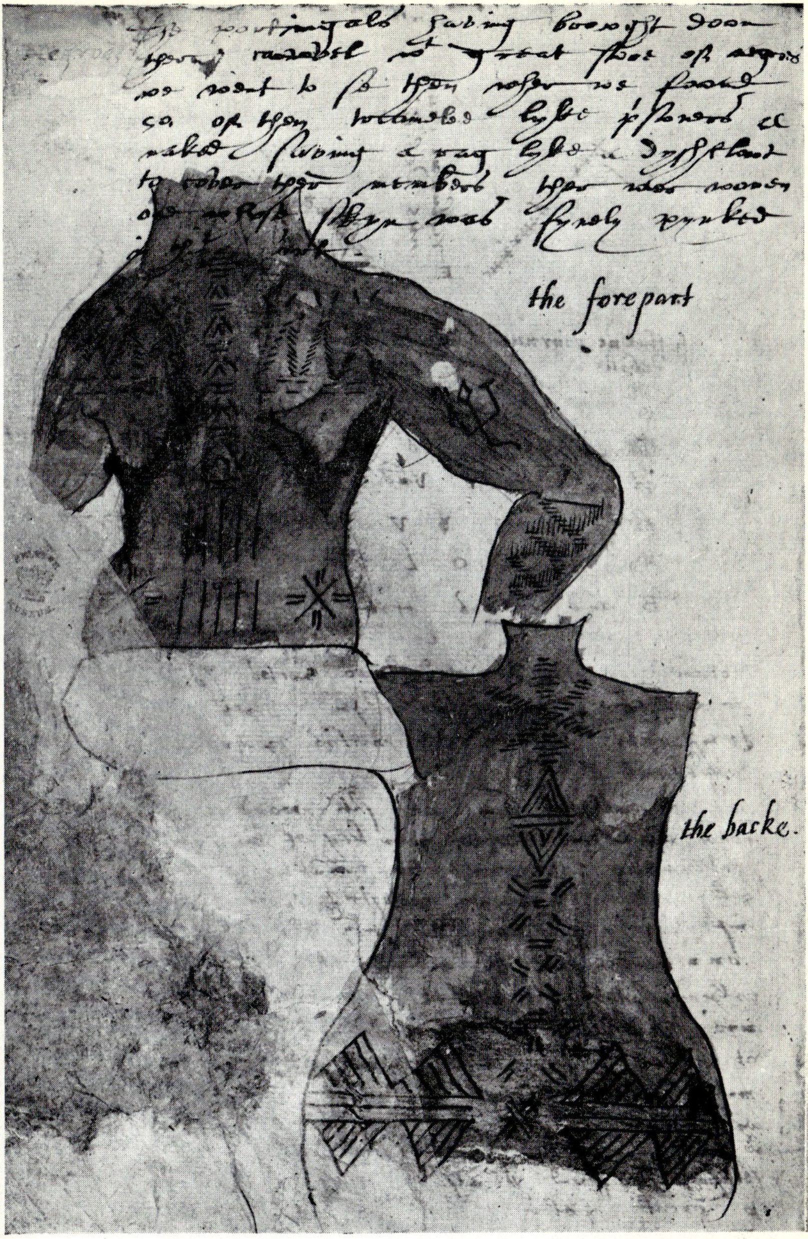

Fig. 16. Madox's sketch of a woman 'fynely pynked'

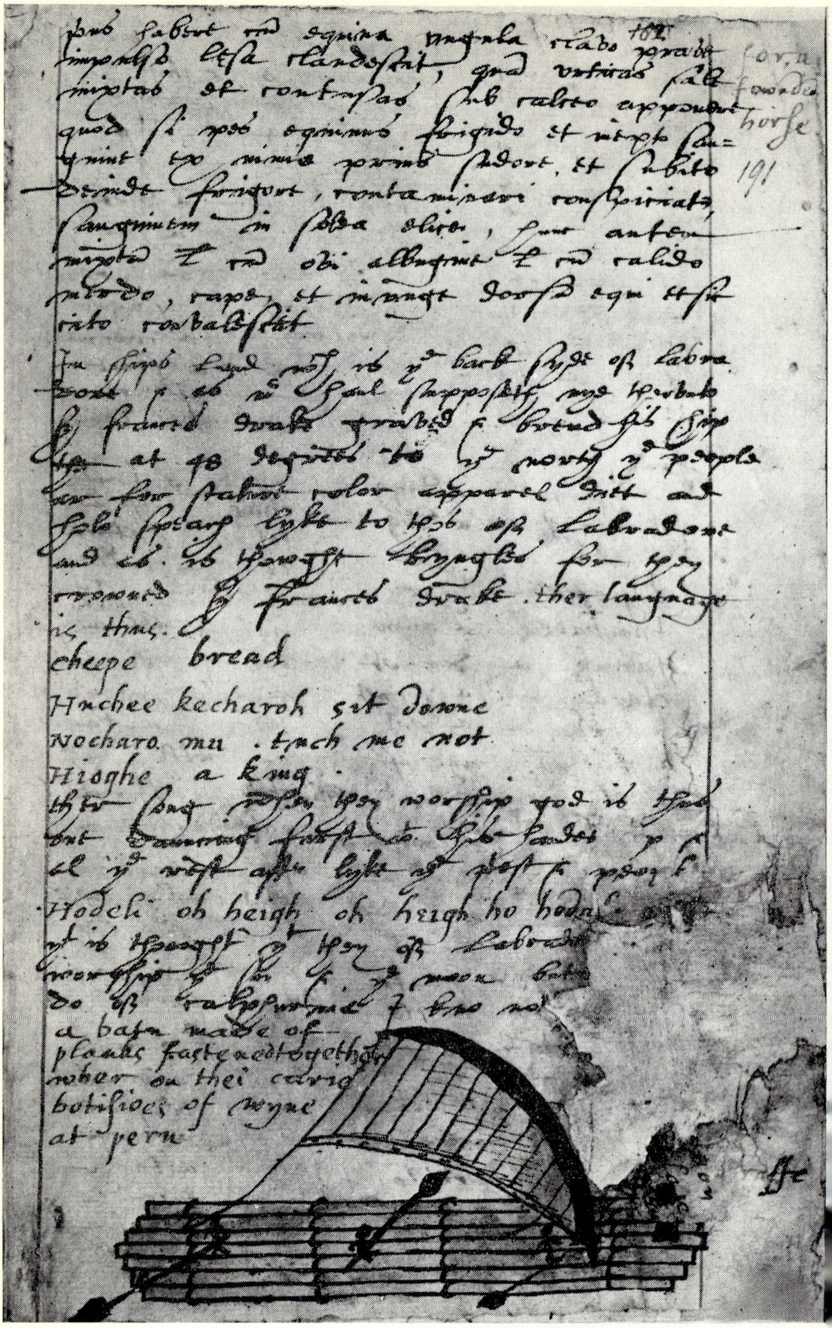

[illegible] 182

[illegible]

for a foundered horse 191

[illegible] ... ther language
is thus.
cheepe bread
Hachee kecharoh sit downe
Nocharo mu . tuch me not
Hioghe a king
[illegible]
Hodeli oh heigh oh heigh ho hoda[illegible]
[illegible]
a batu made of
planks fastened togethor
wher on thei carrie
botishoes of wyne
at peru

Fig. 17. 'A batu'

did not seek lik a sot to hav a pasport and now he shal not if he wold.)

(*Latin*: These writings concerning winds, storms, earthquakes and floods which I placed here I found just as they appeared in old manuscripts. But we must go back to the point where this discussion digressed.

Ward came to dinner with us and after dinner everybody's reasonings are set forth again by which we are shown to be 27 or 28 degrees toward the south, a hundred leagues more or less from the river Januario. Hood, however, swore most solemnly that the port of Plymouth was no better known and more familiar to him than the Straits of Magellan, nor is it possible for ships to anchor and depart there less securely and safely than it is in Catwater or Saltash Water[1] . . . where he was born, nourished and brought up and where now . . . they had flooded the happy pastures by irrigation and thus he longed for his exile no matter where since his account was not believed. But I answer him encouragingly in this matter. Indeed the whole neighborhood claims the pilgrim. (*Latin*: a rash oath)

At night the southeast wind began to inflate its cheeks, then the eastsoutheast, again the northeast, and these three in their turn keep watch as it were. All winds were pleasing to us by which we advanced toward the southwest to water as by a certain plan it was agreed.) // (*Latin*: inconstancy of the winds)

26. [☾ *Mon.*] (*Latin*: [we sailed] almost without design and without benefit except that at dawn I observed certain stars and I drew a chart by which our master (*gubernator*) might proceed toward the Straits. 205v

27. ♂ [*Tues.*] John Smith was caught filching provisions secretly for himself and others, the more boldly as he is in the habit of doing this since many items such as soap, wine, aquavit, clothes and a large number of other things, having been stealthily seized from the common storehouse and repository, lie buried in darkness. For daily we sought to give ourselves opportunity to employ our long-idle hands in pillage and spoils again. God in his wrath permitted that we should be daily afflicted with the private

[1] See above 1 June.

crime of thieves, and for this reason it would be harsh to agree to the punishing of one who either steals very little of value or sparingly and not be pricked in conscience by the crimes of so many at which we all openly contrive. But he is violently threatened and hoysed to the left arm of the sailyard and would have been dunked into the sea unless intervening by prayers, I had not snatched the man from these evils. Would to God that his punishment might cast its spell on us and all others so that we would not again rejoice in thieving.)

(*Latin*: Smithe hoysed to the sailyard)

28. ☿ [*Wed.*] (*Latin*: when today we took the height of the sun – for we saw it for the last time 4 days ago from the circumstance that the winds with uncertain blasts rushing in split almost the entire horizon and blew now from one direction and now from another – we found the antarctic pole elevated no more than 29 degrees although we had expected a more fruitful outcome of our journey . . . toward the southwest. Thus I strongly suspect that the prow of the ship was slowed down by the course of the current because, impeded by a contrary motion and blunted, it appeared to us looking on not to cover the distance with so great speed. For the waves dashed against the prow, swirling with great swiftness along the sides of the ship, as usually happens in the case of a raging and precipitous current . . . up to now they run hurriedly but not with howling winds. We cover 20 miles in the space of 24 hours when one would more readily expect 50 miles.)[1]

(*Latin*: current of the sea and the wind)

3 things rule the world, the pen, the plow, and the sword. *3 th*ings belong to a good surgion, a ladies hand, a lions *ha*rt, a hauks eye.[2]

(*Latin*: triad)

[*29.* ♃ *Thurs.*] (*Latin*: with inflated sails we hold westsouthwest so that putting in at shore we may replenish our scanty store of water with a new supply. There is not enough for boiling peas so we are compelled to eat pork only, for the

(*Latin*: westsouth-west)

[1] Although Madox uses the term *leuca*, he seems to be employing it in the sense of *mile* rather than *league*. See n. 3, p. 229 above for average speed on ocean voyages.

[2] Tilley S1013, where the first example cited is 1585.

beef is little palatable for no other reason I think except that it was at first badly salted at the time when Fernando being in charge of this business cared more about the Hambley heifer than the Netley beef. For it was pickled in London.) //

(*Latin*: provisions)

(*Latin*: It is the best and such as the queen eats with pleasure)

30. ♀ [*Fri.*] *St. Andrews* (*Latin*: [the wind] came to the south which by strong blasts drove us to the west by a violent seizure so that with folded sails loosened to the top we dared to use the lower and larger sails only, and this began with the full moon. 206r

(*Latin*: The south wind)

On the evening of the preceding night something[s were noticed] all of us would call memorable and astonishing: that up to this point our skiff, or ship's boat, tied by a rope at our stern, had been dragging behind us through huge waves; but what seemed to me very much worth noticing and elicited greater admiration on our part was that one of the sailors, John Winston by name, who had been gravely injured in the back by the fall of a cask before we left our native shore, daily worsened and weakened and could not even put food to his mouth and was so worn by emaciation and grievous and slow disease and so vilely polluted with filth that he aroused nausea in those for whom pitch, tallow, sulphur, bitumen, filth, dirt, and bilge water smelled more sweetly than myrrh and marjoram. When we reached Guinea, he strenuously insists that he be allowed to spend one night on shore. This was granted. There he spent almost no night in which he was not bathed by an endless rain and lay in clothes no less soaked than if they had been extracted from the sea. Moreover, attacked by swarms of ants during the day, he was as mordantly assailed as if not vultures but, in truth, flatterers should wish to devour a man. Before we left Guinea, he felt a little better. Four months after he was injured he had so wasted away that by this time we had assigned the man to death. Now, however, having regained his health, his blood, his flesh, his strength, he was ready to perform all duties manfully and lustily. Certainly, not the least cause of this I believe was that the poison dispersed through all his limbs was sucked out from his body by the ants and that

(*Latin*: A certain memorable thing concerning a skiff and concerning a desperately sick man)

the pores of his body opened by their heat exhaled the noxious and pestilent humours. Moreover, the rain like a bath moistened the skin which was somewhat hard and dry and rendered the humours more fluid. And the oysters which he ate and the sweet spring water which he drank in great abundance excited and refreshed the inactive liver and stomach and provided sustenance by which the several parts could be strengthened, whence health followed. Honour and praise be to Christ who remains for all of us the sole head, cause, fountain and origin of life and health.

(*Latin*: a storm

why the waves are lifted up by cold) 206v

Today at dawn a storm arose so that we sailed toward the northwest. During the entire day and night the wind stiffened, the sea swelled with waves, and the unaccustomed cold bit into us with sharpness. The reason I believe that the waves are lifted up by cold and rage with heat or subside and become mild is that the exhalations are easily extracted when the rarified crest of the wave is diminished. But they struggle among themselves and disturb the waves when thus the waters are condensed and are able to boil up.

(*Latin*: the shore is redolent)

Some said today that they smelled the sweetness of flowers when the wind came from the shore, and they were those who could be trusted.)

December ♑

(*Latin*: the Brazilian coast)

1. ♄ [*Sat.*] (*Latin*: Since the sails already worn with age were easily torn from the force of the winds, we made ready new ones for the main yard, which we tied to the sailyard with ropes and rushes. We sighted land in the west trending from the northwest to the southwest where green woods overhang white and chalky cliffs. But what the place is is as yet unknown. However, I think we are about 30 degrees to the south. Would to God we could put to shore here with good omen.

(*Latin*: a torpedo fish birds)

We also saw today a large torpedo fish from which indication we conclude we are not far from shore. On the other hand, birds are seen everywhere so that evidence can scarcely be drawn from them. However, there are some which never leave the shore except unwillingly so if you should see a number of these, know you are not far from land, but if you should sight two or three, say to yourself a single swallow does not make a summer.

After we approached the shore, we sounded and found the depth of the sea to be 35 fathoms, but at the bottom the sand was soft and muddy and blackish. (*Latin*: of what sort the bottom) However, we run toward the north so that we might find a harbour. Finally, we discovered a suitable place in a wide recess with islands and jutting and projecting rocks, safe from the currents of the sea, and there we cast anchor at 10 fathoms.

Pyrgopolynices is sent out to explore who as the tunny fish is timidly wont to do puts on a hundred breastplates (Pyrgopolynices) and arms himself with a hundred shields. Even so, he is not sufficiently safe. He goes up to Hegemon. I have found 207r out something, he says, which can be without danger for us. Speak up. In place of emissaries we shall use the Æthiopians. We will stay in our skiff far beyond the reach of any darts. This is approved. What soldier of the Myrmidons or the Dolopians or of stern Ulysses could refrain from laughing at the utterance of such things. He goes. I send one whom Pyrgopolynices by virtue of his craftiness orders to be summoned on purpose.[1] But the captain of the Francis speedily makes for the shore in his cockboat. Pyrgopolinices is angry. By his regal words he shows himself a man. All laugh. He reaches the shore. They see a wild boar, a huge one so they say. They wound it with a harquebus. They find water. They return. We rejoice. Pyrgopolinices incites Hegemon with complaining. All are indignant. Finally Hypegemon returns laden with (Hypegemon) birds, for he looks out for food for himself very nicely. He brings mainly white storks with sharp beaks which we call herons. (*Latin*: storks) They were thin but tasted delicious to our palate. He also brings plump fat mullets of the best flavour. He is chided because he dared put his foot on shore without our leader and without the guidance of Pyrgopollynices. The man excuses himself but tears at Pyrgopolinices in secret very indignantly and petulantly. He proclaims his own valor and displays his expertness in military affairs.)

[1] The last part of this sentence is written in the margin.

(*Latin*: the loadstone)

2. ⊙ [*G Sun.*] *Advent* (*Latin*: at the rising of the sun [we were] about 900 [leagues] toward the south at 15 degrees by the loadstone when it should have been 20. Here I find that the magnetic poles declined from the celestial poles 10 degrees toward the east so that the common compass by which we are governed shows that part to be in the southern point which is closest to it from the west, from which it results that because of an untried explanation of this matter, we thought we had progressed farther than we afterwards confirmed.[1] For from observing the height of the sun, we found the place to be 12 minutes closer to the equator than 28 degrees. In addition, it also must be noted that the distance between Africa and America is found to be greater than commonly thought, for although, generally, hydrographers indicate 400 leagues, we thought that at least 50 must be added or if I should say 100, I would not err by much.

(*Latin*: 28 degrees latitude

distance between Africa and America)

While visiting Walker, the general began to grow very sick so that he remained on the Edward. All the rest of us on the Gallion dined sumptuously on birds and fish caught with hooks. Then we went to shore. There was a very pleasant space on the sand for walking, and the cliffs which we thought to be of chalk showed themselves now
207v
to be of white and very fine sand, where there was a certain little hut built for fishing and some fragments of an earthen pot. We thought some boat had landed and wintered here for a while, for we do not see how they could have come by land because there was no trail or footpath, the entire area totally deserted and a vast wilderness. Thus with trees in the mountainous places, thorny brambles in some level places, and thickets in the marshy places one found his way with difficulty and with might and main. But the recess, which we call the Bay of Good Comfort, lay open only to the east, otherwise surrounded on all sides by cliffs.

(*Latin*: Bay of Good Comfort, formerly Don Roderigo)[2]

25 of us strained to distinguish certain stakes and long

[1] A large X in brown ink, a colour which Madox generally uses to call attention to an item, has been drawn from the beginning of this entry through the passage.

[2] This is another indication that Madox added to and revised his Diary since their landfall is not identified as taking its name from Dom Rodrigo until after the encounter with the Spanish friars on 6 Dec.

poles which some thought to be fiery wheels by which the approach of the enemy is shown to those living afar, but in reality they were trees burned 10 years or more before with only their trunks standing. We set fire to the grass which spreading amazingly threw out little balls of flame all night and was not extinguished before it reached the banks of a small river.

On our return we fished with a net and in one draught took 600 large fish, that is mullets, at least 18 to 30 fingers (*Latin*: an admirable haul of fish) in length, very fat and of the best flavour, of which I have never tasted the like. Later we took many fine smelts, 12 fingers in length. In the first draught we took fish almost as large as salmon. We marveled and giving praise to God dined elegantly on the Edward. We found bracken in sufficient abundance, petty fern and finger fern and very (*Latin*: herbs) many sweet and fragrant herbs which grow in England such as parsley, yew, . . . and very many others. On the (*Latin*: honey-bearing reeds) side of the south mountain grow many honey-dropping reeds from which sugar is pressed out, which now growing wild through lack of cultivation have lost their savour. But the place by itself has produced a display of gardens as if planted by human hands. Here also grew the (*Latin*: the noble palm) noble palm, similar to a great reed, which produced very delightful nuts not much inferior to dates. Here and there (*Latin*: a . . . pear) along the cliffs grows a fruit similar to an oblong pear, in the center of which was a meat delicate as a strawberry when it matures. But the trunk is thick and shapeless, six or nine feet in height; the egg-shaped leaves were of the thickness of a finger, from which the fruit was produced, 208r succulent but armed with spines.)

3. ☾ [*Mon.*] (*Latin*: I proceed to the mountains together with those who were preparing ties and bands and wooden hoops for the casks. Hyp[e]gem[on] came to this place to Hypegemon fish and because I was swimming here in order to wash my body, he swelled with anger and reported the matter to Hegemon.)

4. ♂ [*Tues.*] (*Latin*: I walk alone on the shore and kill a green snake.)

5. ☿ [*Wed.*] (*Latin*: While the general was ill, I sail with Hood and the viceadmiral to a tiny and rocky island where we caught birds, some of which we roasted, building a bonfire there under the cliff, and although we ate them without bread or salt or drink, nothing ever seemed to me to have tasted more delicious. In the middle of this island, which produces nothing but some brambles where the storks build their nests, is a well which is fed by the sea tide. Here we found crabs and large oysters and small but very shining snails and two rather small mullets.

(*Latin*: hunger the best condiment)[1]

Early in the night I am awakened to watch a wondrous star which was seen by some dancing here and there and sparkling, a will-o'-the-wisp or an apparition of some sort I know not what, for it even comes to the mast and the rigging. On investigation it was found to be nothing more than a winged golden ball or a fly which customarily emits light and fire or sparks at night. In a word, a ridiculous matter, a glowworm.)

(*Latin*: *Ignis fatuus* as fools suppose)

6. ♃ [*Thurs.*] (*Latin*: at daybreak Hypegemon approaches us. He points out a ship going by. Good God, what an uproar, what a flurry, what a hubbub. Who, how, what? Oh, Ah. Delay is hateful. Undress is dangerous. We put on breastplates. There is ranting and babbling. All devour the prize. Milo and Pyrgopolynices are sent out with the skiff attending. They contend about primacy. Great stirring of minds.[2]

(*Latin*: a prize is seen)

Glaucus and I climb a mountain and are washed with

[1] Tilley H819.

[2] As Walker's Diary makes clear, the sailors on the *Edward* first spotted the bark of 46 tons, called *Our Lady of Pity*, at five a.m., and Captain Ward, who was just then rising, immediately went to inform the *Galleon* of the 'prize.' Ordered with Captain Parker to give chase in the *Francis*, with the *Galleon*'s skiff to provide additional aid, Ward first returned to the *Edward* for a 'steele targett etc.' and then set sail before Parker could ready himself, though he later came 'well ynoughe aboorde them.'

After five or six leagues' chase, the *Francis* fired, and the bark struck sail. Ward, Parker, and five others then boarded her, headed – to the chagrin of the two captains – by Tobias Parris, master's mate on the *Edward*. While locking up chests and examining the passengers, the two captains quarrelled and 'hott' words passed between them; 'belyke,' Walker drily notes, 'it was for there auctorytyes in this exercise.'

When the bark was safely riding in the Bay of Good Comfort – Ward having taken one of its sails – Parker who was aboard it with 'dyvers of the Galyon' refused to discharge any of his men in order to share the watch with two from the *Edward*, so that Ward returned to his ship in great displeasure.

southern rain, for up to this point we find the south wind wet, the north wind dry. The prize is brought in, to wit, 7 friars, 2 women, 2 infants, 8 poor souls in a little bark.[1] We exult. But spirits flash and break out into wrath.) (*Latin*: rainy south wind)

7. ♀ [*Fri.*] (*Latin*: a council is called. Milo provokes anger in Pyrgopolynices, denying that he is in command of the people. There is a dispute concerning the dignity and glory of each. There is considerable boasting and pretence on every side. Glaucus complains that his place of honour has been taken from him. Clodius complains that Milo has taken precedence over him on land and sea. Milo believes he has deserved thanks in the matter rather than blame. After much wrangling, he is finally restored to grace.[2] (*Latin*: a quarrelsome deliberation)

There stands in our presence a young man of good birth by the name of John [for Francisco] Torres de Verra[3], a native of Cordova, brought up with his father's brother in the royal palace. He set sail with the royal fleet from the port of San Lucar in Spain on the 9th of December 1581 and [came] to the River Janeiro on the 28th of March. There he 208v transferred himself to the bark of these friars so that proceeding directly to the city of Santa Fe on the river Plate he could go directly to Peru by land with letters in order to ask for help for the new colony in the Straits.

There is here a secluded place where 12 years ago a certain Roderigo spent the winter and died from lack of food, together with all of his companions who could not depart because of their wrecked ship. This seems to us (*Latin*: Cape of Don Roderigo)

[1] As both Ward (*PN* (1589), pp. 660–61) and Walker record, the total number was twenty-one, Madox omitting here to count the Englishman Richard Carter, who was living in Ascension (Asunción), and Juan Pinto, a Portuguese dwelling at the River Plate. According to Ward the '8 poor souls' were 'boyes, and sailers.'

[2] Among matters debated in the council was the issue who should be appointed to 'romage the prize,' whereof 'grewe unkinde, and hot speeches, betweene the Generall, and Master *Parker*, against me,' Ward records, 'concerning authoritie, and government, and also Captaine *Hawkins* finding himself injured, was plaine with them both: so that we were beyond the termes of Commissioners, and fell to plaine brawling and bragging' (*PN* (1589), p. 661). Walker, who because of his frailty, did not attend, heard an account from his captain of the 'verye greate contraversye' between him and Captain Parker, which 'grewe to very unseemlye comparysons' though 'appeased' afterwards.

[3] Don Juan de Torre Vedra, Governor of the River Plate (Taylor, *Fenton*, p. 120 n.). Madox, Ward, and Fenton, and later John Drake in his depositions, give the surname as de Vera (or de Verra).

the more likely since we found certain clay urns within which reposed the bones of men, that is, skulls and the like. We believed that these were left by this group. However, someone else whom we captured reported that here the Indians were in the habit of interring their ancestors in this manner and instituting solemn memorials and commemorations in their honour on set days when, ascending the grave, they salute their shades in the manner of the pagans and feast there.

(*Latin*: Burial of the heathen)

We saw a deer with its young and also a partridge, and we found a fern, its trunk 17 feet in height, its circumference 9 fingers, which our Podalirius so praised that it was not granted to him to take possession of even such a trifle. Afterwards when we observed that it grew here in abundance, the thing was held in no esteem.

(*Latin*: an astounding fern)

Today those two Æthiopians whom Milo had acquired with such burning eagerness took to their heels, and ours commend their flight.

(*Latin*: the Æthiopians flee)

We consult today about the situation which had presented itself to us. First, we discussed those matters which we ascertained diligently, to wit, that in the month of September or thereabouts the fleet sailed from San Luca[r], then forced by storms and winds it returned once or twice; finally on the 9th of December 1581, again with 3000 men of all kinds, all sexes, all ages without distinction and 16 ships (for 4 ships previously damaged by storms are repaired) they sailed.[1] Of these 4 ships which carried 500 select soldiers under the command of Alonso de Sottomaior were destined for Chile. The rest, as they told us and as we read in the letters of Pedro Sarmiento, were making for the Straits of Magellan under the command of Flores de Valdois [de Valdes] in order that, with the erection of defenses on both sides there where the opposing shores are separated by a very narrow space, they could protect the passage so that others would not be permitted

(*Latin*: The explanation of the Spanish fleet)

[1] The expedition to fortify the Strait had initially set out from San Lucar on 25 Sept. 1581 with 23 ships under the general Diego Flores de Valdes. Following a great storm which wrecked 5 of them carrying 800 men before they lost sight of Spain, 16 ships, which included settlers and 10 friars in addition to the soldiers, sailed from Cadiz in Dec. (See *Narratives of Sarmiento*, ed. Markham (1895), pp. 224, 233.)

to pass through.[1] They took provisions for 18 months and 9000 ducats for buying provisions elsewhere – others said 15,000 and also that they have spent 9000[2] – for at that time in Spain there was a very great scarcity of triple-twilled cloth. Corn, powdered pears, and many oils, with which they were well supplied, are of necessity exchanged in the 209r
Terceira Islands. This fleet then came to the Island of St. James [Santiago], which is one of the Cape Verde Islands, on the 9th of January. There it looked for the necessities which the island produced. Then they turned away toward the River Janeiro in Brazil, 23 degrees to the south, [arriving] on the 25th of March following. Here they wintered, preparing their provisions – beef, pork, sugar, honey, wax, hens, ginger and other items of this sort which at first they bought cheaply, viz., 6s a pig, afterward more dearly to be sure, at 24s. Here they pounded casaba flour made from roots with which they prepared bread of the best flavour and much whiter than that made from wheat. For everything they had brought from Spain was spoiled because of worms and internal decay so that 500 or more men perished.[4] The admiral ship is called La Colassa, of about 900 tuns as they say;[5] the Roialla of the same size, but the one that was carrying the governor of Chile was the Trinidad of 300 tuns, and in it were [?] 160 persons of whom 30 were sailors, the rest soldiers. In this port they built a bark, one of their ships having been dashed against the rocks, and thus with 15

(*Latin*: cassaba flour)[3]

[1] Don Diego Flores had been directed to build two forts across from each other in the narrowest part of the Strait, each to be garrisoned with 200 soldiers. As governor and captain general, Sarmiento was to colonise the area. After many false starts, he managed in the early spring of 1584 to designate the site of Nombre de Jesus (setting up a cross where the church was to be built and marking a tree for the execution of justice) and in March established a second settlement called San Felipe, which Cavendish's crew was later to rename Port Famine (*Narratives of Sarmiento*, pp. 209–18, 305 ff.).

[2] The matter within dashes has been inserted in the margin.

[3] For an account of its preparation (Pg. *farina de pão*), see Hawkins, *Observations*, pp. 64–5.

[4] Sarmiento says that upwards of 150 died en route to Brazil and more than 150 at Rio de Janeiro (pp. 240, 242).

[5] 'Dolia' = Sp. *toneladas*: tonnage was computed by the number of wine casks which could be stored in the hold.

The *capitana* of the Spanish fleet (English 'admiral') was the *San Cristóval*, the admiral *San Juan Bautista*; in all, seven of the fleet were royal ships (*Narratives of Sarmiento*, p. 219).

(*Latin*: Friar John)

they sail thence on the 2nd of November.[1] But since there was a friar here, John de Riba Neira [Juan de Rivadeneira] who had lived in Peru 9 years, to wit, in Lima and in the city of Ascension [Asunción] for 6 months, they send a well-born and clever young man with him by the name of Francisco de Torres de Verra so that carried to the river Plate he might cross by land to Cuzco and there implore the help of M. Martin Henry [Don Martin Enriquez], the ruler of all Peru, for those who are trying to establish a colony in the Straits, with as many as 200 [soldiers] on either side, that is *400* in total number, who were in need of provisions and many other things, and they left here two ships for the others who were to return to Spain again. . . .

(*Latin*: preparation in the Straits of Magellan)

(*Latin*: the River Plate supply of horses)

Asked in what manner he would proceed overland, this youth said there was a very large supply of well-bred horses at the river Plate. But the old friar said that travellers for the most part are transported by means of four-wheel carriages, which in some places are drawn by oxen, elsewhere by horses, and there is a passage here from the mouth of the river Plate. There is a city named Santa Fe, 150 leagues distant. For the city called Bone Aieris was 60 leagues distant from the mouth and 90 from Santa Fe. He believes that it was deserted of inhabitants.[2] At other times they go this way. Thence to be sure from Santa Fe to
209v Cordova 50 leagues and then to St. James de la Stera [Santiago del Estero] 80 leagues. A little later to Stalla Verra 50 leagues and then finally to Potosi 150 [leagues] through mountain paths, thence to the city of La Plata 18 leagues. From here to the new colony 70, thence to Cuzco 70, thence to Guamanca [Guamanga] 70. Finally

(*Latin*: Land route to Peru)

[1] The Spaniards having reached Rio de Janeiro on 25 Mar., as Madox records, spent the winter there, and it was during this time that the seven friars met up with them. Their first attempt to reach the Strait was made in Nov. 1582, but on reaching 38° the *San Estevan de Arriola* was disabled and later sank, and the General of the Fleet headed back for Dom Rodrigo. Sarmiento following in the *Santa Maria de Begoña* – later sunk by the English at São Vicente (see pp. 35–8 above) – and Diego de Ribera in the *San Juan Bautista* then encountered the bark with the friars, according to Peter Jeffrey (Otho E VIII, 5 f. 186*v*), four days after the Fenton group had departed and learned of their experience with 'three ships full of English pirates on their way to the Strait, who robbed them of what they had and afterwards returned their boat' (Sarmiento, pp. 240, 251–2).

[2] In his notes recording answers to the interrogations, Madox jots down 'late dispeopled now renued' (Otho E VIII, f. 175).

from here to Lima 80 leagues. All these are Christian cities. Thus the distance from the mouth of the river Plate to Potosi is 480 leagues. From Potosi to Lima 308 leagues. The sum of the distance to this point is 788 Spanish leagues, of which 17 1/2 equal one degree in the heavens.[1] But if you should wish to proceed to the province of Chile, it may be done by the shortest route but one little used on account of the Indians, for the distance from the mouth of the river Plate to Cordova is 200 leagues. Thence to St. John de la Frontiers in Chile 50 leagues. From there to the port of Kokima [Coquimbo] on the Pacific coast, which lies 30 degrees to the south, 50 leagues. Thus Santa Fe is equally distant from the Atlantic sea as from the Pacific, to wit, 150 leagues each way. For the width of the land here is only 300 leagues. A city is found here on the river Plate where a certain Richard Carter of London dwells, whom we took in here. It takes its name from the Ascension and is distant 300 leagues from the mouth of the river and from Santa Fe 130 leagues or more by water. Here a ship of 80 tuns is able to come. Richard Carter

Having taken cognisance of these things, we deliberated particularly whether to send the captives away with the bark or whether to keep them with us or to leave them on shore and take their ship. The general (*praetor*) seemed to favour that last, especially since it could be done with their safety and without danger to us. . . .[2] For indeed Cornicola and I had previously urged that we should concern ourselves lest they come in their boat to the Straits first and there arm their allies against us or flying across the land make known our arrival to all in the area, and thus all hope of obtaining provisions would completely vanish. (*Latin*: deliberation)

I allege a two-fold reason why we should treat these

[1] The Spanish and Portuguese reckoned 17½ leagues (of 4 miles) to a degree; the English 20 leagues (of 3 miles). See Waters, *Navigation*, pp. 64–5 and n.

[2] Walker records that the general had asked Madox 'with M. Jeffrey because he und*erstood the* language,' to persuade the old friar to go ashore in some harbour, whereupon he 'wepte bytterly alledginge the*y wolde* be eaten of the Indyes etc. and desyred *the gene*rall by them to be good unto them etc.'

Although Madox uses the term '*praetor*,' generally applicable to the master Christopher Hall, the referent here seems clearly Fenton. Hall was not one of the Assistants.

innocent souls more gently, the one because we believe in God and expect recompense for our piety or impiety not only here but in the life to come; the other because we must give an accounting of our life and actions to the queen, among whose privy council our reputation, life, liberty and resources would be endangered by these shameful acts. As far as the question of provisions was
210r concerned, I said I was astonished that since we were permitted before to take from any hill or heap or mound so much as could suffice an army, now we despair about a tiny portion. Furthermore, although I oftentimes heard them boast that these two ships could engage the whole Spanish fleet, they are now terrified at the sight of a few cracked and decayed ones. I cannot marvel sufficiently. But this you shall take for certain, if God has determined to bless us with his generosity and grace, it is not possible to take away from us this gift of God even if all our councils and deliberations should become known to all the Spaniards who are everywhere. But if on account of our sins, a calamity should be sent from God, even a little child, all others having been killed, could quickly report the matter to the leaders and stir up the whole region for our destruction. Therefore, it would be better to send these men away unharmed and intact rather than defile our hands with their blood, for to expose them would be to forsake them and to forsake them would be to kill them. Moreover, if they should go with us, they would impede our journey because they would not be able to endure a storm nor would they be able to sail swiftly and thus they would endanger the lives of our sailors. The provisions – candles, wood and other things – would be consumed, for if they dealt out supplies with so much effort and almost with compulsion to our allies sailing on the little Francis, what would they do to strangers? For Hypegemon who pilfered all accounts from the dead purser now feigns that more supplies have been handed over than they have received, and it has been rumored that their viands and other things of that sort are concealed with us.[1]

(*Latin*: For Hood and Hawkins had so assured)

(*Latin*: Hypegemon indeed denies victuals to the bark)

[1] Nicholas Chancellor, the purser of the *Edward*, had died on 29 Sept. On the 7th Fenton, as he notes (p. 118), supplied the *Francis* with three months' victuals

But note Glaucus is now cruel, now compassionate, now for them, now against them. He behaves without reason, like a child. Milo cunningly and I am afraid hypocritically says that it seems to him no harm would threaten us from their liberation. For if they should go away quietly, no one else would be frightened of us, but if they are severely treated, others from their example would be more cautiously on their guard and more ready for vengeance, and they would disseminate the matter as widely as they could. Taylbush and Jeffries and Parker, for they do not call Shaw, assent, nor is there any record made of this deliberation.[1] It was concluded, therefore, that they be sent away in peace but still slightly plucked so as to satisfy our rapacious and greedy sailors in some measure.[2] All the important members of the council supped on the Edward with the exception of Glaucus. There by a solemn oath they

---

and on the following day took occasion to reprove the quartermaster of the *Edward* 'for grudging of victuall for the *Francis*,' 'which,' the Vice-admiral said, 'was answered, and he wel satisfied' (*PN* (1589), p. 661).

[1] Although a decision as to what to do with the bark and its people was deferred, it was determined, as Ward records (p. 660) 'to passe by the streights, notwithstanding the Spaniards.' Omitting any account of this aspect of the deliberations here, Madox records it indirectly by means of the cipher reference below to his entry for 21 Dec.

Walker did not attend the morning council on the *Galleon*, but that night the general, Madox, and Parker supped aboard the *Edward* and sought his opinion which was to the effect 'we nether myghte with charytye or conscyence ether take barke or any thinge from them or hassarde there bodyes upon shore whereby ether the Indyans or wylde beastes shoulde devoure [them] and so we shoulde be gyltye of the sheedinge of ther bloode *which God wold not* leave unreveanged upon us.' Although it was then agreed to let the Spaniards have their bark, the next morning, 'new perswasyons' having been proffered, the Assistants again debated the matter but to the same conclusion (8 Dec. and Ward in *PN* (1589), p. 661).

To his notes on the interrogations of the friars, Madox has added in the margin a passage in cipher (now badly mutilated) commenting on the opinions of the Assistants: 'Ward sayd that using them wel others would . . . but privily he sayd it was no mater. . . . Hawkins inconstant every way. Parker, Madox, Walker . . . wil spend vitayls. Must be un rigd. Can not folo. Wil lose men. Tak sugar, hoopes, succet, nayles, tooles, betisos [Sp. *botijas*, wine jars]' (Otho E VIII, f. 199).

[2] On the 8th Ward and Hawkins brought back sugar and sweetmeats ('some triffling things . . . to supplie our necessities,' Taylor, *Fenton*, p. 119), which, Walker drily notes, the friars 'bestowed upon them *nolens volens* whereof *they* had good store and we wanted.' These were then divided among the ships (Ward, in *PN* (1589), p. 661).

Richard Carter, who was with the bark, later reported that the English had taken 'the wine we carried and the conserves we had made in San Vicente, as well as two or three boxes of nails which they needed to put together a launch . . . to be set up in the South Sea, so that they could use her for going along close to land' (quoted in H. R. Wagner, *Drake's Voyage*, p. 400).

(*Latin*: a Carthaginian covenant) enter into a covenant of friendship but a false and fragile one.[1] *cipher*: Seek mor the 21 December.) //

210v 8. ♄ [*Sat.*] (*Latin*: they take from them a net, sugar, axes, ginger for planting, iron hoops for fastening the casks, (*Latin*: booty) some sweetmeats, bills, keys, all to the value of 10li. However, books, ornaments, etc., we give back, but Milo kept a book and a very great number of trinkets for himself, for he looks to and out for himself as best as possible.[2]

(*Latin*: the guilty one is present) A solemn banquet on the galleon. Ward was there although he had said he would depart, that he cannot put up with such matters, that he would kill Parker, and other nefarious things. The man excuses himself, first tumidly, then timidly. He is asked whether he wishes to behave (*Latin*: heatedly) courteously or not. He promises. They swear again that they will mutually cherish each other without dissembling, and he swears that they will be dearer to him than they were before although they could not be.[3] He talked as if they had been very dear before, but I think they have never been nor can they ever soon become wholly dear to him. I deduce this from the fact that he had stated that that man with whom he was once unfriendly would never afterwards be restored to his favour. And when there is dispute about victualing the little bark, he retorts that many

[1] Recognising that there was scant friendship between the general and Captain Parker on the one hand and the Vice-admiral on the other, Walker had exhorted them that same night to enter into a pact, '*a* perfectyon of Agreement' that should not without great cause be 'any peece dyssolved.' Many words passed, the two chaplains charged unity, and Walker hopefully concluded that he had knit up so perfect a friendship as to prove 'indyssoluble,' but, he added, 'it happened *n*ott.'

[2] Here a deleted passage repeats with slight variation the last sentence in Latin under 7 Dec. dealing with the uneasy truce.

[3] On the morning of the 8th while Walker was still abed, he had been visited by Ward who expostulated on the discourtesies he had received and threatened, unless matters were redressed, to turn '*tay*le to tayle' and depart if his company would go with him, if not, to go ashore and shift for himself. Walker then revealed to Fenton Ward's threat of departure, whereat the general was 'amased.' That night, according to Ward, Walker 'propounded certaine questions to the Generall of unkindnes, by me conceaved against him, which moved him to some cholerike termes with me.' When matters were 'almost being agreed betweene us, then began he to question with Captaine *Hawkins*, which contention was tedious, and not fully ended before supper, and began againe after supper,' so that Ward and Walker did not return to the *Edward* until about ten o'clock that night (*PN* (1589), p. 661).

of us had come together with him from London to Hawkins.[1]

Hawkins was there. Although the general forbade it, he had given tunics . . . especially to Craneus,[2] as if he wished to nourish faction. However Hawkins (my strength can bear with his stupidity) finally requests that the two pieces of cloth he had left come into the common stock.[3] This was granted. This talk lasted far into the night. For here we both dined and supped. Colax is angry because he is excluded.) Glaucus

9. ⊙ G [*Sun.*] *Advent 2* (*Latin*: letters are dug out which . . . that young man had.[4] Nothing else than that which was reported before is discovered. We took Richard Carter who had been living in Ascention along with us; the Edward took the Portuguese [Juan Pinto], the latter willing, the former unwilling.[5] Colax solemnly shows himself on the Edward. He is not admitted. He weeps and complains that he is forsaken. That old friar and Francisco are received there sumptuously, and we give them what they earnestly sought, Latin letters to Furbusher and Acres [directing] that they should not molest them but should hasten to follow us to the Cape of Good Hope.[6] However, this was done on (*Latin*: safe conduct)

1 Apparently recorded as a wholly irrelevant answer.

2 Unidentified.

3 While at Sierra Leone, Hawkins asked the merchants (2 Sept.) to price certain cloths, which he affirmed Alderman Barne and M. Towerson promised could be taken into the adventure. These were so slightly evaluated that Hawkins felt himself badly dealt with and Ward chided the merchants on the *Edward*, his remarks occasioned, as Walker explained, 'by the badd dealings *of the* Galyons merchaunts' (2 Sept.; see also Ward, *PN* (1589), p. 651).

4 These included a letter from Pedro Sarmiento to Martin Enriquez, Viceroy of Peru, detailing the movements of the fleet from the time it had left Spain on 9 Dec. 1581 to the time (Nov. 1582) when it left Rio de Janeiro for the Strait and spelling out the need for 'vitayls, powder and municion.' (A summary made at this time is preserved in Otho E VIII, f. 199.)

5 Born in Limehouse, Carter had been an exile from England for twenty-four years, living on the River Plate for almost twelve; he was taken by Fenton to serve as a pilot. Juan Pinto returned on the *Edward* to England where he was examined by the Privy Council, but through the efforts of Mendoza, he was shipped off to Lisbon. (See Ward in *PN* (1589), p. 660; *CSP, Sp., 1580–86*, pp. 496–7.)

6 According to Mendoza, Frobisher, following on his refusal to sail on the Fenton voyage, intended a rival expedition – variously reported to include four, three, and finally two ships, which was to go through the Strait of Magellan and beat them to the Moluccas. Apparently, Captain George Acres, who had served in the Irish wars, was to accompany him. (See *CSP, Sp., 1580–86*, pp. 313, 341–2, 349, 357; *APC, 1581–82*, pp. 215–16.

purpose lest they should get wind of our journey to the Straits.)[1] //

211r [*10.*] ☾ [*Mon.*] (*Latin*: When now that we are ready to depart, we are left with a south wind blowing though the wind up to now had been northerly. They bring hard and odiferous wood from the shore, of which pieces boiled produce a very fine bath and even potions. Banister said it was the wood of aloe.)

212r *11.* ♂ [*Tues.*] (*Latin*: with Carter as our leader we go fishing toward the northeast where we caught quite a few fish. We saw a most pleasant recess where 1000 ships could anchor in safety and where no force of winds or sea is to be feared. We remained here only a short time because the eastnortheast had begun to blow and the ships seemed to expect our return. Having turned about, they were preparing for tomorrow's light, for sailing at night we should more easily expose ourselves to the dangers of the rocks.)

(*Latin*: a notable port)

12. ☿ [*Wed.*] (*Latin*: the NE and by N wind begins to blow. We sail at the sixth hour. The prow having been turned around by the weight of the anchor and the force of the wind, we were compelled to make a brief circuit with the sails turned back so that we might drive against the sunny shore, and thus avoiding all dangers we departed safely. But the Edward had sailed earlier. After the anchor was raised, they roll up the cable with a revolving engine and put it aside; then by its gravity and weight and the quickened motion of the ship that wing of the beam which the sailors call the cat breaks into pieces and falls and thus the anchor sinks to the bottom, followed likewise by the most rapid unfurling of the cable. But if the floating cylinder, which is made of thin wood, had not disappeared in the waves, they would finally have seen the anchor and

(*Latin*: the NE and by N wind prevails we sail)

(*Latin*: The anchor and cable are endangered)

[1] Athough Walker had argued (7 Dec.) that there was no danger of the friars' revealing information to the Spaniards since they did not, after all, know their destination, it would appear from statements later made by Richard Carter and Fray Juan de Rivadeneira (printed in Wagner, *Drake's Voyage*, pp. 398–402) that members of the crew had boasted only too volubly of their intention to pass through the Strait, a decision that had been taken on 7 Dec. (Ward, *PN* (1589), p. 660).

the cable today. It was recovered with difficulty even with our help and that of the bark, and all this consumed the entire forenoon when we could have sailed a long way.

After dinner a westnorthwest wind blew. We hastened toward the south.[1] Many began to fall sick at the same time. We considered the most likely cause of this the excessive drinking which they had indulged in from a too avid devouring of fish. At night the heavens began to thunder and to sprinkle clouds of dew as it were but very sparingly and slowly. Aeolus also with all his winds begins to faint, and he grows drowsy. Only the south wind seems to be awake, but he moves his limbs only sporadically. This raises a reasonable objection . . . in my mind where, ingenious and practised, he exerts the strength of his power: namely, whether the northern region of the sky and earth is according to Aristotle the fountain, beginning and origin of the waters on account of the severity of the cold as astrologers seem to think who atribute to the north the triple sign of the eagle, to wit, ♋, ♏, ♓ [Cancer, Scorpio and Pisces], and thus it attracts and draws to itself all moisture by a certain force of nature lest at any time a large and abundant source for producing waters should be lacking – as a result all the winds which blow thither bring rains with them; those which go out from there mere exhalations in a drier state, 212v
all moisture having been condensed because of excessive cold, are blown in another direction and bring no rains with them – or whether it is the nature of the northern stars to induce coldness and dryness, even as the bear itself, a cold and dry animal – as it appears from the fact that it quickly grows fat – enjoys cold and snow and is never found – so far as I am able to understand from hearsay reports and old legends – in the southern region of the earth; on the contrary the northern stars delight in rains and heap up clouds. We must, furthermore, examine still more deeply whether the winds are attracted to some end and whether, fearing something hostile, they are

(*Latin*: the westnorthwest wind many fall sick at the same time)

(*Latin*: thunder)

(*Latin*: explanation of the winds)

[1] The friars remained in port, so that when the Spanish fleet arrived four days later, they were informed of their encounter with the English. See Carter's account in Wagner, *Drake's Voyage*, p. 400 and n. 1, p. 252 above.

driven out from some place and flee or whether by some kind of presentiment, they seek out some quiet place congruent to their nature. In the future, God favourably approving, when a freer occasion for investigation concerning these things is granted and books are available in which all opinions are collected, I shall follow up what seems most probable.

(*Latin*: The south wind the lay of the shore)

13. ♃ [*Thurs.*] (*Latin*: we sail toward the west. When we approach the shore, turning our sails, we face toward northwest. This shore is low and sandy and on it we see a funeral pile belching forth smoke and sparks. I do not know whether they did this to frighten us or invite us to trade or to give a signal to their own people or to keep away evil spirits which people here believe can be driven away by torches and firebrands.

On the first of the month when the tranquillity of the waves was violently disturbed by the force of the winds, all the waves which washed the sides of the ship and were broken by dashing against it revealed a distinct rainbow to us; as a result, those who affirm that the rays of the sun, broken into pieces by countless little clouds, are themselves the cause of the appearance of the rainbow argue the more plausibly. At the first watch the north wind again began to bless us with its breezes.)

(*Latin*: the loadstone)

14. ♀ [*Fri.*] (*Latin*: the sun rose at 15 degrees from the east toward the south although last night it set 35 degrees from the west toward the south. I have found up to now that the needle generally indicates that section of the compass which is closest to it from the west. Thus while we think we are sailing toward the south, we are deflected toward the west with the result that the front of America truly trends more toward the setting sun than is shown in the charts and maps of many sailors. All these things square and agree with that which I had written down up to this point and had learned from Francisco de Verra and others.

(*Latin*: thunder and lightning)

213r At the first watch of the night the poles thundered and the sky flashed with frequent fires. It is true we saw very bright flashes of lightning in the port of Guinea, but in comparison with these, they were darkness itself. The inconstant wind turned all around. It ceased, however, in the southeast. Our ship now readily and easily outstripped the Edward. For the last place on which we trod the master had placed 30 tons of ordinary stone at the bottom of the ship in order to stabilise the keel so that, strong as a result of the weight of the ballast and sturdy as the result of a heavier impulsion and force, it furrowed through the seething waves. (*Latin*: Ballast)

15. ♄ [*Sat.*] (*Latin*: we move forward with an inconstant wind. Almost all of us in the whole fleet are afflicted with violent headaches. Many gain some relief by bloodletting.) (*Latin*: universal sickness)

1[6.][1] ⊙ [*G Sun.*] *Advent 3* (*Latin*: we sight a low and sandy land, and at 3 leagues from the shore we sounded and at 20 long fathoms found a blackish sand. Then reversing the sails, we proceed eastward. Soon, however, we proceed southward again with a more generous wind.) (*Latin*: a low shore)

17. ☾ [*Mon.*] (*Latin*: when through fear of the shore we turn from the south toward the east, behold the west wind and the winds from the Straits of Magellan and southwest seize us against our will as it were, and they drove us willy-nilly from the shore.)

(*cipher*: Hear is to be noted that Hood and Fernando be always sik when they com ny the shor. Nando hath cownseled to go bak agayn to rob St. Vinsents and so hom as the master teleth me. The generaul is very fearful to go throo the Strayts becaus of the Spaynards and casteth many dowtes and w[h]er to rob por men was no conshens, now to hurt such as ar able to hurt us agayn is a grudg of conshens. Surly a just judgment of God to mak our cowards manifest, and now see wat *it* is to deal colorably, for had he ment honestl*y* *at* first, theas dowts now had not needed, but Fern*ando a* ravenows theef hath browght the mater to this pas.) (*cipher*: *nota diligenter*)

18. ♂ [*Tues.*] (*Latin*: the greatest calm without wind or tide, as I note, although an object having been let go which

[1] Madox writes '18.'

would float was carried slowly hither and thither while the ship remained continuously immobile.)[1]

19. [☿ *Wed.*] (*Latin*: the eastsoutheast wind blew very strongly. We proceed southwest. Many whales appeared before us, very large like ships, swimming against the wind, long cow-like in appearance but without horns. Hegemon calls me aside, tells me of the dangers. He asks what should be done. He is fearful lest he should seem afraid.) //

213v (*Latin*: deliberations)

20. ♃ [*Thurs.*] (*Latin*: all in the fleet are summoned, the pilots, masters, captains, and gentlemen. The great and urgent danger from the Spanish fleet is propounded. We ask the sailors what is to be done.[2] All clamor for crossing the Staits except our master[3] who thinks we must obtain provisions first and Percy who argues rather in favour of making for the Cape of Good Hope, and Verres, who has shown himself to be the head and source of all evil. To the devil with him. They are excused. We deliberate.[4] Jefries and Shaw think that by making for the Cape of Good Hope, first, we avoid danger; then, we walk in the law as it were. Taylbush prefers to die from the sword in the Straits than from hunger in the archipelago. Walker too believes that this should be attempted if it can be done within a safe observance of the law since there is no hope of going by the Cape of Good Hope on account of lack of

[1] Ward also comments on the calm and 'yet a boylting sea' (*PN* (1589), p. 662).

[2] Having summoned the ships the night before, Fenton called the Assistants together to determine two propositions: whether it were best for them to adventure through the Strait 'considering the force of the enemy . . . there before us' or, if not, 'which way were meetest for us to take.' It was thought good first to hear the opinions of the two captains (Drake and Hawkins) and the two pilots (Hood and Blacollar) who had passed that way with Sir Francis Drake as well as the views of the three masters (Hall, Percy, and Fairweather). See Ward, *PN* (1589), pp. 662–3.

[3] Madox here seems clearly to be reporting the judgement of Christopher Hall since at this point it is the views of the 'sailors' he is recording. Further, this judgement accords with that Madox notes for Hall in the documents of the debate (Otho E VIII, f. 183). Walker quotes him as asserting at this date that he would never consent to go by the Strait 'nor no man els,' for the Spaniards should not 'take hym by the throte for vytay*les*.'

[4] 'Beginning with the yongest in aucthority,' i.e., Peter Jeffrey, merchant on the *Edward*, Fenton heard the several opinions which Madox recorded and the Assistants attested to with their own hands (Ward, *PN* (1589), p. 663); this (mutilated) record is preserved in Otho E VIII, ff. 183–4).

wine. I ask for time to deliberate.[1] Hawkins, Ward and the general do the same. Parker says that of necessity we must go through the Straits but he gives no reasons. Soon Hawkins offers his opinion in writing, to wit, that of necessity we must go through the Straits since there is no possibility otherwise of restoring our provisions, and in this part of his written statement he is vehement.[2]

I coolly suggest that after due preparation we should especially strive to go by the Cape of Good Hope, but if this is not agreeable, through the Straits; if neither is possible, to sell our things honestly and to return home. And this I did because long ago I got wind he was aspiring to a kingdom, not from any suspicion but from manifest evidence – first, evidence of words which imprudently escaped him and now evidence of deeds which point to the goal at which he is aiming.

Ward believes we must obtain provisions before we set out for there. The general expresses the same opinion in writing,[3] and he orders us to decide whether it is better to go 50 leagues up the River [Plate], sailing into the three branches or whether it is better to remain in the port of St. Vincent[4]. . . from ♑ [the Tropic of Capricorn]. All agree on St. Vincent. For what is to be done? One of these must be done. We chose that which is likely to prove the less evil. May God grant that it be so, for I am dubious because I observe he holds Verres dear. At the beginning of the council as all express their opinion in writing,

[1] Madox's separate detailed statement appears in Otho E VIII, f. 195. See below.

[2] Also mutilated, this statement is in Otho E VIII, f. 194. In his brief account of the voyage, dated after the return of the *Galleon* in June 1583, Hawkins specifies those, including Madox, who had been willing to venture the Strait but who in two days were of contrary mind and those who were content to proceed (f. 225*v*).

[3] Deliberating until after supper, Fenton then delivered his written opinion (Otho E VIII, ff. 190–1) to the effect that, as Walker put it, 'he wolde not adventure his shyppes and men upon suche a knowen daunger.'

[4] Richard Carter, who was then interrogated, stated that wine could not be supplied in less than four months though plenty of other provisions would be available but that the river was 'shoale and dangerous' and 'the road 7. leagues from any towne, or place of commoditie.' Thereupon the decision was made to go to São Vicente, the Assistants taking cognisance of these difficulties and, as Ward cryptically noted (*PN* (1589), p. 663), 'the trecherie that might from thence be used, into the Streights by sea, and into *Peru* by land.' Reports of their course sent to these areas would be of significance only if, in fact, they ultimately intended to go to the Moluccas via the South Sea, as Carter later asserted was their intention (Wagner, *Drake's Voyage*, p. 400).

Pyrgopolinices laughs, but afterwards when he notes what others have said, he complains strongly to me that his arguments are wrongly understood. What he wishes he corrects, he inserts, he adds what the others also add.[1] Glaucus is furious.)

(*cipher*: The generaul told me he hoped to do som //
214r notabl thing, which I ges is ether to spoyl St. Vinsent and ther to be king, or to pas to St. Helens and attend [the] Portingal fleet fro Molucas, or to lurk abowt the West India t[i]l the kings treasur com fro Panamau.)[2]

(*Latin*: Reversing our sails we turn back toward the north at dusk. The bitterest complaints arose among the sailors, who now finally think themselves imposed upon. About 33 degrees toward the south.)[3]

21. ♀ [*Fri.*] *St. Thomas* (*Latin*: Pyrgopolinices takes it grievously that he uttered his words without weighing them. He asks to correct them. Clodius agrees. I agree. He asks to be a participant of those things which are under deliberation. I promise, I copy, I hand over. He reads but he says that he wishes to look at the original. See, I want this by your leave. Be content, use a copy. We will keep the original. Both agree. Forthwith he is puffed up and disdainfully goes out of our cabin. Does he go away? Summoned, he returns. But now, my good man, go where your ability calls you. Go and good luck. Drake, bringing a torpedo fish, dined with us.)

Pyrgo-polynices

(*cipher*: After diner in great greef Parker bewayled to me his estat and how by tabl taulk he had been led to this acshon which now he was out of dowt wold never be performed. He muterd how much the generaul hath been beholden to him and his frends and how strayngly he was now used, saying that he wold rather desir to liv hear

[1] See Madox's entries for 21 and 23 Dec. for additional indication of Parker's distraught response to the situation.

[2] See 23 Dec. where Hawkins ascribes to Fenton the same intentions.

[3] Both Walker (20 Dec.) and Ward (*PN* (1589), p. 663) comment on the 'murmuring' of the sailors at their change of course as they feared the expedition was headed home with consequent loss of their 'thirds.'

In his separate opinion, written before they had altered course, Madox takes cognisance of the 'great grutching' of the sailors, first, because they have not 'ther store in al poynts answerable to ther expecta*tion*' and, second, because they say they will starve in the end or return home beggars (Otho E VIII, f. 195).

then return into England with such infamy as we wer lik [to incur]. I pitied the man; inndeed he is very jelos of his reputashon but hath not in him to ma*y*nta*y*n *it*.)

(*Latin*: Opening the register I saw that this matter had indeed been discussed the 7th day of [Decem]ber[1] and when hitherto it had been debated whether it were better to pass the Straits and there to fetch iron for forging and water for the repaired casks, both Hypegemon and Hegemon swear then that they are willing to make a path by force and to snatch themselves as it were even from the middle of the enemy and if the enemy offer any force, they are willing to attend to their coffers and their casks. It is to be noted that Cornicola did not take part in that deliberation and so it is not reported in the minutes. (*cipher*: *nota*)

It is to be noted that Carter said yesterday that at the river Plate there is an abundance of wild beef, pork, hens, honey, wax and saltpeter dug out of the earth. Wines, if one should ask, are produced, for there are vineyards far from the seashore near the center of the land as he himself reported. Thus although it is possible for us to be provided quickly, to wit, in less than a week, with all other things, with wine we could not fully supply ourselves even in 3 months. But of red meat there was the greatest abundance. (*Latin*: products of the river Plate) 214^{v}

Now when there was great consternation of minds and no obscure mutterings concerning these things, lo the wind which had slowly surrendered its reign before to the eastsoutheast, now substituted in its place the northnortheast. Thus while we were being carried for 4 hours toward the northwest and when at dusk we sounded found only 35 cubits, lest we be driven onto the shore, we released and loosened the ropes of our sails from the left, and tying the forward sail tightly to the right, as much as it was possible to do because of the winds, we proceeded toward the eastsoutheast, and the viceadmiral and the bark did the same. (*Latin*: The northnortheast wind opposes us)

The night calm and pleasant with bright stars and with a moderate course with the northnortheast blowing, but

[1] Madox wrote 'kal. 7^{bris}.' There was no meeting of the Assistants on that date; the 7 Dec. deliberation is listed in the Index under *concilium*.

(*Latin*: The bark is lost)

at the tenth hour the bark was seen for the last time.[1] May God grant that it meet with good success.)

(*Latin*: consternation)

22. ♄ [*Sat.*] (*Latin*: no little commotion but confined to secret murmurings. Hegemon bears it with an ill and discontented mind, and he suspects that his [departure] was not without the advice of Glaucus, since a long deliberation had taken place yesterday between him and the captain of the bark. This seems the more probable from the fact that the captain of the bark when he asked for provisions was often threatened that he would be removed and another substituted in his place.[2] Others fear that either because of a broken sailyard or a crushed mast or a gaping hold or some other damage or hindrance it be forced to delay. There is hope, however, that we may finally see it at the port of St. Vincent. But if it turns out not so well, I do not dare admit what I feel, for it carries supplies for 3 months only.

Verres

It would be worth the trouble to see how often Verres was summoned when he acknowledged himself to be in better health, how often he is visited when he feigns himself sick. They conjecture, they call councils, but see how happily it turns out: the shadow is caught, the

[1] The expression 'for the last time' seems curious here, suggesting perhaps that Madox too was aware of Drake's intention to sail for the Strait even as Hawkins (Glaucus) seemed aware (see 22, 30 Dec.) and as others suspected was his intention. Ward simply states that the *Francis* 'by all presumption went roome [at large] in the beginning of the night' (*PN* (1589), p. 663). Walker adds 'we suppose' it to be turned back to the Strait (21 Dec.); and Fenton notes that only eight hours earlier he had made Drake acquainted with the course for São Vicente (Taylor, *Fenton*, p. 121).

In his deposition made at Lima in Jan. 1587, Drake explained that because of the differing opinions about the course they should follow, he and his crew had determined to go to the River Plate for supplies in order to continue the voyage. For the later experiences of Drake and his crew, see pp. 40–2 above.

[2] See 7 Dec. and n. 1, pp. 254–55 above. The victualling of the *Francis* proved a persistent source of conflict between Drake and Ward on the one hand and Fenton and Ward on the other: on 24 June the council (as Fenton noted, p. 91) agreed to supply it and the *Elizabeth* with three months' provisions; this was performed on the 26th, but the following day Fenton had to speak 'sharply' to Ward about his doing so (see 28 June). After it was agreed to sell the *Elizabeth* to the Portuguese, Ward divided up its stores, and presumably the *Francis* received a portion. On 29 Oct. the master of the *Francis* was sent, on Fenton's orders, to the *Edward* to secure a hogshead of pork. Finally, on 7 Dec. the bark was supplied for a second time with three months' stores (*Fenton*, p. 118), though Fenton had once again to speak to Ward two days later about the matter (Ward, *PN* (1589), p. 661). On 26 Dec. Madox records Fenton's suspicions that the *Francis* had defected because of the dissension between Drake and Ward.

A comparable threat to that of removing Captain Drake from his position, it should be recalled, had also been leveled at the master of the *Galleon* (20 Sept.).

substance is lost, and while we shamefully gape after things that belong to others, we lose our own justly and deservedly.

The master (*navarcha*), however, is a vain and arrogant man who has learned to indulge his inclinations at the *Navarcha* expense of others. Hastening his return home, he made an ill thing worse[1] and enhanced the strength of another while catering a little to himself and his own belly.

But this I cannot pass over without laughing, which in 215r common talk has almost become a proverb, to wit, when those two vigorous soldiers, of whom not even Caesar (*Latin*: could determine the braver of the two . . . were charged a tale) with the capture of the little bark before it had come to war and they were only to pursue it with their ships very zealously and publicly, they swear they would either stab with a sword or spear or thrust a lance in the buttocks of him who at the first encounter would not leap into and mount the little vessel boldly, intrepidly, manfully, and instantly.[2] But afterwards those miserable little men [in the bark], astounded and exhausted by the din of battle, having lowered their sails and laid down their arms, would surrender themselves to the power of those pressing upon and pursuing them. Now as victors, these two redouble their voice and declare publicly that whoever, except for the two of them, would dare set foot on the little vessel would be given over to the fish to be devoured, their heads having been cut off with a dagger.

But I remember a certain private soldier as I learned from (*Latin*: hearsay . . . when he had made a stand in an attack against a witty the enemy, the leader and master who followed severely saying) chided and ordered him [not] to precede him. On the contrary, said the rustic, those who lead the choirs at home

[1] Madox's 'hanc commovit camerinam' derives from the Greek proverb *μὴ κινεῖν καμαρίναν ἀκίνητος γαρ ἀμείνων* – to make an ill thing worse.

[2] Madox is referring in slightly disguised form to the actions of Vice-admiral Ward and Captain Parker when they set out to capture the 'prize' of *Our Lady of Pity* with its seven friars (see 6 Dec. and n. 2). In an unfortunately mutilated passage, Walker, recording what the Vice-admiral who was at this time confiding in his chaplain had reported of the event, states that before they came to her they heard Captain Parker deliver great words to the company – '*that* yf they came to any fyghte and *tried to* boorde the barcke whosoever woulde not *wolde* have a pyke or other weapon thruste *in hym* but,' he adds, 'hereof was no neede' (6 Dec.).

and at public prayers occupy the important places by going about the church now also rush forth in order to be seen prominently in front and auspiciously open the way to others, for it is not fitting treatment for one who has been offered at first those things which are harsh and to taste those things which are most bitter if any sweet and dainty gain come his way at the end is not permitted to dip in even his little finger.)[1]

(*Latin*: plans made public)

23. ⊙ [*G Sun.*] *Advent 4* (*Latin*: Hegemon calls together many of us, particularly the master (*navarcha*). He says he has found a way by which it is possible not without an honest and moderate profit and without harm to anyone to return home within 12 months after he purchases here in Brazil sugar, brazilwood, and precious amber, and he openly professes that we have come here not to plunder and steal but to trade.[2] Pyrgopolinices is about to go out of his mind.

(*Latin*: what Glaucus suspects nor vainly)

Glaucus, coming to me secretly, straightaway inquires what we must do. I say I do not know. Come, he says, either we must take the city of St. Vincent and there plant our flag or we must proceed to the island of St. Helens so that when the Portuguese fleet comes there laden with spices from the Indies, we can plunder them utterly or we must lay traps in the Mexican Gulf for the Spanish fleet
215v which every year carries there a great supply of gold and silver; any action of this sort on our part would be criminal and dangerous, nor will I ever approve of it. Here, watch yourself, I said, and say no more. Further, he added, all the sugar that is found here in Brazil has already been sold by contractual agreement to a certain merchant from London, to whom we would be doing an act of injustice if anticipating him, we should buy it for ourselves.[3] Therefore, no way remains except to return home

[1] This passage suggests that the 'private soldier' refers to Tobias Parris, who had been the first to board the 'prize.' Madox was on good terms with him, see 11, 14, 15 May.

[2] If it was concluded that they could not proceed with the voyage, this was the alternative suggested by Madox: 'than must we in my conjecture seek by advise wher we may best vent those commodytyes that we have, and return home with an honest accownt of as lytle losse as may be ether of stock or tyme (Otho E VIII, f. 195; see also 20 Dec. above).

[3] In 1580 at the instigation of John Whithall of São Vicente and Santos (see pp. 34–5 above), a group of adventurers for Brazil had sent out the *Minion*

in disgrace, for the only safe, easy and convenient way that was left through the Straits is now closed to us on account of our fear and timidity. There remains no hope for us of going around the Cape of Good Hope. *Greek*: For it is an impossibility.)

(*Latin*: Why then, said I, are we constrained by such great scruples to make only for this place and not even once to attempt the Straits except under urgent necessity? Did not Drake, he said, accomplish all his actions by (*Latin*: Drake) means of cleverness and planning, who persuaded us that if we should come into the Pacific Ocean we should want to lay waste the coast of Peru, the plunder and glory of which he desired for himself alone.

His story is indeed probable, and for this reason I believe such a great desire had invaded the mind of our Hegemon to make for this place so that he should not be inferior in any way to Drake but even surpass him in many respects. For this he indeed confessed to me once himself. And if Verres, that man full of fear, the foulest glutton and Verres the greatest coward of all who live, had not meddled, our captain, a sly, crafty, purposeless but vain and im- (*Latin*: captain) moderate man, flattering all and creeping into the mind of everybody with disgusting adulation, would have added his support and restored by hope, we should indeed have attempted both those Straits and the strength of the Spanish fleet and all have died fighting rather than they should see our backs in such disgrace and dishonour.

But come, the bark is not to be seen. This depresses the (*Latin*: what the loss of the bark brings to pass) spirit, and because it has departed, then all deliberations become openly known, whence it is that now Hegemon renounces arms, favours honest trading, commends this at length and suddenly, censures the bark at length and suddenly. Whether seriously or feignedly I do not know, for if you look at the man, you will grant that he is able to feign. If you would concede this fact to him, it would be 216r the most suitable for his reputation, the most prudent for his safety. For if he steals, he fears the laws when he returns home and if he should get possession of a kingdom,

stocked with commodities to be exchanged for the 'best, finest, and whitest drie sugers' (*PN* (1589), pp. 638–42).

he will find few who wish to live with him willingly as his subjects. So much by the way.

(*Latin*: Verres perjures himself)

Glaucus reported in addition that he had asked Verres whether he had ever had any conversation with Clodius about St. Helen. He denies it, he appeals to his faith and to his life, and he damns himself to hell if he has heard any mention of this matter, when I know for very certain, and the matter itself is clearer than day, that he has been the persuader and originator of this thing.

(*Latin*: the opinion of Pyrgo-polinices)

Last evening Pyrgopolinices brought his opinion about our last deliberation written in his own hand and he begs that it be admitted.[1] I accept. For I see that the man is in a very alarmed state of mind and that between him and Clodius there are hidden rivalries at work. A man of no native ability or understanding, yet he is extremely avid for praise and not a little fearful, and while he is excessively scrupulous concerning the order and proficiency of the sailors in surveying the land and while he is jealous for his own power, he wishes to prescribe laws by which they can be instructed and desires to extract honour from those who with good cause neglect him either on account of his . . . boorishness or his savageness. They do not tolerate his command, and he appears hateful and peevish. He is of an extravagant mind so that those by whom he is lauded can obtain anything.)

(*Latin*: a tale concerning utensils)

24. ☾ [*Mon.*] (*Latin*: no wind or very weak. Robert Lyddington told me three or four stories, one concerning Mistress Elston of Worcester who, having collected her pewterware so that, polished, it might shine for a certain holiday, then secretly sold it one and all to her husband.

Another concerning Mistress Colding, who engaging in criminal action against her husband and unsheathing the sickle-shaped knife which she always carried hidden under her dress cut off his nose. She was in the habit of hurling the most bitter reproaches at the very trees and petulantly and quarrelsomely to wrangle with them for no other reason but to keep up her habit of chiding and speaking abusively. But when being at an advanced age, it was

[1] Parker's statement in his own hand is preserved in Otho E VIII, f. 196. See also 20 Dec.

predicted she would soon die, she was admonished to come to her senses finally and prepare herself by good deeds for the kingdom of heaven. She laughs, saying, what pleasure 216v indeed do you think there will be for me, wrapped in a white sheet to be thrust as it were into a bag in some narrow corner or vestibule of the house to lie mute and silent? On the contrary, you all know that disagreements, contentions, quarrells, storms and rages have been gratifying to me from the cradle itself. Therefore, let there be a place in hell for me where I may carry around flaming torches and cast disgraceful insults on everyone. After a few months she died, seized by a serious disease and vexed with the worst frenzies, and for three years after her death her home was continually the habitat of satyrs and cacodemons.

The third story he told was of a leader of twelve soldiers fighting before the standard who pressed charges (*Latin*: a very headstrong and extravagant wife) against himself, because he had neglected to wear his cap on two sabbaths, in a certain court of law when there was an inquiry concerning the observance of the statutes.[1] But, he said, a heavier burden lies on my shoulders, for I have a headstrong and disobedient wife who threatens me with many evils and would even bite me to prove more hateful. She swore in public that she would never cover her head with a hat, not because she disliked the ornament but in order that my purse might pay the penalty for her depravity. If I should be included among those who break the laws, it should not ever really be possible for the guilt and rebellious extravagance of wives to be so unjustly redeemed by the money of husbands but it should rather be expiated by penalties on those who deserve them. Although there are many who do not wish their wives to engage in illicit action out of excessive pride, they are not able to overcome and effect this, not even if life and death depend on it.

Jackson[2] related to me that in his presence not far from Lemster a young man came to a sacred chapel with a young girl to betroth her. When it came to the point for

[1] The statute for the wearing of caps passed in the thirteenth year of Elizabeth's reign was designed to protect the artificers of capmaking (*APC*, *1575–77*, p. 36).

[2] Christopher Jackson, a trumpeter.

the minister to ask who gives away the bride, an old man stands up and taking the hand of the bride, places it in the hand of the groom. Do you, said the groom, give this woman to me? I am indeed grateful to you, but lest I should be in your debt, see, I give her back to you gratis. Take her. Saying this, he left the church and climbing on his horse went away, nor was he ever seen there again until the bride had taken another husband.

Snigge

217r

He added that a certain M. Snygg, a wealthy man from Bristol, approached a certain widow of slender means who earned her living by needle and thread. He asks her how many ells of lawn would be required to make a shirt for him. She answers three. And how many, he asks, for a gown for you? Two, she says. Well, he responds, take this money and have both of them ready for the sabbath. See that they are not delayed. Saying this, he went away. On the appointed sabbath he came again at night to the widow. Have you completed, he asks, the things I ordered? Long ago, she says. Very well, responds the man, send the shirt to me. Tomorrow put on your gown and be prepared so that I may marry you at dawn. Saying this, he went away not waiting for any answer. The woman went to Kytchin. She tells him the story. She asks what she should do. Kytchin goes to Snig. He asks him about the matter. The widow is summoned. How, says Snyg, is it proper for widows to go about with so many vain fears, so many scruples, so many trappings of words so that what I had proposed to do secretly is now in the mouth of everyone? I had told you that you would be married to me tomorrow. If the terms please you, prepare yourself. If not, ask for a bill of divorcement lest you become irksome to me. You are not so tender as to blush or reject what you willingly seek. You have age and judgment: so long as time is granted, accept with grace whatever grace is extended to you. Hearing this, the widow assented. On the morrow they celebrate their marriage. They live an honest and tranquil life.

(*Latin*: the Javanese how they drink)

M. Haukins reported that it is the custom of the Javanese to pour a drink into the mouth as it were into a little vase, never touching the cup with their lips lest the breath be vitiated by the stench.)

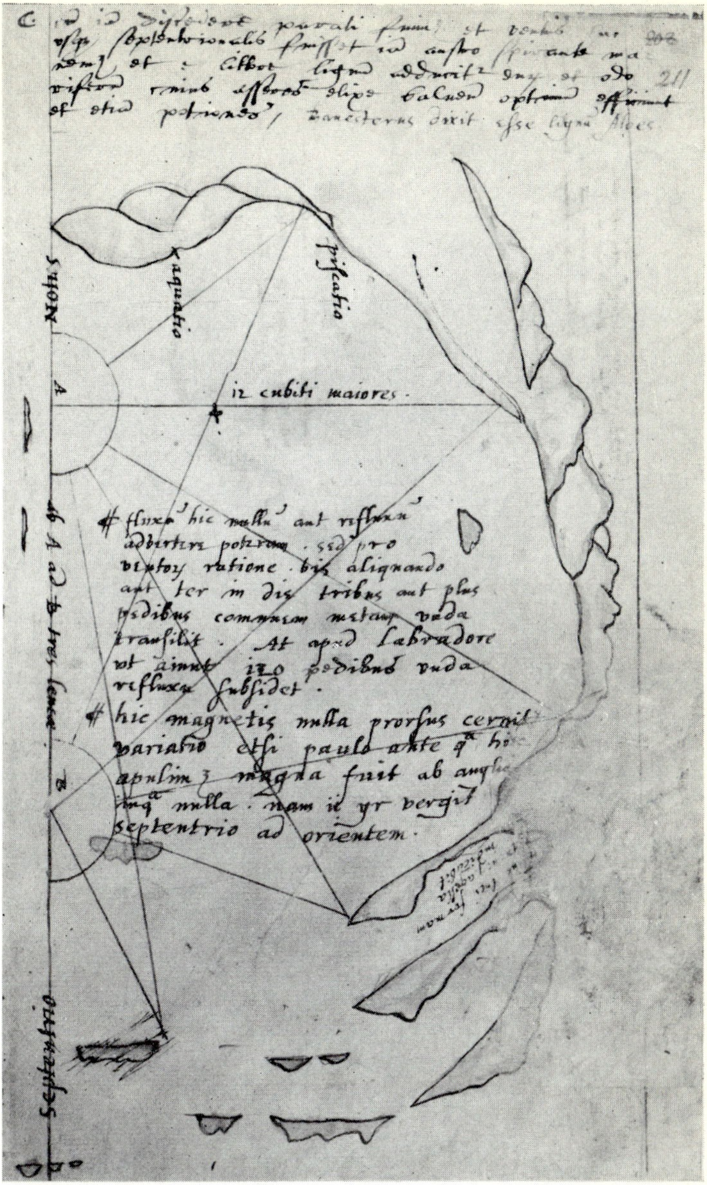

Fig. 18. Madox's chart of the Bay of Good Comfort

The Latin reads: I was not able to perceive any ebb or flow of the tide here, but according to the force of the wind, the water crossed the common limit two or three times now and then by three or more feet. But at Labrador they say the water subsides at ebb tide 120 feet.

Here we observe no variation of the compass at all; although we put in here only a little while ago, I say there was no great variation from England. For the north inclines two degrees to the east.

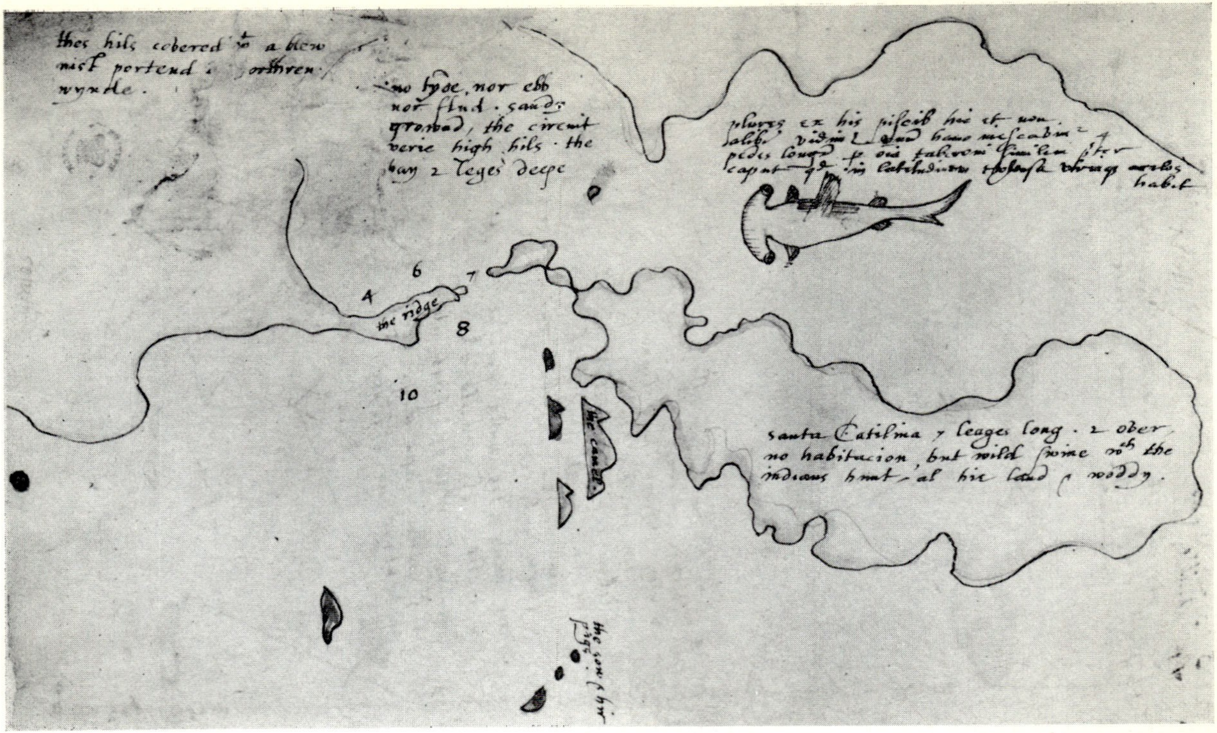

Fig. 19. Madox's chart of Santa Catarina
(North of the Bay of Good Comfort)

The Latin reads: Most of these fish we saw here and nowhere else. With a hook we caught one four feet long, in every way like a tuberon [shark] except its head which, extended in width, has little eyes on both sides.

25. ♂ [*Tues.*] *CHRISTMAS* (*Latin*: we duly celebrate with peas and salted beef and a savoury smoked tongue, and placing the trays and food on the table, we were entertayned with a musical concert, more pleased because the south wind interrupted the assembly in the middle with its dampness. How pleasing was its arrival can be attested by him who knows how harsh its absence was. Looking to the north near the western coastline, we see we are in 30 degrees of southern elevation.

Taylbois, scarcely sober as I think, lost his remarkable hat made of thick camel's hair put together closely and tightly with the application of damp heat by the hands of an artist. And Parker 14 days before similarly lost his made of velvet with a gem in a gold setting. // (*Latin*: Taylbois' hat)

The day was cloudy. Glaucus, indeed, was dressed in splendid holiday attire which when Clodius noticed, he did not even put on a clean shirt. Pyrgopolynices, moreover, at no time was dressed more shabbily, like Barsey,[1] a tasteless good-for-nothing fellow and the most insolent wretch of all men alive who attacked Taylbois with insults because he did not choose to comply with his orders on occasion. For owing to his excessive confidence in Clodius, he is insolent and intolerable.) 217v (*Latin*: a scornful Pyrgopolinices)

26. ☿ [*Wed.*] *St. Stephens* (*Latin*: since it is now made clear to all that we wish to engage in trade, not thievery, Verres who on account of this had hitherto feigned illness, now openly reveals himself. He says no hope remains for us but to go begging for alms like strangers, that he himself is a pauper, that he is in debt, and that he must give 10 marks and a jacket to his servant. The master (*navarcha*) orders him to be of good spirits: have confidence for the greatest gain will come from this. On the contrary, he answers, they do not wish to have any commercial dealings with those who do not have a Portuguese permit. But, said the master (*navarcha*), you have a permit. Certainly, he answers, but now they have pledged allegiance to the Spanish king and therefore I am with good reason the more hateful to them. How so, I ask? Because, he says to (*Latin*: Verres murmurs)

[1] Harry Bardsey, the jeweller; see Oct. 1, n. 2, above.

me, we are at war with the king of Spain. Is that so, I ask? Are you not a subject of our queen? He concedes this. I say there is a treaty between her and the Spanish king, but, he says, a licence has been granted to me by five privy councillors to wage war against the Spaniards. I do not believe it I said. If it were true, go there and fight with whom you wish. Permit us to live honestly. But I do not doubt, he said, that I can bring it about that you too in like manner will become a thief voluntarily. . . . There will be no need I said. Indeed the reasons by which Clodius is induced at last to honest trading, which at first displeased him greatly, are these: the return home of Evans, the loss of the bark which he suspects has returned home because of the dissension between that one [Captain Drake] and Hypegemon. For he believes if we once give ourselves over to piracy, any place suitable for habitation must be contemned and to return home enriched with plunder is
218r neither safe nor honest. And after plundering to return home in poverty is an offense punishable by death. Even if all are charged with the same guilt and all are authors with me in robbing others, yet the harshest blame would fall on me should I return. But to remain is a harsher lot, for I find no one who would willingly wish to die an exile from his country, and I cannot remain alone. Consideration of the matter of supplies does not permit us to continue the journey. There is therefore nothing left except to help our situation by honest trading so far as is permitted or at least not to reduce it to the last farthing.

(*Latin*: The northeast wind) That raging northeast wind hindered us much today, causing us to turn now to the northnortheast, now to the southeast and by frequent winding to retrace our way very often.)

(*Greek*: the north wind) 27. ♃ [*Thurs.*] *St. John* (*Latin*; *Greek*: the fierce north wind opposes us and diverts us toward the eastsoutheast. The sky, however, was still covered with clouds, which I had never noticed before when the north wind was blowing.

(*Latin*: a tale) When certain nobles in England according to custom were coursing the hare with dogs trained for the purpose, some would call out, Come on, black dog; others, come on, brown one; others, I like you more, white one. There happened to be there the master of Towmunt, an Irishman, unaccustomed to this kind of chase and using the English idiom inaptly, who, however, lest he appear totally ignorant if he remained silent, exclaimed loudly, Nay, little cony, you have coursed the best.)

28. ♀ [*Fri.*] *Innocents* (*Latin*: the sky seemed to threaten rain, but no small drops or at any rate very few fell. At night the wind was a little milder, the north now being faint expired in a few hours, in whose reign the northeast wind (*Latin*: the northeast wind) is substituted, more savage, violent and fierce than its father. But now reversing our sails, we turn toward the northnortheast, binding the ropes of the sails and the sailyard strongly to the extreme right.)

29. ♄ [*Sat.*] [*Latin*: almost all the clouds are scattered, but at night it thundered and the sky blazed with frequent lightning. Rain also fell, but not in great quantity, which induced calm. All things become filthy with dew and rust and are covered with an ugly film.) //

30. ⊙ [G *Sun.*] . . . (*Latin*: this night with the eastsoutheast 218v blowing, we head toward the westnorthwest, but again (*Latin*: Eastsoutheast wind Northeast wind) with the eastnortheast and the northeast blowing at night, we head toward the southeast, for sounding at only 30 cubits, we took dark and wet mud.

Today the master gave me a little handkerchief for a *Navarcha* present. Indeed, he is very greedy and fickle, for he hides his bottle of wine in secret, nor does he ever produce it unless he sees me engaged in prayers. Then, indeed, he boldly brings it forth and sucks it out made more palatable with a generous amount of sugar.

Our Podalyrius who hypocritically imagines himself Licinius to be a wise man does likewise, nor does he come to the common table. Thus he indulges himself to the utmost and feasts luxuriously in his own cabin and there consumes more wine than ten others. Further, the master (*navarcha*) told me when I asked about it that the Big Gun cleverly pilfered a tub of soap from the common storehouse, and for this reason he was threatened by Hegemon. But I know this very well and also that the master (*navarcha*) had received no small share of the thing. For he has a disciple and apprentice who, born as it were from his mouth, heaps up these things.

As the day was very calm Hypegemon and Cornicola came to us. There is discussion about the bark. What should be done we do not know. But Hypegemon says that if the bark is not found in the port of St. Vincent, he would publicly make known what he had heard about its leader, who he affirms has in his possession a great quantity of gunpowder and more provision than we suspect who think it equipped for only three months. But our Glaucus, calling me aside, said, let no one be in doubt concerning their safety, for their leader knew many places where he could look for provisions, but if he makes for those openings beyond the Straits and should pass that way, he would come to a continuous sea. But I think it is now doubtful that he will return with great honour, for yesterday around the tenth hour he was in the southern elevation of the Straits.

Glaucus

Here and there there appeared at sea, 20 leagues from the western coast and 30 degrees south, coatings as it were or reddish clouds. We at first thought the water was tinged with sand and mud. Thus it seemed turbid and mixed. As soon as we did not find bottom when sounding, we suspected it to be the sperm of whales. But the water that was brought up was mixed with whitish particles, I do not know what, which once collected together were of a saffron yellow and reddish color. Some thought it was the flower of a reed blown hither from the shore. I declare rather that it is some seed either of insects or little fish or worms or moths.)

219r

La tin: northnortheast wind)

31. ☾ [*Mon.*] (*Latin*: again with the northnortheast blowing we make for the northwest, loosening the cords of the sails from the left and strongly tying them from the fore part to the right. A cloudy and cold day.)

Index: Latin, Greek and Astrological Symbols

Mast	Sept. 20
Drake	Nov. 23, 25; Dec. 23
Current of sea and wind	Oct. 30; Nov. 21; Dec. 12
Borou[gh]s	Nov. 12
Long-tailed monkey	Oct. 29[1]
Council	Nov. 1; Nov. 25; Dec. 7, 27[2]
Colax	Sept. 24; Dec. 9
Diary	Nov. 25
Straits	Sept. 30
Glaucus	Dec. 7, 23, 30
Galba	Nov. 22, 25
Hegemon	Sept. 24, 27, 29; Nov. 22; Dec. 17, 23, 26
Hypegemon	Nov. 11, 19, 25, 27[3]; Dec. 2,[4] 7
Licinius	Oct. 20; Nov. 19; Dec. 30
Menippus	Oct. 1; Nov. 25
Loadstone	Nov. 8, 15; Dec. 2, 14
Master (*navarcha*)	Sept. 20, 21, 24; Dec. 22, 30
Pyrgopolinices	Oct. 13; Dec. 1, 7, 21, 23, 25
Suspicion of Departure	Oct. 24
Verres	Oct. 23; Nov. 1, 21, 22; Dec. 17, 22, 26 //
I was born	11 Nov. 1546 221r
I went to Oxford	24 Jan. 1567
I was admitted to read logic [B.A.]	Nov. 1571, 4 years and 10 months after my arrival
I incepted [M.A.][5]	24 Oct. 1575, 3 years and 11 months after my baccalaureate

[1] The relevance of this reference to a very obscure passage in the Diary is not clear.

[2] Dec. 27 is clearly an error for Dec. 20.

[3] The relevance of this reference is not clear.

[4] Dec. 2 is in error for Dec. 3.

[5] As shown by the next entry, Madox here is using the term *incepi* in place of *licentiatus*, the latter familiar from *Reg. Univ. Oxon* (ed. Clark); *incepi* as used by Madox and *licentiatus* are equivalent on the M.A. level to the *admissum* on the B.A., i.e., they represent the attaining of the degrees except for the final disputations.

I disputed in the Comitia[1]	9 July 1576
I went to Dorchester	15 July 1576 where I remained 2 years and 9 months
I went to Paris	July 1579, the following Oct. back to Dorchester
I was made university lecturer	Nov. 1580, 10 months after my return from Dorchester
I took orders	24 Nov. 1580 ♃ [Thurs.]
and [became] priest	♀ [Fri.] 25
I went to sea	1582 April 1
Deep snow	[1579]
Northern insurrection	[1569]
The Duke [of Norfolk] beheaded	[1572]
The steeple of St. Paul's burned	[1561]
London plague	[1563]
Good Friday sermon at Dorchester	1580 ♀ [Fri.] 1 Apr.
Admitted as Probationer [Fellow]	16 Jan. 1572 ☿ [Wed.]
Fellow	18 Jan. ☉ [Sun.] 1573
I *carried nothing* of the sought fellowship	Nov. 1570, the work of darkness
Made *proc*tor	5 Apr. 15[8]1 ☿ [Wed.][2]

[1] The phrase is used to describe the final exercises of disputation held in St Mary's Church. For the specific questions posed to Madox on this occasion, see p. 11 above.

[2] In noting a series of items relating to the 1570s, Madox assigns the date of his election as proctor to the year 1571 instead of 1581. That this is a simple *lapsus pennae* is indicated by his specifying the date (5 Apr.) and the day of the week (Wed.), which accords with the calendar and the record published by Clark (*Reg.* II.ii.96).

APPENDIX I

MADOX'S REGISTER OR 'BOOKE'*

Accidents of alteration

For the performance of all things aforsayde, our generall and the merchants were very careful so to deale in the execution of the busynes that nothing shold be in anye // poynt swarving from thes directions, 131v
and yet notwithstanding an addition of the fowrth barque, so great was the provision of all things that myght ether serve for our cumfort by the way, or for our credyte at the jorneys end, that all our ships wer very deeply laden, espetially the admirall, and yet some of the saylers complayned that she had not that shifte of cabling and cordage, as to the lenghth of hir viage, and greatnes of hir burden was convenient; this being a thing of all other carfully to be provided, synce all other necessaryes as they sayd myght be boroed by the waye, but as foı ropes, a man wold not impart them to his own father at the sea.

Whyle thes things were a doing by Hampton, word came that capten Carleyl was kept back by an ague, wherof very many were sory, but espetially the tydings did troble mee, because I reposed more cumfort of the viage in the hope of his good curtesy than I did in many other lyklyhoodes of advantedge and had determined with my self also to have remayned with hym wherever he had stayd whyl God wold geve me leave, but yet I trust all for the best. Upon the notyce of his refusall, M. generall, and M. Alderman Barnes did appoynt M. Nycholas Parker to all suche preferments and charges which by commyssion wer to M. Carleyle assygned. And also wher our admyral ship was in the Commission cawled the *Beare Galleon* they thowght yt wold be a name more sownding and significative to cawl her the *Galleon Leicester*, according to the honorable tytle of hir lord and owner. Further wher ther is mention made in the instructions of 2 chests, one to be kept in the Galleon, the other in the Edward, M. Alderman Barnes told us he had receaved of the cowncell but one box, and

* B.L., Cotton MS, Otho E VIII, ff. 131r–143r.

therfore prepared but one chest with three loks, wherunto openly he put the box and locking the same agayn delyvered yt to our generall, and M. sherif Owtread gave the 3 keys to Capten Ward, Capten Hawkins and to mee.

132r *1582. April 29. The fyrste wayinge of anchors*

These things being ernestly in hand, M. Sherif Owtreade (whom wee fownd redy bothe with curtesy of enterteynment and otherwyse to pleasure us) according as by the Cowncel he was requyred, mustered the whole cumpany at his howse, and receaving every mans frank promyse of wylling endeavowr in the service, commended the action unto us, and yn a shorte and good pythy exhortacion dyd declare unto us the favowr of hir Majestie, the bent of hir cownselors, our dutyes by the way, and hope at our returne, and ther delyvred the whole charge to M. Edward Fenton our generall, yn presens of M. Alderman Barns and M. Towrson who did also take noe smal paynes to see all things in ordre dispatched with noe lesse hast for the præparation and tyme, than with advised care for the safety and well ordering of the whole cowrse. So that on Sonday the 29th of Aprill 1582, the rather to get all our men together aboord, which notwithstanding the strayte looking to of our generall, were ever slynking with backerrands to the shore, they thowght not amysse yf conveniently yt might be to waye anchor and faul somwhat lower from the towne, wherfore our generall, whose care was that fyrst in all things Gods name myght be blessed, and next that noe good opportunytye shold be overslacked, invited both them and M. Owtread, the Mayre of Hampton and the whole fleet to dynner aboord the Galleon wher he appoynted me to preach and to handle such matter as I thowght meetest for the tyme. Wher according to the grace geven me from God, from the fyrst verse of the 24 psalme I beat owt the tryal of 3 questions, fyrst shewyng how lawful a thing was travel and merchandyce, and that wee had best ryght to the
132v Indyes, next that wee // myght with safe consciens honestly trafique among the ynfidles making exchange of ware, how ever some think that we cary owt necessaries, and bring home superfluyties, lastly that the appoynted tyme of a mans lyfe can not be shortned, althogh he encownter with a thowsand perils, which questions debated, I exhorted every man to religion and manhood and shewd how both thes must be knyt up in love, and so ended. Which doen after wee had dyned wel and byd many a harty prayer both for hir Majesty and for hir Cowncel and for many of our good frends by name, our Anchors were wayed,

and we fel down with a tyde to Cawshot, wher wee rode the next day taking yn such things as weer wanting.

1 Maii 1582. Our seconde waying at Cawshotte

On May day when we had taken yn as wee supposed all our necessyties and gote our whole cumpany aboorde, the generall, M. Alderman, M. Towrson and M. Caslyn tooke agayn the last muster of them and left the fleet thus ordered:

In the Galleon Leicester	Edward Fenton generawl William Hawkins leiftenent Nicholas Parker capten at land Richard Madox Minister Miles Evans, Mathew Tailboise } merchaunts Christofer Haul master abowt fowrscore for sailers 24 necessarye men beside and a dozen of boies
In the Edward	Luke Warde viceadmirawl John Walker minister Rondol Shawe, Peter Jefrei } merchants Thomas Pearsie master abowt 54 for sailers 16 necesarie men beside and 8 boies //
In the Fraunces	John Drake Capten 133r Wyliam Markam Master 14 saylers. 2 boys
In the Elsabeth	Thomas Skevington Capten Rafe Crane Master 12 saylers. 3 boys

When this muster was taken, we wayd agayn in the name of God, and after we had fawlen a leag toward the Wyght, M. Alderman Barns and his company took ther leave, whom with teares we commended to God bequething both them and al other our owners, hir majesty, and our selvs to the protection of the Almyghtye and so according to the posey of our ship: *Under the conduct of Christ wee forowed the seaze*, and when the next day we had shot of the Nyeldes, a sowthwest wynd aryzing put us in agayne to the Wyght wher we contynued plying of and one, somtymes at Yarmowth, and somtymes at the Cows for the space of twenty days, yn which seazon for the better ordering of the whole viage both in good exercyse and in advised keeping of cumpany, the generall delyvered to eche vessel severall instructions, the coppy wherof hearafter followth.

A Copie of our articles [*2 May 1582*]

Certen Articles, set down by Edward Fenton esquyre, Captayn generall appoynted by hir majesty for the discovery of China and Cataia by the sowthward to be observed by the whole fleet and cumpany under his conduct and government.

1. Fyrst for as muche as in no action can be looked for any good event or successe wher God is not syncerly and dayly honored, you shall therfore cause to be sayd twyse dayly aboord your shipp the usual service appoynted by hir majesty in the church of England. //

133v 2. Item, that you and all those under your charge geve due reverence unto suche as be appoynted ministers of Gods holy word within this fleete upon payn to be punyshed for doing the contrary according to the qualytie of the offence.

3. Item, that you suffer noe swearing, dycing or cards playing, or other vayn talk within your ship upon payn that any one offending in any of those crymes, being by curtesy warned of those fawlts and wil not leave them shall be punyshed sharply for the same.

4. Item, that yf any one of what cawling or condicion he shal be, shal conspire or goe abowt by violence or other ways to take away the lyfe of the generall, his leiftenent, viceadmirall or any other appoynted in auctorytie under hym wherby this viage may be overthroen or hindred, he or they so offending and being detected or convinced therof, by sufficient proofe, shall receave punyshment by death for the same.

5. Item, you shal foloe the admyrall as well by day as by nyght, and geve soe carefull and diligent attendaunce of hym as in noe wyse you loose his cumpany, and that after he shal shew furth his lyght in the poope by nyght all men to foloe hym, and no man to be so bold as go before hym, withowt his lycence or appoyntment, upon payn of punyshment for the same.

6. Item, that every morning by 7 or 8 of the clock you shall not

fayl yf the wether serve you to speak with the admirall, and in the evening abowt 7 of the clock to do the lyke to understand his further pleasure.

7. Item, you shal not ether by day or nyght so nygh as you can be further of from the admyrall than the distance of one Englyshe myle or so near as you may be with your safetynes.

8. Item, that if the admiral shal happen in the nyght to put owt towe lyghts than you shal speedyly repayr unto hym and speak with hym. //

9. Item, that yf any myschance shal happen unto you by day, you 134r
shal presently shoot off one peece and yf by nyght you shal doe the lyke, putting also furth 2 lyghts.

10. Item, no man shal geve chase to sayl or sayles, withowt appoyntment of the Admiral, upon payn to be sharply punyshed for doying the contrarye.

11. Item, that yf any man come up to hayl his feloe in the nyght and knoe hym not shal geve hym this watchword, *yf God be with us,* the other being of our fleet shall answer, *who shal be against us*: to the end that any straunge shipping happening into our cumpanyes, warning may be presently geven to the admirall, ether by hym or the next being of better sayl.

12. Item, that yf by storme or evil wether we shold be seperated, as God forbyd, then you shal dyrect your cowrse for the ylandes of the Canaries to the sowthwest part of the yland cauled Gomæra, wher you shal lye of and one the space of 7 dayes, and yf in that tyme we happen not to meete, then you shal direct your cowrse from thence to the yles of Cape de Verde and to remayn and stay ther abowt the ylands of Bonavista or Maie.

13. Item, the better to knoe on an other afarre of, after we shal happen to have been so seperated, you shal upon the discrying one of an other, so far as yt can be wel discerned, stryke and hoyse the mayn topsayl twyse together very speedyly.

14. Item, that yf any man shal discrye land by day that he presently geve warning by shooting of a peece of ordynance and putting owt of his flag: yf by nyght by the lyke warning and putting furth of 2 lyghts, and stryking of all his sayls he hath abrod.

15. Item, that yf wee shal happen to be trobled with any thik fogs or mysts, and therby have cause to ly at hull, the admyral shal geve warning by a peece and showing of 2 lyghts one above an other, and at his setting of sayl shall doe the lyke, being not cleere. //

134v 16. Item, yf ther shall happen to be any mutynows or disordered person withyn your charge, you shall keepe hym in safety til he may be browght aboord the admirall to receave such condygne punyshment as belongeth to so great an offendowr.

17. Item, that upon putting furth of an ensygne yn the wast of the admirall and shoting of a peece, the resydue of the fleet shal repayre presently to hym and understand the generalls plesure.

18. Item, that yf wee shal happen to encownter or meet with any enemyes, that so nyghe as you can you attend the admirall in such sort as you may rather defend your selvs than be offended of the enemyes.

All the articles and what others shall be fownd necessary for the benyfyte of this service, I requyre in hir majestyes name, and as you will answer the contrary at your perills, faythfully and truly to observe the same. Dated afore Yarmowth aboord the *Galleon Leicester*, the ij of May 1582.

Edwarde Fenton

xxi Maie 1582. Oure first settinge in to the sea.

Munday the 21th of Maye the wynd somewhat harting yn to the northeast, we put owt luckyly (as I trust) into the sea, and stopping certayn tydes, by Thursday folowing, which was the Ascensyon day, we wer gote almost to the Sterte, which when we cold not wether (the gale bloyng stif at the west) we turned to Dartmowth and rode in the range, which place not being comodiows as the wether fel owt,
135r cawsed us on Saturday folowyng // to turne up to Torbay, wher we rode 5 days after. Hear M. Whode, one of our pilots began muche to dislyke with al the tackle of our ship, espetially with the want of cables, wherupon, as I think, he was sent by our generall to Sir Frances Drake for some furnyture, but well I knoe he came with Cables and ropes to us in a fysher boat from Plymmowth, and wyne that Sir Frances bestoed on us. He browght also a letter to M. Hawkyns, in some discurtesy taking yt, that wee wold staye hear, and myght as well have been at Plymmowth, of which fawlt to excuse hym self Captayn Hawkins purposed to ryde to Plymmowth, but the generall was loth he shold, yet notwithstanding he was very desyrows. And now no sooner was he gone away, on Thursday the last of May, but the wynd comyng to the northwest we set sayl in our cowrse, and by Fryday morning had gote past the Stert. Hear when dyvers dyd request that wee myght have edged nye unto Plymmowth to take in the leiftenent and other that were a shore, the generall wold not graunt yt; because,

sayd he, they see the wynd and more meete yt is they make some shifte to come unto mee than I to hynder my cowrse for them. M. Whode, one of our pylotes, being an open mowthede feloe, began hearat chafingly to swear, and cawlyng to the Frawncys, willed hir to stand yn for M. Hawkins; but the generall forbad yt, wherby grew great grutching and choler, but anon the wynde meeting us at west sowtherly enforced us of necessyty to Plymmowth wher we rode in the sownd.

Hear M. Hawkins cam aboord and requested our general to go ashore, but he refused, than returned he back with the Plymmowth men, taking yt unkindly that the generall shold not of curtesy do ether Sir Frances or hym self that æstimation, as to geve hym credyt before his own people, and yn my // conjecture yt wold have been a great 135v
cause of love and contentment, wher contraryly things fel owt with bytternes and grutching. For one the moroe mornyng the wynd comyng fayr, the master requested twyse that he myght send the pynnase a shore for the cumpany that was ther, but when yt cold not be grawnted, yet seeyng the importance of the matter, sent yt notwithstanding. Anan ther was shot of a warning peece and after the generall comaunded to way anchor, but when the saylers fyrst had lyngered and after flatly denayed, the general in choler demaunded the cause; answer was made that yn as muche as ech man went upon his venter, they wold not rune headlong into an unknoen coast withowt those pylots that were appoynted by the cowncel, adding moreover that M. Whood fownd hym self so muche aggreeved, that he wold not returne agayne tyl he knew how he shold be used; the generaul bad them way up anchors, or he wold hang up hym that refused. The master than pacifyed the mariners with gentil words, requesting them to way and to spread a topsayl in the wynd, that the absent myght make the more hast, and promysed to lynger for ther takyng yn. So did they, but when we had lyngered abowt an howr with a flyttering sayl, and cold not see them come we spread more canvase and away wente sheere. The viceadmirall cam after and so dyd the Elsabeth, but nether cold we see our pynnyse nor the Frances. Abowt noone Capten Ward cam aboord the galleon, requesting our generall to cast abowt for the rest of our cumpany; the generall answered that they owght to have geven better attendance. Captain Ward replying, // sayd that 136r
fel not now so muche in consyderation what they shold have done, (for that was manifest) but the thing beyng allredy past what was best for us to doe, adding that wynde we myght have commodius hearafter, but

men shold we fynde noe more, being once hence departed. To this the generall rejoyned that he wold go into Fawmowth and ther take up a new supply of saylers to furnysh our complement, but when yt was declared that ther they wer not to be had, and that the generall saw all men very lothe to goe withowt the cumpany, he was content to stand back, so that abowt 2 howrs after, the Frances came with the leiftenent, the pilotes and the rest, having left behynd them one Henry Kyrkman whom they accused of yl behaviour towards them. Our general cauled them and as many of his assystants as were aboord into his cabyn and soberly admonyshed them of ther fawlts, axyng of M. Whood wherin he fownd hym self agreeved that he shold speak such words as he had doen to the disquyeting of the whole cumpany. He answered agayn that he thowght great scorn not to be cawled to cownsel abowt waying the anchors at all tymes, but when M. Hall had excused hym self therof, declaring that hytherto that thing had needed no delyberation, for every man saw and knew what was to be doen on this coast, but hearafter he shold be cawled yf yt wold please hym. The generall seeing some weaknes thowght better to knyt up thyngs yn love, than now to begyn with punyshment, and therfore exhorting us al to a frendly agreement, pardoning and promysing to forget this fawlt, with shaking of handes they wear all dismist. I pray God grawnt us harty love among our selvs and a reverent regard of duty towards our owners. //

136v *Junij 2, 1582. The processe of our viage from Ingland.*

On Saturday nyght being the second of June, we last set eye on the Leyzard of Ingland; wherfore on Whytsonday, not withowt teares in our prayers, we comended the safety of hir majesty and the cowncel, the Muscovy merchants, and all our frends, to almyghty God, desyring that after the honest dispatch of our busynes, we myght at our returne fynd them in safety. Which God grawnt. And so with a good north wynd we held our course (as I suppose by the direction of Furdinando) sowthwest and sowth, purposyng to passe between the yland of Launceroti and Barbary, the cause wherof (being muche owt of our way) I can not gesse (althoe we wer born in hand that they went to fetch an east wynd) but that some of the leaders were caried with hope to meete with a Carvel of sugar and Canarie wynes, for discrying on Saturday folowyng a hulk at the sea, wonder yt was to see on what an edge every mans teath in maner wer set on, seeking by all means possyble a cause and quarel to hir, pretending fyrst that she was a

French man of war, and many other reconings, but the general wold not consent to offer them any wrong, and on the moroe being Trynyty Sonday when both I in the gallion and M. Walker in the Edward, had spoken in our sermons ageynst this pretence, and shewed openly the purpose of our viage, and exhorted them to performe the same with an honest care of upryght dealing, many fel to a private grutching hearat, and those of whose conscience before wee had good hope dyd // not styck to affyrme openly that wee wer bownd in duty 137r
to spoyl all papists, as enemyes to God and our soverayn, of what cuntrey so ever they were. Which begynning browght us into some fear what yssue this eger desyre of them myght bring with yt. When we were thwart the straytes M. Owtreads ship cauled the Brydget, which hytherto had kept us cumpany, now departed from us sowth-west toward Tenaryfe, we holding due sowth. By hir wee sent letters to Ingland as our last farewel.

On Sonday the 17 of June in the mornyng wee had syght of the Canaries, and fynding our selvs to the west of Launcerota and also almost past yt, so that our fyrst purpose cold take no effect, we bended now more to the west leaving both yt and Forteventura on the larboord, and shooting between Grawnd Canary and Tenaryfe, by the 20th of June, we had passed the Tropique of Cancer, sayling stil at pleasure before the wynde, but now began to be many speeches among us, some fynding fault with the Elsabeth, of whom they desyred to be ryd, some greevowsly accusyng Richard Grafton that had dealt yl with us for all kynd of provision, espetialy green billet, and fusty meale, some complayning for lack of water, by reason that our ships being at fyrst pestered with muche lumber, cold take yn but smale quantytye therof at Ingland. Wherfore the tyme being fayre, and somwhat caulme the general cawled on Mydsomer day his assystants together, to take advyce of such things as shold be needful. //

Junij 24th. 1582. The firste consultatione healde in the Galleone Leicester on midsomer day, at 2 degrees of longitude and 18 of northren latitude. 137v

Being athwart the Cape Blanco within 18 degrees to the lyne of equalyty yn as muche as the generall had appoynted the ylands of Bonavista or Mayo to be places of our meeting yf any misfortune shold sever us, and in as muche as many wer desyrows ther to refresh them selvs and to be furnyshed with water, the sea beyng peaseable and lytle wynde, he assembled aboord the Galleon all those whome yt pleased the Cownsel to appoynte for assystants unto hym in this action and when we wer come together he shewed us wrytten in a paper 2 questions to be consydered of in this maner.

24 Junij, 1582. Matters to be consydered of as foloweth, viz. Latitude 18. 1. To see what cowrse wee shal hold from the ylands of Cape de Verde and what tyme wee shal remayn ther for our watring.

2. To see the barques provided of all things necessary, as well with victuals as with Cards and platts.

When he had red thes questions and proceded into some discowrse of his owne opinion in the case, at last he put us to consyder whether yt were best water at thes ylandes or noe, and yf wee thowght so requysyte, than to which yland wee shold goe, and so gave me the paper to wryte every mans reason and opynion. //

138r These questions as I ymagined being somwhat intricate because on thing was set down and an other thing was proposed, and the question also that was proposed stoode on 2 poyntes, I wylled them fyrst to answer what they thowght of the watring at thes ylands and yf hearof they dyd agree, than myght be thowght upon which yland was fyttest for our servyce.

Hearunto Captayne Warde answerethe that in as muche as he had aboord hym, in the vyceadmirall, very smale store of water and that very unholsome and corrupte, and because the cumpanye myght the better fresh them selvs both by washing of ther clothes and by romedging of the ship, which was scarsely yet in any good trym, and because also those vytuales which the barques wanted myght be put into them, he thowght yt needfull espetially at some of thes ylands to water.

Captayne Hawkins was also of the same mynde adding moreover that wher dowt was made by the generall whether wee shold hear fynd any water or noe, that the hynderaunce wold not be great to seeke and yf we fownd any than myght our desyre be performed, yf not wee myght the sooner be goene.

Thes reasons wer lyked of all the rest particularly, and wee were all desyrows that so yt myght be, wherupon the generall adjoyned his consent, althoe he seemed wyllyng to have goen further.

Than for the place wher, and which of thes ylands wee referred to the pylots, who told us Bona Vista was the fyttest and moste lykely place, so that wee all fully determyned, yf pleased God, to seeke Bona Vista. //

138v Than tuching the furnyture of the 2 barques, because wee knew not how far God myght by tempest or otherwyse seperate them from us, nor how soone, and that we cold not leave them in such cases utterly distressed, yt was therfore fully agreed upon by general consent, that at Bona Vista they shold take yn owte of the shipps victuals for three moneths, over and above that portion which they had aboord alredy, and that they shold be thorowly provided of all other ther wants what so ever.

This being doen the generawll cawled the pylotes, demawnding of them that yn as muche as wee were to passe into the sowtheast sease by the Cape of Good Hope, which was the best place of rende vow next after this watring, who affyrmed that the ryver of Plate was the best and the only place that they knewe. Upon this informatyon the generawl consenting pronownsed that yt shold be soe, but M. Walker not well lyking hearwith desyred the generall that this matter myght also be proposed to the delyberation of his assystants, partly because he supposed this place to be far owt of our way, partly because being come thither wee shold be caried ether by necessytye or by pretences, agaynst our commission to passe throwe the Straytes of Magellanus wherunto he saw many throe desyre of purchase, as they cawl yt, much enclyned. The pylotes hearunto constantly avowched that of necessyty they must come withyn a hundred leagwes of this place to fet a wynd to cary us unto the Cape of Good Hope, and comyng so nye by constraynt yt wold be no hynderaunce // at all, the case ryghtly 139r
consydered, to put yn with the ryver, both to refresh our men, and to furnysh oure watring, syth other harboroe than this they knew not til wee shold come to the yle of Java, which was a long streche. This peremptory speach by those that professed knoledge hearin cut of M. Walker, and other of us that were lothe to have tuched in America, because whatever myght be objected was answered with wyndes and tydes and currents and reconyngs, which fel not, as they sayd, into our consyderations. Wherfore to this poynt also wee wholy consented and subscrybed our names as hear followeth. Edward Fenton, Luke Warde, William Hawkins, Nycholas Parker, Richard Madox, John Walker, Myles Evans, Rondolph Shawe, Mathew Taylboyse, Peter Jeffreys.

When I had of all this made a breif note in that paper which the generall had begune, I told them that the thing must be presented in a booke at our returne before hir majesties honorable Cowncel and willed them therfore that in respect of the disordered handelyng I myght digest yt in my booke according to ther true meaning althogh yt shold somwhat differ in wordes and that than they wold set ther handes to the booke, but in any case yt cold not be graunted that other

139v coppy shold be taken than the originall, wherfore // for the better credyte of this booke, I have annexed at the end therof all those oryginall copyes which are fyrmed with our own handes.

At this present also Captayn Parker in as muche as the general had appoynted hym in styd of Captayn Carleyl to have the ordering of all at the shore, requested that he myght be alowed to choose hym self a leiftenent and corporalls for the better performance of his service. Hearunto was answered by the generall that so many officers in suche smale cawses wold but make the common shares in the ende to fawll short, to which he replyed that rather than that objection shold take place he wold owte of his owne share alowe a larges unto his offycers, but the generall rejoyning told hym that he knew as yet no great land servyce but to fet in a barico of water at a tyme of neede which myghte be doen withowt any such ceremonye. As for leiftenent, he wold suffer noe more in the fleet than his owne, and with that wee arose, and for this tyme departed.

Junij 26. 1582. Of the Ilandes of Cape de Verde
(*Margin*: Latitude 16)

One Tuesday morning being the 26th of June wee descryed land on the west of us which some sayd was Bonavista, some sayd La Sel, but when in the after noone we had anchored in a fayr bay on the
140r sowtheast syde of yt, our // pylates pronownsed playnly that yt was Bonavista, but yet confessed that they were never hear before, nether knew whether we shold therin fynde water or noe. Wherupon the generall was in purpose to be goen, but when I perceaved the drifte of thes good men to be suche, that bringing us to an exigent of water and beverage, than must we be constreyned to fil yt in wher ever wee mette with yt, and when our fethers were once lymed in pillage, and our handes anoynted with spoyle, wee wold not styck to chop up from the fyngers endes to the hard elboes (which was the doctryne that they dayly tawght) and when I perceaved that the whole fleete began greatly to grutch and murmure at so sodayn departure, withowt any tryall, contrary to determination and apoyntment, I advyzed the generaul to send his pynasse a shore, certyfiyng hym that wher ther be such fayre wooddy hills, ther was also to be fownd in some parte or other spryngs of fresh water. Hearupon capteyn Ward in one pynase and capteyn Parker in an other were sent to make serche, with store of men and municion among whom I was also crept to see what wold become of the matter, but when wee had rowed abowt a myle, one

of our people espied a cupple of goates with long beardes, advauncyng them selvs on the syde of a sandy hil, and a lytle kyd after them, streyt wyse ech gave other warnyng to beware, for ther were towe harnesed men on horsebacke and a dogge folowing them. Than was he cownted the manlyest soldier that cold lyft his buckler hyest over his head, and plant his peece in // best redynes. 140v

To conclude whether yt were the dread of thes goates, which I suppose, or the rut of the shore, which they than aledged, or any other meaning which is hydden from mee, but at the shore our boates cam not, notwithstanding Captayne Ward sent owt 2 of his men, which swam aland and broght us word back of a fayre river, of plenty of goates, of some great cattell, but no evident sygne of people: with this tydings we returned aboord seing by the way fysh and byrds in great abundance. When the general hard that ther was such a rut at the shore, that he myght not easyly land his boates, he determyned not to stay hear because wee wer now before the sone, and yt wer joperdy both of tornadoes, of qualmes and of contrary wyndes yf the sone throe our lyngring shold overtake us. This being appoynted, on the morow cam the viceadmiral complayning greatly that we shold so depart in as much as he stood in some distresse of water, wherfore the generall goyng aboord hym and fynding that true, gave hym a tune of water owt of the Galleon and so in the name of God, as I hope, wee proceaded forward in our viage.

Junij 27. 1582. From the iles of Cape de Verde to the coast of Guiny

On Thursday the 27 of June we wayed anchors, having a fayr northren wynde. The master wold have had us kept due sowth, but our pylats wold needly dyrect // our cowrse to the sowthsowtheast, 141r affyrming that of necessyty we must fet an east wynd upon the coast of Guyny, or els cold wee never get throe, for otherwyse great daunger ther was lest on the sodayn wee myght be embayed on the sholds which lye betwyxt the yle of Ascention and Capo de los Baxos, on the coast of Bresyl, which was not past 700 leages of, or therabowt. These and such lyke reasons constantly and sternly avowched by thes old beaten saylers set me and others newe to schole. Ymagening for certaynty that ether Aolus or Neptune dyd keepe ther martes at appoynted places, wher wee myght purvey and furnysh our selvs of such wynds as sholde be necessary for us, but whether this poynt of doctryne be not always fyrme, or whether we were unworthy to fynd yt true, I knoe not, but according to the pylots speach the master was overruled, so that the larboord tack aboord wee hawled to the sowthsowtheast and on St. Peters day, being the 29th of June, being within 14 degrees of the lyne wee mett with a sowth wynd so that we were constrayned to runne fyrst upon one boord and after on an other with smale advantedge a great while, meeting the wynd most comonly sowth and sowthwest, so that the northeast wynde whom our pilots heald in an obligation, upon very negligens had broken his band, nether cold wee devise in what cowrt best to sue hym, nor with what maner of wryt unlesse yt were a Latitat unto Boreas, who thoe he be head borowe and highe sherif of the seaz yet is he so lynked in kynred with this defendant that wee cold hope but for a cold shuyt [*sic*] in so de[s]perate a cause.

Of our people some began to wax syck and some dyed. //

141v *Julij 20. 1582. The first sight of the land of Gwynie and a consultacion.*

(*Margin*: Latitudo septentrionalis 6.) Uppon Fryday the 20th of July after wee had for 4 or 5 days together rune upon a sowth east boord having the wynd at sowthwest and by sowth wee descryed in the morning a very high land at east northeast, beyond the expectacion of our pylots, which land they deemed to be ether Capo de Verga or Capo de Palmas, but the generall not meaning to tuche upon yt gave warning and cast to the offward which whan the viceadmyral espied he cam aboord us with his master and his pylote wyshing that wee shold rather stand yn with some harborowe for the relief of our cumpanyes than to lye bweltyng at the sea withowt advauntadge. The generall therfore both to be advized thearin and also to lern some certenty of the place cawled the master and pilots and some other to shew ther reconyngs and platts, who did somwhat dowt of the place but supposed that we were within 4 degrees of the lyne by accownt of the ships, for the sune nor star had not been taken yn 10 days before. The leiftenent and M. Whood who had coasted this place before and Blaccollar affirmed yt to be Capo de Palmas, but M. Evans and I which wold gladly have shewed some lyklyhoodes why we cold not be soe nye the lyne, were cut of with peremptory pronunciations, as thoe therby we cawled ther knoledge in dowte and so incurred the penalty of presumption. After this question was thus concluded wee grewe in //
142r some speach of watring hear. The general was lothe to go aland in any place uppon the coast of Guynye, fearing, as he sayd, lest the contagion of the cuntrey wold rather be occasion of more sycknes to his people than any recovery of strenth. M. Hawkins told that Sir Frances Drake even in this monethe and within 2 days of this tyme watered at the

Serra Liona and fownd no annoyance at all. M. Whood sayd yt was a villanows place for while Sir Fransis dyd ther stay to water they set on the potage pot with ryse every meale. M. Hawkins added moreover that his uncle had comended this place unto hym. The generall replyed that hear his uncle had lost many men. I was of opinion that somtyme when men were so lost as was not expedient for all the world to knoe, yt was a very probable report to saye that the contagios murren of the shore had baned them, and wher the Portingals speak evil of yt I rather commend ther wyts than beleeve ther words which seeke to make all other men afrayd to serch owt that wherin them selvs fynd sweetnes and comodytie, and into this mynde was I browght the rather for that I cold never hear grownd of reason why or how yt shold be so unholsome, but only bare wordes wherunto I cold geve but bare credit. Our master, perceaving that none of the pilates knew the shore aright, was desirows rather to keepe the sea than to fawl in to a road wher both our men and tackle myght be joperded. M. Ferdinando sayd that the Portingales do water and vitayle hear from January to May but further he knew not. When the generall saw many desyrows to water and that the sowth wynd stood so stif in opinion as ten Nestors cold not have persuaded hym to yeld an ynch of his hold, wherbye // we were out of hope to gayn owght at the sea, 142v
the generall demaunded whether yt were better to keepe the east shore or to hawle back agayn northweaste to the Sera Liona. M. Hawkins shewed that the further we trended eastward the more daunger were wee yn both of embaying and of qualmes, nether did any man ther knoe place of herberowe, but to the Serra Liona myght wee goe withowt losse of way and in a qualme ryde withowt hazard or with any land breez put of to our advantedge. M. Evans desyred that wee myght hold on to the eastward which was our way, not dowting but by advysed cowrse wee myght with this wynd duble the Cape of Good Hope, but Blaccoller told hym that in so doing he myght be put into a bay and ther lye half a yere withowt wynd or water, for the current, sayth he, setts to the land and ther is not a breth of ayre sturring. This did the other pilots constantly affyrme, being lyke to Vergills fame which is *tam ficti pravique tenax quam nuncia veri*, and althoe of thes matters they knew not muche, yet when so ever the Cape of Good Hope cam in talk, as thoe the name of good hope had put them owt of all hope of pillage, which was the thing they desyred, the pylots ever in Pylats voyce cried *crucifige* and ther voyces prevayled for the generaul appoynted to go back to the Serra Liona except the wynde changed

to further us in owr way, and upon this resolution he dismissed the cumpany, not commytting this as an act in the register because yt was but a familier debating between hym and the pilots espetially, althoe other present were bold to utter what they thowght. //

143r *Julij 21. 1582. Of certaine things which fell owt after this time.*

When wee had rune all nyght to the northwest on Saturday abowt noone the wynde mett us agayn at the sowthwest wherupon the general cawsed to turne our course and put up agayn for the ryver of Plate, but now in putting of and on we were on all sydes so embayed with the land that the master had work ynoghe to cleere hym self of yt. Nowe happen unto us dyvers qualmes.

APPENDIX II

THE DIARY OF JOHN WALKER: 1582–83*

[May, June]

[May 1, Tues.] Parted from Southampton . . . where after devyne servyce *with M.* . . . *of* Hampshyre, M. Alderman Barns and M. *Towrson and M. Caslyn*, merchauntes of London, the maior of S*outhampton* . . . and dyvers other gentlemen of good estym*ation having* ended, M. Captayne Warde and I wente to the Edw*ard* . . . the other gentlemen stayd with our generall M. Ed*ward Fenton* and about 1 of the clocke we hoysed sayles and *with the* . . . sounde of trumpetts in both these shyppes [and] with the s*hooting of* certayne greate ordynaunce we sayled ii leages whe*re* both we and two other small barkes the Francys, M. John Drake ca*ptayne* and *the* Elyzabethe, M. Skevington being captayne we rode at Ankor untyll a xi of the clock *on* May day whence we sayled with a ~~moste prosperous~~ [*dele*] wy*nde* being northeaste, yet drawinge towardes nyghte by reason of *the* daunger of rockes in that coste, we caste anckor over agaynst Yarmothe. 202r

[Wed.] The seconde of Maye we sayled with the lyke *northeaste* wynde into the meane sea but before nyght the wynd*e* came aboute to the weste and so we were constrayned to returne to the same harboure of Yarmothe and there we ancorded enew and stayde ther*e* untyll the vth day [Sat.] in the afternone and then the wynde and weather growinge ext*remely foul, the wynde* south south weste we were constrayned to returne two leages u*nto* Southhampton and there we ancored at the Cowes the same nygh*t and* there stayed.

* Walker's Diary appears in Cotton MS, Otho E VIII (ff. 202–17, 160–4, and 218–23) which was badly damaged in the fire of 1731. Thanks to the other documentation, it has been possible to reconstruct some of the mutilated passages. These reconstructions are printed in italic; inadvertent omissions are in brackets. In Walker's hand, the final letters for *they, them, ther* frequently tail off if they may be said to exist at all; I have accepted this characteristic practice as a kind of abbreviation in order to avoid spattering the text with brackets.

[Sun., Mon.] Upon the vi I preached. Upon the vii I went to New-
7 porte in the yle of *Wyghte* and there dyned at one M. Iles, ther new chosen baylyfe where *were* presente M. Browne, M. Baker, both preachers and late studentes of Chryste Churche in Oxon. with dyvers other magystrates of that towne.

[Tues., Wed.] The 8 we had the wynde at the northeaste and hoysed
8 our sayles towardes *the* seas but ancored at Yarmothe and the ixth
9 we fearinge fowle wether . . . came to the Cowes agayne.

[Thurs.] The xth the generall, M. Captay*ne* Parker, M. Maddoxx and
10 other supped with M. Captayne Warde in our Edwarde.

[Fri.] *The* xith we had the communyon mynystered in our shypp
11 where I pre*ached* a sermon of the supper of the Lorde.

[Sat.] The xii Sir Edwarde Ho*rsey* beinge on shore in the yle of
12 Wyghte, our generall, M. Captay*ne* Warde, M. Captayne Parker and I went unto hym where we were almoste *ii* howres, vidz. fro a xi of the clocke untyll one in the afternone.

[Sun.] T*he* xiiith I preached in the Edwarde and after dynner about ii
202 of the cl*ocke* // *M. Madd*oxx, M. Lewys and I *were at Newporte* all that day and the nyghte. . . .

[Wed.] The *xvi*th one M. Colman came with commyssyon and ser*ved M. Boze*.

[Thurs.] The xvii the wynde came easte and we sayled *about ii of the clocke* to the south weste and there we stayd the x*viii and on the xix in* the afternoone and then we came to the Cowes agayne. . . .

[Sun.] *The xxth I prea*ched upon the 16 [:23] of John: *si quid petieritis patrem* etc. After ser*vice we dyned on* the Frauncys with captayne Drake: at what tyme the wyn*de came from the easte* and with that wynde we sayled welneere to Yarmouth *wher at n*yghte we ancored.

[Mon.] The xxith we had a northe easte wyn*de* . . . so came to the sea and about iiijor of the clock we ancored within iii *leages of St. Albons* or thereaboutes. To Portelande the same nyghte with the next tyde . . . *al*moste over agaynste Portlande and there ancored in the morninge.

[Tues.] The xxiith *we lay at ancor till the* nexte tyde. Aboute a xi of the clocke in the afternoone sayled and on . . . the xxiii [Wed.] over agaynste Exmouth about xii of the clocke at the eb we sayled iii or iiii^{or} leages further and there ancored about xii of the clock*e*. *The* same nyghte we sayled further and ancored aboute vii of the clocke the*r* . . . almost over agaynste Dartemouthe. The same day we *wayed* with a mery wynde into the sea but were enforced backe agayne to D*art*mouth rode and there we contynued untyll the xxviiith [Mon.] and then in the morning we went backe agayne to Tor Bey and there ancored and stayde untyll the las*t of* May [Thurs.] and in the afternoone about iiii^{or} a clocke we sett sayle and *came* into Plymmouthe Sounde the fyrste of June [Fri.] in the afternoone and there rod. Aboute vi of the clocke, M. Maddox and I wente ashore and supped with captayn*e* Hawykyns, captayne Drake, M. Whytacres at M. Whooddes house, pylate in the Gallyon, but after supper we came aboorde.

[Sat.] The 2 we sett sayle about vi of the clocke in the morninge and sayled alonge the coste of Englande and that nyghte we passed the Lyzard with a good wynde. Captay*ne* Hawkyns lefte beh*ind hys man* [Henry Kirkman].

[Sun.] The 3 beinge Whytsunday I preached of concorde and of the comming of the Holy Ghost and the same day was sea sycke and so contynued untyll the vith day [Wed.], all whyche tyme we had the wynde at north and by east for the most parte and so untyll the ixth.

[Sat.] The 9 at 10 of the clocke in the morninge we mett with a shyppe of *Lu*beck *goinge* upon the Spanyshe seas of whom we learned newes that the kinge of Spayne had prepared (at there comminge from St. Lucas) ix shyppes to go to the Yndies and 11 to the Strayghtes of Brasyle, and that in one of these 11 *go* 50 monkes. At thys tyme we were in 38 degrees from the equynoctyal // . . . . *The xiii* [Wed.] in 35 degrees . . . and 15 [Fri.] . . . we 203r
had the wynde at northe and kept *south southwest*.

[Sat.] *The 16* . . . in the morninge we dyscryed land *which was* some of the Canaria ylandes which lay easte. . . .

[Sun.] The 17 in the morninge we saw the graunde Canar*ie* at easte of us as before and sayled betwyxte Taneryf *and Fortventura* leavinge the Canaries on our lefte hande. This day I pr*eached*. . . . In the afternoone captayne Ward the viceadmirall, the Master, and the pilate wente in our *skyffe to* the Elysabeth who made in to the shore of the Graunde *Canarie* one myle, to the ende to make the lande perfecte and aboute . . . clocke came aboorde the Edwarde agayne. We sawe the pyke of *Teneryf* whyche is thoughte to be in heyghte 54 myles.

[Mon.] The 18 in the morninge there came a calme but in the after noo*ne* the wynde blew a good gale and so contynued at the N.

[Tues., Wed.] The 19 and 20 the same wynde contynued. Upon the 20 in the morninge we entered (as I take it) in to the tropyck Cancer and at noone had the sun for our zenith. (margin: *trop*yck).

[Thurs.] The 21 we had all day a calme but at nyghte the wynde blewe as befor.

[Fri.] The 22 allmoste at nyghte the vyceadmyrall and I in our skyffe wente aboorde the gallyon and because it was nyghte and the wynde blew I was fearefull to enter the skyffe and so stayed all nyghte in the gallyon.

[Sat.] The 23 I lykewyse contynued there.

[Sun.] The 24 M. vyceadmyrall with the master, merchauntes, and pylote came aboorde the galyon where conclusion was had of wateringe at Bonavista, an ylande of Cape Verde and lykewyse of our course to Ryo de Plate there lykewyse to water and refreshe our selves. After supper I came aboorde the Edwarde wherof I was verye gladd for I lyked not the badd enteringe into a shyppe, the wynde blowinge.

[Mon.] The 25 we beinge at dynner (and ther eatinge of a flyinge fyshe which dyd fly into the Elyzabeth and geven us be the captayne) we saw many of these flyinge fyshes. Some of them dyd fly a flyghte shoote [a bow shot]. The fyshe is as bygge as a hearinge and some a greate deale bygger and hathe ii wynges of good lenghe, a verye delyca*te* fyshe to taste. Not ii howers after we sawe a whale. //

203v [26, Tues.] *The vyceadmyrall took a tortuse with a shell* lyke to a horne of *yvory and of such h*ardnesse that a carte goinge laden *could ryde on* her. She goethe on her bellye but . . . bellye of the lyke hardnesse and her . . . close to that she goethe on. She was of *the strength to* *carrie me s*yttynge upon her backe layinge my legges a crosse . . . She was taken ingendringe with her mate, this beinge *so* she was very monstrous to looke [on], her necke covered with a *roughe* skynne and lyke an oxe skynne but not hearye, her headde had *a very* harde shell, her fleshe to looke lyke to veale and is in taste. *About ii* of the clock in the afternoone M. Captayne Warde wente with *the skyff* to enter the lande to seeke for freshe water, but when they cam to shore the sea wente to hyghe that they were not able *to bring the boat ashor*. Only ii of our men, vidz. [Thomas] Russell and Markes [Towghts] swoemed a lande where *were great* store of goates but no freshe water for they were not paste halfe *way* in the lande.

[Wed.] The nexte daye in the morninge beinge the 27 we *wer* to have watered and have proved further (for doubtless there was plenty) but the Generall wolde not staye but in the after n*oone* set sayle and awaye they wente. Notwithstandinge the ii barkes d*id go* neere the shore and founde a convenyente landynge place, for one . . . went upon lande. Ther departure (wantinge water) was agaynst Captayne Wardes w*yll* and myne.

[Thurs.] The 28 we descryed the ylande of Maio and had a good gale betweene the N. and the E.

[Fri.] The 29 in the afternoone a greate calme whych contynued untyll the fyrste of Julye and then a very lyttle wynde.

[July]

[Sun.] The 1 of July I preached *ex* Luca the 15 [:4] *de ove perdita* etc.

[Mon.] The 2 we had a good gale begynnynge in the morninge but not contynuinge untyll nyght. This tyme there was found abuses amongste some of the companye which dyd not alyttle greeve our captayne, consyderinge the greate care he contynuallie had to keepe them in peace: *causa propterea quid biberunt, illo ignoto: aliquantulum vini et cervisiae; capiunt mori* etc.

[Tues.] The 3 the Captaynes greyfe was suche and so increased by reas*on* of the premysses that he grewe towardes sycknesse, but at lenghe by Goddes helpe he recovered, castinge his care upon

Chryste. This daye I delyvered lessons unto them of the want they should sustayne lackinge a guyde etc. //

204r [Sun.] *The 8 I preached* ex Luca 6 [:36] *estote misercordes. The sm*ythe dyed and was caste ore boorde. . . . *The* 13, 14, and 15 we had the wynde at S com*inge now* in a daungerous clymate in latitude 7 degrees where . . . they have, for we had almoste no sunne shyne but wynd. . . .

[Sun.] *The 15* I preached *ex* 1 Peter 3 [:8] *estote unanimes* etc.

[Mon.–Thurs.] *The* 16, 17, 18, and 19 we had the wynde at Soth and had mutche *rayne and fogg.*

[Fri.] *The* 20 in the morninge about ix of the clocke we fell upon the *coste of Gu*inea when as all the cunnyinge maryners thoughte us *50 leag*es of that place. The curraunt ranne very stronge along *the coste.* We thoughte our selves to be within 4 *degrees of the lyne* and *on th*e 21 we lay alonge the coste but went *not in* with the sh*ore*. Yett our vyce admyrall and I used all meanes possyble to have h*is* men refreshed but the generall withstoode us etc.

[Sun.] The 22 I preached *ex* Matheo 5 [:20]: *nisi iustitia vestra* etc.

[Mon.] The 23 we bore of from the coste of Guinea, but contynuall*y* we had greate showers of rayne and the ayre verye dystemperate. This nyghte one Roberte [Wood] a trumpeter dyed.

[Tues.] The 24 we had a more temperate ayre.

[Wed.] The 25 William Dye [Dee], a sayler departed this lyfe.

[Thurs.] The 26 M. Maddoxe, Captayne Hawkyns and Captayne Drake came aboorde us where we were merye with a dolphyn our vyce admyrall had kylled that morninge. Abou*t* 4 of the clocke M. Maddox in our boate was sett aboorde the gallyon. Captayne Hawkyns wente aboorde the barke Frauncys with Captayne Drake. I sente a leter by M. Maddox to the generall wherein I sorowed the greate sycknesse happened amongste our companye (for then had we 30 men infected with some sycknesse) and lykewyse the wante of water, complayning of our not wateringe at the ylandes of Cape Verde etc.

[Fri.] The 27 the ayre grewe to be verye temperate with some sonne shynynge. //

[28, Sat.] *The generall* reproved *the vyce admyrall with* these wordes, 204[v]
vidz., I . . . wyll rule and I knowe what is go*od to be done. I will be* obeyed and wyll commaunde everye man in th*e company, the hin*deste and the beste with many suche w*ordes.* Our Captayne M. W*ard to thes* greate speaches reAwneswered nothinge more t*han in* the manner, defendinge the good husbandrye was *that we shold* water, but in truthe the cause he [Fenton] so hardelye dea*lt was* for a Jelosye he conceyved agaynste me by reason of *a letter* M. Maddox sente me that daye by M. Banister whyche leter *he in*tercepted and redde, (but the same beinge in Latyn he *could not under*stand it for that he understoode not Latyn perfectlye) and ymagin*yng* some secrett practyses betwyxte us two after many re*marks* on his syde bytterly passed, we ceassed our talke, I desyring *a* more pryvate place to speake in, for he spoke openly to all *within* hearinge. The generall wente downe with our Captayne into the h*old* and I to salute M. Banister who tolde me of a letter M. Maddox *sent* me but intercepted by the Generall. We passed the tyme for *i* or ii howres in veywinge our sycke people and in some other conf*erence* but my wordes were they never so reasonable were unpleasa*nt* to the Generall. Styll he standinge upon his aucthorytye, as tho*ugh* I wente about to infrynge the same. At lenghe he and our vyce admyrall syttinge above in the poope I demaunded openly for a letter M. Maddox sente me which I understoode he had: he dynyed not the letter but sayde he had to talke with me about it. The vyce admyrall departed and he entered speache in . . . manner chargynge me with M. Maddox letteres. I excused my selfe as ygnoraunte of any matter betwyxte us that myghte concerne hym and the lyke I thoughte I myghte saflye say of M. Maddox, but he wolde accepte no excuse but urged me styll with the letter. I requested to see the same who graunted I shoulde see it but not have it: when I had readd it and perceyved the matter in the. . . . // other shyppinge yf we took*e* 205[r]
. . . *w*herwithall our men broughte from those . . . restytutyon when we come home to En*glande* . . . *colde* he do it lawfully or no: I sayde he myght *but that evil shold* not be done that good may insue: upon this . . . but in the ende I perswaded hym it w*ere unlawfull* to take any thinge which is not our owne. Other mat*ters he offered and* lyke motyons, but I lyked of no one proposytyon be*inge one and* all repugnaunt agaynste the worde of God. In fyne *we conclud*ed in frendeshyppe, savinge that in these questions

of *spoiling oth*er mens goodes, for thereunto wolde I not nether (by Godds *grace*) *agree or* consente unto. And in truthe I spoke my opynyon verye fr*eely and* I perceyved he was purposed to goe into the South Seas but *thereu*nto wylle not I agree. About 6 of the clocke receyving *fr*endely vale, they went aboorde, but his comminge was to no end . . . of betteringe our condytyon more then this: one M. Cottonn a gent*leman in the Gallyon* wrote unto me (with whom I had very small famylyarytye): the ge*ne*rall lykewyse intercepted his letter but that letter after he had shewed me the same and I readd it, he kepte it but wolde not delyver it for some wordes conteyned there: which were that he was sorye there was no better agreement amongste us: but (in truthe) what his meaninge was herein I understoode not. Before the Generall and I ceassed talkinge, I requested hym verye earnestlye to deale with Ferdynand the pylote to deale with more contynence in his conversatyon and with more modestie in his speaches, for that they were (as I affyrmed) offensyve to God, and nothinge chrystyanlyke, for that he rejoysed in thinges starke naughte*y*, bragginge in his sondrye pyracyes. The generall dyd assure me of Amendement And so we departed. //

205v [Tues.] *The 31 at 4* degrees and all the *wynd from* the S.

[August]

[Wed.] *The firste* of Auguste in the afternoone about 3 *of the clocke* the *general* shewed his flagge in the waste of the shy*ppe and shot off a p*eece whereat the vyceadmirall, the merch*ants* [Randoll Shaw and Peter Jeffrey], *the p*ylote [Thomas Blacollar], and I wente aboorde, where we concluded (a cou*nsel having byn* called) upon dyvers consyderatyons to returne to *the coa*ste of Guinea to the ryver of Surleona to water: . . . we caste about and kepte our course for the moste *N*. . . .

[Thurs.] The seconde we made our way as before.

[Fri.] The thirde there dyed in the Galyon ii men, the one be*ing* [Edward] Stokes a younge man, a plott drawer, the other a baker [David Evans] an*d* lykewyse this day dyed one of our men, a cowper. In the afternoo*ne* aboute 6 of the clocke we dyscryed lande.

[Sat.] The 4 in the morninge we bore in with the coaste of Guinea suppos*ing* the same to have byn Surleona but we founde it a mayne land and a fayre baye called Cape de Monte for the bark Elysabethe wente harde a shore and there ancored, and some of our men wente a shore where they founde freshe water and a ponde of freshe fyshe and dyvers frutes as pomegranates and sawe lyttle howses but no people but because the bay was open to the sea we wolde not staye there but made into the sea and sayled a longe the coaste and founde it all a meyne lande contrary to all our plottes and cardes as we ymagyned but it happened otherwyse for we were farre of Surleona and that was parte of Matrobomba.

[Sun.] The 5 I preached *ex* Math. 7 [: 15] *cavete a pseudoprophetis* [attendite falsis prophetis] and this was a day of rayne for the moste parte all day, and styll we sayled in syght of the fyrme lande whyche is all full of trees and a lowe lande but lyklye to be verye full of frutes, // [6, 7, Mon., Tues.] . . . but styll upon . . . sayle at 206r 10 of the clocke . . . contynually the water ebbeth and *flows* . . . *sup*posed towardes Surleona: but . . . *a*heed came suche a hawse and suche gr*eate rayne and fog* . . . that we were constrayned to Ancore. . . . loste the syghte of the Elyzabethe which . . . that the ancor of the barke the nyghte bef*ore* and they constrayned to sett sayle in the nyghte, but. . . .

[8, Wed.] The nexte the Elyzabeth ovetooke us; this *day at* 11 of the clocke one of our Saylors whose name is Markes [Towghts] was possessed of a *spirit and I* by the power of God throughe me his mynyster he was dyspos*sessed* and . . . we sayled alonge the shore of Guynea from *5 in the afternoone* but ancored everye nyghte.

[Thurs.] And the 9 we fell *in with Surleona* and ancored within a leage of the watringe place.

[Fri.] *The* 10 we halled in to the shore for there blewe no wynd. . . . *A*bout 10 of the clocke with that tyde we came to ancor *a mile short of the watringe place.* And same day in the afternoone the vyceadmirall and I with some more of our companye tooke *our* skyffe and wente to shore desyrous to knowe what the countrey was . . . and gardinge our selves we wandered in the woodde*s* beinge wylde wyldernes*se* where we sawe man*y* kyndes of trees and greate dyversytyes of frutes and founde many lymmons growinge whereof we broughte greate store aboorde; we sawe the footinge of certeyne beastes and lykewyse the dunging whiche we ymagyned to be of elephantes. The countrey is full of trees and wooddes but verye frutefull with grasse. There be many monckeyes and parats whereof I sawe greate nomber. The countrey is a very wylde wyldernesse. I saw a tall . . . a beaste and rubbed the heyghte wherof I code not reach by 1/4 of a yard.

[Sat.] The 11 I wente a shore in the common wateringe place where I met M. Maddox and others of the galyon: M. Maddox and I with iii more [Evans, Cotton, and Fairweather] wente ii myles into the countrey but sawe no more then before I sa*we*.

[Sun.] The 12 we had a communyon and I preached *ex* Luca 16 [:2] *redde rationem* vil*licationis tuae*. In the Afternoone the generall sente M. Maddox and the master of the gallyon to me to requeste me to goe aboorde the Elysabethe. //

206v [13, Mon.] *We assembled aboorde the Galyon* where we harde *M. Skevingtons accusation and agreed to give* the master [Rafe Crane of the bark *Elizabeth*] worthy punyshm*ent* . . . *ap*poynted which was to sytt in the by*lboes*: *punish*ment folowed but mytygated at our req*uest*. *He* was not in ther 10 Minutes. We dyned aboord *the Galyon*: *after* dyner I came to the Edwarde etc.

[14, Tues.] The generall came aboorde the Edwarde with whom I *had con*ference a longe space, bothe concernynge our present estat*e and a*ccydences as were lyke to happen in the voyage. After *dyned I*, the generall and vyce Admirall together and wente a shore *where we fou*nde M. Maddox and dyvers others of the Galyon: I . . . washed my selfe in the freshe water and afterwarde went up into the woodd where I sawe dyvers sortes of fr*utes* and trees where out yssued, the same beinge cutt, dyvers so*rtes* of gummes: as some redde whych I judged to be dragons*eede*, some whyte as mylke but beinge a lyttle dryed it wolde ho*ld* lyke byrde lyme or. . . . The frutes were very gr*een* and the trees with blossomes whereby I gather that it was the springe not withstandinge the sonne was there zenith; for t*he* sonne broughte greate store of rayne and the sonne beinge . . . ther of wolde be hot ynouughe to rypen the frutes and *make* a sommer. About v of the clocke Captayne Hawkins came to us and broug*ht* with hym some fresh fyshe which we had after sodd in the kettle wherein the water was made hott for the washynge of our clothes: and lykewyse we had greate store of oysters sodde whereof th*ere* is greate aboundaunce growinge upon the trees whyche grow*e* by the sea syde, the trees so standinge that at a full sea the water flowethe up the bodyes of the trees so farre as the oysters growe, but when it ebbe they stande without water: the trees are lyke our wyllowes or olers [alders], as bygge as a mans legge or Arme. We supped with this dyett in the woodd by a runninge water which yeelded us good drincke: afterwarde we came a boorde, but it was within nyghte before we came aboorde: it is seene there commonly every nyghte upon *the* coaste greate lyghteninge and thunderinge *and* all nyghte commonly rayne. We sawe a reere mouse [sea bat] in the *woo*dde as bygge at [*sic*] a henne. The trees are alwayes full of lemmons. //

[15, Wed.] *This* thinge is to be noted . . . almoste 40 of our men syck *with scur*by: it takethe them in there legges. . . . *m*ayme and makethe them lame, the flesh bec*omes soft and swell*eth in the knees: lykewyse they are very so*re* . . . that there teethe growe loose and there gummes *swell*; *God be* praysed we see some of them to amende of there m*ouths, scouring* them with the yuce of lymmons and there legges to be be*tter by bathy*nge them in runninge freshe water and walkinge on the sh*ore*. 207r

[16, Thurs.] . . . *tod*ay we receyved certayne thinges from the Elysabeth for dyvysy*on between the* Generall and the vyceadmirall of suche thinges as were lefte un*divided*.

[17, Fri.] . . . we tooke in more water and broughte to our shyppes the tym*ber squar*ed and framed for our foremaste. In the afternoone I went aboorde the *gal*lyon, the generall beinge then at shore, who came aboorde before *I w*ente away, and because I tolde hym the vyceadmirall was sycke, he ca*me wit*h me to the Edwarde and there supped, he and Captain Parker.

[Sat.] *T*he 18 about a 11 of the clocke in the forenoone we dyscryed a verye lyttle boate call*ed a* cannow comminge rowinge towarde our shyppes with 3 men in it whom we ymagyned to be Negroes; Captain Parker manned the pynnyse of the galyon and to shore they rowed to take in the men that were on shore for we suspected the Negroes had be*gun to* come downe upon us: the vyceadmirall he manned his skyffe and takinge M. Jeffrey one of our merchauntes with hym who caryed a whyte flagge in the poope of the boate in token of peace: and by that tyme the boate was a lyttle from the shyppe the cannowe was come to the galyon (who in deede were Portyngales) and fayling *of* there holde were caste a sterne by reason of the goinge of the tyde but our skyffe meetinge them tooke them in and so wente aboorde the Galyon: who were well inte*r*tayned of the generall, of whom we learned the state of this countrey: (for they we*re* merchauntes and used this countrey [to] traffycke, the cheyfe of them dwelleth and [*sic*] San tyago, an yl*and* of Cape de Verde) certyfyinge us that the kinges neere dwellinge were cruell to chrystyans etc. and that the kinge of Spayne had sente xx seale [sail] of shyppes who were gone to the Straytes of Magellane and lykewyse vi shyppe*s* of Frenche men who were gone the same way in to the South *sea* wh*ych* French men as they sayde watered at the same place we *were*.... ||

207v [19, Sun.] *I preached ex* Luca the 19: Jesus . . . Ther wente a shore to solac*e themselves the men of* bothe our boates: we wente up the woo*dd and to the oister* bay were be a marveylous aboundaunce of *trees of* straunge proportyon: there we mett with captayne *Hawkyns, captayne Parker, and some* of the galyons men. There we dys*cryed* . . . syde by the wyldernesse and afterwarde we came to *the Edwarde and* they to the Galyon.

[20, Mon.] . . . the vyceadmirall tooke the skyffe and with hym the master and pylott and wente to e*xplore the bay*s and ryvers in the harbour: I wente to the generall with whom I *spent the* daye sometymes in conference with him: otherwhyles in other exercyses and *talk with* M. Maddox: at nyghte the viceadmirall sente the skyffe for me and I ca*me aboorde*.

[Tues.] *T*he 21 in the morninge the vyceadmyrall and I wente aboorde the galyon to the gener*all*. *Th*e generall with the master and M. Maddox and captayne Parker were gone into the ryver to dyscove*r the nature thereof*. We had broken our faste with some freshe fyshe which Captayne Hawkyns cawsed *to be* made ready for us: we tooke 2 nettes to goe a fyshing up into the *ryver* that goeth from oyster bay into the wooddes, where when we were land*ed we* sett our nettes, for the tyde beganne to go out: as we were thus busye we cha*unced* to espye a greate crocodyle in the water, whom we besett with our nettes *but* coulde not take hym: at lenghe after mutche beatinge up and downe af*ter* hym, we sett our selfes in order, some with calyvers, some with fyshgygges, *some* with speares and other with swordes and targetts, purposinge to fyghte it out with hym with whom we had mutche a doe to avoyde the daunger of hym. At laste Captayne Hawkins caste a fyshgygge in into hym under the hynder legge whereat he made at the neereste man and withall gaped with his mouthe which was monstrous to looke upon: the viceadmirall beinge ready with his calyver shott into his mouth which intered into his throte whereat he was amased but yett yeelded not: the pylot [Blacollar] shot his fysh*gygge* at hym who lefte some peeces of it in the fore legge. Dyvers stroked *hy*m with swordes, with pykes but coulde nothinge hurte hym: in truthe we had verye warlyke battayle with hym, but in fyne we conquered hym and // . . . 208r

*After we ky*lled hym we broughte hym to the *Gallyon where he was opened and flayed, in* whose belly was gravell and *his hart did smel* as muske and so dyd he hym selfe. . . . *After* we had passed the tyme in myrthe and had *groen weary, we wente* aboorde our owne shyppe. When this beaste *was skynned ther was founde* under his eares muske and under his fore*legges gr*aynes *of* muske. Certayne men of this countrey dyd *not thinke that* we durste attempte the kyllinge of this beaste for he *feedeth on land and u*sed to eate the Negroes whom he met withall nyghe the s*hore*.

[Wed.] *The 22* the Portyngales accordinge to there promyse came with *other Portingales and Negroes and broug*hte the ryce and the ellephantes teethe for the barke Elyz*abeth*: *the vyc*eadmirall and I wente aboorde the Galyon, he fyrste in the skyffe and after I, to the Generall where we *met with th*e Portyngales whom we saluted: the cheyfe Portyngale gave the *generall a* Negro boy. At dynner we enquyred of the Portyngales the state and c*ondition of th*is countrey and of the lawes used by the people under there king. (*Lewis Henriques on*e of these Portyngales dwelleth here). He tolde us the chyefeste we*alth* of the kynges is (one kynge called Farma, the other Toro) there . . . *sla*ves, some ryce, some elephaunte teeth and some golde. When any merch*aunt de*syrethe to buy bonde slaves, the kynge within 10 dayes wyll provyd*e* 300 or 400 which they wy*nne* by warres of there enemyes. The king hathe 2 or 300 wyves who worke for his wealthe in gatheringe of ryce, etc. The fyrste wyfe is the cheyfeste and her sone injoyeth the crowne: yf she [be] barren, then the nexte, etc.: yf the kynge

dye leavinge his sonnes under yeares of dyscretyon to governe, then he appoyntethe the eldest of his kynred to be his proctectour who shall governe the kyngedome but yf the kynges sone duringe this protectours lyfe come to his yeares, yet he, the protectour, wyll be kynge duringe his owne lyfe. They have *legem talionis*, an eye for an eye, a tothe for a tothe: for he that kylleth shall *be* kylled, and yf he escape then shall dye the reste of his kynred; yf anie be in debte and have not to pay, he shall sell all he hathe: at laste than *must he be* solde hym selfe to make restytutyon: when the kynge dyethe, his concubyn*s* or wyves shalbe put to deathe with hym: yf a man be taken in adulter*y* havinge a wyfe he shall fyne [pay a fine] for it, but she shall goe free, because he (said they) myght have had ynoughe of fleshlye appetyte with his wyfe, but the woman not of one man. This people knowethe
208v there is a god but // . . . elephaunts teeth . . . wh*o is buryed with h*is beste wyves and some plate whom they say *will intercede for them*: *they* thinke there soles walke on earthe etc.

[23, Thurs.] . . . wente aboorde the Galyon for . . . the other concerninge there merchaundyse: our *master and carpenters went aland. It* was a daye of mutche rayne and so was eve*ry day*. This day we tooke a sea hedgehogge.

[24, Fri.] Being Saint Barthelmewes daye the Generall and Captain Parker came *to see the vy*ceadmirall. After dynner the vyceadmirall, Captayne Parker, M. Maddox, and I . . . wente a shore, and our men to gather lymmons. Captayne Parker and I went *to the* wooddes where we came into a fayre launde [glade or pasture] convenyent to hu*nt wy*lde beastes whereof there are greate nomber: but before we colde co*me back it* rayned so mutche that we were well wett: neere unto the lymmons . . . there is a tre lyke unto an ashe tree of marveylous grow*th b*othe in the compasse which is 13 fadomme and in the manner of growing *which was* indented with walls rysynge from the roote to the myddeste of the tree: a*nd* at nyghte we came aboorde.

[Sat.] The 25 the Portyngales who boughte the barke Elyzabeth came aboorde the Edwarde and *ther* dyned: at dynner he tolde us of kynge Ferma, a notable wytche who wolde d*o* woonderfull thinges, as transforme hym selfe in any lykenesse etc. and so wolde h*is* sonne, and yf he laye with a woman all nyghte, in the morninge he wolde kyll her and eat her yf he lyke her not and that yf merchauntes seeke trafycque, they presente hym with a peece of wyne, and he geveth them for there safe conduycte no wrytinge but only a slave to wayte on them, but yf he geve them one of his wyves to goe with them that is a sure conduycte.

[Sun.] The 26 Captayne Hawkyns and dyvers of the galyon came to heare me preach and I preached *ex* Luca 18 [:10]: *duo ascendebant in templum* etc. and they that came dyned with the vyceadmirall and after dynner we all together wente a shore and there we sawe the goinge of an elephaunt whom we folowed // *but saw him not.* 209r

[27, Mon.] ... find some on shore ... but the galyon. ...

[28, Tues.] *The Port*yngales came and broughte us he*nnes and oren*ges with whom the merchauntes had some *trafficque* of the Negroes. The Generall dyslyked with the men *for there s*ellinge them commodytyes very cheape for they had not 2 [double] of a *value*. ...

[29, Wed.] . . . the vyceadmiral with Captayne Parker and other that they tooke with them s*et out* to hunte the elyphaunte but prevayled not and at lenghe *returned w*eary.

[30, Thurs.] ... our longe boate wente to be rygged a shore and our skyffe was se*nt out* to fyshe and in the afternoone about 4 of the clocke the generall w*ith Captayne Parker* and Captayne Drake came aboorde the Edwarde and broughte with them *the Negroes and Por*tyngales whom the generall examyned concerninge thinges solde by some of our fleete but he founde no cause in them of offend*ing. The* generall and the other supped with us and after supper Captayne Drake made a dyscours*e of* some of Sir Frauncys Drakes voyage and allso his extremytyes *on h*is voyage: this done they departed to there shyppes.

[Fri. The 31 I sente my man Yevan [Evan Wyn] to gather lemmons: in the afternoone our skyffe came aboorde whyche in the morninge wente a fyshinge and broughte good store of fyshe: the Portyngales stayd supper and beinge nyghte before we wente to supper, we called for candles (the table beinge covered under an Awninge upon the sommer decke) but presentlye there happened suche aboundaunce of contynuall lyghteninge without ceasinge that the same mynystered suffycyent lyghte to suppe by, but afterwarde there folowed greate thunder and rayne. This daye one of our merchauntes, M. Jeffrey shott with a goonn at a buffe and stroke her but she escaped.

[September]

[Sat.] The fyrste of September aboute 4 of the clocke in the morninge the wynde beinge NE: (for everye day moste commonly before it was at SW: and betwyxte the S and W:), we wayed ancor and
209v hoysed our sayles to // *depart but the wind was sla*cke which presently *calmed*.... Here harde by the sh*ore were great piles of shells the* Negroes had made and some ty*mes of the year they come hither but now b*e gone: there houses are mad lyke . . . with the boughes of the palmyto tr*ee* . . . and a lyttle scaffolde of forkes whereon theye. . . . *They* goe all naked; this place is full of palmito tr*ees through* all the countrey. The meate of it is good which grow *60 or 70 foot* uppe; And where it is reported that the Coaste of Gu*ynea is d*aungerous in contagyon of sycknesse we founde it ve*ry whol*esome more then sycknesse which we had with eatinge *the fru*tes of the countrey and I take the frutes which men have ea*ten* to cause the sycknesse when they have complayned of the sonn *and* of the ayre: after the generall was gone from *us*, the Vyceadmirall and I with some other wente throughe the wood*ds to* the necke of a lande unto a very fayre bay and there w*e* wente alonge the sea more then a myle and then returned *to the baye* where we went a fyshinge agayne and caughte greate s*tore* of good fyshe and after we had cut a palmito we came *a*boorde.

[Sun.] The seconde we sett sayle in the morninge havinge the winde easterly. I preached *ex* Marco 7 [:37]: *omnia bene fecit* etc. In the after noone Captayne Hawkyns came aboorde us to have the merchauntes pryce certayne clothes he saythe M. Alderman Barnes and M. Towersone had promysed should be taken into the adventure. Our merchauntes wente aboorde with hym to the Galyon but pryced them so hardely that Captayne Hawkins thought hym ill dealte withall etc. After our merchauntes came aboorde some wordes passed from the vyceadmirall but occaysyoned there unto by the badd dealinges *of the* Galyons merchauntes.

[3, Mon.] This day having sayled . . . // *the Generall* went aboord *us and determined* to goe in but the tyde not servinge *we were carried northward with the flud.* 210r

[Tues.] *On the fourthe day by n*eglygence the quarter masters lett *goe an ancor and cable* and we lett fall another.

[Wed.] *On the fifthe day we rod*de into the shore to our wateringe place and there *ancored athwart the* bay: this day the Portyngales came aboorde us.

[Thurs.] *On the sixte day in* the after noone we wente a shore to fyshe with our nett and ca*ught great store and took part aboord the Galyon to the* generall.

[7, Fri.] . . . in the afternoone the vyceadmirall with the Generall wente to fyshe *in the accustomed bay* but the Generall before nyghte came to the barke Frauncys *to suppe* beinge invyted by Captayne Drake where I lykewyse supped and t*here lay a*boorde the barke all nyghte: the vyceadmirall stayed with his men a sh*ore all nyghte* and tooke greate store of fyshe as mullets whereof he *sent some to the g*enerall.

[Sat.] *The* 8 our men wente to fyshe and came home very late: this day we wente *to our w*oonted rode.

[Sun.] *The* 9 I preached in the barke Elyzabeth *ex* Luca 10 [:23]: *beati occuli* and there I mynys*tered* communion and after wente aboorde the galyon. Our captayne wente a fyshinge and *br*oughte home great store: Smythe our paynter was buryed a shore: the *vyce*admyrall sett up a forge on the shore and garded the place with men all nyghte, Captayne Parker hym selfe remayninge with them.

[Mon.] The 10 the vyceadmyrall wente early in the morninge to shoote at a pellycane but by myshappe his peece wente of and myssed them: Captayne Hawkins and M. Maddox ca*me* aboorde to make mery with me and stayed there untyll the vyceadmyrall came and then departed. M. Maddox and M. Hall came and supped with the vyceadmyrall but I was sent for with the Frauncys skyffe to supp aboorde the Frauncys: my man watched on shore with Captayne Parker: *sinapium* [i.e. mustard, see Madox's Diary, 10 Sept.].

[Tues.] The *11* the vyceadmyrall wente with the longe boate wente [*sic*] to sweepe for our cable and Ancor but myssed it: I wente aboorde the Galyon where I founde the generall ready to goe to shore to Captayne Parker who requested my company with whom I and M. Maddox went and there we dyned. After dynner M. Maddox and I with some other wente after certayne buffes which my man broughte worde he had seene amongste the lymmon trees but we founde none, and then we sett on fyre a
210v greate grounde con*sisting* .... || *The Generall and M. Maddox* came aboorde with me to the *Edwarde and supped and they went* aboorde and I to bed.

[Wed.] *The 12* certayne Portyngale marchauntes abyding far *up in the* countrey came downe to us, with whom we ba*rgained to receive at the rate of* 5 bushels of ryce for 3 of salte: I wente with the vyceadmirall *and the Portyngales* aboorde the Galyon and there dyned, with whom we *had dyscour*ce concerninge the state of the countrey etc. After dynner *the vyceadmirall and Captayne* Hawkyns went to shore to Captayne Parker and I to sleepe: after . . . a whyle the generall called for me with whom I had . . . a large dyscourse of all matters in particularytye y*ssues that con*cerne this voyage as our returninge to the ylands of Cape de Verd*e for* our gayninge of wyne etc. but I wolde not yeelde which yf we obtayned not (*inquit*) *our* voyage were utterly overthrowne. The generall and M. Ma*ddox* wente with me to the vyceadmyrall to supper, for the Portyngal*es* were invyted to suppe aboorde the Edwarde with the vyceadmirall. After supper everye one departed to there shyppes and I to bedd. Th*is* nyghte we had 2 turnadoes. Our skyffe drove away but was founde a*gayn*.

[Thurs.] The 13 our men wente a shore to mende our foresayle. The Port*yn*gales were aboorde us, and from us went up into the countrey w*ith* our skyffe (for they had borowed it) to fetche the ryce. This nyghte the campe broke up on shore for captayne Parker by myshappe of a shrubbe receyved hurte in his legge and the turnadoes with wynde and rayne so ve*x*ed them that the bellowes were lefte unwatched and the forge unlooked to.

[Fri.] The 14 our carpenters and our men wente to cutt woodd. At nyghte came aboorde: our saylers murmured for wantinge there suppers and at there small allowaunce for which cause they wolde not sett the watche. The master [Thos. Percy] came into the Captayns Cabbyn where he and I were alone and made there complaynte and grudgynge knowen, who presentley wente forthe amongste them and appeased them with promyse to amende there myslykinge when upon juste cause they myslyked, and with frendelye and wyse perswasyons satysfyed ther myndes. I stayed walkinge upon the hatches untyll 12 of the clocke and then went abedd where I dreamed straungly of my . . . Englande etc. //

[15, Sat.] . . . we two I with a pyke and . . . *went to* the wooddes and [at] lenghe came to the *oister bay where the men had oysters rost*inge in the oven: there I nett a baskett full *and cooked them over* the fyre and the vyceadmyrall and I eate them and were *content with* brookes ale. In the oyster baye one [Thomas] Russell, a man of *the Edwarde tooke a* fyshe which had foughte with a crocadyle and beinge *bytten by the cro*cadyle was constrayned to enter the ose at the shore. . . . *The* fyshe had in her headd a thinge of 20 ynches or there ab*oute like an* arminge sworde of greate strenghe growinge out of her *head* close with the grounde. This sworde (for so I may call it) had . . . 23 thorny pyckes of an ynche longe growinge out of it and on *the other side* . . . 22 so that it was a sawe on both sydes. Our vyceadmyrall hathe. . . . After this about 5 of the clocke we came aboorde havynge *geven* one halfe of the fyshe to the generall, vidz. the hyndermoste parte ther*of in* leng[h]e aboute 5 foote: the other halfe we sodd and eate her which tasteth *lyke unto* a sharke. This nyghte we had a turnado. 211r

[Sun.] The 16 I preached *ex* Luca 17 [:12]: *de decem leprosis*. After dynner the vyceadmyrall and I wente aboorde the generall and there we passed all the afternoone and supped. I and M. Maddox complayned to the other *de miserrimis nostris casibus* etc. Afterwarde we came aboorde aboute 8 of the clocke. This day the generall gave his men new lyveryes of brodd cloth of popyngay greene.

[Mon.] The 17 in the afternoone the vyceadmirall, captayne Parker and bothe the masters [Hall and Percy] wente to sounde the sande on the northerne syde the Surliona and so returned before nyght home agayne etc.

[Tues.] The 18 I wente to shore to angle where I mett captayne Hawkins and captayne Parker wh*o* appoynted to meete me there, where we had merye pastyme with hookinge the lyttle fyshe:

afterwarde we had fyshed we wente to the byrdes nestes which were buylded with greate arte, the same hanginge upon lyttle sprygges over the water. The mouthes or entraunce of the nestes made hanginge downewarde to defende them from monkeyes and Auntes. At lenghe we came aboorde and I went then w*ith them* to supper with the generall. After supper the vyceadmirall sente his bo*ate* for me. //

211ᵛ [19, Wed.] *I talked with the* generall who was *aboord us. The vyceadmirall* was returned from *Pellicane Bay where he shot* a herne. Captayne Parker and M. Maddox *and M. Cotton supped* alltogether, and after supper they depar*ted* to the Galyon. *The generall dicit mihi de insula Saint Hellena* and *de impera. . . .*

[20, Thurs.] . . . *th*e Portingales broughte downe a carvell loded with *Ne*groes slaves: the vyceadmirall wente with the longe boate to sh*oot. Walter Hooker kylled* a monkey which we eate the lyver then and I dyd ea*t the le*gs and the bodye the nexte daye.

[Fri.] The 21 in the morninge the generall sente for the vy*ceadmirall and* me, who at our comminge made knowen unto us an injury *re*ceyed at M. Haulls handes, which was (amongste other w*ordes be*twyxte them) that he sayde he woulde be master whether the genera*ll wold* or no etc. The generall callinge us together into his cabbyn *which* were the vyceadmirall, the leyfetenaunt [Hawkins], captayne Parker, M. Maddox and I, s*ent* for the master and layd open his faulte. The master excused hym s*elfe* as cleere of any juste cryme, and spoke somewhat playnely etc. Th*e gen*erall replyed and sayde, durste he speake suche wordes to *the* queene? Yf he durste not, why dared he presume to speak to hym? After many suche lyke wordes the master was commaunde*d to* departe: and then I beganne the [*sic*] intreate the generall *to mit*ygate the matter with some clemencye (for the wordes the ge*nerall* did charge hym with were justyfyed [confirmed] by the leyfetennaunt) who consented (for he sware he shoulde be dysplaced) upon this condicion that the master shoulde kneele unto hym at dyvyne service tyme and confesse his fau*lte* and aske pardon. The vyceadmirall replyed that althoughe he had her majesties commyssyon yett he had not her royaltye etc. In fyne we concluded that the master shoude confesse the faulte and requeste the generalls frendeshyppe wherunto he wyllynglye condyscended [consented], which at prayer tyme he performed. The vyceadmirall and I departed to our shyppe ymedyatelye. After dynner the vyceadmirall and I in our boate wente a shore where we angled in a lyttle ryver and tooke some lyttle fyshes with which pastyme we recreated our selves 2 howres. Afterwarde we wente thence and passinge *o*ver the lawnds and interinge the wooddes we espyed M. Maddox. . . . // *It would not a*stonyshe me consy*dering they* had 212r *cursed* there nati*v*ity . . . for they laye fettered together *like prisoners*, . . . eatinge there meate lyke dog*s*. . . . we wente aboorde: after supper came the Portyngale from the *carvel and* there promysed the vyceadmirall a Negro: he wente *ashore and I to* bed.

[Sat.] *The* 22 the vyceadmyrall and I wente to Pellycane Bay to shoote but we were so pelted with rayne that I beinge but in *c*amblett [light wool and cotton cloth] was wett throughe to my skynne: one of our company *shot at a* peacocke and stroke her, who runne into the bushes and we *folowing* her happened upon a bees nest who troubled us so sore w*ith stingin*ge us that we were fayne for our beste defence to beta*ke to* our feete: the vyceadmirall seeinge this battall betwyxte us and them *h*elde his hatt aboute his eares and styll laughinge at the sk*yrm*yshe wente thence: in the ende the boate came for us and *we lea*vinge peacocke and all wente a boorde.

[Sun.] The 23 I preached *ex* Math: 6 [:24]: *nemo potest duobus dominos servire* etc. Whyle I was preachinge the captayne Portyngale [Matthew Ferdinando] with more of his company came aboorde and broughte the vyceadmirall his promysed Negroe which is a chylde of viii yeares: they dyned with us: and after dynne*r* the vyceadmirall and I wente aboorde the Galyon to see the generall where we stayed all daye and stayed supper. Afterwarde we came a boorde, but whyle we were there the Portyngale captayne came aboorde and fayne wolde have byn gone with his carvell to whom we gave Awneswere that for asmutche as they had our skyffe with them up the ryver and xii barrells of Salte for the which salte we shoulde have had 20 barrels of ryce, we thoughte it no reason to suffer them to departe untyll bargayne[s] were performed because they were straungers unto us and thereupon *we* concluded that he should go and fetche downe our skyffe and ryce which he promysed to do. //

212v [24, 25 Mon., Tues.] *M. Maddox* and I wente to the Fra*uncys wher Willyam Markham was* very sycke and speachlesse: abo*ut* . . . *in the afternoone* he dyed and that nyghte was bury*ed* . . . in the wooddes. After he was buryed I *came aboord*: the vyceadmyrall called me and the master to his cabby*n wher he gave us a* rehersall of an intente the generall had (for th*e generall was a*boorde us that afternoone) to go backe to the ylandes *of Cape de Verde* and there to staye and gyve chase to everye shyppe *he colde fynde* to thende to furnyshe hym selfe of a longe tyme provy*sion for a* further purpose, and requyred our opynions: to whom I *awnes*wered (for in truthe I knewe all the generalls purpose bef*ore as* he had dealte pryvately with me: but coulde not wynne *me*) to returne backe were not only an overthrowe of our whole v*oyage* but suche and so greate a dyscredyte to the churche of God and *my* professyon that the enemye myghte have greate cause of try*umphe* to heare that 2 professours of the gospell shoulde in so noble actyon become pyrates and I wyshed rather to dye then any *suche* myscheyfe shoulde happen unto us with many other wordes to th*at* ende, *idque lacrimis*: the master in lyke manner was unwyllinge *to* retyre backe etc. The vyceadmirall when he harde my wordes dyd not on*ly* rejo[y]se but shewed what it was to leave so noble a enterpryse so and n*ot* to go on in our voyage and allso verye greately with zeale preferred my opynyons sayinge and protestynge that with the losse of his lyfe he wolde performe the opynyon the nobylytye of Englande had of hym and good wyll the merchaunts dyd beare *and would* beare hym: and we concluded by the helpe of God to gett forwarde, whether the generall dyd or no: but fyrste we thought *u*s needefull to perswade hym to go on the voyage: because we wolde not do any thinge rashelye etc.
213r In fyne the vyceadmyrall gave // *promyse that we woulde go* for*ward to* the Moluccoes but . . . and there to have inhabyted and *traffyqued with the* shyppes had come that way from the Yndes.

[Wed.] *The 26* verye early I wente with M. Maddox to shore who *caused us to go* alonge eastewarde on the Southe shore in the woo*ddes wher never* ther any of our fleete ever went untyll we came ov*er a ry*ver that goes to Ygaryna, a towne of the Negroe*s*. . . . . We bewayled our myseryes etc. and concluded to make trya*l whether* we coulde wynne the generall to goe on the voyage. *We* returned and so came a boorde: this day one of our sayl*ors*

*La*wrence Tryppe dyed and at nyghte I buryed hym on shor*e*. *Th*is daye the kinge sente his sonne and his chamberlayne to the Generall with a pres*ent of* a monkey and an elephauntes toothe who sente the kinge backe agayne a yar*d and 1/2* of stammell [linsey-woolsey, usually dyed red] and to his queene a wroughte smocke and a lookinge glasse.

[Thurs.] *The* 27 the vyceadmyrall in the morninge takinge the master with hym, very earlye wente to shoote *the* pellycane and to fyshe with the new nett who broughte good store of fyshe aboorde. *In* the meane season the Negroe chamberlayne came aboorde the Edwarde, whom *I* receyved and intertayned in the vyceadmiralls absence (who was wyllynge and consented I thanke hym of that I dyd): the Negro broughte hym an elephauntes toothe but because he was not a boorde he wolde not leave it behynde hym. I gave the Negro a buffe yelow gyrdle which he receyved with greate curtesye. This daye our men had greate pleasure in huntynge buffes.

[Fri.] The 28 the vyceadmirall, M. Maddox and I with other wente a fyshynge where we had good pastyme and at nyghte came home and supped alltogether aboorde the Edwarde etc.

[Sat.] The 29 beinge St. Mychells day at after dynner the vyceadmirall and I havinge determyned before to deale playnely with the generall for the goinge forwarde (yf it pleased God) in our pretended voyage. When we came aboorde hym the vyceadmirall began to commu*n*e with hym concerninge the Portyngales who had taken our skyffe etc. At lenghe the vyceadmirall upon that occasyon called me and M. Maddox unto hym to aske our opynyons what he myghte do in conscyence in respecte of that matter etc. We replyed as we thought beste etc. Whereupon I beganne to speake of our goinge to the ylandes of Cape de Verde // . . . who be heere . . . for he was stayed in his *design*. 213v
The vyceadmirall at lenghe takinge . . . wolde not take effecte, verye chrysty*anly*. . . . whether he did goe on or no, yett he wolde by go*ing have* respected the honorable voyage, his dutye to her m*ajesties pryvye* councell and the love he bore to the merchauntes . . . allso donne etc. When the generall sawe how he was p*resentlye reso*lved with hym to take parte with us and to be as forwarde and *it was agreed to this* end upon this conclusyon after many more

wordes amongste *those who* were presente: Captayne Haukyns, Captayne Parker, M. Maddox and I. We stayed *to* supper: and after supper we wente to the Portyngales shyppe *and* tooke there sayles from them because we suspected they w*olde have* byn gone: and so have deceyved us of our skyffe and the ryce we ba*rgayned* with them for: the vyceadmyrall sente for the master [Percy], the pylote [Blacollar], and the 2 merch*aunts* [Shaw and Jeffrey] into his cabbyn to whom he made knowen the generalls devyse and pur*pose.*

[Sun.] The 30 in the morninge our men broughte a boorde a mons*trous* fyshe which they had taken in a nett beinge 7 foote in lenghe and 4 and a *half* in thycknesse only havinge 2 legges before: her mouthe lyke the m*outh* of a cow and therefore we tooke it for a sea cowe: the meate was *very* good and delycate. Upon the occasyon of this straunge fyshe the vycea*dmyrall* sente for the generall to come see it: where after vewe thereof the generall wente into the vyceadmiralls cabbyn where were lykwyse with hym captayne Hawkins, captayne Parker, M. Maddox and I and makinge offer of matter for the voyage beganne to tell us of some extremytyes lyke to happe for wante of foode which was Awneswered by all men etc.: then he alledged the greatnesse of our shyppes, how unfytt they were for dyscoverye etc. That matter was debated of and the 2 pylottes, M. Whoode and M. Blacke-coller, were called, and there opynyons asked: we concluded our [men] shoude fynde water ynoughe etc. Then the generall wolde of us what way was moste fytt whether throughe Magellanns
214r Strayghtes or by Cape of Good Hope // . . . as good and to hav*e* . . . but the vyceadmirall as he dyd before *spoke* . . . of the voyage etc. All with which . . . some harde speeches betw*yxt Captain Hawkins and Captain* Parker but was appeased by us and so parted frendes: this done *we went to serv*is: but because it was 12 of the clocke I dyd not preache. . . . *The* reste dyned aboorde us. [In] the meane *season* the Portyngales comminge downe the ryver with the ry*ce for our salt*, we all wente to walke on the shore and returned *to the Ed*warde agayne and there supped with the meate of the sea cow . . . *a* very good banquett: this after noone we tooke in some ryce: in *the morning*e amongste other conference and talke the generall made a great doub*te of the* passage of our shyppes for there greatnesse and more affyrmed that our

marchandy*ze at the Mol*uccas wolde not buy us vytayles. This I harde M. Whoodd affyrme.

[October]

[Mon.] *The* fyrste of October early in the morninge the generall sente for the vyceadmyrall and me: when we came thyther he called us to gether, vidz. the viceadmyrall, Captayne Hawkins, Captayne Parker, M. Maddox and me and there made manyfeste dyvers injuryes he sustayned at M. Evans handes etc. M. Evans was called for and there denyed nothinge; he was urged with all but earnestlye desyred to be dysmyssed and that he rather wolde be in Eingland than heere: and that the Portyngales wolde carrye hym home etc., as appeareth by the Artycles wherunto are our handes. Upon which cause we consented he shoulde go: yett notwithstanding M. Maddox and I labored with hym to staye with us, and procured M. Taylboys to entreate his stayinge but prevayled not. At afternoone M. Maddox and I went a shore and there *promissis datis tamquam fratres in Christo . . . permanere* we came aboorde and after supper the vyceadmyrall, Captayne Hawkyns, Captayne Parker and I wente aboorde the Portyngales to buy some of there slaves (for dyvers of our men were deadde) where we perswaded Yevans to staye with moste earneste requestes where with any man myghte well have byn moved, but he was obstynate etc. We had 4 Negroes and there we had a boy which the vyceadmyrall exchaunged for a boy he had before. This done we came aboorde etc. //

[2, Tues.] . . . *about 9 of* the clocke it fell calme and so we *ancored near* 214v
the fishing bay and in the afternoone the master and I *went fyshing* with our nett and broughte some fyshe. . . . About 10 of the clocke there was a turn*ado*.

[3, Wed.] At 2 of the clocke in the morninge we had the wynde . . . *we* wayed ancor and made our way for the moste parte west; *about* 11 of the clock came a calme and we ancored over agaynst Matrobombe: about 2 *of the clocke* in the afternoone I fell sodenly sycke with a vehemente vomyting *and ex*treme purging: Captayne Hawkins came aboorde and there supped. At afternoone there came a turnado and we wayde ancor and wente *6 leages* SW. All this nyghte I was sore sycke.

[Thurs.] The 4 in the morninge Captayne Hawkins in our skyffe went aboorde who *sente* me certayn spyces. This day we had no greate wynde but so . . . made our way NW. At nyghte it fell calme and so contynued *all* nyghte.

[Fri.] The 5 in the morninge I prayse God I felte my selfe somewhat *re*covered but was very weake and feeble. This day was extreeme*ly hot* and all day calme. We sawe a greate [store] of fyshe about our shypp as sha*rke* and bonytoes whereof we tooke 2 sharke of a greate byggnesse.

[Sat.] The 6 we had the wynde at NE: and made our way SSW. but no greate wynde. We had greate plentye of fyshe and foule all alonge the seas in so mutche that the vyceadmyrall with others at his appoynment wente to shoote at foule in the skyffe and kylld 12 and came aboorde and afterwarde he and M. Blackoller kylled with there fysegygges such store that we eate nothinge but foule and freshe fyshe: we had greate pastyme this daye with takinge of so greate sharkes that 3 men colde scarse drawe them into the boate: we tooke 2 greate sharks at nyghte which we heaved overboorde for the other plenty we had of fyshe: a sharke is 10 foote in lenghe. This day I *was* lett bloodd in the ryghte arme. //

215r [Wed.] *On the 10* the ge*nerall came to see* how we dyd (as he affyr*med and found me re*covered of my healthe) but the vyc*eadmyrall* . . . *w*ente . . . vidz. . . . etc. who *when they were in their* boate we shott of two great peeces *to cause the Gallyon* come roome to take in the generall.

[Thurs.] *The 11* in the morninge we had a lyttle Turnado and a freshe *g*ale at N. In the afternoone the gale freshed and we wente *till 9 the next day*.

[Fri.] *The 12* we had a good gale at the N and to the E warde. We made *south and west* and sometymes SSW.

[Sat.] *The* 13 day lyttle wynde: this day by the sonne we were in 6 degrees.

[Sun.] *The 14* I preached *ex* Matheo 22 [:34, 35, 36] *de phariseo interrogante de mandatis* etc. After dyn*ner Captayne* Drake came aboorde and broughte us a peece of a porpase which he had kyll*d that* day at sermon tyme (for we sawe hym take it). After from us he wente aboor*de the* Galyon and broughte Captayne Hawkyns with hym . . . and supped with us and *th*ence they wente to the Frauncys: this daye was all day calme and *hote*.

[Mon.] The 15 in the morninge Captayne Drake sente his skyffe for the vyceadmyrall and me to dyne in the barke Frauncys where we founde Captayne Hawkyns and there we passed the greateste part of the day in good felowshyppe. At nyghte we came a boorde. It was all daye calme.

[Tues.] The 16 all daye callme: this daye we tooke 2 verye goodlye dolphyns, one of 4 foote in lenghe and the other of 5: we founde in there bellyes many other fyshe as flyinge fyshe etc. Ther colour is very fyne to beholde, his fynne growinge all alonge from his headd downe his backe to his tayle, his colour is bright *h*ue of azure speck[led]. [John] Roberts, Markes [Towghts], [Robert] Parker, and the [*sic*] [John] Collyns, the goonners boy were whypped at the capstyn for robbynge the stuards roome of beere, byskett and cheese. //

. . . 30 in . . . reasonable gales when the . . . dyd not blowe it was quyte calm. . . . 215v

[21, Sun.] *The 21 I preached ex Matt.* 9 [:5] *fili bono omnio esto dimittuntur tibi peccata* etc. . . .

[Mon.] *The 22* in the morninge at 2 of the clocke we had a turn*ado. It was* verye calme but styll rayne: at noone we had a *calme and m*utche rayne and a hyghe sea: we went SSW. . . .

[Tues.] *The 23* we loste the syghte of the gallyon but the Frau*ncys went roome with* us which was by reason the nyghte before we shewe*d our flag* . . . *th*e galyon shewed none.

[Wed.] *T*he 24 we had a good gale at SE and made our way SSWest. We were in 3 degrees 10 mynuts. At nyghte we bore up with the *Galyon* and haled eche other which was our comforte for we had not spoken *with them* . . . of many dayes before.

[Thurs.] The 25 we had a freshe gale at SE and by E. We wente w*est and* by southe. At nyghte the wynde skanted and we went SW.

[Fri.] The 26 we wente the same course: SW and by S. . . .

[Sat.] The 27 as before.

[Sun.] The 28 I preched *ex* Matheo 22 [:2] *de similitudine regni coelorum*. . . . Heere we were verye nyghe the lyne and founde the place verye . . . good temperature as in Einglande in May or June. The wynd this day scanted.

[Mon.] The 29 we wente SW and by S. This day the master of the bar*ke Frauncys* came aboorde us from the generall for a hogshead of porke who told us the generall had geven commandement to his goner to shoot at them for ther keepinge so mutche into the wether etc.

[Tues.] The 30 we were under the equynoctyall cyrcle. At nyghte the wynde came larger and the fyrste watche we wente S and by W.

[Wed.] The laste day we had the wynde all day at SE and went *S*W and by W: at 4 of the clocke the wynde came aboute an*d* we went for 2 howres SE but after it fell calme. //

[November]

216r [1, 2 Thurs., Fri.] . . . coulde and to make there way to *the cost of Brasile*, then came aboorde agayne: we wente *hence and* had the wynde larger then before and wente SSW and *by* W. . . . I sett the sonne in the morninge . . . at E and by S and did sett at W and by South . . . beinge but one degree from the equator.

[Sat., Sun.] *The 3* and 4 we had the wynde somewhat larger at S and by E . . . good SW and by S but we went S and sometymes S and *by west. I* preched *ex* Joh. 4 [:46] *de regulo cuius filius infirmabatur* etc.

[Mon., Tues.] *The 5* and 6 the wynde came to the E and we wente south then S *and by west*. . . . *I* tooke the sonne in 5 degrees 20 mynuts.

[Wed., Thurs.] The 7 and 8 as bef*ore*. . . .

[Fri.] The 9 about 3 of the clocke in the morninge I fell daungerously syc*k of* a burninge Cala[n]ture. All that day I sweatt and burned extremely.

[Sat.] *The* 10 I was lett bloodd.

[Sun.] *The* 11 the generall hearinge of my sycknesse came to vysytt *me* with whom came Captayne Parker, M. Maddox, M. Banyster and all the gen*tle*men in the Galyon. They broughte with them conserves of dyvers sortes and sweete meates in great quantytye: now I beganne to growe sycker *and* more weake. M. Maddox stayde with me all nyghte which was a very sycke nyghte to me.

[Mon.] The 12 I tooke a glyster and so dyd 3 tymes after.

[Tues.–Fri.] The 13, 14, 15, and 16 I was in greate daunger of deathe but I prayse God I was ready when soever the Lorde had called. I had made my wyll and testament and had dysposed all thinges orderly: the vyceadmyrall and M. Maddox were my executors.

[Sat.] The 17 I was in suche extremyte that I thoughte my selfe paste all recoverye, and so dyd all aboute me: and therefore fyrste I prepared my selfe to dye and after sente for the master, the pylate and there // *took leave of them* . . . they all commyttynge me to the 216v
mercy of God: they of the Galion and they of the Fr*auncys in th*is extremytye of myne came then gre*atlie grieving but* chefyest to take there leave of me: all *this time I was* extreme sycke, my stomacke burninge *could not* be quenched notwithstandinge I had waters of . . . which the Generall and Captayne Parker gave me besy*des those things which M. Banyster* had at commaundemente, in effecte all the *waters and* all the conserves etc. that he had which was. . . . The vyceadmyrall lett fall many a teare for me . . . whyle there was no day but ether the generall, Captayne *Parker and M. Maddox* or some other came to vysytte me as the leyfetennaunte *Hawkins and* others. All this nyghte they had a verye prosperous *gale*. . . . for styll they wolde byd me be of goodd cheare for they *had* a fayr wynd. We sayled alonge the coaste of Brasy*lle* within 40 or 50 leages of the shore where we wer in 30 degrees to the Southwarde. We romaged for water. . . . //

[December]

[1, Sat.] . . . in which A*ncored* . . . *a*nd came in to a bay and *the* 217r
Generall named it the Bay of Good Comforte and there *we thanked* God for our safe comminge thyther for me . . . *having for* 3, 4 dayes

very foule wether. The vyceadm*yrall met with a rocke in the sea and* kylled verye good foule.

[Sun., Mon.] *On the seco*nde the generall came aboorde to see me and s*uddenly fell syc*ke and scoured up and downe: the vyceadmyrall *sent for Captayne Parker and M. Banyster to* see hym: after his two fyttes which were vehe*ment he fell* a sleepe and all the gentlemen departed to dyne at *the Galyon*. The generall stayed with me all that day. In the after *noone the v*yceadmyrall wente a shore and tooke his nett with hym and tooke *in a single* draughte 600 greate mulletes and 5 greate bases, and coming *aboo*rde they all supped aboorde us: All this whyle from the *9 of* November untyll the 2 of December I never came fourthe *from* my bedd in so mutche that now I am so weake that I can nether sytt nor stande. All the fleshe is consumed of my bodye and I lyke to an anatomye but I hope to God to recover my strenghe for this beinge the thirde daye I feele my selfe a little stronger.

[Tues.] The 4 I wente forth of the cabbyn and walked upon the hatches but founde my selfe so feeble that I scarse was able to stande.

[Wed.] The 5 I lykewyse growe stronge I prayse God and am able somewhat to walke. //

160r [Thurs.] 1582: 6 die Decembre.

On the 6 of December about 5 of the clocke in the morn*ing* our men dyscryed a barke saylynge alonge *the* shore not farre from the entraunce of the porte where were our shyppes at ancor: vidz. in the porte *o*f Don Dondrygo [Dom Rodrigo] aboute 28 degrees in latitude to the *W* and S from the equynoctyall lyne. Worde of this barke was presently broughte to the vyceadmyrall who was then in rysynge from his bed: he withall speede dyspatched hym selfe with the newes to the Generall: who stayed not longe there but (in his owne skyffe wherein he went) came backe to the shyppe syde and called for some furnyture of defence as a steele targett etc. Away [he] wente to the barke Frauncys (whyther some were gone out of the Galyon before to make her ready for she shoulde fetche in this sayde barcke): ymedyatelye they hoysed sayles so that before Captayne Parker coulde be readye and come from the Galyon (for he was appoynted by the Generall to go with the

Vyceadmyrall), they were under sayle, yett he came well ynoughe aboorde them. The wynde was northerly and therefore coulde they not gett forthe of harbour but were towed forthe with the Edwardes skyffe and the Galyons. The Galyons skyffe was sente with the barke to geve ayde yf neede were, etc. They had not sayled more then 4 or 5 leages but they were so nyghe that they shott at her // whereupon she stroke sayl and . . . *be*fore they came 160v
to her they *hard Captayne Parker deliver* greate wordes to the company . . . *that* yf they came to any fyghte and *tried to* boorde the barcke whosoever woulde not *wolde* have a pyke or other weapon thruste *in hym* but hereof was no neede for the vyce-*admyrall, Captayne* Parker and feiv more wente aboorde them w*ith* one Tobias the masters mate in the Edward fyrste, whereat the captay[n]es were dyspleased. A*ll they founde* in the barke was 21 persons: whereof 7 *were* fryers and 2 were women with a yonge chyld *all* Spanyardes. The chestes were looked in *and the* keyes taken from the owners and what was *there* they quyckly had searched. The wynde being*e a stoute gale at the south* they were constrayned to come to ancor: about . . . the clocke the wynde turned and came at S. . . . The two barkes, the Frauncys and the pryse se*tt sayle* (for they called the barke a pryse) and came *in* to harbour about 4 of the clocke but whyle thinges were a doinge there fell a contravers*y be*twyxte the vyceadmyrall and Captayne Parker and hott word*es* p*assed*. Belyke it was for there auctorytyes in this ex*ercise*. When they were in harbour and at Ancor the fry*ers* from the Frauncys (for thyther they were caryed before) *were* sente aboorde the Generall, whyther lykewys*e* the vyce-admyrall wente but came into the rode in the pryse: there the fryers delyvered suche thinges th*at they were* enquyred of: which were of the fleete gone to the Straytes etc. // *Th*e vyceadmyrall 161r
came aboorde whom I per*ceyved to be dis*pleased: I enquyred what *troubled him and he said* he was not well dealte withall by *those* of the Galyon for the generall had geven *comm*aundement that all shoulde departe the pryse *excepte* Captayne Parker and his 2 men and that he should sende two more to them to watche there all nyghte, whom he sayde shoulde have byn M. Symberbe and M. Wylkes: but when he came by the pryse and called to Captayne Parker and tolde hym the *order for* the Generalls men that these of the Galyon shoulde come aboorde (for there were dyvers of the Galyon with Captayne Parker) but they wolde not, whereupon

he came away and sente none. Other matters in bryefe he tolde me whyche after I learned more at large.

[Fri.] The 7 the vyceadmyrall went aboorde the Galyon who stayed not there longe but M. Jeffrey was sent for who after was appoynted with M. Taylebush was appoynted [*sic*] to go aboorde the pryse and to take an Inventorye of all thinges in her: the generall at this tyme called the commyssyoners to consulte what myghte be done in these causes (I my selfe was not there for I was sycke and then began to recover. I had the Callenture and kepte my bed 17 dayes) where there happened a verye greate contraveryse betwyxte the vyceadmyrall and Captayne Parker whereupon they grewe to very unseemlye comparysons etc. but was
161v appeased afterward. // . . . it was there determyned and thoug*hte on whether* to take the barke from the Spanyarde*s or* sett them on shore in the wylde wyl*dernesse or* to carrye them alonge with us to the Stray*ts of Ma*gellane, but to carrye them thyther . . . there vyttayles wolde be spente whereof *was* no greate plenty and therefore the ge*nerall asked* M. Maddox with M. Jeffrey because he und*erstood the* language to perswade the olde fryer rather *to go a* shore in some harbour they knewe then to ta*ke* a voyage in hande: the olde fryer who was cheyfe father wepte bytterly alledginge the*y wolde* be eaten of the Indyes etc. and desyred *the gene*rall by them to be good unto them etc. At Sur*vyce* tyme the Generall came aboorde with the *vyceadmyrall* to suppe with hym and to conferre concerninge th*ese* matters and to have my opynyon: M. Maddox and *Captayne* Parker were lykewyse there: the Genera*ll began* to tell me what benefyte God had sente in *to our* handes as these men for by them they unders*tood* that the kynge of Spaynes fleete was gone to the Strayghtes there to fortyfye and that they wer*e 16* shyppes with 3000 persons who wyntered in the ry*ver* of Januarye and went thence the xxx of October, and that 4 of the shyppes were for Chylye in the South Seas with 500 very choyse men [under Don Alonso de Sotomayor]: the
162r nomber that shoulde fortyfye the Strayghtes wer 360. // . . . *The name of the Generall of the Spanysh fleete* was Don Flores etc. and that *he was the cheyfe of t*he reste, whereof one of the reste *was a man of* good accounpte called Don Francisco [de Torre Vera] . . . etc. and that these men *w*ere *in*habyters at ryver of Plate, the*re* . . . *h*avinge obtayned leave of the governour *of the* countrey to go to

Spayne 2 yeares synce *to fetc*he more fryers. Other matters *he to*lde me of lyke cause, which for brevytye I *omyt*. This beinge tolde he shewed me the *grea*te hurte these men myghte do us in our voyage *yf* we lett them go to the Ryver of Plate, consyder*ing that yf* we were to vytayle in the South Seas *then* they myghte sende over by lande in shorte *spa*ce to the portes there: whereby we myghte *be* prevented etc. and therefore requyred my opynyo*n*. I desyred pacyence to speake my mynde with lybertye which was graunted. Fyrste I in verye ample manner shewed what was chrystyan charytye and the effectes thereof and after that what was a good conscyence and the effect etc. Whereupon after a verye longe dyscourse I concluded that we nether myghte with charytye or conscyence ether take barke or any thinge from them or hassarde there bodyes upon shore whereby ether the Indyans or wylde beastes shoulde devoure [them] and so we shoulde be gyltye // of the sheedinge of ther bloode *which God wold not* leave 162v unreavenged upon us and *I shewed that* the hurte they myghte do us by *sending to the ports was none* for that they were ygnoraunte *of our intentions*. The Generall and the reste havinge *hard, they* used some speaches to and fro but verye *soone* all concluded to lett them have there barke and to go on there voyage. By this tyme *supper* was readye, beinge now 9 of the clocke. *We supt* and were mery and thanked God for his be*nefytes*. At after supper I verye earnestly *asked* the Generall and the reste presente to geve *me leave* to saye somewhat more which was graunte*d* . . . *I* presentely, *ex abrupto*, begann to showe wha*t bown*tyfull love was and of concorde I sayde the *lyke* and alledged reasons and examples to approve th*e* . . . *benef*yte of them bothe, etc. and of the contrary *even* as mutche, spendinge in both halfe an ho*ur*. The reason that moved me thereunto was *that* I ether suspected or knewe betwyxe the Ge*nerall* and Captayne Parker on one parte and the vyce-admyrall on the *other* was but *mediocris amitia imo dissimulata. In* fyne I expounded my selfe and shewed my *opy*nyon, requestynge them to Joyne together in a p*act, a* perfectyon of Agreement that shoulde not be without greate [cause] any peece dyssolved: heere now I passed many wordes: but I charged as a dyvyne *myny*ster to unytye and so dyd M. // *Maddox*. . . . in the ende they 163r con*sent*inge I dyd knytt up so perfec*t frendship that I hoped a*s was indyssoluble: but it happened *no*tt. . . . Hereupon they went home and I to *bed f*or my headd dyd ake and I was sycke.

[8, Sat.] *The next* day in the morninge earlye I lyinge in *bed*d the vyceadmyrall came to me and burste out *th*ese wordes that for his parte he was nott yett *satis*fyed in the frendeshyppe and that he had receyved *dys*curtesyes at the Generalls handes and that unlesse *these* and other matters were reformed he wolde not *con*clude to the frendeshyppe but wolde turne *tay*le to tayle and wolde goe from hym yf his *cump*any wolde go with hym. I replyed that his *cum*pany wolde not leave the generall with *ow*t juste cause, then (sayde he) I wylbe sett on *s*hore and shyfte for my selfe etc. I tolde hym *I* was hartelye sorye to heare this and wylled *hym to let me* understande his gryefes and that I doubted not but *t*o *r*edresse them etc. He tolde me, saynge the Generall thynkes to tye me to that obedyence that when I come into a harbour I shall not go ashore without askinge hym leave and I see no suche reason and other matters which I wyll tell when tyme serves etc. I tolde hym how mutche I myslyked of dyssentyon and because the occasyons geven to leave companyes myghte be occasyon of the overthrowe of our voyage I wolde shewe the Generall what he
163v sayd etc. and that I doubted not but upon this extremytye // . . . to make a more perfecte fre*ndeshyppe then the*se wolde have byn etc. which he a*greed to. He* and I were bydden to dynner to the *Galyon. I* was desyrous to goe because I . . . and there I shoulde talke with them. . . . The day before sente me a platter. . . . *When* we wente aboorde ymedyate the commy*ssoners* intred into councell and the matter was ag*eyn* for the Spanyardes and fryers, what shoul*de we do* with them for new perswasyons had *bin offered*. Many reasons were tossed to and fro: the *lefte*tennaunt wolde have had them sett on s*hore* but I stoode to my olde matter and in end *wi*th the good consent of the Generall and *the* vyceadmyrall it was concluded as before. W*hen* they sygnyfyed so mutche to the olde frye*r and* Don Frauncysco who dyned there with us, *they* rejoysed thereat etc. The vyceadmyrall and the le*ft*ennaunt went with them aboorde the barke *wher* they had some sugar and sweete meates which *the* fryers bestowed upon them *nolens volens* whereof *they* had good store and we wanted. In the mea*n* season I sygnyfyed unto the Generall *the* dyscontented mynde of the vyceadmirall in all thing*s* as is before. The Generall amased hereat say*d* he thoughte he wolde deny the goinge from hym but I sayde I wolde justyfye it, and that I knewe he wolde not denye
164r any thinge // . . . *A*bout 5 of the clocke came ab*oorde the sugar and*

sweet meates: at after supper the Generall *and the commy*ssyoners urged the vyceadmyrall with what *he myslyke*de and because I reported it the Generall *did c*all me to speake it agayn: I beganne to *open* the matter in everye poynte in effecte as *befor*e: the vyceadmyrall denyed nothinge: then the *Gen*erall requyred of whether he thoughte hym *sel*fe to good to by vyceadmyrall where her majestie had *ap*poynted hym Generall etc. who Awneswered *he did not* but used further wordes shewinge his greyfe *whereupon* many things and wordes passed and all myldlye *a*wneswered and well objected: in the ende *I* desyred as I had broched this matter and *no*w that it was come to this poynte and extasye [bewilderment] *th*ey wolde geve me leave to speake in the matter: which graunted I earnestelly requested *t*he generall to forgett what had byn sayde and done etc. and the lyke to the vyceadmyrall etc. and that now they wolde geve me leave as Goddes mynyster to make them frendes. After mutche adoe it was graunted and all concluded frendes with a chrystyan promyse, the performaunce whereof I charged them under Goddes name fullfyll: which they vowed and so God contynue it: after this about 10 of the clocke the vyceadmyrall and I went a boorde havinge invyted them to meete the Gentleman // *Don Frauncysco* and the fryer the nexte daye *beinge* 164v
Sundaye.

[Sun.] The 9 the Generall, the leyft*ennaunt*, *Captayne Parker*, *M.* Maddox, Don Francysco and the fryer *dyned aboorde* us: the Generall tooke into his one of *there ma*ryners [Richard Carter, alias Juan Perez] to be his pylote upon this coast*e and the* vyceadmyrall tooke another [Juan Pinto] etc. and so when th*e wynd* served us to leave the rode which was *the 11*. . . .

[10, Mon.] . . . *the vyceadmyrall and his men goinge again to fysh* lefte the barke and men there and wente *to descry the lande*. . . . //

[Tues.] *The 11 the v*yceadmyrall *went to fysh and lackyng* for wynde to 218r
carrye us further . . . *we* wente a shore where I sawe a verye wylder*nesse so over*growen that no man is able to travayle any thinge at *any ty*me there is suche deepenesse of fogge and mosse that *we sunk our le*gge eche steppe up to the thyghe: we founde dyvers *jars of yearth* in the grounde and a mans scull. We myghte descerne *wher a* house had byn buylded. At nyghte I came aboorde ag*ayne. We being ashore the vyceadmyrall* was warpinge to gett

forthe of the rode for the wy*nd came* fayre at NNE. Upon this shore our two Negroes wente forthe . . . we never sawe them synce.

[Wed.] *On the* 12 in the morninge we sett sayle out of the Baye of Good *Cumforte* called by the Portyngales Porte Don Dondrygo, for there was he *and* his shyppinge caste away. It standeth in 28 degres to the S from *the* equynoctyall lyne. We had a very fayre wynde at NE and went S and by W.

[Thurs.] The 13 the wynde came at S and inforced us to beate up and downe. At laste towardes the eveninge we were allmoste aboorde the shore where we sawe certayne great fyers.

[Fri.] The 14 in the morninge the wynde came aboute to the N and we wente S and by W: at nyghte we had the wynd contrarye.

[Sat.] The 15 we had the wynde at South and by that meanes beate it up and downe sometymes nyghe the shore within 3 or 4 leages where we sawe greate fyers which the people of the countrey made to geve warninge from place to place that shyppes were upon there coaste. The people are of greater stature then any Englyshe man. They be of 7 or 8 foote hyghe (for so the Spanyarde that is in our
218v shyppe dothe tell us) // . . . and his ba*rke* . . . nothinge: then the vyc*eadmyrall* . . . and dyscharged him selfe of *prov*isyon: the vyceadmyrall tooke order that *it should be* more carefully looked unto.

[Sun.] *The* 16 I preached *ex* Math. 11 . . . *contra sanguinis effusionem* etc. At nyghte the *wynd lar*ged and we upon one boorde went S and by E. . . .

[Mon.] The 17 we had the wynd verye large at W and *went* S and by W but at nyghte the wynde came contrarye.

[Tues.] The 18 all day calme.

[Wed.] The 19 the wynde was easterly and we wente SSW but *at* nyghte altered.

[Thurs.] The 20 (The Generall havinge called us the nyghte before) . . . *the vyceadmyrall and* the marchauntes [Shaw and Jeffrey], the master [Percy] and pylott [Blacollar] and I wente aboorde the Ad*myrall* where we dyned and after dynner the Generall made k*noen* unto us the cause of his assemblynge of us: which was sett d*owne* in 2 questyons: the fyrste was that he was advertised of a S*panysh* fleete gone to the Strayghtes of Magellane who were in nomber [16] shyppes and were gone oute of the Ryver of January the xxxth of Oc*tober* with 3000 men with women and chyldren in them whereof 360 were to *forty*fye the Strayghtes by way of bullwarke, upon which cause he moved by what meanes we beste myghte escape there daunger and passe the Strayghtes or whether it were necessary to go that way. The 2 questyon was yf we went that way what course were beste to be kepte etc., whereupon the masters and pylotes were called who coulde assure us of no safetye to passe and escape there force but they doubted not there strenghe etc. When they had sayd what they coulde and woulde they departed. Then dyd the generall demaund our opynyons. The merchauntes, M. Shawe and M. Jeffrey, wolde have // *us go by the Cape of Good Hope and make for* 219r the Mo*luccas* for suche a tyme that *it requireth to go by the Strayghts En*glyshe natures coulde not lyve *without vitayles and* as this voyage was lyke to contynue *800 leages afte*r we moste passe the Strayghtes to the Molucc*as* . . . . *Rather than l*eaving our voyage unperformed, I thought it *beste to go by the Strayghtes and since by report* we only ymagyned this fleete to . . . upon Spanyardes) to passe the Strayghtes by . . . *w*ayes whom to annoy we wolde be lothe: and to fear *ther forces before we see them* I thoughte greate follye, and that suche a voyage *colde* not be performed without some daunger: for sayde *I* si deus *nobiscum quis contra nos*. Captayne Parker: he in effecte sa*yd the* lyke and so dyd the lyefetennaunt but in other termes: the *vyc*eadmyrall he shewed the greate daungers of the passage and alledge*d e*yghte reasons to approve the same: and therefore concluded that *it* were better to seeke releyfe upon the coaste of America or Brasyle *for* a convenyent place to trymme up our decayed caske etc., which coulde not be done in the Strayghtes where we determyned to do it and after this done to proceede as shoulde seeme good to the generall and his assystauntes. The generall requyred a tyme to yeelde his opynyon, who at after supper gave up his mynde in wrytinge to this effecte that he wolde not adventure his shyppes and men upon suche a knowen daunger, and had many sounde reasons to establyshe that he spoke and in fyne concluded that he wolde not go throughe the Strayghtes but wolde furnyshe hym selfe of necessaryes upon this coaste and therefor put us to choyse whether we wolde

venter into the Ryver of Plate 50 leages up the Ryver whyther we were promysed to be safely broughte by one Carter whom we had then a boorde us *where we* shoulde have vyttayles of all sortes
219v suffycyent . . . // opynyon which was *of all* consented and this I. . . . *The* leyfetennaunt and M. Maddox requ*ested time to write* there opynyons or to consyder of th*em* . . . *It was* graunted and so Awneswered as is before *put down. It was* paste 9 of the clocke and then the vyce*admyrall and* the reste came aboorde and ymedyately we caste *about wh*ereat our men greatly murmured fearinge *the loss o*f the voyage. This day M. Hall sayde there vytayles was *much decayed and he* wolde never consente to goe to the Strayghtes nor no man els: for h*e said the Spanysh should* not take hym by the throte for vytay*les*.

[Fri.] The xxi beinge S. Thomas day at afte*r* dyvyne servyce the vyceadmyrall made knowen *to our men* the cause of their goinge backe who at laste *were* satysfyed. This day it was all day calme: at *nyght* the wynde came NNE and blewe there a styffe *gale* all nyghte. At the begynnynge of this nyghte we los*t* syghte of the barke Frauncys whom we suppose to be *turned* back to the Strayghtes of Magellane.

[Sat.] The 22 this wynde contynued.

[Sun.] The 23 it came more southerlye. I preached *ex* Joh. I [:23] *dirigite vi*am Domini.

[Mon.] The 24 at NE.

[Tues.] The 25 beinge Chrysmas day I preached *ex* Luca 2 [:10] *ecce annuntio vobis gaud*ium magnum. At our dynner the wynde sudde*n*ly came to the S and there contynued 2 howres.

[Wed., Thurs.] The 26 and 27 at NNE. This day we went aboorde the generall.

[Fri.–Mon.] The 28, 29, 30, 31 the wynd at northerlye.

[January 1583]

[Tues.] The fyrste of January the wynde at nygh Southerly.

[Wed., Thurs.] The 2 and 3 as before.

[Fri.] The 4 the wynde S and we fell with the lande aboute the latitude of 28: 54 mynuts: at nyghte caste about etc. //

[5, Sat.] *The* wynde came to the NE: we were *within 3 leages of the shore* with the wind at N. 220r

[13, Sun.] I preached *ex* Luca 2 [:48] *fili quid fec*istis nobis sic. *The* general, Captayne Parker, and M. Maddox came aboorde *where they supped. At*... of the clocke the wynde came large and we were *within 4 leages of the shore. The wind ca*lminge we fell with a hygh lande in a greate bay and wente . . . but about a xi of the clocke the wynde came fayre and *we wente a* longe the shore. . . .

[14, Mon.] The wynde was at S and at nyghte the Generall ancored ... but the vyceadmyrall doubtinge our grounde tackelynge wolde *not* but wente of and on all that nyght: and in the morninge [15, Tues.] *we kept* the weather to our admyrall and 3 or 4 leages further [to]wardes *the windward* . . . we made it up and downe sometyme upon on boorde sometyme on another: *we* did not beare roome to the Admyrall. This nyghte we loste the syghte *of the* admyrall.

[Wed.] *The 16* we had a badd wynde and towardes nyghte we sayled to a lyttle rounde *ylande* [they name it Faulcon Island] where we ancored 4 leages from the mayne lande.

[Thurs.] The 17 we sett sayle in the afternoone, the wynde then E and by S.

[Fri.] *The* 18 we had no wynde to profytte us. About the myddeste of *the* seconde watche we be chaunce at the sea mett with the Gallyon who [had] byn at an ylande [called Citron Island by Ward; Burnt Island by Fenton] 10 leages from shore . . . *w*here they had water for they wanted and good store of fowle.

[Sat.] The 19 the vyceadmyrall, the master and I wente aboorde where I stayed but they in our skyffe wente to see the ylande and broughte fowle with them. In the meane season about a xi of the clocke the wynde came fayre and we wente NE and NNE.

[Sun.] The 20 I preached. . . . At dynner tyme we dys*cr*yed certayne boates who came from St. Vyncent with flagges *o*f truce: 2 wente to the Generall and one came to us. // *One Portyngale* who *at lenghe* 220v comminge *to the Generall* . . . for the same: he syg*nyfyed he had* Artycles concerninge the *trafficking* etc. This done he with the res*te departed. Then went the vy*ceadmyrall to sounde the channel: within one *hour the generall summoned hym* and me to supper and afterwarde came the *vyceadmyrall when* we dyscryed a cannowe with a flagge of truce *with xii men aboord* who were well intertayned: for there were 2 . . . *from the* towne: one was an Italyan that had dwelled *at Genoa* [Joffo Dore], the other a Portyngale [Stephano Riposo] The generall sygnyfyed *t*hat we were Einglyshe men and were merchauntes come *to tra*ffycke as with Chrystyans etc. and that he had wrytt*en to the* governour of the countrey to that intente etc. The*y* Awnes*wered that* there countrey was very poore, and that the cheyfeste thing was sugar and conserves etc. We concluded with greate frende*shyppe* and growinge towardes nyghte they desyred to departe and promys*ed to come* the nexte daye agayne with Awneswere to the generall: th*e cannowe* was manned with Indyans who were wholy naked and ro*wed the* boate with shovells 20 on a syde etc. We gave them a vo*lley of* shott and thence they wente: the generall dyd not wr*yte by* these men for he had wrytten before by one that came *to* hym in the morninge.

[Mon.] The 21 I wente aboorde the generall and aboute 4 of the cloc*ke* the same men with one other of the cheyfe, a Dutchman [Paulo Bedeves], in the cann*owe* came with Awnsewere and broughte a bull and a hogge with other s*uche vittayles.* There Awneswere was that the kinge of Spayne had sente the governour and geven them strayghte charge that they should not traffycke with any natyon but especyally with no Einglyshe men for that not longe synce there was [an] Einglyshe man who had byn in the southe seas and upon that coast and at Chyla had taken greate
221r store of golde and sylver etc. And that there // *fore they colde not trade with* our shyppes. We shoulde *have provysions* etc. Many speaches passed *and then the generall de*maunded his pynnyse to be manne*d and the long boat as gu*ard for the generall: with trumpetts, dr*um and fife in the skyffe with* the vyceadmyrall and so the generall, the vyce*admyrall and Captayne Parker accompanied* them a leage almoste in there waye with contyn*uall musick and* soundynge of trumpetts and drumes and fyfes: *at ther* goinge of we gave them a vollew of shott. *We gave them* certayne notes to

be resolved on for our provysy*ons which they pr*omysed to bringe worde of etc. After we had taken our le*ave in order* to recreate ourse[l]ves we wente to walke a shore and . . . mette Captayne Parker who was in the Gallyons longe boa*te with ce*rtayne small shott: and thence we came a boorde the Edward and there *supp*ed together. This day dyed Roberte Rose [Rosse] and Gryffyn [Davis].

[Tues.] *On the* 22 in the morninge earlye we of the Edward, vidz. the commyssyoners, wente aboorde the Galyon where *with* the generall, it was concluded to sende the governour and the 3 that *h*ad taken paynes betwyxte us a presente, which was certayne brodd *c*lothe: the merchauntes were dyspatched away in the Admyralls pynnyse to carrye the same: who mett by the way neere the towne *the Portyngale* wyllinge them to returne and certyfe the generall that as yett they had not concluded but shoulde have presently Awneswers etc. After this and there returne we sygned with our handes the cause of our comminge to St. Vyncentes etc. and there we all supped and [then] came aboorde.

[Wed.] The 23 in the morninge the generall with other gentlemen in his *s*kyffe, the vyceadmyrall and I with some more wente a shore to see the castle and manner of the countrey in that place to the intente to sett up our forges etc. Afterwarde the generall with Captayne Parker came aboorde the Edward and there dyned and afterwardes // 221v

[Thurs.] *On the 24th came aboord an Einglishman named John Whitehall.* He sayde the towne of S*antos had been fortifyed* etc. In the meane season we proce*ede to our ordinarie business. Then came a cannow* where was the Portyngales that br*oughte awneswere from the* governour, which awneswere was that they *colde not traffycke* because of the kinges commaundement for they *woulde be sentenced* to deathe yf they dyd deale with us: but we sh*olde have dyvers sortes* of vytayles broughte us the nexte day: and that *the Captayne* wolde meete the generall and conferr with hym wh*ere-upon* we concluded to meete hym etc. so they departed. After d*ynner* we gave them certayne brodde clothe for ther paynes *and suffered them to depart*. . . . Aboute 4 of the clocke there came in to the harbour 3 shyppes of Spanyardes, beinge the kynges fleete, fyrste the admyrall then the vyce *admirall shewed* there

flagges and Auncyentes [insignia] dysp*l*ayed in verye gallaunte so*rte* . . . at us beinge before them in harbour. . . . ancored. The meane whyle we beinge unready and our mery*ners a* shore, fell to make our greate ordynaunce in readyness and dyspa*tched a* boate to fetche our men from shore who were workinge and washinge. *The* Admyrall sente lykewyse for his men and prepared his shyppe (for *we* knewe they wolde fyghte with us). The nyghte approched and we w*orked* harde. The vyceadmirall tooke his skyffe and wente aboorde the admyrall *where they* conferred what to be done. I encouraged our people to be of good com*forte* and shewed the [~~quarrel~~ (*dele*)] vyctor*ies* wolde be honorable (yf they wolde begynne w*ith* us) and wylled them to resolve them selves in Chryste etc. All the begynninge *of* the nyghte untyll 10 of the clocke all our men labored verye harde: the Spanyardes perceyvinge our unreadynesse about 10 of the clocke lett slyppe there ancors and lett dryve upon us, purposinge to have boorded us. The vyceadmirall of the fleete lett dryve overthwarte our admyralls hause [across the stem of the ship] untyll they came within calyver shott and then within the reach of a pyke that the one talked to the other. The vyceadmirall seeinge them so nyghe called to the generall byddinge him shoote and so the admirall shott, and foughte with them valyauntlye. The vyceadmirall dyd the lyke: greate was the fyghte on ether syde which contynued untyll 4 or 5 of [the] clocke in the morninge and then ceased: so
222r soone as it was daye // lighte. . . . About 6 of the *clocke the vyce-admirall dyd c*all to knowe whether th*ey shold way and drive down to them.* The generall bade hym go fyrste on and *we had this day one* verye hott breakefaste fyghtinge. . . . 4 howres all whyche tyme the general was *at ancor for the r*ope wolde not worke: at lenghe he came and then *battled* verye stoutely, the vyceadmirall beinge wearye fell *back* . . . . then [the] generall shott them verye stoutley. In truth the *fight was so* fierce that the lyke hathe seldome byn seene: it con*tynued all d*ay untyll 4 of the clocke: the vyceadmirall and I wente in the *skyffe to the* generall to consulte what myghte be moste convenyent to be do*ne*. . . . the reere admirall of the Spanyardes seeing us putt *out from our* shyppe, shott at us but God be thanked they myssed us. After we *came a*boorde the general the enemye shott at the Edward many shotts *but the* general was out of the reache of there shott: the Edward lykewyse . . . for the fyghte was so cruell that our men in both shyppes *were*

allmoste. . . . There were slayne in our admirall 1 man and 8 hurte, *in the* vyceadmirall [~~4~~ (dele)] 5 slayne and 8 or so hurte. The Edwarde was shott throughe in many places and *so w*as the admirall. Many hurtes we both received in our shyppes. At lenghe we . . . the Spanyarde to understand there force: they certyfyed that in *the* whole there were of souldyers and maryners 760 and odd: in the vyceadmirall *th*at we suncke were 222 men and that these were the cheyfe souldyers the kynge of Spayne hathe. The shyppes were one 600, another 500, and another 400. When the fleete came out of [~~Spayne~~ (*dele*)] January [Rio de Janeiro] they were 16 shyppes whereof 5 were caste away ether at sea or in harbour: 12 of them were 38 degrees to the S goinge for Magellanns Strayghtes and fyndynge the wynde contrarye and the weather colde, intended to returne and so dyd, and came to St. Catelina where they mett with the barke we before mett with (the souldyers provyded for Chyla wente by lande from ryver of Plate). The Spanyardes and fryers in the barke tolde them of us and that we were gone to the Strayghts of Magellane or to St. Vyncente whereupon they concluded 8 to goe to the Strayghts and 4 to St. Vyncent to looke for us but one of the 4 they loste in the way but tooke in there men *in*to the other 3.
Many other // . . . that we were out of hope . . . or otherwyse any 222v
refreshinge, . . . with many souldyers and Indyans . . . etc. After conclusyon to goe hence (upon suspyty*on of the* other fleete) and causes before alledged, the vyceadmirall. . . . *He* that wyll ryghtely ponder the greate power of God wh*o did save us* from the force of these Spanyardes or Spanyshe kings fleete *will have me*ate cause to prayse the Lorde God with an humble harte. . . . *we* were in the bay of Don Rodrygo and wente thence upon the *12 of December.* The Monday after the whole fleete came in thyther, and besyde*s* *we commynge* to the S and they commynge to the N, it pleased God that they . . . sawe us not and where we determyned to water at ryver of *Plate yf* the wynde had served us we had fallen into there handes . . . for there they were then: and further when we agreed to re*turn to* this coaste of Brasyle to seeke refreshinge, we were purposed yf *the wynde* had not served well to have gone to St. Catelina and then ha*ve come* upon them where they were at our passinge by, and more yf the*y* had stayed but 1 or 2 dayes longer they had founde us in a marv*elous* unreadynesse for that we intended the nexte day to sett up our forg*es and* make our

ovens and take up our merchaundyse etc. or yf they had *come* 1 or 2 dayes sooner they had founde us with our shyppes unryg*ged:* these causes and manye others oughte to enforce us to yealde *the* Lorde immortall thankes etc. This countrey yeeldethe greate store of *fish and* all sorte of frutes as plantaynes, potatoes, pyne apples, etc. The cheyfe ynhabyt*ants* are Portyngales who have subjecte unto them infynyte nombre of Indyans who go a*bout* naked both men and women. They use them as slaves or as we do horses to tyll the grounde etc.

[Sat.] The 26 we fetched in some water from the shore, arminge our selves with calyvers to defende them that caryed the water to the boates. The generall came aboorde the Edwarde to comforte the men that were hurt*e* and to geve them all thankes for there greate manhoodd in defendinge our selves etc. About 10 of the clocke at nyghte we wayed ancor and sett sayle with a verye smalle gale for we sayled all day in the mouthe of the harbour but ther shyppes were gone up to the towne the nyghte before whyche is 3 myles from the place we foughte. //

223r . . . of this yland, but . . . ancor to come neere. *The crew* was so busye, some about fyllynge *the c*aske and other in lyftynge downe greate ord*inaunce* . . . and there chambers in the holde that . . . we wolde: afterwarde we went to way ancor . . . with greate daunger for before that our men were . . . capstone. The cable broke and we enforced to s*eeke them* in the longe boate and skyffe wente to way the *ancor* . . . approched and we fell to the lee warde not able to *come nere the A*dmyrall nor any rode. Our men and boates were in daung*er of* loosinge, but Goddes wyll was that within nyghte we es*pied them* a headd and with mutche ado we recovered them. The*n* . . . we seeinge our presente extremytye in respecte of the *lee* shore made into the sea makinge our way S and by E *wher we* stoode of all nyghte.

[Tues.] *T*he 29 in the morninge we havinge loste the Admirall the vyceadmirall *m*oved this questyon, callinge the assystaunce and the cheyfe of *t*he shyppe to hym: whether we myghte fetche the Admirall where we suspected hym to ryde and what were beste to be done: the master, pylott, and masters mate affyrmed that it was impossyble to reatche the ylande and what to do they knewe not for the safetye of our lyves more then to beare of into the sea: whereunto we all condescended the vyceadmirall confyrminge it, in hope to meete our Admirall at sea. We bore of SE and sometymes SE and by S.

[Wed.] The 30 we wente as before.

[Died Feb. 5]

INDEX

Titles and authors of works cited in the introduction and notes are included here, indicated in the latter case by the abbreviations 'n' and 'nn'. Where bibliographical details are given they will be found at the initial reference. The index was compiled by A. M. Quinn.